History of Modern India

BIPAN CHANDRA

Orient BlackSwan

All rights reserved. No part of this book may be modified, reproduced or utilised in any form, or by any means, electronic or mechanical, including photocopying, recording or by any information storage and retrieval system, in any form of binding or cover other than in which it is published, without permission in writing from the publisher.

HISTORY OF MODERN INDIA

ORIENT BLACKSWAN PRIVATE LIMITED

Registered Office
3-6-752 Himayatnagar, Hyderabad 500 029 (Telangana), India
e-mail: centraloffice@orientblackswan.com

Other Offices
Bengaluru, Chennai, Guwahati, Hyderabad, Kolkata,
Mumbai, New Delhi, Noida, Patna, Visakhapatnam

© Orient Blackswan Private Limited 2009
First published 2009
Reprinted 2009, 2010, 2011, 2012, 2013, 2014,
 2015, 2016, 2017, 2018, 2019 (twice), 2020
This Edition 2020
Reprinted 2021, 2022

ISBN: 978 93 90122 55 4

Maps cartographed by
Sangam Books (An imprint of The Agricultural Development Commercial Credit and Industrial Investment Company Private Limited)

Maps
© Government of India, Copyright 2017.
The responsibility for the correctness of internal details rests with the publisher.

The territorial waters of India extend into the sea to a distance of twelve nautical miles measured from the appropriate base line.

The external boundaries and coastlines of India agree with the Record/Master Copy certified by the Survey of India.

The spellings of names in these maps have been taken from various sources.

Typeset by
Bukprint, Delhi

035691

Printed in India at
B.B. Press, Noida

Published by
Orient Blackswan Private Limited
3-6-752 Himayatnagar, Hyderabad 500 029 Telangana, India
e-mail: info@orientblackswan.com

Contents

Preface   *vii*

1. **The Decline of the Mughal Empire**   1
   Causes of the Decline of the Mughal Empire

2. **Indian States and Society in the Eighteenth Century**   19
   Decay of the Mughal Empire • Hyderabad and the Carnatic • Bengal • Awadh • Mysore • Kerala • Areas around Delhi • Bangash Pathans and Rohelas • The Sikhs • The Rise and Fall of the Maratha Power • Social and Economic Conditions of the People • Education • Social and Cultural Life

3. **European Penetration and the British Conquest of India**   53
   A New Phase in Europe's Eastern Trade • The Growth of the East India Company's Trade and Influence, 1600–1714 • The Anglo-French Struggle in South India • British Occupation of Bengal • Dual System of Administration of Bengal • Wars Under Warren Hastings (1772–85) and Cornwallis (1786–93) • Expansion under Lord Wellesley (1798–1805) • Expansion under Lord Hastings (1813–22) • The Consolidation of British Power (1818–57)

4. **The Structure of Government and the Economic Policies of the British Empire in India, 1757–1857**   86
   The Structure of Government • British Economic Policies in India (1757–1857) • Land Revenue Policy

Contents

5. **Administrative Organisation and Social and Cultural Policy** — 108
   Civil Services • Army • Police • Judicial Organisation • The Rule of Law • Equality before Law • Social and Cultural Policy • Humanitarian Measures • Spread of Modern Education

6. **Social and Cultural Awakening in the First Half of the Nineteenth Century** — 128
   Rammohun Roy • Derozio and Young Bengal • Debendranath Tagore and Ishwar Chandra Vidyasagar • Pioneers of Reform in Western India

7. **The Revolt of 1857** — 140
   General Causes • The Immediate Cause • The Beginning and Course of the Revolt • The Weaknesses of the Revolt and its Suppression

8. **Administrative Changes after 1858** — 158
   Administration • Changes in the Army • Public Services • Relations with the Princely States • Administrative Policies • Racial Antagonism • Foreign Policy

9. **The Economic Impact of British Rule** — 181
   Disruption of the Traditional Economy • Ruin of Old Zamindars and Rise of New Landlordism • Stagnation and Deterioration of Agriculture • Poverty and Famines

10. **The Nationalist Movement: 1858–1905** — 199
    Consequence of Foreign Domination • Administrative and Economic Unification of the Country • Racial Arrogance of the Rulers • Predecessors of the Indian National Congress • The Programme and Activities

of the Early Nationalists • Economic Critique of
Imperialism • Constitutional Reforms • Administrative
and Other Reforms • Role of the Masses • Attitude of the
Government • Evaluation of the Early National
Movement

11. **Religious and Social Reform after 1858**   219

    Religious Reform • Religious Reform in Maharashtra
    • Ramakrishna and Vivekananda • Swami Dayanand and
    the Arya Samaj • The Theosophical Society • Sayyid
    Ahmad Khan and the Aligarh School • Muhammad
    Iqbal • Religious Reform among the Parsis
    • Religious Reform among the Sikhs • Emancipation
    of Women • Struggle Against Caste

12. **The Nationalist Movement: 1905–18**   243

    Recognition of the True Nature of British Rule
    • Growth of Self-Respect and Self-Confidence
    • Growth of Education and Unemployment • International
    Influences • Existence of an Aggressive Nationalist School
    of Thought • A Trained Leadership • The Anti-Partition
    Movement • The Swadeshi and Boycott • The Role of
    Students, Women, Muslims and the Masses • All-India
    Aspect of the Movement • Growth of the Revolutionary
    Struggle • Growth of Revolutionary Nationalism • The Home
    Rule Leagues • Lucknow Session of the Congress (1916)

13. **The Struggle for Swaraj: 1919–27**   276

    The Montagu-Chelmsford Reforms • The Rowlatt
    Act • Gandhiji and His Ideas • Champaran Satyagraha
    (1917) • Ahmedabad Mill Strike • Satyagraha against
    the Rowlatt Act • Jallianwala Bagh Massacre

14. **The Struggle for Swaraj: 1927–47**   298
    Emergence of New Forces • Boycott of the Simon
    Commission • Poorna Swaraj • Nationalist Politics
    1935–39 • The Peasants' and Workers' Movements
    • Congress and World Affairs • People's Struggle in the
    Princely States • Growth of Communalism
    • Post-War Struggle

Books for Further Reading   335

Index   339

Preface

The book presents an overview of the history of what was known as British India. The text is largely based on my own research on nationalism and colonialism in India, and on a large number of scholarly works published in this area.

Challenging and revising old imperialist and nationalist historiographies, the book moves away from the historico-political narrative to emphasise the mutual interrelationships between history, politics, economics, sociology and other related subjects. The book attempts to study wider social forces, movements, institutions and individuals in order to understand why certain events happened and analyses the consequences of such developments within a chronological framework.

The book examines the social, economic and political conditions in India in the eighteenth century in an attempt to explain why India fell prey to the British East India Company and later to the British Crown. It goes on to detail the political, administrative and economic impact of British rule in India. The economic exploitation of India through trade and investment is emphasised as the primary *raison d'être* of British rule. The foreign policies of British India, like the wars with Nepal and Afghanistan or the conquest of Burma, also find mention in the book. The indigenous movements of various tribes and peasants across India are discussed. In the beginning, they rose and struggled in the traditional manner, resulting in major tribal and peasant uprisings throughout the country, which culminated in the revolt of 1857, though peasant and tribal uprisings continued even after. An effort has been made to juxtapose various strands of protest against British rule, so that the readers can develop their own opinion of the impact of British rule in the subcontinent.

I also examine the response of the Indian people to the emergence and growth of British rule. Realising the significance of the decline of Indian culture and society by the eighteenth century, the Indians organised several social and religious reform movements in the nineteenth century. This awakening in the nineteenth century not only adopted Western technology, like the printing press, to protest against British exploitation, but also resulted in assimilating Indians into prevailing world standards.

The last five chapters deal with the emergence of the nationalist movement in India, through the formation of the Indian National Congress, to the attainment of Indian independence. A detailed account is provided of the different strands that emerged within the national movement, like the moderate, the extremist and the revolutionary. The emergence of the mass phase of the Indian national movement under the leadership of Mahatma Gandhi is dealt with extensively, without ignoring the multiple strands represented by Bhagat Singh, Jawaharlal Nehru, Subhas Bose and Jai Prakash Narayan. Certain individuals, who were the key figures in the national movement, have been discussed thoroughly, with an aim to showcase their contribution to the cause of Indian independence. The growth of communalist forces and the opposition of the nationalist movement towards its spread is also innovatively presented.

BIPAN CHANDRA   March 2009

ONE

The Decline of the Mughal Empire

The Mughal Empire, the envy of its contemporaries for almost two centuries, declined and disintegrated during the first half of the eighteenth century. The Mughal emperors lost their power and glory and their empire shrank to a few square miles around Delhi. In the end, in 1803, Delhi itself was occupied by the British army and the proud Mughal emperor was reduced to the status of a mere pensioner of a foreign power. A study of the process of decline of this great Empire is most instructive. It reveals some of the defects and weaknesses of India's medieval social, economic and political structure which were responsible for the eventual subjugation of the country by the English East India Company.

The unity and stability of the Empire had been shaken up during the long and strong reign of Aurangzeb; yet, in spite of his many harmful policies, the Mughal administration was still quite efficient and the Mughal army quite strong at the time of his death in 1707. Moreover, the Mughal dynasty still commanded respect in the country.

On Aurangzeb's death, his three sons fought among themselves for the throne. The 65-year-old Bahadur Shah emerged victorious. He was learned, dignified, and able. He followed a policy of compromise and conciliation, and there was evidence of the reversal of some of the narrow-minded policies and measures adopted by Aurangzeb. He adopted a more tolerant attitude towards the Hindu chiefs and rajas. There was no destruction of temples in his reign. In the beginning, he made an attempt to gain greater control over the Rajput states of Amber and Marwar (Jodhpur) by replacing Jai Singh with his younger brother Vijai Singh at Amber and by forcing Ajit Singh of Marwar to submit to Mughal authority. He also made an attempt to garrison the cities of Amber and Jodhpur. This attempt was, however, met with firm resistance. This may have made him recognise the folly of his actions for he soon arrived at a settlement with the two states, though the settlement was not magnanimous. Though their states were restored to the Rajas Jai Singh and Ajit Singh, their demand for high *mansabs* and the offices of *subahdars* of important provinces such as Malwa and Gujarat was not accepted. His policy towards the Maratha *sardars* (chiefs) was that of half-hearted conciliation.

While he granted them the *sardeshmukhi* of the Deccan, he failed to grant them the *chauth* and to satisfy them fully. He also did not recognise Shahu as the rightful Maratha king. He thus let Tara Bai and Shahu fight for supremacy over the Maratha kingdom. The result was that Shahu and the Maratha *sardars* remained dissatisfied and the Deccan continued to be susceptible to disorder. There could be no restoration of peace and order so long as the Maratha *sardars* fought one another as well as against the Mughal authority.

Bahadur Shah had tried to conciliate the rebellious Sikhs by making peace with Guru Gobind Singh and giving him a high *mansab* (rank). But when, after the death of the Guru, the Sikhs once again raised the banner of revolt in the Punjab under the leadership of Banda Bahadur, the emperor decided to take strong measures and himself led a campaign against the rebels, who soon controlled practically the entire territory between the Sutlej and the Jamuna, reaching the close neighbourhood of Delhi. Even though he succeeded in capturing Lohgarh, a fort built by Guru Gobind Singh north-east of Ambala at the foothills of the Himalayas, and other important Sikh strongholds, the Sikhs could not be crushed and in 1712, they recovered the fort of Lohgarh.

Bahadur Shah conciliated Chatarsal, the Bundela chief, who remained a loyal feudatory, and the Jat chief Churaman, who joined him in the campaign against Banda Bahadur.

There was further deterioration in the field of administration in Bahadur Shah's reign. The position of state finances worsened as a result of his reckless grants of jagirs and promotions. During his reign, the remnants of the royal treasure, amounting in 1707 to some 13 crores of rupees, were exhausted.

Bahadur Shah was groping towards a solution to the problems besetting the empire. Given time, he might have revived the imperial fortunes. Unfortunately, his death in 1712 plunged the Empire once again into civil war.

A new element entered Mughal politics in this and the succeeding wars of succession. While previously the contest for power had been between royal princes, and the nobles had merely aided the aspirants to the throne, now ambitious nobles became direct contenders for power and used princes as mere pawns to capture the seats of authority. In the civil war following Bahadur Shah's death, one of his less able sons, Jahandar Shah, won because he was supported by Zulfiqar Khan, the most powerful noble of the time.

Jahandar Shah was a weak and degenerate prince who was wholly devoted to pleasure. He lacked good manners and dignity and decency. During his reign, the administration was virtually in the hands of the extremely capable and energetic Zulfiqar Khan, who had become his *wazir*. Zulfiqar Khan believed that it was necessary to establish friendly relations with the Rajput rajas and the Maratha *sardars* and to conciliate the Hindu chieftains in general in order to strengthen his own position at the Court and to save the Empire. Therefore, he rapidly reversed the policies of Aurangzeb. The hated *jizyah* was abolished. Jai Singh of Amber was given the title of Mirza Raja Sawai and appointed governor of Malwa; Ajit Singh of Marwar was awarded the title of Maharaja and appointed governor of Gujarat. Zulfiqar Khan confirmed the earlier private arrangement that his deputy in the Deccan, Daud Khan Panni, had concluded with the Maratha king Shahu in 1711. By this arrangement, the Maratha ruler was granted the *chauth* and *sardeshmukhi* of the Deccan on the condition that these collections would be made by Mughal officials and then handed over to the Maratha officials. Zulfiqar Khan also conciliated Churaman Jat and Chhatarsal Bundela. Only towards Banda and the Sikhs did he continue the old policy of suppression.

Zulfiqar Khan made an attempt to improve the finances of the Empire by checking the reckless growth of jagirs and offices. He also tried to compel the *mansabdars* (nobles) to maintain their official quota of troops. An evil tendency encouraged by him was that of *ijarah* or revenue-farming. Instead of collecting land revenue at a fixed rate as under Todar Mal's land revenue settlement, the government began to contract with revenue farmers and middlemen to pay the government a fixed amount of money while they were left free to collect whatever they could from the peasant. This led to increased oppression of the peasant.

Many jealous nobles secretly worked against Zulfiqar Khan. Worse still, the emperor too did not give him his trust and cooperation in full measure. The emperor's ears were poisoned against Zulfiqar Khan by unscrupulous favourites. He was told that his *wazir* was becoming too powerful and ambitious and might even overthrow the emperor himself. The cowardly emperor dared not dismiss the powerful *wazir*, but he began to intrigue against him secretly. Nothing could have been more destructive of healthy administration.

Jahandar Shah's inglorious reign came to an early end in January 1713 when he was defeated at Agra by Farrukh Siyar, his nephew. Farrukh Siyar owed his victory to the Saiyid brothers, Abdullah Khan and Husain Ali Khan Baraha, who were therefore given the offices of *wazir* and *mir bakshi*, respectively. The two brothers soon acquired dominant control over the affairs of the state. Farrukh Siyar lacked the capacity to rule. He was cowardly, cruel, undependable and faithless. Moreover, he allowed himself to be influenced by worthless favourites and flatterers.

In spite of his weaknesses, Farrukh Siyar was not willing to give the Saiyid brothers a free hand but wanted to exercise personal authority. On the other hand, the Saiyid brothers were convinced that administration could be carried on properly, the decay of the Empire checked, and their own positions safeguarded only if they wielded real authority and the emperor merely reigned without ruling. Thus, there ensued a prolonged struggle for power between Emperor Farrukh Siyar and his *wazir* and *mir bakshi*. Year after year, the ungrateful emperor intrigued to overthrow the two brothers; year after year, he failed. In the end, in 1719, the Saiyid brothers deposed and killed him. In his place, they raised to the throne in quick succession two young princes who died of consumption. The Saiyid brothers now made the 18-year-old Muhammad Shah the Emperor of India. The three successors of Farrukh Siyar were mere puppets in the hands of the Saiyids. Even their personal liberty to meet people and to move around was restricted. Thus, from 1713 until 1720, when they were overthrown, the Saiyid brothers wielded the administrative power of the state.

The Saiyid brothers adopted the policy of religious tolerance. They believed that India could be ruled harmoniously only by associating Hindu chiefs and nobles with the Muslim nobles in governing the country. Again, they sought to conciliate and use the Rajputs, the Marathas and the Jats in their struggle against Farrukh Siyar and the rival nobles. They abolished the *jizyah* immediately after Farrukh Siyar's accession to the throne. Similarly, the pilgrim tax was abolished from a number of places. They won over to their side Ajit Singh of Marwar, Jai Singh of Amber, and many other Rajput princes by giving them high positions of influence in the administration. They made an alliance with Churaman, the Jat chieftain. In the later years of their administration, they reached an agreement with King Shahu by granting him the *swarajya* (of Shivaji) and the right to collect the *chauth* and *sardeshmukhi* of the six provinces of the Deccan. In return, Shahu agreed to support them in the Deccan with 15,000 mounted soldiers.

The Saiyid brothers made a vigorous effort to contain rebellions and to save the Empire from administrative disintegration. They failed in these tasks mainly because they were faced with constant political rivalry, quarrels, and conspiracies at the court. This continued friction in the ruling circles disorganised and even paralysed administration at all levels. Lawlessness and disorder spread everywhere. The financial position of the state deteriorated rapidly as zamindars and rebellious elements refused to pay land revenue, officials misappropriated state revenues, and central income declined because of the spread of revenue farming. As a result, the salaries of the officials and soldiers could not be paid regularly and the soldiers became indisciplined and even mutinous.

Even though the Saiyid brothers had tried hard to conciliate and befriend all sections of the nobility, a powerful group of nobles headed by Nizam-ul-Mulk and his father's cousin, Muhammad Amin Khan, began to conspire against them. These nobles were jealous of the growing power of the two brothers. The deposition and murder of Farrukh Siyar frightened many of them: if the emperor could be killed, what safety was there for mere nobles? Moreover, the murder of the emperor created a wave of public revulsion against the two brothers. They were looked down upon as traitors—persons who had not been 'true to their salt' (*namak haram*). Many of the nobles of Aurangzeb's reign also disliked the Saiyid alliance with the Rajput and the Maratha chiefs and their liberal policy towards the Hindus. These nobles declared that the Saiyids were following anti-Mughal and anti-Islamic policies. They tried to rouse the fanatical sections of the Muslim nobility against the Saiyid brothers. The anti-Saiyid nobles were supported by Emperor Muhammad Shah, who wanted to free himself from the control of the two brothers. In 1720, they succeeded in treacherously assassinating Husain Ali Khan, the younger of the two brothers. Abdullah Khan tried to fight back, but was defeated near Agra. Thus ended the domination of the Mughal Empire by the Saiyid brothers, known in Indian history as 'king makers'.

Muhammad Shah's long reign of nearly 30 years (1719–48) was the last chance of saving the Empire. There were no quick changes of imperial authority as in the period 1707–20. When his reign began, Mughal prestige among the people was still an important political factor. The Mughal army and particularly the Mughal artillery was still a force to reckon with. Administration in northern India had deteriorated, but had not broken down yet. The Maratha *sardars* were still confined to the south, while the Rajput rajas continued to be loyal to the Mughal dynasty. A strong and farsighted ruler supported by a nobility conscious of its peril might still have saved the situation. But Muhammad Shah was not the man of the moment. He was weak-minded and frivolous and overly fond of a life of ease and luxury. He neglected the affairs of state. Instead of giving full support to able *wazirs* such as Nizam-ul-Mulk, he fell under the evil influence of corrupt and worthless flatterers and intrigued against his own ministers. He even shared in the bribes taken by his favourite courtiers.

Disgusted with the fickle-mindedness and suspicious nature of the emperor and the constant quarrels at the court, Nizum-ul-Mulk, the most powerful noble of the time, decided to follow his own ambition. He had become the *wazir* in 1722 and made a vigorous attempt to reform the administration. He now decided to leave the emperor and his empire to their fate and to strike out on his own. He relinquished his office in October 1724 and marched south to found the state of Hyderabad in the Deccan. "His departure was symbolic of the flight of loyalty and virtue from the empire." The physical break-up of the Mughal Empire had begun.

The other powerful and ambitious nobles now began to utilise their energies to carve out semi-independent states. Hereditary nawabs owing nominal allegiance to the emperor at Delhi rose in many parts of the country, for example in Bengal, Hyderabad, Avadh, and the Punjab. Everywhere petty zamindars, rajas and nawabs raised the banner of rebellion and independence. The Maratha *sardars* began their northern expansion and overran Malwa, Gujarat and Bundelkhand. Then, in 1738–39, Nadir Shah descended upon the plains of northern India, and the Empire lay prostrate.

Nadir Shah had risen from shepherd boy to *Shah* (king) by saving Persia from sure decline and disintegration. In the beginning of the eighteenth century Persia, hitherto a powerful and far flung empire, was under the weak rule of the declining Safavi dynasty. It was threatened by internal rebellions and foreign attacks. In the east, the Abdali tribesmen revolted and occupied Herat, and the Ghalzai tribesmen detached the province of Qandahar. Similar revolts occurred in the north and west. In Shirvan, religious persecution of the *Sunnis* by fanatical *Shias* led to rebellion. Here, "*Sunni mullahs* were put to death, mosques were profaned and turned into stables, and religious works were destroyed." In 1721, the Ghalzai chief of Qandahar, Mahmud, invaded Persia and occupied Isfahan, the capital. Russia under Peter the Great was determined to push southward. Peter began his invasion of Persia in July 1722 and soon forced Persia to sign away several of her provinces on the Caspian Sea, including the town of Baku. Turkey, deprived of most of her European possessions, also hoped to make good the loss at Persia's cost. In the spring of 1723, Turkey declared war on Persia and rapidly pushed through Georgia, and then penetrated south. In June 1724, Russia and Turkey signed a treaty dividing all northern and most of western Persia between them. At this stage, in 1726, Nadir emerged as a major supporter of Tahmasp and his most brilliant commander. In 1729, he won back Herat after defeating the Abdalis and expelled the Ghalzais from Isfahan and central and southern Persia. After long and bitter warfare, he compelled Turkey to give back all conquered territory. In 1735, he signed a treaty with Russia receiving back all seized territory. The following year, he deposed the last of the Safavi rulers and made himself the Shah. In the following years, he reconquered the province of Qandahar.

Nadir Shah was attracted to India by the fabulous wealth for which it was always famous. Continual campaigns had made Persia virtually bankrupt. Money was needed desperately to maintain his mercenary army. Spoils from India could be a solution. At the same time, the visible weakness of the Mughal Empire made such spoliation possible. He entered Indian territory towards the end of 1738, without meeting any opposition. For years the defences of the north-west frontier had been neglected. The danger was not fully recognised till the enemy had occupied Lahore. Hurried preparations were then made for the defence of Delhi, but the faction-ridden nobles refused to unite even in sight of the enemy. They could not agree on a plan for defence or on the commander of the defending forces. Disunity, poor leadership, mutual jealousies and distrust could lead only to defeat. The two armies met at Karnal on 13 February 1739 and the invader inflicted a crushing defeat on the Mughal army. Emperor Muhammad Shah was taken prisoner and Nadir Shah marched on to Delhi. A terrible massacre of the citizens of the imperial capital was ordered by Nadir Shah as a reprisal against the killing of some of his soldiers. The greedy invader took possession of the royal treasury and other royal property, levied tribute on the leading nobles, and plundered the rich of Delhi. His total plunder has been estimated at 70 crores of rupees. This enabled him to exempt his own kingdom from taxation for three years! He also carried away the famous Koh-i-nur diamond and the jewel-studded Peacock Throne of Shahjahan. He compelled Muhammad Shah to cede to him all the provinces of the Empire west of the river Indus.

Nadir Shah's invasion inflicted immense damage on the Mughal Empire. It caused an irreparable loss of prestige and exposed the hidden weakness of the Empire to the Maratha *sardars* and the foreign trading companies. The central administration was paralysed temporarily. The invasion ruined imperial finances and adversely affected the economic life of the country. The impoverished nobles began to rack-rent and oppress the peasantry even more in an effort to recover their lost fortunes. They also fought one another over rich jagirs and high offices more desperately than ever. The loss of Kabul and the areas to the west of the Indus once again opened the Empire to the threat of invasions from the north-west. A vital line of defence had disappeared.

The Decline of the Mughal Empire

It is surprising indeed that the Empire seemed to revive some of its strength after Nadir Shah's departure, even though the area under its effective control shrank rapidly. But the revival was deceptive and superficial. After Muhammad Shah's death in 1748, bitter struggles and even civil war broke out among unscrupulous and power hungry nobles. Furthermore, as a result of the weakening of the north-western defences, the Empire was devastated by the repeated invasions of Ahmed Shah Abdali, one of Nadir Shah's ablest generals, who had succeeded in establishing his authority over Afghanistan after his master's death. Abdali repeatedly invaded and plundered northern India right down to Delhi and Mathura between 1748 and 1767. In 1761, he defeated the Marathas in the Third Battle of Panipat and thus dealt a big blow to their ambition of controlling the Mughal emperor and thereby dominating the country. He did not, however, found a new Afghan kingdom in India. He and his successors could not even retain the Punjab, which they soon lost to the Sikh chiefs.

As a result of the invasions of Nadir Shah and Abdali and the suicidal internal feuds of the Mughal nobility, the Mughal Empire had by 1761 ceased to exist in practice as an all-India Empire. It remained merely as the Kingdom of Delhi. Delhi itself was a scene of 'daily riot and tumult'. The descendants of the Grand Mughals no longer participated actively in the struggle for the Empire of India; rather, the various contenders for power found it politically useful to hide behind their name. This gave the Mughal dynasty a long lease of life on the nominal throne of Delhi.

Shah Alam II, who ascended the throne in 1759, spent the initial years as an emperor wandering from place to place far away from his capital, for he lived in mortal fear of his own *wazir*. He was a man of some ability and ample courage. But the Empire was by now beyond redemption. In 1764, he joined Mir Qasim of Bengal and Shuja-ud-Daula of Awadh in declaring war upon the English East India Company. Defeated by the British at the Battle of Buxar, he lived for several years at Allahabad as a pensioner of the East India Company. He left the British shelter in 1772 and returned to Delhi under the protective arm of the Marathas. The British occupied Delhi in 1803 and from that year until 1857, when the Mughal dynasty was finally extinguished, the Mughal emperors merely served as a political front for the English. In fact, the continuation of the Mughal monarchy after 1759, when it had ceased to be a military power, was due to the powerful hold that the Mughal dynasty had on the minds of the people of India as a symbol of the political unity of the country.

CAUSES OF THE DECLINE OF THE MUGHAL EMPIRE

When a mighty empire like that of the Mughals decays and falls, it is because many factors and forces have been at work. The beginnings of the decline of the Mughal Empire are to be traced to the strong rule of Aurangzeb. Aurangzeb inherited a large empire, yet he adopted a policy of extending it further to the farthest geographical limits in the south at great expense in men and materials. In reality, the existing means of communication and the economic and political structure of the country made it difficult to establish a stable centralised administration over all parts of the country. Thus Aurangzeb's objective of unifying the entire country under one central political authority was, though justifiable in theory, not easy in practice.

One of the basic failures of Aurangzeb lay in the realm of statesmanship. He was not willing to accept to the full the Maratha demand for regional autonomy, failing to grasp the fact that Shivaji and other Maratha *sardars* represented forces which could not be easily crushed. Akbar, placed in similar circumstances, had made an alliance with the Rajput princes and chiefs. Aurangzeb too would have been well-advised to win over the Maratha *sardars*. Instead, he chose to suppress them. His futile but arduous campaign against the Marathas extended over many years; it drained the resources of his empire and ruined the trade and industry of the Deccan. His absence from the north for over 25 years and his failure to subdue the Marathas led to deterioration in administration; this undermined the prestige of the Empire and its army, led to the neglect of the vital north-west frontier, and encouraged provincial and local officials to defy central authority and to dream of independence. Later, in the eighteenth century, Maratha expansion in the north weakened central authority still further.

Aurangzeb's conflict with some of the Rajput states also had serious consequences. Alliance with the Rajput rajas with the consequent military support was one of the main pillars of Mughal strength in the past. Aurangzeb himself had in the beginning adhered to the Rajput alliance by raising Jaswant Singh of Marwar and Jai Singh of Amber to the highest of ranks. But his short-sighted attempt later to reduce the strength of the Rajput rajas and to re-extend imperial sway over their lands led to the withdrawal of their loyalty from the Mughal throne. Wars with the Rajput rajas further weakened the empire and encouraged separation.

The strength of Aurangzeb's administration was challenged at its very nerve centre around Delhi by the Satnami, Jat and Sikh uprisings. Even though the number of people involved in these uprisings was not large, they were significant because they were popular in character—peasants formed their backbone. All of them were to a considerable extent the result of the oppression of the Mughal revenue officials over the peasantry. They showed that the peasantry was deeply dissatisfied with feudal oppression by zamindars, nobles and the state.

Aurangzeb's religious orthodoxy and his policy towards the Hindu rulers seriously damaged the stability of the Mughal Empire. The Mughal state in the days of Akbar, Jahangir and Shahjahan was basically a secular state. Its stability was essentially founded on the policy of non-interference with the religious beliefs and customs of the people, fostering of friendly relations between Hindus and Muslims, opening the doors of the highest offices of the state to nobles and chiefs belonging to different regions and professing different religions. The Mughal alliance with the Rajput rajas was a visible manifestation of this policy. Aurangzeb made an attempt to reverse this policy by imposing the *jizyah*, destroying several Hindu temples in the north, and placing certain restrictions on the Hindus. In this way, he tended to alienate the Hindus, split Mughal society and, in particular, widened the gulf between the Hindu and the Muslim upper classes. But the role played by Aurangzeb's religious policy in causing the decay of Mughal power should not be over-stressed. This policy was followed only in the latter part of his reign. It was speedily abandoned by his successors. As we have seen earlier, the *jizyah* was abolished within a few years of Aurangzeb's death. Amicable relations with the Rajput and other Hindu nobles and chiefs were soon restored, and some of them, such as Ajit Singh Rathor and Sawai Jai Singh, rose to high offices under the later Mughals. Relations with King Shahu and the Maratha *sardars* were also developed along political rather than religious lines. It should also be kept in mind that the Rajput, Jat, Maratha and Sikh chieftains of the eighteenth century did not behave as champions of the Hindus. Power and plunder were more important considerations to them than religious solidarity. They were often as ruthless in fighting and looting the Hindus as the Muslims were. In fact, neither the Hindus nor the Muslims formed a homogeneous community at that time. The upper classes of both religious groups formed the ruling class, while the peasants and artisans, Hindu or Muslim, formed the underprivileged majority of society. Sometimes the Hindu and Muslim nobles and chiefs used religion as a weapon of propaganda to achieve their political aims. But even more often, they formed mutual alliances against fellow co-religionists for gaining power, territory, or money. Moreover, both the Hindu and Muslim nobles, zamindars and chiefs ruthlessly oppressed and exploited the common people, irrespective of their religion. The Hindu peasantry of Maharashtra or Rajputana paid as high an amount in land revenue as did the Hindu or Muslim peasantry in Agra or Bengal or Avadh. Moreover, cordial cultural and social relations prevailed between the Hindu and Muslim upper classes of India.

If Aurangzeb left the Empire with many problems unsolved, the situation was further worsened by the ruinous wars of succession which followed his death. In the absence of any fixed rule of succession, the Mughal dynasty was always plagued after the death of a king by a civil war between the princes. These wars of succession became extremely fierce and destructive during the eighteenth century. They resulted in great loss of life and property. Thousands of trained soldiers and hundreds of capable military commanders and efficient and tried officials were killed. Moreover, these civil wars loosened the administrative fabric of the Empire. The nobility, the backbone of the Empire, was transformed into warring factions. Many of the local chiefs and officials utilised the conditions of uncertainty and political chaos at the centre to consolidate their own position, to acquire greater autonomy, and to make their offices hereditary.

The weaknesses of Aurangzeb's reign and the evils of the wars of succession might still have been overcome if able, farsighted, and energetic rulers had appeared on the throne. Unfortunately, after Bahadur Shah's brief reign came a long reign of utterly worthless, weak-willed and luxury-loving kings. After all, in an autocratic, monarchical system of government the character and personality of the ruler do play a crucial role. At the same time, this single factor need not be given too much importance. Aurangzeb was neither weak nor degenerate. He possessed great ability and capacity for work. He was free of the vices common among kings and lived a simple and austere life. He undermined the great empire of his forefathers not because he lacked character or ability, but because he lacked political, social and economic insight. It was not his personality but his policies that were out of joint.

Apart from the personalities of the Mughals, the strength of the Mughal Empire lay in the organisation and character of its nobility. The weakness of the king could have been successfully overcome and covered up by an alert, efficient, and loyal nobility. But the character of the nobility had also deteriorated. Many nobles lived extravagantly and beyond their means. Many of them became ease-loving and fond of excessive luxury. Even when they went out to fight, they surrounded themselves with comforts and frequently took their families with them. They were often poorly educated. Many of them even neglected the art of fighting. Earlier, many able persons from the lower classes had been able to rise to the ranks of nobility, thus infusing fresh blood into it. Later, the existing families of nobles began to monopolise all offices, barring the way to fresh entrants. Not all the nobles, however, had become weak and inefficient. A large number of energetic and able officials and brave and brilliant military commanders came into prominence during the eighteenth century, but most of them did not benefit the Empire because they used their talents to promote their own interests and to fight each other rather than serve the state and society.

In fact, contrary to popular belief, the major weakness of the Mughal nobility during the eighteenth century lay not in the decline in the average ability of the nobles or their moral decay, but in their selfishness and lack of devotion to the state and this, in turn, gave birth to corruption in administration and mutual bickering. In order to increase their power, prestige, and income, the nobles formed groups and factions against each other and even against the king. In their struggle for power, they took recourse to force, fraud, and treachery. Their mutual quarrels exhausted the empire, affected its cohesion, led to its dismemberment, and, in the end, made it an easy prey to foreign conquerors. And the most guilty in this respect were precisely those nobles who were active and able. It is they who shattered the unity of the Empire by carving out their own private principalities. Thus, the decadence of the later Mughal nobility lay not so much in private vice as in a lack of public virtue and political foresight and in its devotion to the short-sighted pursuit of power. But these characteristics were not the monopoly of the Mughal nobility at the centre. They were found in equal measure among the rising Maratha chiefs, the Rajput rajas, Jat, Sikh, and the Bundela chiefs, the new rulers of autonomous provinces, and the other innumerable adventurers who rose to fame and power during the troubled eighteenth century.

One of the major causes of the growing selfishness and cliquishness of the nobles was the paucity of jagirs and the reduced income of the existing jagirs at a time when the number of nobles and their expenditure was going up. So there ensued intense mutual rivalry among them for possession of the existing jagirs. The heart of the matter perhaps was that no arrangement could have been made that would satisfy all the nobles, for there were just not enough offices and jagirs for all. The paucity of jagirs had some other consequences. The nobles tried to get the maximum income from their jagirs at the cost of the peasantry. They tried to transform their existing jagirs and offices into hereditary ones. To balance their own budgets, they tended to appropriate *khalisah* (crown) lands, thus intensifying the financial crisis of the central government. They invariably reduced their expenditure by not maintaining their full quota of troops and thus weakened the armed strength of the Empire.

A basic cause of the downfall of the Mughal Empire was that it could no longer satisfy the minimum needs of its population. The condition of the Indian peasant gradually worsened during the seventeenth and eighteenth centuries. While at no time perhaps was his lot happy, in the eighteenth century his life was "poor, nasty, miserable and uncertain". The burden of land revenue went on increasing from Akbar's time. Moreover, constant transfer of nobles from their jagirs also led to great evil. They tried to extract as much from a jagir as possible in the short period of their tenure as jagirdars. They made heavy demands on the peasants and cruelly oppressed them, often in violation of official regulations. After the death of Aurangzeb, the practice of *ijarah* or farming the land revenue to the highest bidder, who was permitted to raise what he could from the peasantry, became more common both on jagir and *khalisah* (crown) lands. This led to the rise of a new class of revenue farmers and talukdars, whose extortions from the peasantry often knew no bounds.

All these factors led to stagnation and deterioration in agriculture and the impoverishment of the peasant. Peasant discontent increased and came to the surface. There are some instances of peasants leaving the land to avoid paying taxes. Peasant discontent also found an outlet in a series of uprisings (the Satnamis, the Jats, the Sikhs, etc.), which eroded the stability and strength of the Empire. Many ruined peasants formed roving bands of robbers and adventurers, often under the leadership of the zamindars, and thus undermined law and order and the efficiency of the Mughal administration.

As a matter of fact, agriculture was no longer producing enough surplus to meet the needs of the Empire, of constant warfare, and of the increased luxury of the ruling classes. If the Empire was to survive and regain its strength and if the people were to go forward, trade and industry alone could provide the additional economic resources. But it was precisely in trade and industry that stagnation was most evident. No doubt the establishment of a large empire encouraged trade and industry in many ways and India's industrial production increased to a marked extent. Both in the quality of its products and their quantity, Indian industry was quite advanced by contemporary world standards. But unlike in Europe at this time, Indian industry did not make any new advances in science and technology. Similarly, the growth of trade was hampered by bad communications and by the self-sufficient nature of village economy. Moreover, emphasis on land as a source of wealth and government revenue led to the neglect of overseas trade and the navy. Perhaps not even the best of kings and nobles could have changed this situation. In the absence of scientific and technological development and a social, economic, and political revolution, India lagged behind Europe economically and politically and succumbed to its pressure.

An important socio-political cause of the downfall of the Mughal Empire was the absence of the spirit of political nationalism among the people. This was because India at the time lacked the elements which constitute a modern nation. The people of India did not feel that they were all Indians, nor were they conscious of oneness or of having common interests, even though elements of cultural unity had existed in the country for centuries. Therefore, there did not exist the ideal of living and dying for one's nation. Instead, people were loyal to persons, tribes, castes, and religious sects.

In fact, no group or class in the country was deeply interested in maintaining the unity of the country or the Empire. Such unity as did exist was imposed from above by strong rulers. The peasants' loyalty was confined to their village and caste. Moreover, they took little interest in the politics of the Empire, nor did they identify its interests with their own. They realised that they had little stake in it and that even its defence from external aggression was not their concern. The zamindars tended to rebel against any central authority which showed signs of weakness. They were opposed to a strong, centralised state that curbed their power and autonomy.

The nobles had been earlier imbued with an exalted notion of loyalty to their dynasty. But this was mainly based on the high offices and privileges they obtained in return. With the decline of the dynasty, the nobles placed their self-interest and ambition above loyalty to the state and attacked the very unity of the Empire by carving out autonomous principalities. Even those who rebelled against the Empire, for example, the Marathas, the Jats, and the Rajputs, were interested in consolidating their regional, tribal, or personal power and had no notion of fighting for a nation called India or for its unity. The reality was that the existing character of the Indian economy, social relations, caste structure, and political institutions was such that the time was not yet ripe for the unification of Indian society or for its emergence as a nation.

The Mughal Empire might have continued to exist for a long time if its administration and armed power had not broken down, mostly as a result of the factors discussed above. There was rapid decline in the administrative efficiency of the Empire during the eighteenth century. Administration was neglected and law and order broke down in many parts of the country. Unruly zamindars openly defied central authority. Even the royal camp and Mughal armies on the march were often plundered by hostile elements. Corruption and bribery, indiscipline and inefficiency, disobedience and disloyalty prevailed on a large scale among officials at all levels. The central government was often on the verge of bankruptcy. The old accumulated wealth was exhausted, while the existing sources of income were narrowed. Many provinces failed to remit provincial revenues to the centre. The area of the *khalisah* lands was gradually reduced as emperors tried to placate friendly nobles by granting jagirs out of these lands. The rebellious zamindars regularly withheld revenue. Efforts to increase income by oppressing the peasantry produced popular reaction.

Ultimately, the military strength of the Empire was affected. During the eighteenth century, the Mughal army lacked discipline and fighting morale. Lack of finance made it difficult to maintain a large army. Its soldiers and officers were not paid for months, and, since they were mere mercenaries, they were constantly disaffected and often verged on a mutiny. Again, the noblemen-cum-commanders did not maintain their full quota of military contingents because of their own financial troubles. Moreover, the civil wars resulted in the death of many brilliant commanders and brave and experienced soldiers. Thus, the army, the ultimate sanction of an empire and the pride of the Mughals, was so weakened that it could no longer curb the ambitious chiefs and nobles or defend the Empire from foreign aggression.

The final blow to the Mughal Empire was given by a series of foreign invasions. Attacks by Nadir Shah and Ahmad Shah Abdali, which were themselves the consequences of the weakness of the Empire, drained it of its wealth, ruined its trade and industry in the north, and almost destroyed its military power. Finally, the emergence of the British challenge took away the last hope of the revival of the crisis-ridden Empire. In this last fact lies the most important consequence of the decline of the Mughal Empire. None of the Indian powers rose to claim the heritage of the Mughals for they were strong enough to destroy the Empire, but not strong enough to unite it or to create anything new in its place. They could not create a new social order which could stand up to the new enemy from the West. All of them represented the same moribund social system as headed by the Mughals and all of them suffered from the weaknesses which had destroyed the mighty Mughal Empire. On the other hand, the Europeans knocking at the gates of India had the benefit of coming from societies which had evolved a superior economic system and which were more advanced in science and technology. The tragedy of the decline of the Mughal Empire was that its mantle fell on a foreign power which dissolved, in its own interests, the centuries-old socio-economic and political structure of the country and replaced it with a colonial structure. But some good was destined to come out of this evil. The stagnation of Indian society was broken and new forces of change emerged. This process, because it grew out of a colonial contact, inevitably brought with it extreme misery and national degradation, not to mention economic, political, and cultural backwardness. But it was precisely these new forces of change that were to provide the dynamism of modern India.

Two

Indian States and Society in the Eighteenth Century

Decay of the Mughal Empire

With the gradual weakening and decline of the Mughal Empire, local and regional political and economic forces began to arise and assert themselves and politics began to undergo major changes from the late seventeenth century onwards. During the eighteenth century, from the debris of the Mughal Empire and its political system rose a large number of independent and semi-independent powers such as the Bengal, Awadh, Hyderabad, Mysore and Maratha kingdoms. It is these powers which the British had to overcome in their attempt at supremacy in India.

Some of these states, such as Bengal, Awadh and Hyderabad, may be characterised as 'succession states'. They arose as a result of the assertion of autonomy by governors of Mughal provinces with the decay of the central power. Others, such as the Maratha, Afghan, Jat and Punjab states, were the product of rebellions by local chieftains, zamindars and peasants against Mughal authority. Not only did the politics in the two types of states or zones differ to some extent from each other, but there were also differences among all of them because of local conditions. Yet, not surprisingly, the overall political and administrative framework was very similar in nearly all of them. There was, of course, also a third zone comprising of areas on the south-west and south-east coasts and of north-eastern India, where Mughal influence had not penetrated to any degree.

The rulers of all the eighteenth-century states tried to legitimise their position by acknowledging the nominal supremacy of the Mughal emperor and by seeking his approval as his representatives. Moreover, nearly all of them adopted the methods and spirit of Mughal administration. The first group of states (succession states) inherited functioning Mughal administrative structures and institutions; others tried to adopt and adapt in varying degrees this structure and institutions, including the Mughal revenue system. The rulers of these states established law and order and viable economic and administrative structures. They curbed, with varying degrees of success, the lower local officials and petty chiefs and zamindars who constantly fought with higher authorities for control over the surplus produce of the peasant, and who sometimes succeeded in establishing local centres of power and patronage. They also conciliated and accommodated these local chiefs and zamindars who desired peace and law and order. In general, there was in most of the states decentralisation of political authority, with chiefs, jagirdars and zamindars gaining in economic and political power. The politics of these states were invariably non-communal or secular, the motivations of their rulers being similar in economic and political terms. These rulers did not discriminate on religious grounds in public appointments, civil or military; nor did the rebels against their authority pay much attention to the religion of the rulers. There is, therefore, little warrant for the belief that the decline and break-up of the Mughal Empire was followed by 'anarchy' or breakdown of law and order in different parts of India. In fact, whatever anarchy in administration and economy existed in the eighteenth century usually followed British wars of conquest and British intervention in the internal affairs of the Indian states.

None of these states, however, succeeded in arresting the economic crisis which had set in during the seventeenth century. All of them remained basically rent-extracting states. The zamindars and jagirdars, whose number and political strength constantly increased, continued to fight over the income from agriculture, while the condition of the peasantry continued to deteriorate. While these states prevented any breakdown of internal trade and even tried to promote foreign trade, they did nothing to modernise the basic industrial and commercial structure of their states. This largely explains their failure to consolidate themselves or to ward off external attack.

Hyderabad and the Carnatic

The state of Hyderabad was founded by Nizam-ul-Mulk Asaf Jah in 1724. He was one of the leading nobles of the post-Aurangzeb era. He played a leading role in the overthrow of the Saiyid brothers and was rewarded with the viceroyalty of the Deccan. From 1720 to 1722, he consolidated his hold over the Deccan by suppressing all opposition to his viceroyalty and organising the administration on efficient lines. From 1722 to 1724, he was the *wazir* of the Empire. But he soon became disgusted with that office as the Emperor, Muhammad Shah, frustrated all his attempts at reforming the administration. So he decided to go back to the Deccan where he could safely maintain his supremacy. Here, he laid the foundations of Hyderabad State which he ruled with a strong hand. He never openly declared his independence from the central government, but in practice he acted like an independent ruler. He waged wars, concluded peace, conferred titles, and gave jagirs and offices without reference to Delhi. He followed a tolerant policy towards the Hindus. For example, a Hindu, Puran Chand, was his Dewan. He consolidated his power by establishing an orderly administration in the Deccan on the basis of the jagirdari system along the Mughal pattern. He forced the big, turbulent zamindars to respect his authority and kept the powerful Marathas out of his dominions. He also made an attempt to rid the revenue system of its corruption. But after his death in 1748, Hyderabad fell prey to the same disruptive forces as were operating in Delhi.

The Carnatic was one of the *subahs* of the Mughal Deccan and as such came under the Nizam of Hyderabad's authority. But just as in practice the Nizam had become independent of Delhi, so also the Deputy Governor of the Carnatic, known as the Nawab of Carnatic, had freed himself of the control of the Viceroy of the Deccan and made his office hereditary. Thus, Nawab Saadutullah Khan of Carnatic had made his nephew, Dost Ali, his successor without the approval of his superior, the Nizam. Later, after 1740, the affairs of the Carnatic deteriorated because of the repeated struggles for its nawabship, and this provided an opportunity to European trading companies to directly interfere in Indian politics.

Bengal

Taking advantage of the growing weakness of the central authority, two men of exceptional ability, Murshid Quli Khan and Alivardi Khan, made Bengal virtually independent. Even though Murshid Quli Khan was made Governor of Bengal as late as 1717, he had been its effective ruler since 1700, when he was appointed its Dewan. He soon freed himself from central control, though he regularly sent a large tribute to the emperor. He established peace by freeing Bengal of internal and external danger. Bengal was now also relatively free of major uprisings by zamindars. The only three major uprisings during his rule were, first, by Sitaram Ray, Udai Narayan and Ghulam Muhammad, and then by Shujat Khan, and finally by Najat Khan. After defeating them, Murshid Quli Khan gave their zamindaris to his favourite, Ramjivan. Murshid Quli Khan died in 1727, and his son-in-law Shuja-ud-din ruled Bengal till 1739. In that year, Alivardi Khan deposed and killed Shuja-ud-din's son, Sarfaraz Khan, and made himself the Nawab.

These three Nawabs gave Bengal a long period of peace and orderly administration and promoted its trade and industry. Murshid Quli Khan effected economies in the administration and reorganised the finances of Bengal by transferring large parts of jagir lands into *khalisah* lands by carrying out a fresh revenue settlement, and by introducing the system of revenue-farming. He recruited revenue farmers and officials from local zamindars and merchant-bankers. He also granted agricultural loans *(taccavi)* to the poor cultivators to relieve their distress, as well as to enable them to pay land revenue in time. He was thus able to increase the resources of the Bengal government. But the system of revenue-farming led to increased economic pressure on the zamindars and peasants. Moreover, even though he demanded only the standard revenue and forbade illegal cesses, he collected the revenue from the zamindars and peasants with utmost cruelty. Another result of his reforms was that many of the older zamindars were driven out, and their place taken by upstart revenue-farmers.

Murshid Quli Khan and the succeeding Nawabs gave equal opportunities for employment to Hindus and Muslims. They filled the highest civil posts and many of the military posts with Bengalis, mostly Hindus. In choosing revenue farmers, Murshid Quli Khan gave preference to local zamindars and *mahajans* (money-lenders), who were mainly Hindus. He thus laid the foundations of a new landed aristocracy in Bengal.

All three Nawabs recognised that the expansion of trade benefited the people and the government, and therefore encouraged all merchants, Indian and foreign. They provided for the safety of roads and rivers from thieves and robbers by establishing regular *thanas* and *chowkies*. They checked private trade by officials. They prevented abuses in the customs administration. At the same time, they made it a point to maintain strict control over foreign trading companies and their servants and prevented them from abusing their privileges. They compelled the servants of the English East India Company to obey the laws of the land and to pay the same customs duties as were being paid by other merchants. Alivardi Khan did not permit the English and the French to fortify their factories in Calcutta and Chandernagore. The Bengal Nawabs proved, however, to be short-sighted and negligent in one respect. They did not firmly put down the increasing tendency of the English East India Company after 1707 to use military force, or to threaten its use, to get its demands accepted. They had the power to deal with the Company's threats, but continued to believe that a mere trading company could not threaten their power. They failed to see that the English Company was no mere company of traders, but the representative of the most aggressive and expansionist colonialism of the time. Their ignorance of, and lack of contact with, the rest of the world was to cost the state dearly. Otherwise, they would have known of the devastation caused by the Western trading companies in Africa, South-East Asia, and Latin America.

The Nawabs of Bengal neglected to build a strong army and paid a heavy price for it. For example, the army of Murshid Quli Khan consisted of only 2000 cavalry and 4000 infantry. Alivardi Khan was constantly troubled by the repeated invasions of the Marathas and, in the end, had to cede a large part of Orissa to them. And when, in 1756–67, the English East India Company declared war on Siraj-ud-Daulah, the successor of Alivardi, the absence of a strong army contributed much to the victory of the foreigner. The Bengal Nawabs also failed to check the growing corruption among their officials.

Even judicial officials, the *qazis* and *muftis*, were given to taking bribes. The foreign companies took full advantage of this weakness to undermine official rules and regulations and policies.

AWADH

The founder of the autonomous kingdom of Awadh was Saadat Khan Burhan-ul-Mulk, who was appointed Governor of Awadh in 1722. He was an extremely bold, energetic, iron-willed, and intelligent person. At the time of his appointment, many rebellious zamindars had raised their heads everywhere in the province. They refused to pay the land tax, organised their own private armies, erected forts, and defied the Imperial Government. For years, Saadat Khan had to wage war upon them. He succeeded in suppressing lawlessness and disciplining the big zamindars, and thus increasing the financial resources of his government. He won over the chieftains and zamindars through various concessions. Moreover, most of the defeated zamindars were also not displaced. They were usually confirmed in their estates after they had submitted and agreed to pay their dues (land revenue) regularly.

Saadat Khan also carried out a fresh revenue settlement in 1723. He is said to have improved the lot of the peasant by levying equitable land revenue and by protecting him from oppression by the big zamindars.

Like the Bengal Nawabs, he too did not discriminate between Hindus and Muslims. Many of his commanders and high officials were Hindus, and he curbed refractory zamindars, chiefs, and nobles, irrespective of their religion. His troops were well-paid, well-armed, and well-trained. His administration was efficient. He, too, continued the jagir system. Before his death in 1739, he had become virtually independent and had made the province a hereditary possession. He was succeeded by his nephew Safdar Jang, who was simultaneously appointed the *wazir* of the Empire in 1748 and granted in addition the province of Allahabad.

Safdar Jang brought a long period of peace to the people of Awadh and Allahabad before his death in 1754. He suppressed rebellious zamindars, won over others and made an alliance with the Maratha

Indian States and Society in the Eighteenth Century

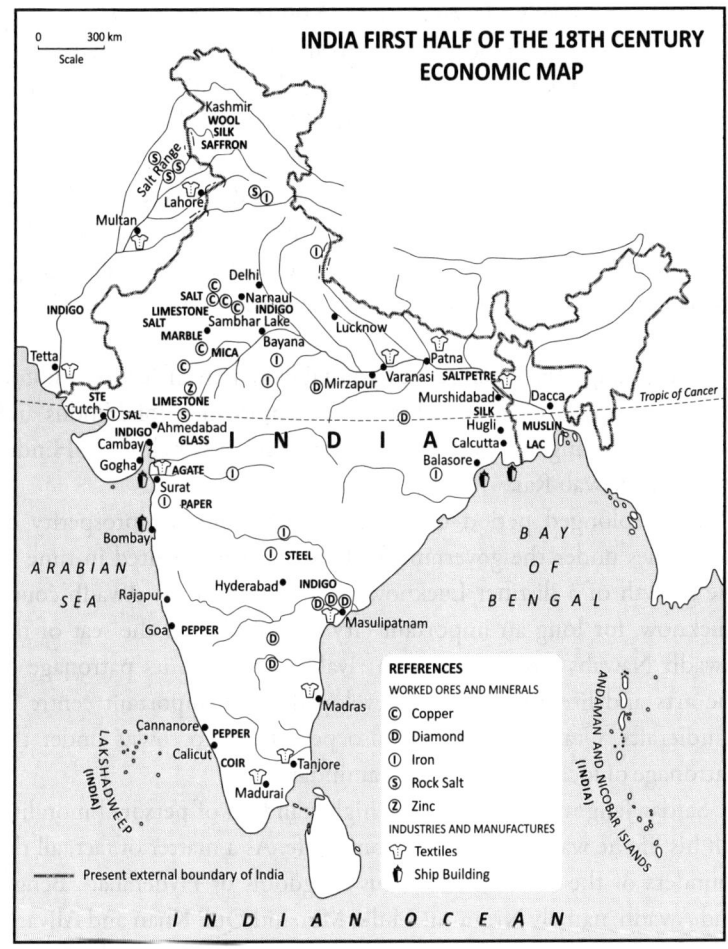

sardars so that his dominion was saved from their incursions. He was able to win the loyalty of Rajput chieftains, *shaikhzadas*. He carried on warfare against the Rohelas and the Bangash Pathans. In his war against the Bangash Pathans in 1750–51, he secured Maratha military help by paying a daily allowance of Rs 25,000 and Jat support by paying Rs 15,000 a day. Later, he entered into an agreement with the Peshwa, by which the Peshwa was to help the Mughal Empire against Ahmad Shah Abdali and to protect it from such internal rebels as the Indian Pathans and the Rajput rajas. In return, the Peshwa was to be paid Rs 50 lakh, granted the *chauth* of the Punjab, Sindh, and several districts of northern India, and made the Governor of Ajmer and Agra. The agreement failed, however, as the Peshwa went over to Safdar Jang's enemies at Delhi, who promised him the governorship of Awadh and Allahabad.

Safdar Jang also organised an equitable system of justice. He too adopted a policy of impartiality in the employment of Hindus and Muslims. The highest post in his government was held by a Hindu, Maharaja Nawab Rai.

The prolonged period of peace and of economic prosperity of the nobles under the government of the Nawabs resulted in time in the growth of a distinct Lucknow culture around the Awadh court. Lucknow, for long an important city of Awadh and the seat of the Awadh Nawabs after 1775, soon rivalled Delhi in its patronage of the arts and literature. It also developed as an important centre of handicrafts. Crafts and culture also percolated to towns under the patronage of local chieftains and zamindars.

Safdar Jang maintained a very high standard of personal morality. All his life he was devoted to his only wife. As a matter of fact, all the founders of the three autonomous kingdoms of Hyderabad, Bengal and Awadh, namely Nizam-ul-Mulk, Murshid Quli Khan and Alivardi Khan, and Saadat Khan and Safdar Jang, were men of high personal morality. Nearly all of them led austere and simple lives. Their lives give lie to the belief that all the leading nobles of the eighteenth century led extravagant and luxurious lives. It was only in their public and political dealings that they resorted to fraud, intrigue and treachery.

Mysore

Next to Hyderabad, the most important power that emerged in south India was Mysore under Haidar Ali. The kingdom of Mysore had preserved its precarious independence ever since the end of the Vijayanagar Empire and had been only nominally a part of the Mughal Empire. Early in the eighteenth century two ministers, Nanjaraj (the Sarvadhikari) and Devraj (the Dulwai), had seized power in Mysore, reducing the king, Chikka Krishna Raj, to a mere puppet. Haidar Ali, born in 1721 in an obscure family, started his career as a petty officer in the Mysore army. Though uneducated, he possessed a keen intellect and was a man of great energy, daring and determination. He was also a brilliant commander and a shrewd diplomat.

Haidar Ali soon found his opportunity in the wars which involved Mysore for more than twenty years. Cleverly using the opportunities that came his way, he gradually rose in the Mysore army. He soon recognised the advantages of Western military training and applied it to the troops under his own command. He established a modern arsenal in Dindigal in 1755 with the help of French experts. In 1761, he overthrew Nanjaraj and established his authority over the Mysore state. He extended full control over the rebellious *poligars* (warrior chieftains and zamindars) and conquered the territories of Bidnur, Sunda, Sera, Canara and Malabar. A major reason for his occupation of Malabar was the desire for access to the Indian Ocean. Though illiterate, he was an efficient administrator. He was responsible for introducing the Mughal administrative and revenue system in his dominions. He took over Mysore when it was a weak and divided state and soon made it one of the leading Indian powers. He practised religious tolerance and his first Dewan and many other officials were Hindus.

Almost from the beginning of the establishment of his power, he was engaged in wars with the Maratha *sardars*, the Nizam, and the British. In 1769, he repeatedly defeated the British forces and reached the walls of Madras. He died in 1782 in the course of the second Anglo-Mysore War and was succeeded by his son Tipu.

Sultan Tipu, who ruled Mysore till his death at the hands of the British in 1799, was a man of complex character. He was, for one, an innovator. His desire to change with the times was symbolised in the introduction of a new calendar, a new system of coinage, and new scales of weights and measures. His personal library contained books on such diverse subjects as religion, history, military science, medicine, and mathematics. He showed a keen interest in the French Revolution. He planted a 'Tree of Liberty' at Srirangapatam and he became a member of a Jacobin Club. His organisational capacity is borne out by the fact that in those days of general indiscipline among Indian armies, his troops remained disciplined and loyal to him to the last. He tried to do away with the custom of giving jagirs, and thus increase state income. He also made an attempt to reduce the hereditary possessions of the *poligars* and to eliminate the intermediaries between the state and the cultivator. However, his land revenue was as high as that of other contemporary rulers—it ranged up to one-third of the gross produce. But he checked the collection of illegal cesses, and he was liberal in granting remissions.

His infantry was armed with muskets and bayonets in the European fashion which were, however, manufactured in Mysore. He also made an effort to build a modern navy after 1796. For this purpose, he established two dockyards, the models of the ships being supplied by the Sultan himself. In personal life, he was free from vices and kept himself free from luxury. He was recklessly brave and, as a commander, brilliant. He was fond of saying that it was "better to live a day as a lion than a lifetime as a sheep". He died fighting at the gates of Srirangapatam in pursuance of this belief. He was, however, hasty in action and unstable in nature.

As a statesman he, more than any other eighteenth-century Indian ruler, recognised to the full extent the threat that the English posed to south India as well as to other Indian powers. He stood forth as the steadfast foe of the rising English power. The English, in turn, looked upon him as their most dangerous enemy in India.

Though not free from contemporary economic backwardness, Mysore flourished economically under Haidar Ali and Tipu, especially when seen in contrast to its immediate past or with the rest of the country. When the British occupied Mysore after defeating and killing Tipu in 1799, they were surprised to find that the Mysore peasant was much more prosperous than the peasant in British-occupied Madras. Sir John Shore, Governor-General from 1793 to 1798, wrote later that "the peasantry of his dominions are protected and their labour encouraged and rewarded". Another British observer wrote of Tipu's Mysore as "well cultivated, populous with industrious inhabitants, cities newly founded and commerce extending". Tipu also seems to have grasped the importance of modern trade and industry. In fact, alone among the Indian rulers, he understood the importance of economic strength as the foundation of military strength. He made some attempts to introduce modern industries in India by importing foreign workmen as experts and by extending state support to many industries. He sent emissaries to France, Turkey, Iran and Pegu Myanmar to develop foreign trade. He also traded with China. He even tried to set up a trading company on the pattern of European companies and thus sought to imitate their commercial practices. He tried to promote trade with Russia and Arabia by setting up state trading institutions in the port towns.

Some British historians have described Tipu as a religious fanatic. But this is not borne out by facts. Though he was orthodox in his religious views, he was in fact tolerant and enlightened in his approach toward other religions. He gave money for the construction of the image of goddess Sarda in the Shringeri Temple after the latter was looted by Maratha horsemen in 1791. He regularly gave gifts to this temple as well as to several other temples. The famous temple of Sri Ranganath was situated barely 100 yards from his palace. But while he treated the vast majority of his Hindu and Christian subjects with consideration and tolerance, he was harsh on those Hindus and Christians who might directly or indirectly aid the British against Mysore.

KERALA

At the beginning of the eighteenth century, Kerala was divided up among a large number of feudal chiefs and rajas. The four most important states were those of Calicut, under the Zamorin, Chirakkal, Cochin and Travancore. The kingdom of Travancore rose to prominence after 1729 under King Martanda Varma, one of the leading statesmen of the eighteenth century. He combined rare foresight and strong determination with courage and daring. He subdued the feudatories, conquered Quilon and Elayadam, and defeated the Dutch, thus ending their political power in Kerala. He organised a strong army on the Western model with the help of European officers and armed it with modern weapons. He also constructed a modern arsenal. Martanda Varma used his new army to expand northwards and the boundaries of Travancore soon extended from Kanyakumari to Cochin. He undertook many irrigation works, built roads and canals for communication, and gave active encouragement to foreign trade.

By 1763, all the petty principalities of Kerala had been absorbed or subordinated by the three big states of Cochin, Travancore and Calicut. Haidar Ali began his invasion of Kerala in 1766 and in the end annexed northern Kerala up to Cochin, including the territories of the Zamorin of Calicut.

The eighteenth century saw a remarkable revival in Malayalam literature. This was due in part to the rajas and chiefs of Kerala, who were great patrons of literature. Trivandrum, the capital of Travancore, became, in the second half of the eighteenth century, a famous centre of Sanskrit scholarship. Rama Varma, successor of Martanda Varma, was himself a poet, scholar, musician, renowned actor, and a man of great culture. He conversed fluently in English, took a keen interest in European affairs, and regularly read newspapers and journals published in London, Calcutta and Madras.

Areas around Delhi

The Rajput States

The principal Rajput states took advantage of the growing weakness of Mughal power to virtually free themselves from central control while at the same time increasing their influence in the rest of the Empire. In the reigns of Farrukh Siyar and Muhammad Shah, the rulers of Amber and Marwar were appointed governors of important Mughal provinces such as Agra, Gujarat and Malwa.

The Rajputana states continued to be as divided as before. The bigger among them expanded at the cost of their weaker neighbours,

Rajput and non-Rajput. Most of the larger Rajput states were constantly involved in petty quarrels and civil wars. The internal politics of these states were often characterised by the same type of corruption, intrigue, and treachery as prevailed at the Mughal court. Thus, Ajit Singh of Marwar was killed by his own son.

The most outstanding Rajput ruler of the eighteenth century was Raja Sawai Jai Singh of Amber (1681–1743). He was a distinguished statesman, law-maker, and reformer. But most of all, he shone as a man of science in an age when Indians were oblivious of scientific progress. He founded the city of Jaipur and made it a great seat of science and art. Jaipur was built upon strictly scientific principles and according to a regular plan. Its broad streets are intersected at right angles.

Jai Singh was, above everything else, a great astronomer. He erected observatories with accurate and advanced instruments, some of them of his own invention, at Delhi, Jaipur, Ujjain, Varanasi and Mathura. His astronomical observations were remarkably accurate. He drew up a set of tables, entitled Zij Muhammadshahi, to enable people to make astronomical observations. He had Euclid's "Elements of Geometry" translated into Sanskrit, as also several works on trignometry, as well as Napier's work on the construction and use of logarithms.

Jai Singh was also a social reformer. He tried to enforce a law to reduce the lavish expenditure which the Rajputs had to incur on their daughters' weddings. This had given rise to the evil practice of female infanticide. This remarkable prince ruled Jaipur for nearly 44 years, from 1699 to 1743.

The Jats

The Jats, a caste of agriculturists, lived in the region around Delhi, Agra and Mathura. Jat peasants around Mathura revolted under the leadership of their Jat zamindars in 1669, and then again in 1688. These revolts were crushed, but the area remained disturbed. After the death of Aurangzeb, they created disturbances all around Delhi. Though originally a peasant uprising, the Jat revolt, led by zamindars, soon became predatory. They took active part in the Court intrigues at Delhi, often changing sides to suit their own advantage. The Jat state of Bharatpur was set up by Churaman and Badan Singh. Jat power reached its highest glory under Suraj Mal, who ruled from 1756 to 1763 and who was an extremely able administrator and soldier and a very wise statesman. He extended his authority over a large area which extended from the Ganga in the east to the Chambal in the south, the Subah of Agra in the west to the Subah of Delhi in the north. His state included, among others, the districts of Agra, Mathura, Meerut and Aligarh. He tried to lay the foundations of an enduring state by adopting the Mughal revenue system. A contemporary historian has described him as follows:

> Though he wore the dress of a farmer and could speak only his own Braj dialect, he was the Plato of the Jat tribe. In prudence and skill, and ability to manage the revenue and civil affairs he had no equal among the grandees of Hindustan except Asaf Jah Bahadur.

After his death in 1763, the Jat state declined and was split up among petty zamindars, most of whom lived by plunder.

Bangash Pathans and Rohelas

Muhammad Khan Bangash, an Afghan adventurer, established his control over the territory around Farrukhabad, between what are now Aligarh and Kanpur, during the reigns of Farrukh Siyar and Muhammad Shah. Similarly, during the breakdown of administration following Nadir Shah's invasion, Ali Muhammad Khan carved out a separate principality, known as Rohilkhand, at the foothills of the Himalayas between the Ganga in the south and the Kumaon hills in the north, with its capital at first at Aolan in Bareilly and later at Rampur. The Rohelas clashed constantly with Awadh, Delhi and the Jats.

The Sikhs

Founded at the end of the fifteenth century by Guru Nanak, the Sikh religion spread among the Jat peasantry and other lower castes of the Punjab. The transformation of the Sikhs into a militant, fighting community was begun by Guru Hargobind (1606–45). It was, however, under the leadership of Guru Gobind Singh (1666–1708), the tenth and last Guru of the Sikhs, that they became a political and military force. From 1699 onwards, Guru Gobind Singh waged constant war against the armies of Aurangzeb and the hill rajas. After Guru Gobind Singh's death, the institution of Guruship came to an end and the leadership of the Sikhs passed to his trusted disciple Banda Singh Bahadur. Banda Singh Bahadur rallied together the peasants and the lower castes of the Punjab from Delhi to Lahore, and carried on a vigorous though unequal struggle against the Mughal army for eight years. He was captured in 1715 and put to death. There were several reasons for his failure. The Mughal centre was still strong. The upper classes and castes of Punjab joined forces against Banda Singh Bahadur for his championship of the lower castes and rural poor.

The invasions of Nadir Shah and Ahmad Shah Abdali and the consequent dislocation of Punjab administration gave the Sikhs an opportunity to rise once again. They soon began to fill the political vacuum. Between 1765 and 1800, they brought the Punjab and Jammu under their control. The Sikhs were organised into 12 *misls* or confederacies which operated in different parts of the province. These *misls* fully cooperated with one another. They were originally based on the principle of equality, with all members having an equal voice in deciding the affairs of a *misl* and in electing its chief and other officers. Gradually, the democratic and plebian character of the *misls* disappeared, and powerful feudal chiefs and zamindars dominated them.

The Punjab under Ranjit Singh

At the end of the eighteenth century, Ranjit Singh, chief of the Sukerchakia *misl*, rose to prominence. A strong and courageous soldier, an efficient administrator, and a skilful diplomat, he was a born leader of men. He captured Lahore in 1799 and Amritsar in 1802. He soon brought all Sikh chiefs west of the Sutlej under his control and established his own kingdom in the Punjab. Later, he conquered Kashmir, Peshawar, and Multan. The old Sikh chiefs were transformed into big zamindars and jagirdars. He did not make any changes in the system of land revenue promulgated earlier by the Mughals. The amount of land revenue was calculated on the basis of 50 per cent of the gross produce.

Ranjit Singh built up a powerful, disciplined, and well-equipped army along European lines with the help of European instructors. His new army was not confined to the Sikhs. He also recruited Gurkhas, Biharis, Oriyas, Pathans, Dogras, and Punjabi Muslims. He set up modern foundries to manufacture cannon at Lahore and employed Muslim gunners to man them. It is said that he possessed the second best army in Asia, the first being the army of the English East India Company.

Ranjit Singh had great capacity for choosing his ministers and officials. His court was studded with outstanding men. He was tolerant and liberal in religious matters. He patronised not only Sikh, but also Muslim and Hindu holy men. Many of his important ministers and commanders were Muslims and Hindus. The most prominent and trusted of his ministers was Fakir Azizuddin, while his finance minister was Dewan Dina Nath. His was a state based on equal opportunities for all. Political power was not used for exclusive Sikh benefit. On the other hand, the Sikh peasant was as oppressed by Sikh chiefs as was the Hindu or Muslim peasant. In fact, the structure of the Punjab as a state under Ranjit Singh was similar to the structure of the other Indian states of the eighteenth century.

When the British forbade Ranjit Singh in 1809 to cross the Sutlej and took the Sikh states east of the river under their protection, he kept quiet for he realised that his strength was no match for the British. Thus, by his diplomatic realism and military strength, he temporarily saved his kingdom from English encroachment. But he did not remove the foreign threat, he only left it for his successors. And so, after his death, when his kingdom was torn by an intense internal struggle for power, the English moved in and conquered it.

THE RISE AND FALL OF THE MARATHA POWER

The most important challenge to the decaying Mughal power came from the Maratha kingdom, which was the most powerful of the succession states. In fact, it alone possessed the strength to fill the political vacuum created by the disintegration of the Mughal Empire. Moreover, it produced a number of brilliant commanders and statesmen needed for the task. But the Maratha *sardars* lacked unity, and they lacked the outlook and programme necessary for founding an all-India empire. And so they failed to replace the Mughals. They did, however, succeed in waging continuous war against the Mughal Empire, till they destroyed it.

Shahu, the grandson of Shivaji, had been a prisoner of Aurangzeb since 1689. Aurangzeb had treated him and his mother with great dignity, honour, and consideration, paying full attention to their religious, caste, and other needs, hoping perhaps to arrive at a political agreement with Shahu. Shahu was released in 1707 after Aurangzeb's death. Very soon, a civil war broke out between Shahu at Satara and his aunt Tara Bai at Kolhapur, who had carried out an anti-Mughal struggle since 1700 in the name of her son, Shivaji II, after the death of her husband Raja Ram. Maratha *sardars,* each of whom had a large following of soldiers loyal to himself alone, began to side with one or the other contender for power. They used this opportunity to increase their power and influence by bargaining with the two contenders for power. Several of them even intrigued with the Mughal viceroys of the Deccan. Arising from the conflict between Shahu and his rival at Kolhapur, a new system of Maratha government was evolved under the leadership of Balaji Vishwanath, the Peshwa of King Shahu. With this change began the second period—the period of Peshwa domination— in Maratha history, in which the Maratha state was transformed into an empire.

Balaji Vishwanath, a brahmin, started life as a petty revenue official and then rose step by step. He rendered Shahu loyal and useful service in suppressing his enemies. He excelled in diplomacy and won over many of the big Maratha *sardars* to Shahu's cause. In 1713, Shahu made him his Peshwa or the *mukh pradhan* (chief minister). Balaji Vishwanath gradually consolidated Shahu's hold and his own over the Maratha *sardars,* and over most of Maharashtra except for the region south of Kolhapur where Raja Ram's descendants ruled. The Peshwa concentrated power in his office and eclipsed the other ministers and *sardars*. In fact, he and his son Baji Rao I made the Peshwa the functional head of the Maratha empire.

Balaji Vishwanath took full advantage of the internal conflicts of the Mughal officials to increase Maratha power. He had induced Zulfiqar Khan to grant the *chauth* and *sardeshmukhi* of the Deccan.

In the end, he signed a pact with the Saiyid brothers. All the territories that had earlier formed Shivaji's kingdom were restored to Shahu, who was also assigned the *chauth* and *sardeshmukhi* of the six provinces of the Deccan. In return Shahu, who had already recognised, though nominally, Mughal suzerainty, agreed to place a body of 15,000 cavalry at the emperor's service, to prevent rebellion and plundering in the Deccan, and to pay an annual tribute of 10 lakhs of rupees. He also walked barefoot and paid obeisance at the tomb of Aurangzeb at Khuldabad in 1714. In 1719, Balaji Vishwanath, at the head of a Maratha force, accompanied Saiyid Hussain Ali Khan to Delhi and helped the Saiyid brothers in overthrowing Farrukh Siyar. At Delhi, he and the other Maratha *sardars* witnessed at first hand the weakness of the Empire and were filled with the ambition of expansion in the north.

For the efficient collection of the *chauth* and *sardeshmukhi* of the Deccan, Balaji Vishwanath assigned separate areas to Maratha *sardars*, who kept the greater part of the collection for their expenses. This system of assignment of the *chauth* and *sardeshmukhi* also enabled the Peshwa to increase his personal power through patronage. An increasing number of ambitious *sardars* began to flock round him. In the long run, this was to be a major source of weakness of the Maratha Empire. Already the system of *watans* and *saranjams* (jagirs) had made the Maratha *sardars* strong, autonomous, and jealous of central power. They now began to establish their control in the distant lands of the Mughal Empire, where they gradually settled down as more or less autonomous chiefs. Thus, the conquests of the Marathas outside their original kingdom were not made by a central army directly controlled by the Maratha king or the Peshwa, but by *sardars* with their own private armies. During the process of conquest, these *sardars* often clashed with one another. If the central authority tried to control them too strictly, they did not hesitate to join hands with enemies, be they the Nizam, the Mughals, or the English.

Balaji Vishwanath died in 1720. He was succeeded as Peshwa by his 20-year-old son Baji Rao I. In spite of his youth, Baji Rao was a bold and brilliant commander and an ambitious and clever statesman. He has been described as "the greatest exponent of guerrilla tactics after Shivaji". Led by Baji Rao, the Marathas waged numerous campaigns against the Mughal Empire, trying to compel the Mughal officials to first, give them the right to collect the *chauth* of vast areas, and second, to cede these areas to the Maratha kingdom. By 1740, when Baji Rao died, the Marathas had won control over Malwa, Gujarat, and parts of Bundelkhand. The Maratha families of Gaekwad, Holkar, Sindhia, and Bhonsle came into prominence during this period.

All his life, Baji Rao worked to contain Nizam-ul-Mulk's power in the Deccan. The latter, on his part, constantly intrigued with the Raja of Kolhapur, the Maratha *sardars* and Mughal officials to weaken the Peshwa's authority. Twice the two met on the field of battle and both times the Nizam was worsted and compelled to grant the Marathas the *chauth* and *sardeshmukhi* of the Deccan provinces.

In 1733, Baji Rao started a long campaign against the Sidis of Janjira and, in the end, expelled them from the mainland. Simultaneously, a campaign against the Portuguese was started. In the end, Salsette and Bassein were captured. But the Portuguese continued to hold their other possessions on the west coast.

Baji Rao died in April 1740. In a short period of 20 years, he had changed the character of the Maratha state. From the kingdom of Maharashtra it had been transformed into an empire, expanding in the north. He, however, failed to lay the firm foundations of an empire. New territories were conquered and occupied, but little attention was paid to their administration. The chief concern of the successful *sardars* was with the collection of revenues.

Baji Rao's 18-year-old son Balaji Baji Rao (known more widely as Nana Saheb) was the Peshwa from 1740 to 1761. He was as able as his father, though less energetic. King Shahu died in 1749 and by his will left the management of state affairs in the Peshwa's hands. The office of the Peshwa had already become hereditary and the Peshwa was the *de facto* ruler of the state. Now he became the official head of the administration and, as a symbol of this fact, shifted the government to Poona, his headquarters.

Balaji Baji Rao followed in the footsteps of his father and further extended the empire in different directions, taking Maratha power to new heights. Maratha armies now overran the whole of India. Maratha control over Malwa, Gujarat and Bundelkhand was consolidated. Bengal was repeatedly invaded and, in 1751, the Bengal Nawab had to cede Orissa. In the south, the state of Mysore and other minor principalities were forced to pay tribute. In 1760, the Nizam of Hyderabad was defeated at Udgir and compelled to cede vast territories yielding an annual revenue of Rs 62 lakh. In the north, the Marathas soon became the power behind the Mughal throne. Marching through the Gangetic Doab and Rajputana, they reached Delhi where, in 1752, they helped Imad-ul-Mulk to become the *wazir*. The new *wazir* soon became a puppet in their hands. From Delhi, they turned to the Punjab and soon brought it under control after expelling the agent of Ahmad Shah Abdali. This brought them into conflict with the doughty warrior-king of Afghanistan, who once again marched into India to settle accounts with the Maratha power.

A major conflict for mastery over north India now began. Ahmad Shah Abdali soon formed an alliance with Najib-ud-Daulah of Rohilkhand and Shuja-ud-Daulah of Awadh, both of whom had suffered at the hands of the Maratha *sardars*. Recognising the great importance of the coming struggle, the Peshwa despatched a powerful army to the north under the nominal command of his minor son, the actual command being in the hands of his cousin Sadashiv Rao Bhau. An important arm of this force was a contingent of European-style infantry and artillery commanded by Ibrahim Khan Gardi. The Marathas now tried to find allies among the northern powers. But their earlier behaviour and political ambitions had antagonised all these powers. They had interfered in the internal affairs of the Rajputana states and levied huge fines and tributes upon them. They had made large territorial and monetary claims upon Awadh. Their actions in the Punjab had angered the Sikh chiefs. Similarly, the Jat chiefs, on whom they had also imposed heavy fines, did not trust them. They had, therefore, to fight their enemies all alone, except for the weak support of Imad-ul-Mulk. Moreover, the senior Maratha commanders constantly bickered with one another.

The two forces met at Panipat on 14 January 1761. The Maratha army was completely routed. The Peshwa's son, Vishwas Rao, Sadashiv Rao Bhau, and numerous other Maratha commanders perished on the battlefield, as did nearly 28,000 soldiers. Those who fled were pursued by the Afghan cavalry and robbed and plundered by the Jats, Ahirs, and Gujars of the Panipat region.

The Peshwa, who was marching north to help his cousin, was stunned by the tragic news. Already seriously ill, his end was hastened and he died in June 1761.

The Maratha defeat at Panipat was a disaster for them. They lost the cream of their army and their political prestige suffered a big blow. Most of all, their defeat gave an opportunity to the English East India Company to consolidate its power in Bengal and south India. Nor did the Afghans benefit from their victory. They could not even hold the Punjab. In fact, the Third Battle of Panipat did not decide who was to rule India, but rather, who was not. The way was therefore cleared for the rise of British power in India.

The 17-year-old Madhav Rao became the Peshwa in 1761. He was a talented soldier and statesman. Within a short period of 11 years, he restored the lost fortunes of the Maratha empire. He defeated the Nizam, compelled Haidar Ali of Mysore to pay tribute, and reasserted control over northern India by defeating the Rohelas and subjugating the Rajput states and Jat chiefs. In 1771, the Marathas brought back Emperor Shah Alam to Delhi, who now became their pensioner. Thus, it appeared as if Maratha ascendancy in the north had been recovered.

Once again, however, a blow fell on the Marathas for Madhav Rao died of consumption in 1772. The Maratha empire was now in a state of confusion. At Poona, there was a struggle for power between Raghunath Rao, the younger brother of Balaji Baji Rao, and Narayan Rao, the younger brother of Madhav Rao. Narayan Rao was killed in 1773. He was succeeded by his posthumous son, Sawai Madhav Rao. Out of frustration, Raghunath Rao went over to the British and tried to capture power with their help. This resulted in the First Anglo-Maratha War.

The Peshwa's power was now on the wane. At Poona, there was constant intrigue between the supporters of Sawai Madhav Rao, headed by Nana Phadnis, and the partisans of Raghunath Rao. In the meantime, the big Maratha *sardars* had been carving out semi-independent states in the north, which could seldom cooperate. Gaekwad at Baroda, Bhonsle at Nagpur, Holkar at Indore and Sindhia at Gwalior were the most important. They had established regular administrations on the pattern of Mughal administration and possessed their separate armies. Their allegiance to the Peshwas became more and more nominal. Instead, they joined opposing factions at Poona and intrigued with the enemies of the Maratha empire.

Among the Maratha rulers in the north, Mahadji Sindhia was the most important. He organised a powerful European-style army, comprising equally of Hindu and Muslim soldiers, with the help of French and Portuguese officers and gunners. He established his own ordnance factories near Agra. He also established control over Emperor Shah Alam in 1784. From the emperor, he secured the appointment of the Peshwa as the Emperor's Deputy *(Naib-i-Munaib)*, on the condition that Mahadji would act on behalf of the Peshwa. But he spent his energies intriguing against Nana Phadnis. He was also a bitter enemy of Holkar of Indore. He died in 1794. He and Nana Phadnis, who died in 1800, were the last of the great soldiers and statesmen who had raised Maratha power to its height in the eighteenth century.

Sawai Madhav Rao died in 1795 and was succeeded by Baji Rao II, son of Raghunath Rao. The British had by now decided to put an end to the Maratha challenge to their supremacy in India. They divided the mutually warring Maratha *sardars* through clever diplomacy and then overpowered them in separate battles during the Second Maratha War, 1803–05, and the Third Maratha War, 1816–19. While other Maratha states were permitted to remain as subsidiary states, the house of the Peshwas was extinguished.

Thus, the Maratha dream of controlling the Mughal Empire and establishing their own empire over large parts of the country could not be realised. This was basically because the Maratha empire represented the same decadent social order as the Mughal Empire and suffered from the same underlying weaknesses. The Maratha chiefs were very similar to the later Mughal nobles, just as the *saranjami* system was similar to the Mughal system of jagirs. So long as there existed a strong central authority and the need for mutual cooperation against a common enemy, the Mughals, they remained united in a loose union. But at the first opportunity, they tended to assert their autonomy. If anything, they were even less disciplined than the Mughal nobles. Nor did the Maratha *sardars* try to develop a new economy. They failed to encourage science and technology or to take much interest in trade and industry. Their revenue system was similar to that of the Mughals, as was their administration. Like the Mughals, the Maratha rulers were also mainly interested in raising revenue from the helpless peasantry. For example, they too collected nearly half of the agricultural produce as tax. Unlike the Mughals, they failed to even provide sound administration to the people outside Maharashtra. They could not inspire the Indian people to any higher degree of loyalty than the Mughals had succeeded in doing. Their dominion, too, depended on force and force alone. The only way the Marathas could have stood up to the rising British power was to have transformed their state into a modern state. This they failed to do.

SOCIAL AND ECONOMIC CONDITIONS OF THE PEOPLE

India in the eighteenth century failed to make progress economically, socially or culturally at an adequate pace. The increasing revenue demands of the state, the oppression of the officials, the greed and rapacity of the nobles, revenue-farmers and zamindars, the marches and counter-marches of the rival armies, and the depredations of the numerous adventurers roaming the land made the life of the people quite wretched.

The India of those days was also a land of contrasts. Extreme poverty existed side by side with extreme riches and luxury. On the one hand, there were the rich and powerful nobles steeped in luxury and comfort, on the other, backward, oppressed and impoverished peasants living at the bare subsistence level and having to bear all sorts of injustices and inequities. Even so, the life of the Indian masses was by and large better at this time than it was after over 100 years of British rule at the end of the nineteenth century.

Indian agriculture during the eighteenth century was technically backward and stagnant. The techniques of production had remained stationary for centuries. The peasant tried to make up for technical backwardness by working very hard. He, in fact, performed miracles of production; moreover, he did not usually suffer from shortage of land. But, unfortunately, he seldom reaped the fruits of his labour. Even though it was his produce that supported the rest of the society, his own reward was miserably inadequate. The state, the zamindars, the jagirdars, and the revenue-farmers tried to extract the maximum amount from him. This was as true of the Mughal state as of the Maratha or Sikh chiefs, or other successors of the Mughal state.

Even though Indian villages were largely self-sufficient and imported little from outside and the means of communication were backward, extensive trade within the country and between India and other countries of Asia and Europe was carried on under the Mughals. India imported pearls, raw silk, wool, dates, dried fruits, and rose water from the Persian Gulf; coffee, gold, drugs, and honey from Arabia; tea, sugar, porcelain, and silk from China; gold, musk and woollen cloth from Tibet; tin from Singapore; spices, perfumes, arrack, and sugar from the Indonesian islands; ivory and drugs from Africa; and woollen cloth, metals such as copper, iron, and lead, and paper from Europe. India's most important article of export was its cotton textiles, which were famous all over the world for their excellence and were in demand everywhere. India also exported raw silk and silk fabrics, hardware, indigo, saltpetre, opium, rice, wheat, sugar, pepper and other spices, precious stones, and drugs.

Since India was on the whole self-sufficient in handicrafts and agricultural products, it did not import foreign goods on a large scale. On the other hand, its industrial and agricultural products had a steady market abroad. Consequently, it exported more than it imported and its trade was balanced by the import of silver and gold. In fact, India was known as a sink of precious metals.

Historians differ on the state of internal and foreign trade during the pre-colonial period of the eighteenth century. According to the dominant view, constant warfare and disruption of law and order in many areas during the eighteenth century harmed the country's internal trade. Many trading centres were looted by the contestants for power and by foreign invaders. Many of the trade routes were infested with organised bands of robbers, and traders and their caravans were regularly looted. Even the road between the two imperial cities, Delhi and Agra, was made unsafe by the marauders. Moreover, with the rise of autonomous provincial regimes and innumerable local chiefs, the number of custom houses or *chowkies* grew by leaps and bounds. Every petty or large ruler tried to increase his income by imposing heavy customs duties on goods entering or passing through his territories. All these factors had an injurious effect on long-distance trade. The impoverishment of the nobles, who were the largest consumers of luxury products in which trade was conducted, also injured internal trade. Other historians believe that the effect of political changes and warfare on internal trade has generally been exaggerated. The impact on foreign trade was also complex and differential. While sea trade expanded, overland trade through Afghanistan and Persia was disrupted.

Political factors which hurt trade also adversely affected urban industries. Many prosperous cities, centres of flourishing industry, were sacked and devastated. Delhi was plundered by Nadir Shah; Lahore, Delhi and Mathura by Ahmad Shah Abdali; Agra by the Jats; Surat and other cities of Gujarat and the Deccan by Maratha chiefs; Sarhind by the Sikhs, and so on. Similarly, in some areas artisans catering to the needs of the feudal class and the court suffered as the fortunes of their patrons declined, leading to the decline of cities like Agra and Delhi. The decline of internal and foreign trade also hit them hard in some parts of the country. Nevertheless, some industries in other parts of the country gained as a result of expansion in trade with Europe, owing to the activities of the European trading companies. Moreover, the emergence of new courts and local nobility and zamindars led to the growth of new cities such as Faizabad, Lucknow, Varanasi and Patna and the recovery, to some extent, of production by artisans.

Even so, India remained a land of extensive manufactures. Indian artisans still enjoyed fame the world over for their skill. India was still a large-scale manufacturer of cotton and silk fabrics, sugar, jute, dye-stuffs, mineral and metallic products like arms, metalware, and saltpetre and oils. The important centres of the textile industry were Dacca and Murshidabad in Bengal; Patna in Bihar; Surat, Ahmedabad and Broach in Gujarat; Chanderi in Madhya Pradesh; Burhanpur in Maharashtra; Jaunpur, Varanasi, Lucknow and Agra in Uttar Pradesh; Multan and Lahore in the Punjab; Masulipatam, Aurangabad, Chicacole and Vishakhapatnam in Andhra; Bangalore in Karnataka; and Coimbatore and Madurai in Tamil Nadu. Kashmir was a centre of woollen manufactures. Ship-building industry flourished in Maharashtra, Andhra and Bengal. Writing about the great skill of Indians in this respect, an English observer wrote: "In ship-building they probably taught the English far more than they learnt from them." The European companies bought many Indian-made ships for their use.

In fact, at the dawn of the eighteenth century, India was one of the main centres of world trade and industry. Peter the Great of Russia was led to exclaim: "Bear in mind that the commerce of India is the commerce of the world and ... he who can exclusively command it is the dictator of Europe."

Once again, historians disagree whether there was overall economic decline as a result of the decay of the Mughal Empire and the rise of a large number of autonomous states, or whether trade and agricultural and handicraft production continued to grow in some parts of India while they were disrupted and declined in others, with overall trade and production not suffering any sharp decline. But in fact, the question is not of some progress here and some decline there but of basic economic stagnation. While the Indian economy was quite resilient and there was a certain continuity in economic life, there was no greater effervescence or buoyancy in economic activities in the eighteenth century than what was there in the seventeenth century. On the other hand, there was a definitely declining trend. At the same time, it is true that there was less economic distress or decline in agricultural and handicraft production in the Indian states of the eighteenth century than was to result from the impact of British colonialism in the eighteenth and nineteenth centuries.

EDUCATION

Education was not completely neglected in eighteenth-century India. But it was on the whole defective. It was traditional and out of touch with the rapid developments in the West. The knowledge which it imparted was confined to literature, law, religion, philosophy and logic, and excluded the study of physical and natural sciences, technology and geography. Nor did it concern itself with a factual and rational study of society. In all fields, original thought was discouraged and reliance placed on ancient learning.

The centres of higher education were spread all over the country and were usually financed by nawabs, rajas, and rich zamindars. Among the Hindus, higher education was based on Sanskrit learning and was mostly confined to brahmins. Persian education, being based on the official language of the time, was equally popular among both Hindus and Muslims.

Elementary education was quite widespread. Among the Hindus, it was imparted through town and village schools, while it was imparted among the Muslims through the Maulvis in *maktabs* situated in mosques. In these schools the young students were taught reading, writing and arithmetic. Though elementary education was mostly confined to the higher castes like brahmins, Rajputs and vaishyas, many persons from the lower castes also often received it. Interestingly enough, the average literacy was not less than what it was under the British later. Warren Hastings even wrote in 1813 that Indians had in general "superior endowments in reading, writing and arithmetic than the common people of any nation in Europe." Though the standard of primary education was inadequate by modern standards, it sufficed for the limited purposes of those days. A very pleasant aspect of education then was that the teachers enjoyed high prestige in the community. A bad feature of it was that girls were seldom given education, though some women of the higher classes were an exception.

SOCIAL AND CULTURAL LIFE

Social life and culture in the eighteenth century were marked by stagnation and dependence on the past. Despite a certain broad cultural unity that had developed over the centuries, there was no uniformity of culture and social patterns all over the country. Nor did all Hindus and all Muslims form two distinct societies. People were divided by religion, region, tribe, language and caste. Moreover, the social life and culture of the upper classes, who formed a tiny minority of the total population, was in many respects different from the life and culture of the lower classes.

Caste was the central feature of the social life of Hindus. Apart from the four varnas, Hindus were divided into numerous castes (*jatis*), which differed in their nature from place to place. The caste system rigidly divided people and permanently fixed their place in the social scale. The higher castes, headed by the brahmins, monopolised all social prestige and privileges. Caste rules were extremely rigid. Inter-caste marriages were forbidden. There were restrictions on inter-dining among members of different castes. In some cases, persons belonging to the higher castes would not take food touched by persons of the lower castes. Castes often determined the choice of profession, though exceptions occurred on a large scale. For example, brahmins were involved in trade and government service and held zamindaris. Similarly, many *shudras* achieved worldly success and wealth and used them to seek higher ritual and caste ranking in society. In many parts of the country, caste status had become quite fluid. Caste regulations were strictly enforced by caste councils, panchayats and caste chiefs through fines, penances (*prayaschitya*) and expulsion from the caste. Caste was a major divisive force and an element of disintegration in eighteenth-century India. It often split Hindus living in the same village or region into many social atoms. It was, of course, possible for a person to acquire a higher social status through the acquisition of high office or power, as the Holkar family had done in the eighteenth century. Sometimes, though not often, an entire caste would succeed in raising itself in the caste hierarchy.

Muslims were no less divided by considerations of caste, race, tribe and status, even though their religion enjoined social equality on them. The Shia and Sunni nobles were sometimes at loggerheads on account of their religious differences. The Irani, Afghan, Turani and Hindustani Muslim nobles and officials often stood apart from one another. A large number of Hindus who had converted to Islam carried their caste into the new religion and observed its distinctions, though not as rigidly as earlier. Moreover, the *sharif* Muslims, consisting of nobles, scholars, priests and army officers, looked down upon the *ajlaf* or lower-class Muslims in a manner similar to that adopted by the higher-caste Hindus towards the lower-caste Hindus.

The family system in eighteenth-century India was primarily patriarchal, that is, the family was dominated by the senior male member and inheritance was through the male line. In Kerala, however, the family among Nairs was matrilineal. Outside Kerala, women were subjected to nearly complete male control. They were expected to live as mothers and wives only, though in these roles they were shown a great deal of respect and honour. Even during war and anarchy, women were seldom molested and were treated with respect. A European traveller, Abbe J.A. Dubois, commented at the beginning of the nineteenth century: "A Hindu woman can go anywhere alone, even in the most crowded places, and she need never fear the impertinent looks and jokes of idle loungers. ... A house inhabited solely by women is a sanctuary which the most shameless libertine would not dream of violating." But the women of the time possessed little individuality of their own. This does not mean that there were no exceptions to this rule. Ahilya Bai administered Indore with great success from 1766 to 1796. Many other Hindu and Muslim ladies played important roles in eighteenth-century politics. While women of the upper classes were not supposed to work outside their homes, peasant women usually worked in the fields and women of the poorer classes often worked outside their homes to supplement the family income. The *purdah* was common mostly among the higher classes in the north. It was not practised in the south.

Boys and girls were not permitted to mix with one another. All marriages were arranged by the heads of the families. Men were permitted to have more than one wife but, except for the well-off, they normally had only one. On the other hand, a woman was expected to marry only once in her lifetime. The custom of early marriage prevailed all over the country. Sometimes children were married when they were only three or four years of age.

Among the upper classes, the evil customs of incurring heavy expenses on marriages and of giving dowry to the bride prevailed. The evil of dowry was especially widespread in Bengal and Rajputana. In Maharashtra, it was curbed to some extent by energetic steps taken by the Peshwas.

Two great social evils of eighteenth-century India, apart from the caste system, were the custom of *sati* and the condition of widows. Sati involved the rite of a Hindu widow burning herself along with the body of her dead husband. It was mostly prevalent in Rajputana, Bengal, and other parts of northern India. In the south, it was uncommon and the Marathas did not encourage it. Even in Rajputana and Bengal, it was practised only by the families of rajas, chiefs, big zamindars and upper castes. Widows belonging to the higher classes and higher castes could not remarry, though in some regions and in some castes, for example among non-brahmins in Maharashtra, the Jats and people of the hill-regions of the north, widow remarriage was quite common. The lot of the Hindu widow was usually pitiable. There were all sorts of restrictions on her clothing, diet, movements, etc. In general, she was expected to renounce all the pleasures of the world and to serve selflessly the members of her husband's or her brother's family, depending on where she spent the remaining years of her life. Sensitive Indians were often touched by the hard and harsh life of the widows. Raja Sawai Jai Singh of Amber and the Maratha General Prashuram Bhau tried to promote widow remarriage, but failed.

Culturally, India showed some signs of exhaustion during the eighteenth century, but the eighteenth century was no Dark Age. The creativity of the people continued to find expression, cultural continuity with the preceding centuries was maintained and local traditions continued to evolve. At the same time, culture remained wholly traditionalist. Cultural activities of the time were mostly financed by the Royal Court, rulers and nobles, chiefs and zamindars, whose impoverishment led to their gradual neglect. The most rapid decline occurred precisely in those branches of the arts which depended on the patronage of kings, princes and nobles. This was true most of all of Mughal architecture and painting. Many of the painters of the Mughal school migrated to provincial courts and flourished at Hyderabad, Lucknow, Kashmir and Patna. At the same time, new schools of painting were born and achieved distinction. The paintings of the Kangra and Rajputana schools revealed new vitality and taste. In the field of architecture, the Imambara of Lucknow reveals proficiency in technique, but a decadence in architectural taste. On the other hand, the city of Jaipur and its buildings are an example of continuing vigour. Music continued to develop and flourish in the eighteenth century, both in the north and the south. Significant progress was made in this field in the reign of Muhammad Shah.

Poetry in nearly all the Indian languages tended to lose its touch with life and become decorative, artificial, mechanical and traditional. Its pessimism reflected the prevailing sense of despair and cynicism, while its content reflected the impoverishment of the spiritual life of its patrons, the feudal nobles and kings.

A noteworthy feature of the literary life of the eighteenth century was the spread of the Urdu language and the vigorous growth of Urdu poetry. Urdu gradually became the medium of social intercourse among the upper classes of northern India. While Urdu poetry shared the weaknesses of contemporary literature in other Indian languages, it produced brilliant poets like Mir, Sauda, Nazir and, in the nineteenth century, that great genius, Mirza Ghalib. Hindi, too, was developing throughout the century.

Similarly, there was a revival of Malayalam literature, especially under the patronage of the Travancore rulers Martanda Varma and Rama Varma. One of the great poets of Kerala, Kunchan Nambiar, who wrote popular poetry in the language of daily usage, lived at this time. Eighteenth-century Kerala also witnessed the full development of *Kathakali* literature, drama and dance. The Padmanabhapuram palace, with its remarkable architecture and mural paintings, was also constructed in the eighteenth century.

Tayaumanavar (1706–44) was one of the best exponents of *sittar* poetry in Tamil. In line with other sittar poets, he protested against the abuses of temple-rule and the caste system. Music, poetry and dance flourished under the patronage of the Tanjore court in the first half of the eighteenth century. In Assam, literature developed under the patronage of the Ahom kings. Dayaram, one of the great lyricists of Gujarat, wrote during the second half of the eighteenth century. *Heer Ranjha*, the famous romantic epic in Punjabi, was composed at this time by Warris Shah. For Sindhi literature, the eighteenth century was a period of enormous achievement. Shah Abdul Latif composed his famous collection of poems, *Risalo*. Sachal and Sami were the other great Sindhi poets of this century.

The main weakness of Indian culture lay in the field of science. Throughout the eighteenth century, India remained far behind the West in science and technology. For the last 200 years, Western Europe had been undergoing a scientific and economic revolution that was leading to a spate of inventions and discoveries. The scientific outlook was gradually pervading the Western mind and revolutionising the philosophical, political and economic outlook of the Europeans and their institutions. On the other hand, the Indians, who had in earlier ages made vital contributions to the fields of mathematics and natural sciences, had been neglecting the sciences for several centuries. The

Indian mind was still tied to tradition; both the nobles and the common people were superstitious to a high degree. The Indians remained almost wholly ignorant of the scientific, cultural, political and economic achievements of the West; they failed to respond to the European challenge. The eighteenth-century Indian rulers showed little interest in things Western, except in their weapons of war and techniques of military training. Except Tipu, they were content with the ideological apparatus they had inherited from the Mughals and other sixteenth and seventeenth-century rulers. There were, of course, some intellectual stirrings—no people or culture can be totally stagnant. Some changes and advances in technology were being made, but their pace was very slow and their scope severely limited, so that on the whole they were negligible compared to advances in Western Europe. This weakness in the realm of science was to a large extent responsible for the total subjugation of India by the most advanced country of the time.

The struggle for power and wealth, economic decline, social backwardness and cultural stagnation had a deep and harmful impact on the morals of a section of the Indian people. The nobles, in particular, degenerated in their private and public life. The virtues of loyalty, gratitude and faithfulness to their pledged word tended to disappear in the single-minded pursuit of selfish aims. Many of the nobles fell prey to degrading vices and excessive luxury. Most of them took bribes when in office. Surprisingly enough, the common people were not debased to any marked extent. They continued to exhibit a high degree of personal integrity and morality. For example, the well-known British official John Malcolm remarked in 1821:

> I do not know the example of any great population, in similar circumstances, preserving through such a period of changes and tyrannical rule, so much virtue and so many qualities as are to be found in a great proportion of the inhabitants of this country.

In particular, he praised "the absence of the common vices of theft, drunkenness, and violence." Similarly, Cranford, another European writer, observed:

Their rules of morality are most benevolent: and hospitality and charity are not only strongly inculcated but I believe nowhere more universally practised than amongst Hindus.

Friendly relations between the Hindus and Muslims were a very healthy feature of life in eighteenth-century India. Even though the nobles and chiefs of the time fought one another incessantly, their fights and their alliances were seldom based on distinctions of religion. In other words, their politics were essentially secular. In fact, there was little communal bitterness or religious intolerance in the country. All people, high or low, respected one another's religion and a spirit of tolerance, even harmony, prevailed. "The mutual relations of Hindus and Muslims were those of brothers among brothers." This was particularly true of the common people in the villages and towns who fully shared one another's joys and sorrows, irrespective of religious affiliations.

Hindus and Muslims cooperated in non-religious spheres, such as social life and cultural affairs. The evolution of a composite Hindu–Muslim culture, or of common ways and attitudes, continued unimpeded. Hindu writers often wrote in Persian, while Muslim writers wrote in Hindi, Bengali and other vernaculars, often dealing with subjects of Hindu social life and religion, such as Radha and Krishna, Sita and Ram, and Nal and Damyanti. The development of Urdu language and literature provided a new meeting ground between Hindus and Muslims.

Even in the religious sphere, the mutual influence and respect that had been developing in the last few centuries as a result of the spread of the Bhakti Movement among Hindus and Sufism among Muslims continued to grow. A large number of Hindus worshipped Muslim saints and many Muslims showed equal veneration for Hindu gods and saints. Many local cults and shrines had both Hindu and Muslim followers. Muslim rulers, nobles and commoners joyfully joined in Hindu festivals such as Holi, Diwali and Durga Puja, just as Hindus participated in the Muharram processions and Hindu officials and zamindars presided at other Muslim festivals. The Marathas supported the shrine of Shaikh Muinuddin Chishti in Ajmer and the Raja of Tanjore supported the shrine of Shaikh Shahul Hamid of Nagore. We have already seen how Tipu gave financial support to the Shringeri Temple, as also to other temples. It is noteworthy that Raja Rammohun Roy, the greatest Indian of the first half of the nineteenth century, was influenced in an equal measure by the Hindu and Islamic philosophical and religious systems.

It may also be noted that religious affiliation was not the main point of departure in cultural and social life. The ways of life of upper-class Hindus and Muslims converged much more than the ways of life of upper-class and lower-class Hindus or of upper-class and lower-class Muslims. Similarly, regions or areas provided points of departure. People of one region had far greater cultural synthesis, irrespective of religion, than people following the same religion spread over different regions. People living in the villages also tended to have a different pattern of social and cultural life than that of the town dwellers.

Three

European Penetration and the British Conquest of India

A New Phase in Europe's Eastern Trade

India's trade relations with Europe go back to the ancient days of the Greeks. During the Middle Ages, trade between Europe and India and South-East Asia was carried on along several routes. The Asian part of the trade was carried on mostly by Arab merchants and sailors, while the Mediterranean and European part was the virtual monopoly of the Italians. Goods from Asia to Europe passed through many states and many hands. Yet, trade remained highly profitable.

The old trading routes between the East and the West came under Turkish control after the Ottoman conquest of Asia Minor and the capture of Constantinople in 1453. Moreover, the merchants of Venice and Genoa monopolised the trade between Europe and Asia and refused to let the new nation-states of Western Europe, particularly Spain and Portugal, have any share in the trade through these old routes. The West European states and merchants therefore began to search for new and safer sea routes to India and the Spice Islands in Indonesia, then known as the East Indies. They wanted to break the Arab and Venetian trade monopolies, bypass Turkish hostility, and open direct trade relations with the East. They were well-equipped to do so, as great advances in ship-building and the science of navigation had taken place during the fifteenth century. Moreover, the Renaissance had generated a great spirit of adventure among the people of Western Europe.

The first steps were taken by Portugal and Spain whose seamen, sponsored and controlled by their governments, began a great era of geographical discoveries. In 1492, Columbus of Spain set out to reach India and discovered America instead. In 1498, Vasco da Gama of Portugal discovered a new and all-sea route from Europe to India.

He sailed round Africa via the Cape of Good Hope and reached Calicut. He returned with a cargo which sold for 60 times the cost of his voyage. These and other navigational discoveries opened a new chapter in the history of the world. The seventeenth and eighteenth centuries were to witness an enormous increase in world trade. The vast new continent of America was opened to Europe and relations between Europe and Asia were completely transformed.

Another major source of early capital accumulation or enrichment for European countries was their penetration of Africa in the middle of the fifteenth century. In the beginning, the gold and ivory of Africa had attracted the foreigner. Very soon, however, trade with Africa centred around the slave trade. In the sixteenth century, this trade was a monopoly of Spain and Portugal. Later, it was dominated by Dutch, French and British merchants. Year after year, particularly after 1650, thousands of Africans were sold as slaves in the West Indies and in North and South America. The slave ships carried manufactured goods from Europe to Africa, exchanged them on the coast of Africa for African slaves, took these slaves across the Atlantic and exchanged them for the colonial produce of plantations or mines, and finally brought back and sold this produce in Europe. It was on the immense profits of this triangular trade that the commercial supremacy of England and France was to be based. A great deal of West European and North American prosperity was based on the slave trade and the plantations worked by slave labour. Moreover, the profits of slave trade and the slave-worked plantations provided some of the capital which financed the Industrial Revolution in the eighteenth and nineteenth centuries. A similar role was later played by the wealth extracted from India.

In the sixteenth century, European merchants and soldiers also began the long process of first penetrating and then subjecting Asian lands to their control. Portugal had a monopoly over the highly profitable Eastern trade for nearly a century. In India, Portugal established its trading settlements at Cochin, Goa, Diu and Daman. From the beginning, the Portuguese combined the use of force with trade. In this, they were helped by the superiority of their armed ships, which enabled them to dominate the seas. A handful of Portuguese soldiers and sailors could maintain their position on the seas against the much more powerful land powers of India and Asia. By threatening Mughal shipping, they also succeeded in securing many trading concessions from the Mughal emperors.

Under the viceroyalty of Alfonso D'Albuquerque, who captured Goa in 1510, the Portuguese established their domination over the entire Asian coast, from Hormuz in the Persian Gulf to Malacca in Malaya and the Spice Islands in Indonesia. They seized Indian territories on the coast and waged constant war to expand their trade and dominions and safeguard their trade monopoly from their European rivals. Nor did they shy away from piracy and plunder. They also indulged in inhuman cruelties and lawlessness. In spite of their barbaric behaviour, their possessions in India survived for a century because they enjoyed control over the high seas, their soldiers and administrators maintained strict discipline, and they did not have to face the might of the Mughal Empire as south India was outside Mughal influence.

In the latter half of the sixteenth century, England and Holland, and later France, all growing commercial and naval powers, waged a fierce struggle against the Spanish and Portuguese monopoly over world trade. In this struggle, the latter had to go under. The English and the Dutch merchants were now able to use the Cape of Good Hope route to India and so join in the race for empire in the East. In the end, the Dutch gained control over Indonesia and the British over India, Sri Lanka, and Malaya.

In 1602, the Dutch East India Company was formed and the Dutch States General—the Dutch parliament—gave it a charter empowering it to make war, conclude treaties, acquire territories and build fortresses. The main interest of the Dutch lay not in India but in the Indonesian Islands of Java, Sumatra, and the Spice Islands where spices were produced. They soon turned out the Portuguese from the Malay Straits and the Indonesian Islands and, in 1623, defeated English attempts to establish themselves there. They also established trading depots at Surat, Broach, Cambay and Ahmedabad in Gujarat in west India, Cochin in Kerala, Nagapatam in Madras, Masulipatam in Andhra, Chinsura in Bengal, Patna in Bihar, and Agra in Uttar Pradesh. In 1658, they also conquered Sri Lanka from the Portuguese.

The English merchants looked greedily at the Asian trade. The success of the Portuguese, the rich cargoes of spices, calicoes, silk,

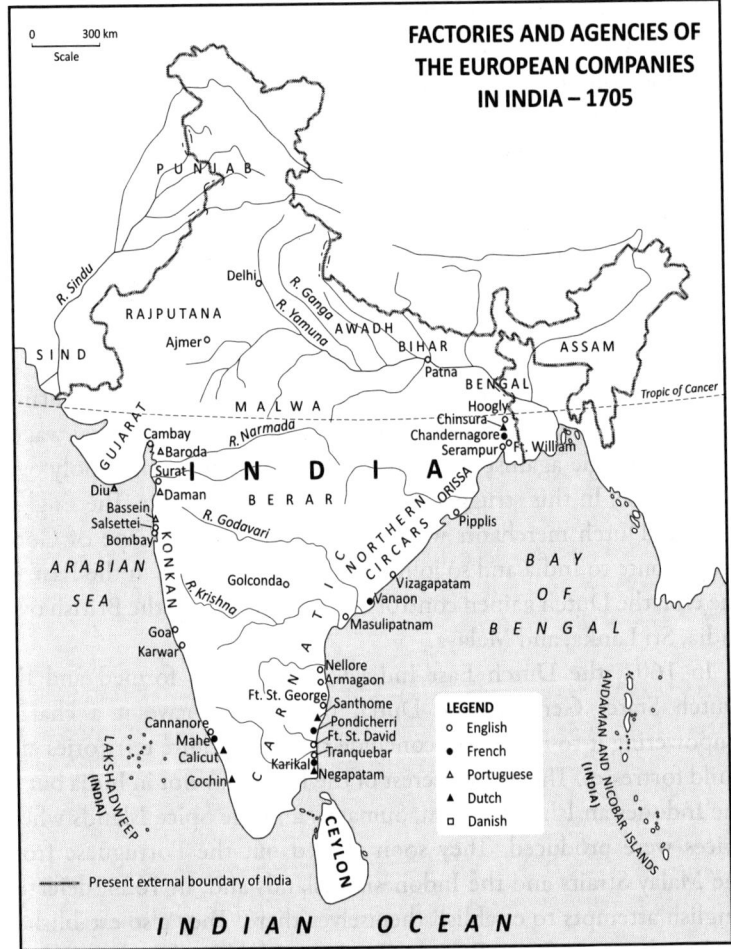

gold, pearls, drugs, porcelain, and ebony they carried and the high profits they made inflamed the imagination of the merchants of England and made them impatient to participate in such profitable commerce. An English association or company to trade with the East was formed in 1599 under the auspices of a group of merchants known as the Merchant Adventurers. The company, popularly known as the East India Company, was granted a royal charter and the exclusive privilege to trade in the East by Queen Elizabeth on 31 December 1600. In 1608 it decided to open a 'factory', the name given at the time to a trading depot, at Surat on the west coast of India and sent Captain Hawkins to Jahangir's court to obtain royal favours. Consequently, the English Company was given permission by a royal *farman* to open factories at several places on the west coast.

The English were not satisfied with this concession. In 1615, their ambassador Sir Thomas Roe reached the Mughal court. Roe succeeded in getting an imperial *farman* to trade and establish factories in all parts of the Mughal Empire. In 1662, the Portuguese gave the island of Bombay to King Charles II of England as dowry for marrying a Portuguese princess. Eventually, the Portuguese lost all their possessions in India except Goa, Diu and Daman. The English Company fell out with the Dutch Company over the division of the spice trade of the Indonesian Islands. The intermittent war in India between the two powers, which had begun in 1654, ended in 1667, when the English gave up all claims to Indonesia while the Dutch agreed to leave alone the English settlements in India.

THE GROWTH OF THE EAST INDIA COMPANY'S TRADE AND INFLUENCE, 1600–1714

The English East India Company had very humble beginnings in India. By 1623, it had established factories (trading posts) at Surat, Broach, Ahmedabad, Agra, and Masulipatam. From the very beginning, it tried to combine trade and diplomacy with war and control of the territory where their factories were situated.

Conditions in the south were more favourable to the English as they did not have to face a strong Indian government there. The great Vijayanagar Kingdom had been overthrown in 1565 and its place taken by a number of petty and weak states. It was easy to appeal to their greed or overawe them with armed strength. The English opened their first 'factory' in the south at Masulipatam in 1611. But they soon shifted the centre of their activity to Madras, the lease of which was granted to them by the local Raja in 1639. The Raja authorised them to fortify the place, administer it, and coin money on condition of payment to him of half of the customs revenue of the port. Here, the English built a small fort around their factory called Fort St. George.

Interestingly enough, from the very beginning this company of profit-seeking merchants was also determined to make Indians pay for the conquest of their own country. For example, the Court of Directors of the Company wrote to the Madras authorities in 1683:

> ... we would have you to strengthen and fortify our Fort and Town (Madras) by degrees, that it may be terrible against the assault of any Indian Prince and the Dutch power of India.... But we must needs desire you so to continue your business (but with all gentleness) that the inhabitants may pay the full charge of all repairs and fortifications...

The island of Bombay was acquired by the East India Company from the British government in 1668 and was immediately fortified. In Bombay the English found a large and easy-to-defend port. For that reason, and because English trade was threatened at the time by the rising Maratha power, Bombay soon superseded Surat as the headquarters of the Company on the west coast.

In eastern India, the English Company had opened its first factories in Orissa in 1633. In 1651, it was given permission to trade at Hugli in Bengal. It soon opened factories at Patna in Bihar, Balasore in Orissa and Dhaka and other places in Bengal. It now desired that in Bengal too it should have an independent settlement. It dreamt of establishing political power in India, which would enable it to compel the Mughals to allow them a free hand in trade, to force Indians to sell cheap and buy dear, to keep the rival European traders out and to make its trade independent of the policies of the Indian powers. Political power would also make it possible for it to appropriate Indian revenues and thus to conquer the country with its own resources. Such plans were explicitly put forward at the time. In 1687, the directors advised the Governor of Madras to:

... establish such a policy of civil and military power and create and secure such a large revenue to maintain both as may be the foundation of a large, well-grounded, secure English dominion in India for all time to come.

In 1689, they declared:

The increase of our revenue is the subject of our care, as much as our trade: 'tis that must maintain our force, when twenty accidents may interrupt our trade; 'tis that must make us a nation in India ....

Hostilities between the English and the Mughal emperor broke out in 1686 after the former had sacked Hugli and declared war on the emperor. But the English had seriously misjudged the situation and underestimated Mughal strength. The Mughal Empire under Aurangzeb was even now more than a match for the petty forces of the East India Company. The war ended disastrously for them. They were driven out of their factories in Bengal and compelled to seek refuge in a fever-stricken island at the mouth of the Ganga. Their factories at Surat, Masulipatam, and Vishakhapatam were seized and their fort at Bombay besieged. Having discovered that they were not yet strong enough to fight the Mughal power, the English once again became humble petitioners and submitted "that the ill crimes they have done may be pardoned". They expressed their willingness to trade under the protection of the Indian rulers. Obviously, they had learnt their lesson. Once again they relied on flattery and humble entreaties to get trading concessions from the Mughal emperor.

The Mughal authorities readily pardoned the English folly as they had no means of knowing that these harmless-looking foreign traders would one day pose a serious threat to the country. Instead, they recognised that foreign trade carried on by the Company benefited Indian artisans and merchants, and thereby enriched the State treasury. Moreover, the English, though weak on land, were, because of their naval supremacy, capable of completely running Indian trade and shipping to Iran, West Asia, Northern and Eastern Africa and East Asia. Aurangzeb therefore permitted them to resume trade on payment of Rs 150,000 as compensation. In 1698, the Company acquired the zamindari of the three villages Sutanati, Kalikata, and Govindpur, where it built Fort William around its factory. The villages soon grew into a city, which came to be known as Calcutta. In 1717, the Company secured from Emperor Farrukh Siyar a *farman* confirming the privileges granted in 1691 and extending them to Gujarat and the Deccan. But during the first half of the eighteenth century, Bengal was ruled by strong Nawabs such as Murshid Quli Khan and Alivardi Khan. They exercised strict control over the English traders and prevented them from misusing their privileges. Nor did they allow them to strengthen fortifications at Calcutta or to rule the city independently. Here, the East India Company remained a mere zamindar of the nawab.

Even though the political ambitions of the Company were frustrated, its commercial affairs flourished as never before. Its imports from India into England increased from £500,000 in 1708 to £1,795,000 in 1740. British settlements in Madras, Bombay and Calcutta became the nuclei of flourishing cities. Large numbers of Indian merchants and bankers were attracted to these cities. This was due partly to the new commercial opportunities available in these cities and partly to the unsettled conditions and insecurity outside them, caused by the break-up of the Mughal Empire. By the middle of the eighteenth century, the population of Madras had increased to 300,000, that of Calcutta to 200,000 and that of Bombay to 70,000.

The Charter of 1600 granted the East India Company the exclusive privilege of trading east of the Cape of Good Hope for a period of 15 years. The Company was a strictly closed corporation or a monopoly. In India, a factory of the Company was generally a fortified area within which the warehouse (stores), offices and houses of the Company's employees were situated. It is to be noted that no manufacture was carried on in this 'factory'.

The Company's servants were paid very low salaries. Their real income, for which they were so keen to take service in India, came from the permission the Company granted them to carry on private trade within the country, while trade between India and Europe was reserved for the Company.

The Anglo-French Struggle in South India

The English East India Company's schemes of territorial conquests and political domination, which had been frustrated by Aurangzeb at the end of the seventeenth century, were revived during the 1740s because of the visible decline of Mughal power. Nadir Shah's invasion had revealed the decay of the central authority. But there was not much scope for foreign penetration in western India where the vigorous Marathas held sway, and in eastern India where Alivardi Khan maintained strict control. In southern India, however, conditions were gradually becoming favourable to foreign adventurers. While central authority had disappeared from there after Aurangzeb's death, the strong hand of Nizam-ul-Mulk Asaf Jah was also withdrawn by his death in 1748. Moreover, the Maratha chiefs regularly invaded Hyderabad and the rest of the south, collecting *chauth*. These raids resulted in politically unsettled conditions and administrative disorganisation. The Carnatic was embroiled in fratricidal wars of succession.

These conditions gave the foreigners an opportunity to expand their political influence and control over the affairs of the south Indian states. But the English were not alone in putting forward commercial and political claims. While they had, by the end of the seventeenth century, eliminated their Portuguese and Dutch rivals, France had appeared as a new rival. For nearly 20 years, from 1744 to 1763, the French and the English were to wage a bitter war for control over the trade, wealth and territory of India.

The French East India Company was founded in 1664. It was firmly established at Chandernagore near Calcutta and Pondicherry on the east coast. The latter was fully fortified. The French Company had some other factories at several ports on the east and the west coasts. It had also acquired control over the islands of Mauritius and Reunion in the Indian Ocean.

The French East India Company was heavily dependent on the French government, which helped it by giving it treasury grants, subsidies and loans, and in various other ways. Consequently, it was largely controlled by the government, which appointed its directors after 1723. State control of the Company proved quite harmful to it. The French state of the time was autocratic, semi-feudal, and unpopular, and suffered from corruption, inefficiency, and instability. Instead of being forward-looking, it was decadent, bound by tradition, and in general unsuited to the times. Control by such a state could not but be injurious to the interests of the Company.

In 1742, war broke out in Europe between France and England. This war soon spread to India, where the two East India Companies clashed with each other. In 1748, the general war between England and France ended. Though war had ended, the rivalry in trade and over the possessions in India continued and had to be decided one way or another.

Dupleix, the French Governor-General at Pondicherry at this time, now evolved the strategy of using the well-disciplined, modern French army to intervene in the mutual quarrels among Indian princes and, by supporting one against the other, securing monetary, commercial or territorial favours from the victor. Thus, he planned to use the resources and armies of the local rajas, nawabs, and chiefs to serve the interests of the French Company and to expel the English from India. The only barrier to the success of this strategy could have been the refusal of Indian rulers to permit such foreign intervention. But the Indian rulers were guided not by patriotism, but by a narrow-minded pursuit of personal ambition and gain. They had little hesitation in inviting the foreigners to help them settle accounts with their internal rivals.

In 1748, a situation arose in the Carnatic and Hyderabad which allowed full scope to Dupleix's talents for intrigue. In the Carnatic, Chanda Sahib began to conspire against Nawab Anwaruddin, while in Hyderabad the death of Asaf Jah, Nizam-ul-Mulk, was followed by civil war between his son Nasir Jang and his grandson, Muzaffar Jang. Dupleix seized this opportunity and concluded a secret treaty with Chanda Sahib and Muzaffar Jang to help them with his well-trained French and Indian forces. In 1749, the three allies defeated and killed Anwaruddin in a battle at Ambur. The latter's son, Muhammad Ali, fled to Trichinopoly. The rest of the Carnatic passed under the dominion of Chanda Sahib, who rewarded the French with a grant of 80 villages around Pondicherry.

In Hyderabad, too, the French were successful. Nasir Jang was killed and Muzaffar Jang became the Nizam or Viceroy of the Deccan. The new Nizam rewarded the French Company by giving it territories near Pondicherry as well as the famous town of Masulipatam. He gave a sum of Rs 500,000 to the Company and another Rs 500,000 to its troops. Dupleix received Rs 2,000,000 and a jagir worth Rs 100,000 a year. Moreover, he was made honorary governor of Mughal dominions on the east coast, from the river Krishna to Kanya Kumari. Dupleix stationed his best officer, Bussy, at Hyderabad with a French army. While the ostensible purpose of this arrangement was to protect the Nizam from enemies, it was really aimed at maintaining French influence at his court. While Muzaffar Jang was marching towards his capital, he was accidentally killed. Bussy immediately raised Salabat Jang, the third son of Nizam-ul-Mulk, to the throne. In return, the new Nizam granted the French the area in Andhra known as the Northern Sarkars, consisting of the four districts of Mustafanagar, Ellore, Rajahmundry and Chicacole.

The French power in south India was now at its height. Dupleix's plans had succeeded beyond his dreams. The French had started out by trying to win Indian states as friends; they had ended by making them clients or satellites.

But the English had not been silent spectators of their rival's successes. To offset French influence and to increase their own, they had been intriguing with Nasir Jang and Muhammad Ali. In 1750, they decided to throw their entire strength behind Muhammad Ali. Robert Clive, a young clerk in the Company's service, proposed that French pressure on Muhammad Ali, besieged at Trichinopoly, could be released by attacking Arcot, the capital of the Carnatic. The proposal was accepted and Clive assaulted and occupied Arcot with only 200 English and 300 Indian soldiers. As expected, Chanda Sahib and the French were compelled to raise the seige of Trichinopoly. The French forces were repeatedly defeated. Chanda Sahib was soon captured and killed. The French fortunes were now at an ebb as their army and its generals had proved unequal to their English counterparts. In the end, the French government, weary of the heavy expense of the war in India and fearing the loss of its American colonies, initiated peace negotiations and agreed in 1754 to the English demand for the recall of Dupleix from India. This was to prove a big blow to the fortunes of the French Company in India.

The temporary peace between the two Companies ended in 1756 when another war between England and France broke out. At the very beginning of the war, the English managed to gain control over Bengal. This has been discussed later in this chapter. After this event, there was little hope for the French cause in India. The rich resources of Bengal turned the scales decisively in favour of the English. The decisive battle of the war was fought at Wandiwash on 22 January 1760 when the English general, Eyre Coot, defeated Lally. Within a year the French had lost all their possessions in India. The war ended in 1763 with the signing of the Treaty of Paris. The French factories in India were restored, but they could no longer be fortified or even adequately garrisoned with troops. They could serve only as centres of trade; and now the French lived in India under British protection. The English, on the other hand, ruled the Indian sea. Freed of all European rivals, they could now set about the task of conquering India.

During their struggle with the French and their Indian allies, the English learnt a few important and valuable lessons. First, in the absence of nationalism in the country, they could advance their political schemes by taking advantage of the mutual quarrels of the Indian rulers. Second, the Western-trained infantry, European or Indian, armed with modern weapons and backed by artillery, could defeat the old-style Indian armies with ease in pitched battles. Third, it was proved that the Indian soldier, trained and armed in the European manner, made as good a soldier as the European. And since the Indian soldier too lacked a feeling of nationalism, he could be hired and employed by anyone willing to pay him well. The English now set out to create a powerful army consisting of Indian soldiers, called sepoys, and officered by Englishmen. With this army as its chief instrument and the vast resources of Indian trade and territories under its command, the English East India Company embarked on an era of wars and territorial expansion.

British Occupation of Bengal

The beginnings of British political sway over India may be traced to the Battle of Plassey in 1757, when the English East India Company's forces defeated Siraj-ud-Daulah, the Nawab of Bengal. The earlier British struggle with the French in south India had been but a dress rehearsal. The lessons learnt there were profitably applied in Bengal.

Bengal was the most fertile and the richest of India's provinces. Its industries and commerce were well-developed. The East India

Company and its servants had highly profitable trading interests in the province. The Company had secured valuable privileges in 1717 under a royal *farman* by the Mughal emperor, which had granted it the freedom to export and import their goods in Bengal without paying taxes and the right to issue passes or *dastaks* for the movement of such goods. The Company's servants were also permitted to trade, but were not covered by this *farman*. They were required to pay the same taxes as Indian merchants. This *farman* was a perpetual source of conflict between the Company and the Nawabs of Bengal. For one, it meant loss of revenue to the Bengal government. Second, the power to issue *dastaks* for the Company's goods was misused by the Company's servants to evade taxes on their private trade. All the Nawabs of Bengal, from Murshid Quli Khan to Alivardi Khan, had objected to the English interpretation of the *farman* of 1717. They had compelled the Company to pay lump sums to their treasury, and firmly suppressed the misuse of *dastaks*. The Company had been compelled to accept the authority of the Nawabs in the matter, but its servants had taken every opportunity to evade and defy this authority.

Matters came to a head in 1756 when the young and quick tempered Siraj-ud-Daulah succeeded his grandfather, Alivardi Khan. He demanded that the English trade on the same basis as in the times of Murshid Quli Khan. The English refused to comply as they felt strong after their victory over the French in south India. Instead of agreeing to pay taxes on their goods to the Nawab, they levied heavy duties on Indian goods entering Calcutta, which was under their control. All this naturally annoyed and angered the young Nawab, who also suspected that the Company was hostile to him and was favouring his rivals for the throne of Bengal. The breaking point came when, without taking the Nawab's permission, the Company began to fortify Calcutta in expectation of the coming struggle with the French, who were stationed at this time at Chandernagore. Siraj rightly interpreted this action as an attack upon his sovereignty. How could an independent ruler permit a private company of merchants to build forts or to carry on private wars on his land? In other words, Siraj was willing to let the Europeans remain as merchants, but not as masters. He ordered both the English and the French to demolish their fortifications at Calcutta and

Chandernagore and to desist from fighting each other. While the French Company obeyed his order, the English Company refused to do so, for its ambitions had been whetted and its confidence enhanced by its victories in the Carnatic. It was now determined to remain in Bengal even against the wishes of the Nawab, and to trade there on its own terms. It had acknowledged the British government's right to control all its activities; it had quietly accepted restrictions on its trade and power imposed in Britain by the British government; its right to trade with the East had been extinguished by the Parliament in 1693 when its Charter was withdrawn; it had paid huge bribes to the King, the Parliament, and the politicians of Britain (in one year alone, it had to pay £80,000 in bribes). Nevertheless, the English Company demanded the absolute right to trade freely in Bengal, irrespective of the Bengal Nawab's orders. This amounted to a direct challenge to the Nawab's sovereignty. No ruler could possibly accept this position. Siraj-ud-Daulah had the statesmanship to see the long-term implications of the English designs. He decided to make them obey the laws of the land.

Acting with great energy but with undue haste and inadequate preparation, Siraj-ud-Daulah seized the English factory at Kasimbazar, marched on to Calcutta, and occupied Fort William on 20 June 1756. He then retired from Calcutta to celebrate his easy victory, letting the English escape with their ships. This was a mistake, for he had underestimated the strength of his enemy.

The English officials took refuge at Fulta near the sea, protected by their naval superiority. Here, they waited for aid from Madras and, in the meantime, organised a web of intrigue and treachery with the leading men of the Nawab's court. Chief among these were Mir Jafar, the *Mir Bakshi*, Manick Chand, the Officer-in-Charge of Calcutta, Amichand, a rich merchant, Jagat Seth, the biggest banker of Bengal, and Khadim Khan, who commanded a large number of the Nawab's troops. From Madras came a strong naval and military force under Admiral Watson and Colonel Clive. Clive reconquered Calcutta in the beginning of 1757 and compelled the Nawab to concede all the demands of the English.

The English, however, were not satisfied; they were aiming high. They had decided to instal a more pliant tool in Siraj-ud-Daulah's place. Having joined a conspiracy organised by the enemies of the young Nawab to place Mir Jafar on the throne of Bengal, they presented the youthful Nawab with an impossible set of demands. Both sides realised that a war to the finish would have to be fought between them. They met for battle on the field of Plassey, about 30 km from Murshidabad, on 23 June 1757. The fateful Battle of Plassey was a battle only in name. In all, the English lost 29 men while the Nawab lost nearly 500. The major part of the Nawab's army, led by the traitors Mir Jafar and Rai Durlabh, took no part in the fighting. Only a small group of the Nawab's soldiers led by Mir Madan and Mohan Lal fought bravely and well. The Nawab was forced to flee and was captured and put to death by Mir Jafar's son Miran.

The Battle of Plassey was followed, in the words of the Bengali poet Nabin Chandra Sen, by "a night of eternal gloom for India". The English proclaimed Mir Jafar the Nawab of Bengal and set out to gather the reward. The Company was granted the undisputed right to free trade in Bengal, Bihar and Orissa. It also received the zamindari of the 24 Parganas near Calcutta. Mir Jafar paid a sum of Rs 17,700,000 as compensation for the attack on Calcutta to the Company and the traders of the city. In addition, he paid large sums as 'gifts' or bribes to the high officials of the Company. Clive, for example, received over two million rupees, Watts over one million. Clive later estimated that the Company and its servants had collected more than 30 million rupees from the puppet Nawab. It was also understood that British merchants and officials would no longer be asked to pay any taxes on their private trade.

The Battle of Plassey was of immense historical importance. It paved the way for British mastery over Bengal, and eventually, over the whole of India. It boosted British prestige and, by a single stroke, raised them to the status of a major contender for the Indian empire. The rich revenues of Bengal enabled them to organise a strong army and meet the costs of the conquest of the rest of the country. Control over Bengal played a decisive role in the Anglo-French struggle. Lastly, the victory at Plassey enabled the Company and its servants to amass untold wealth at the cost of the helpless people of Bengal. As British historians Edward Thompson and G.T. Garrett have remarked:

> To engineer a revolution had been revealed as the most paying game in the world. A gold lust unequalled since the hysteria that took hold of the

Spaniards of Cortes' and Pizarro's age filled the English mind. Bengal in particular was not to know peace again until it had been bled white.

Even though Mir Jafar owed his position to the Company, he soon regretted the bargain he had struck. His treasury was quickly emptied by the demands of Company's officials for presents and bribes, the lead in the matter being given by Clive himself. As Colonel Malleson has put it, the single aim of Company's officials was "to grasp all they could; to use Mir Jafar as a golden sack into which they could dip their hands at pleasure". The Company itself was seized with unsurpassable greed. Believing that the *kamdhenu* had been found and that the wealth of Bengal was inexhaustible, the directors of the Company ordered that Bengal should pay the expenses of the Bombay and Madras Presidencies and purchase out of its revenue all the Company's exports from India. The Company was no longer to merely trade with India, it was to use its control over the Nawab of Bengal to drain the wealth of the province.

Mir Jafar soon discovered that it was impossible to meet the full demands of the Company and its officials who, on their part, began to criticise the Nawab for his inability to fulfil their expectations. And so, in October 1760, they forced him to abdicate in favour of his son-in-law, Mir Qasim, who rewarded his benefactors by granting the Company the zamindari of the districts of Burdwan, Midnapore, and Chittagong, and giving handsome presents totalling 29 lakhs of rupees to the high English officials.

Mir Qasim, however, belied English hopes, and soon emerged as a threat to their position and designs in Bengal. He was an able, efficient, and strong ruler, determined to free himself from foreign control. He realised that a full treasury and an efficient army were essential to maintain his independence. He therefore tried to prevent public disorder, to increase his income by removing corruption from revenue administration, and to raise a modern and disciplined army along European lines. All this was not to the liking of the English. Most of all, they disliked the Nawab's attempts to check the misuse of the *farman* of 1717 by the Company's servants, who demanded that their goods, whether destined for export or for internal use, be free of duties. This injured the Indian merchants, as they had to pay taxes from which the foreigners were given complete exemption.

European Penetration and the British Conquest of India

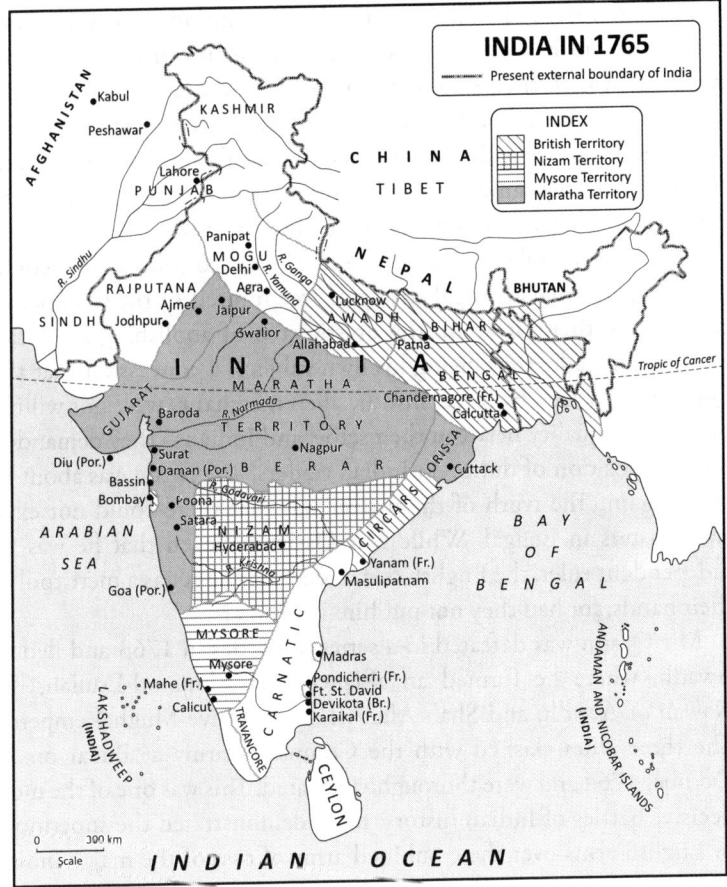

Moreover, the Company's servants illegally sold the *dastaks* or free passes to friendly Indian merchants who were thereby able to evade the internal customs duties. These abuses ruined the honest Indian traders through unfair competition and deprived the Nawab of a very important source of revenue. In addition to this, the Company and its servants forced the Indian officials and zamindars to give them presents and bribes. They compelled the Indian artisans, peasants and merchants to sell their goods cheap but buy dear from them. People who refused were often flogged or imprisoned. These years have been described by a recent British historian, Percival Spear, as "the period of open and unashamed plunder". In fact, the prosperity for which Bengal was renowned was being gradually destroyed.

Mir Qasim realised that if these abuses continued, he could never hope to make Bengal strong or free himself of the Company's control. He therefore took the drastic step of abolishing all duties on internal trade, thus giving his own subjects a concession that the English had seized by force. But the alien merchants were not willing to tolerate equality between themselves and Indians. They demanded the reimposition of duties on Indian traders. The battle was about to begin again. The truth of the matter was that there could not exist two masters in Bengal. While Mir Qasim believed that he was an independent ruler, the English demanded that he act as a mere tool in their hands, for had they not put him in power?

Mir Qasim was defeated in a series of battles in 1763 and fled to Awadh, where he formed an alliance with Shuja-ud-Daulah, the Nawab of Awadh, and Shah Alam II, the fugitive Mughal emperor. The three allies clashed with the Company's army at Buxar on 22 October 1764 and were thoroughly defeated. This was one of the most decisive battles of Indian history, for it demonstrated the superiority of English arms over the combined army of two of the major Indian powers. It firmly established the British as masters of Bengal, Bihar and Orissa and placed Awadh at their mercy.

Clive, who had returned to Bengal in 1765 as its Governor, decided to seize the chance of power in Bengal and to gradually transfer the authority of government from the Nawab to the Company. In 1763, the British had restored Mir Jafar as Nawab and collected huge sums for the Company and its high officials. On Mir Jafar's death, they placed his second son, Nizam-ud-Daulah, on the throne and as a reward to themselves, made him sign a new treaty on 20 February 1765. By this treaty, the Nawab was to disband most of his army and to administer Bengal through a Deputy *Subahdar* who was to be nominated by the Company, and who could not be dismissed without its approval. The Company thus gained supreme control over the administration (or *nizamat*) of Bengal. The members of the Bengal Council of the Company once again extracted nearly 15 lakhs of rupees from the new Nawab.

From Shah Alam II, who was still the titular head of the Mughal Empire, the Company secured the *Diwani,* or the right to collect the revenue of Bihar, Bengal and Orissa. Thus, its control over Bengal was legalised and the revenues of this most prosperous of Indian provinces placed at its command. In return, the Company gave him a subsidy of 26 lakhs of rupees and secured for him the districts of Kora and Allahabad. The emperor resided in the fort of Allahabad for six years as a virtual prisoner of the English.

The Nawab of Awadh, Shuja-ud-Daulah, was made to pay a war indemnity of five million rupees to the Company. Moreover, the two signed an alliance by which the Company promised to support the Nawab against an outside attack, provided he paid for the services of the troops sent to his aid. This alliance made the Nawab a dependent of the Company.

Dual System of Administration of Bengal

The East India Company became the real master of Bengal, at least from 1765. Its army was in sole control of its defence and the supreme political power was in its hands. The Nawab depended for his internal and external security on the British. As the *Diwan,* the Company directly collected its revenues, while through the right to nominate the Deputy *Subahdar,* it controlled the *nizamat* or the police and judicial powers. This arrangement is known in history as the 'dual' or 'double' government. It held a great advantage for the British: they had power without responsibility. The Nawab and his officials had the responsibility of administration, but not the power to discharge it. The weaknesses of the government could be blamed on the Indians, while its fruits were gathered by the British. The consequences for the people of Bengal were disastrous: neither the Company nor the Nawab cared for their welfare.

The Company's servants now had the whole of Bengal to themselves and their oppression of the people increased greatly. We can quote Clive himself:

> I shall only say that such a scene of anarchy, confusion, bribery, corruption, and extortion was never seen or heard of in any country but Bengal; nor such and so many fortunes acquired in so unjust and rapacious a manner. The three provinces of Bengal, Bihar, and Orissa, producing a clear revenue of £3 millions sterling, have been under the absolute management of the Company's servants, ever since Mir Jafar's restoration to the *subahship;* and they have, both civil and military, exacted and levied contributions from every man of power and consequence, from the Nawab down to the lowest zamindar.

The Company's authorities, on their part, set out to gather the rich harvest and drain Bengal of its wealth. They stopped sending money from England to purchase Indian goods. Instead, they purchased these goods from the revenues of Bengal and sold them abroad. These were known as the Company's Investment and formed a part of its profits. On top of all this, the British government wanted its share of the rich prize and, in 1767, ordered the Company to pay it £400,000 per year.

In the years 1766, 1767 and 1768 alone, nearly £5.7 million were drained from Bengal. The abuses of the 'dual' government and the drain of wealth led to the impoverishment and exhaustion of that unlucky province. In 1770, Bengal suffered a famine which, in its effects, proved to be one of the most terrible famines known in human history. People died in lakhs and nearly one-third of Bengal's population fell victim to its ravages. Though the famine was due to the failure of the rains, its effects were heightened by the Company's policies.

WARS UNDER WARREN HASTINGS (1772–85) AND CORNWALLIS (1786–93)

The East India Company had by 1772 become an important Indian power and its directors in England and officials in India set out to consolidate their control over Bengal before beginning a new round of conquests. However, their habit of interfering in the internal affairs of the Indian states and their lust for territory and money soon involved them in a series of wars.

In 1766, they joined the Nizam of Hyderabad in attacking Haidar Ali of Mysore. But Haidar Ali forced the Madras Council to sign a peace-treaty on his terms. Then, in 1775, the English clashed with the Marathas. An intense struggle for power was taking place at that time among the Marathas, between the supporters of the infant Peshwa Madhav Rao II, led by Nana Phadnis, and Raghunath Rao. The British officials in Bombay decided to intervene on behalf of Raghunath Rao. They hoped thus to repeat the exploits of their countrymen in Madras and Bengal and reap the consequent monetary advantages. This involved them in a long war with the Marathas, which lasted from 1775 to 1782.

This was a dark hour indeed for British power in India. All the Maratha chiefs were united behind the Peshwa and his chief minister, Nana Phadnis. The southern Indian powers had long been resenting the presence of the British among them, and Haidar Ali and the Nizam chose this moment to declare war against the Company. Thus, the British were faced with the powerful combination of the Marathas, Mysore and Hyderabad. Abroad, they were waging a losing war in their colonies in America, where the people had rebelled in 1776. They also had to counter the determined design of the French to exploit the difficulties of their old rival.

The British in India were, however, led at this time by the energetic, and experienced Governor-General, Warren Hastings. He acted with firm resolve and determination. Neither side won and the war came to a standstill. Peace was concluded in 1782 with the Treaty of Salbai, by which the status quo was maintained. It saved the British from the combined opposition of Indian powers.

This war, known in history as the First Anglo-Maratha war, did not end in victory for either side. But it did give the British 20 years of peace with the Marathas, the strongest Indian power of the day. The British utilised this period to consolidate their rule over the Bengal Presidency, while the Maratha chiefs frittered away their energy in bitter mutual squabbles. Moreover, the Treaty of Salbai enabled the British to exert pressure on Mysore, as the Marathas promised to help them in recovering their territories from Haidar Ali. Once again, the British had succeeded in dividing the Indian powers.

Meanwhile, war with Haidar Ali had again started in 1780. Repeating his earlier exploits, Haidar Ali inflicted one defeat after another on the British armies in the Carnatic and forced them to surrender in large numbers. He soon occupied almost the whole of the Carnatic. But once again, British arms and diplomacy saved the day. Warren Hastings bribed the Nizam with the cession of Guntur district and gained his withdrawal from the anti-British alliance. During 1781–82, he made peace with the Marathas and thus freed a large part of his army for use against Mysore. In July 1781, the British army under Eyre Coote defeated Haidar Ali at Porto Novo and saved Madras. After Haidar Ali's death in December 1782, the war was carried on by his son, Tipu Sultan. Since neither side was capable of overpowering the other, peace was signed between them in March 1784 and both sides restored all conquests. Thus, though the British had been shown to be too weak to defeat either the Marathas or Mysore, they had certainly proved their ability to hold their own in India.

The third British encounter with Mysore was more fruitful from the British point of view. The peace of 1784 had not removed the grounds for struggle between Tipu and the British; it had merely postponed the struggle. The authorities of the East India Company were acutely hostile to Tipu. They looked upon him as their most formidable rival in the south and as the chief obstacle standing between them and complete domination over south India. Tipu, on his part, thoroughly disliked the English, saw them as the chief danger to his own independence and nursed the ambition to expel them from India. War between the two began again in 1789 and ended in Tipu's defeat in 1792. By the treaty of Seringapatam, Tipu ceded half his territories to the English and their allies and paid 330 lakhs of rupees as indemnity.

EXPANSION UNDER LORD WELLESLEY (1798–1805)

The next large-scale expansion of British rule in India occurred during the Governor-Generalship of Lord Wellesley, who came to India in 1798 at a time when the British were locked in a life-and-death struggle with France all over the world.

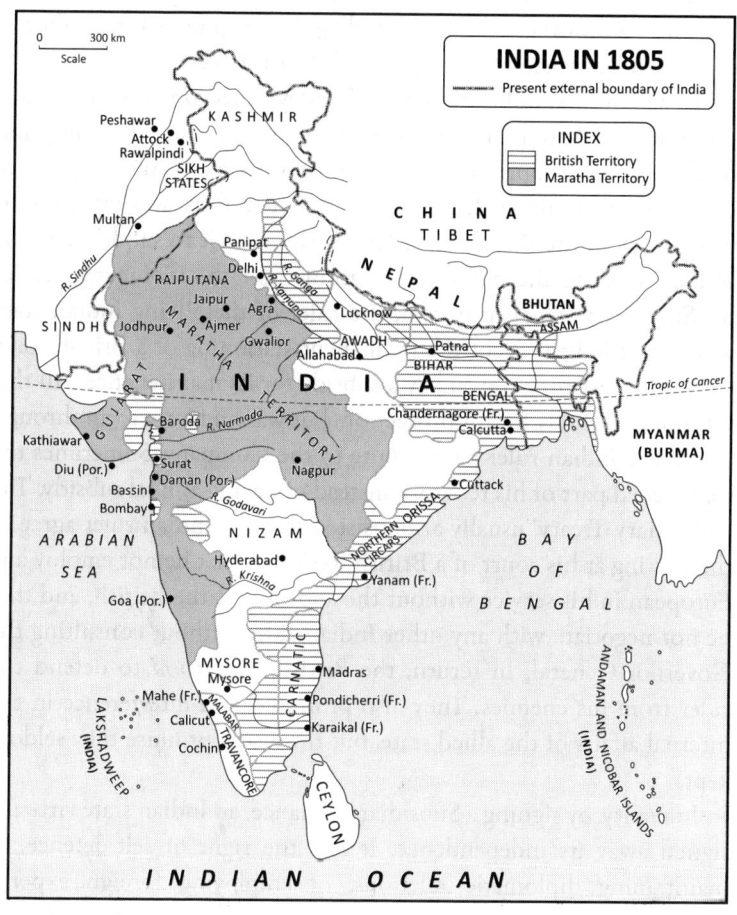

Till then, the British had followed the policy of consolidating their gains and resources in India and making territorial gains only when this could be done safely, without antagonising the major Indian powers. Lord Wellesley decided that the time was ripe for bringing as many Indian states as possible under British control. By 1797 the two strongest Indian powers, Mysore and the Marathas, had declined in power. Political conditions in India were propitious for a policy of expansion: aggression was easy as well as profitable.

To achieve his political aims, Wellesley relied on three methods: the system of 'Subsidiary Alliances', outright war, and the assumption of the territories of previously subordinated rulers. While the practice of helping an Indian ruler with a paid British force was quite old, it was given definite shape by Wellesley, who used it to subordinate the Indian states to the paramount authority of the Company. Under his Subsidiary Alliance system, the ruler of the allying Indian state was compelled to accept the permanent stationing of a British force within his territory and to pay a subsidy for its maintenance. All this was done allegedly for his protection, but was, in fact, a form through which the Indian ruler paid tribute to the Company. Sometimes the ruler ceded part of his territory instead of paying annual subsidy. The 'Subsidiary Treaty' usually also insisted that the Indian ruler agree to the posting at his court of a British Resident, that he not employ any European in his service without the approval of the British, and that he not negotiate with any other Indian ruler without consulting the Governor-General. In return, the British undertook to defend the ruler from his enemies. They also promised non-interference in the internal affairs of the allied state, but this was a promise they seldom kept.

In reality, by signing a Subsidiary Alliance, an Indian state virtually signed away its independence. It lost the right of self-defence, of maintaining diplomatic relations, of employing foreign experts, and of settling its disputes with its neighbours. In fact, the Indian ruler lost all vestiges of sovereignty in external matters and became increasingly subservient to the British Resident, who interfered in the day-to-day administration of the state. In addition, the system tended to bring about the internal decay of the protected state. The cost of the subsidiary force provided by the British was very high and, in fact, much beyond the paying capacity of the state. The payment of the arbitrarily-fixed and artificially-bloated subsidy invariably disrupted the economy of the state and impoverished its people. The system of Subsidiary Alliances also led to the disbanding of the armies of the protected states. Lakhs of soldiers and officers were deprived of their livelihood, spreading misery and degradation in the country. Moreover, the rulers of protected states tended to neglect the interests of their people and to oppress them, as they no longer feared them. They had no incentive to be good rulers as they were fully protected by the British from domestic and foreign enemies.

The Subsidiary Alliance system was, on the other hand, extremely advantageous to the British. They could now maintain a large army at the cost of the Indian states. This enabled them to fight wars far away from their own territories, since any war would occur in the territories either of the British ally or of the British enemy. They controlled the defence and foreign relations of the protected ally and had a powerful force stationed at the very heart of his lands, and could, therefore, at a time of their choosing, overthrow him and annex his territories by declaring him 'inefficient'. As far as the British were concerned, the system of Subsidiary Alliances was, in the words of a British writer, "a system of fattening allies as we fatten oxen, till they were worthy of being devoured".

Lord Wellesley signed his Subsidiary Treaties with the Nizam of Hyderabad in 1798 and 1800. In lieu of cash payment for the subsidiary forces, the Nizam ceded part of his territories to the Company.

The Nawab of Awadh was forced to sign a Subsidiary Treaty in 1801. In return for a larger subsidiary force, the Nawab was made to surrender to the British nearly half of his kingdom, consisting of Rohilkhand and the territory lying between the Ganga and the Jamuna. His own army was virtually disbanded and the British had the right to station their troops in any part of his state.

Wellesley dealt with Mysore, Carnatic, Tanjore and Surat even more sternly. Tipu of Mysore would, of course, never agree to a Subsidiary Treaty. On the contrary, he was not reconciled to the loss of half of his territory in 1792. He worked incessantly to strengthen his forces for the inevitable struggle with the British. He entered into negotiations for an alliance with Revolutionary France. He sent missions to Afghanistan, Arabia and Turkey to forge an anti-British alliance.

The British army attacked and defeated Tipu in a brief but fierce war in 1799, before French help could reach him. Tipu still refused to beg for peace on humiliating terms. He proudly declared that it was "better to die like a soldier, than to live a miserable dependent on the infidels, in the list of their pensioned rajas and nabobs". He met a hero's end on 4 May 1799 while defending his capital Seringapatam. His army remained loyal to him to the very end.

Nearly half of Tipu's dominions were divided between the British and their ally, the Nizam. The reduced Kingdom of Mysore was restored to the descendants of the original rajas from whom Haidar Ali had seized power. A special treaty of Subsidiary Alliance was imposed on the new raja, by which the Governor-General was authorised to take over the administration of the state in case of necessity. Mysore was, in fact, made a complete dependency of the Company.

In 1801, Lord Wellesley forced a new treaty upon the puppet Nawab of Carnatic, compelling him to cede his kingdom to the Company in return for a pension. The Madras Presidency as it existed till 1947 was now created, by attaching the Carnatic to territories seized from Mysore, including the Malabar. Similarly, the territories of the rulers of Tanjore and Surat were taken over and their rulers pensioned off.

The Marathas were the only major Indian power left outside the sphere of British control. Wellesley now turned his attention towards them and began aggressive interference in their internal affairs.

The Maratha empire at this time consisted of a confederacy of five big chiefs, namely the Peshwa at Poona, the Gaekwad at Baroda, the Sindhia at Gwalior, the Holkar at Indore and the Bhonsle at Nagpur, the Peshwa being the nominal head of the confederacy. But all of them were engaged in bitter fratricidal strife, blind to the real danger from the rapidly advancing foreigner.

Wellesley had repeatedly offered a Subsidiary Alliance to the Peshwa and Sindhia. But the far-sighted Nana Phadnis had refused to fall into the trap. However, when on 25 October 1802, the day of the great festival of Diwali, Holkar defeated the combined armies of the Peshwa and Sindhia, Peshwa Baji Rao II rushed into the arms of the English and on the fateful last day of 1802, signed the Subsidiary Treaty at Bassein.

The victory had been a little too easy and Wellesley was wrong in one respect: the proud Maratha chiefs would not surrender their great tradition of independence without a struggle. But even in this moment of their peril they would not unite against their common enemy. When Sindhia and Bhonsle fought the British, Holkar stood on the sidelines and Gaekwad gave help to the British. When Holkar took up arms, Bhonsle and Sindhia nursed their wounds.

In the south, the British armies led by Arthur Wellesley defeated the combined armies of Sindhia and Bhonsle at Assaye in September 1803 and at Argaon in November. In the north, Lord Lake routed Sindhia's army at Laswari on 1 November and occupied Aligarh, Delhi and Agra. Once again, the blind emperor of India became a pensioner of the Company. The Maratha allies had to sue for peace. Both Sindhia and Bhonsle became subsidiary allies of the Company. They ceded part of their territories to the British, admitted British Residents to their courts and promised not to employ any Europeans without British approval. The British gained complete control over the Orissa coast and the territories between the Ganga and the Jamuna. The Peshwa became a disgruntled puppet in their hands.

Wellesley now turned his attention towards Holkar, but Yeshwant Rao Holkar proved more than a match for the British and fought British armies to a standstill. Holkar's ally, the Raja of Bharatpur, inflicted heavy losses on Lake, who unsuccessfully attempted to storm his fort. Moreover, overcoming his age-old antagonism to the Holkar family, Sindhia began to think of joining hands with Holkar. On the other hand, the shareholders of the East India Company discovered that the policy of expansion through war was proving costly and reducing their profits. The Company's debt had increased from £17 million in 1797 to £31 million in 1806. Moreover, Britain's finances were getting exhausted at a time when Napoleon was once again becoming a major threat in Europe. British statesmen and the directors of the Company felt that the time had come to check further expansion, put an end to ruinous expenditure, and to digest and consolidate Britain's recent gains in India. Wellesley was, therefore, recalled from India and the Company made peace with Holkar in January 1806 by the treaty of Raighat, giving back to the Holkar the greater part of his territories.

Wellesley's expansionist policy had been checked near the end. All the same, it had resulted in the East India Company becoming the paramount power in India. A young officer in the Company's judicial service, Henry Roberclaw, wrote (in about 1805):

> An Englishman in India is proud and tenacious, he feels himself a conqueror amongst a vanquished people and looks down with some degree of superiority on all below him.

EXPANSION UNDER LORD HASTINGS (1813–22)

The Second Anglo-Maratha War had shattered the power of the Maratha chiefs, but not their spirit. They made a desperate last attempt to regain their independence and old prestige in 1817. The lead in organising a united front of the Maratha chiefs was taken by the Peshwa, who was smarting under the rigid control exercised by the British Resident. The Peshwa attacked the British Residency at Poona in November 1817. Appa Sahib of Nagpur attacked the Residency at Nagpur, and Madhav Rao Holkar made preparations for war.

The Governor-General, Lord Hastings, struck back with characteristic vigour. He compelled Sindhia to accept British suzerainty, and defeated the armies of the Peshwa, Bhonsle and Holkar. The Peshwa was dethroned and pensioned off at Bithur near Kanpur. His territories were annexed and the enlarged Presidency of Bombay brought into existence. Holkar and Bhonsle accepted Subsidiary forces. To satisfy Maratha pride, the small kingdom of Satara was founded out of the Peshwa's lands and given to the descendant of Chatrapati Shivaji, who ruled it as a complete dependent of the British. Like other rulers of Indian states, the Maratha chiefs too existed from now on at the mercy of British power.

The Rajputana states had been dominated for several decades by Sindhia and Holkar. After the downfall of the Marathas, they lacked the energy to reassert their independence and readily accepted British supremacy.

Thus, by 1818, the entire Indian subcontinent excepting the Punjab and Sindh had been brought under British control. Part of it was ruled directly by the British and the rest by a host of Indian rulers over whom the British exercised paramount power. These states had virtually no armed forces of their own, nor did they have any independent foreign relations. They paid heavily for the British forces stationed in their territories to control them. They were autonomous in their internal affairs, but even in this respect they acknowledged British authority, wielded through a Resident. They were on perpetual probation.

The Consolidation of British Power (1818–57)

The British completed the task of conquering the whole of India from 1818 to 1857. Sindh and the Punjab were conquered and Awadh, the Central Provinces and a large number of other petty states were annexed.

The Conquest of Sindh

The conquest of Sindh occurred as a result of the growing Anglo-Russian rivalry in Europe and Asia and the consequent British fears that Russia might attack India through Afghanistan or Persia. To counter Russia, the British government decided to increase its influence in Afghanistan and Persia. It further felt that this policy could be successfully pursued only if Sindh was brought under British control. The commercial possibilities of the river Sindh were an additional attraction.

The roads and rivers of Sindh were opened to British trade by a treaty in 1832. The chiefs of Sindh, known as *Amirs*, were made to sign a Subsidiary Treaty in 1839. And finally, in spite of previous assurances that its territorial integrity would be respected, Sindh was annexed in 1843 after a brief campaign by Sir Charles Napier, who had earlier written in his diary: "We have no right to seize Sind, yet we shall do so, and a very advantageous, useful humane piece of rascality it will be". He received seven lakhs of rupees as prize money for accomplishing the task.

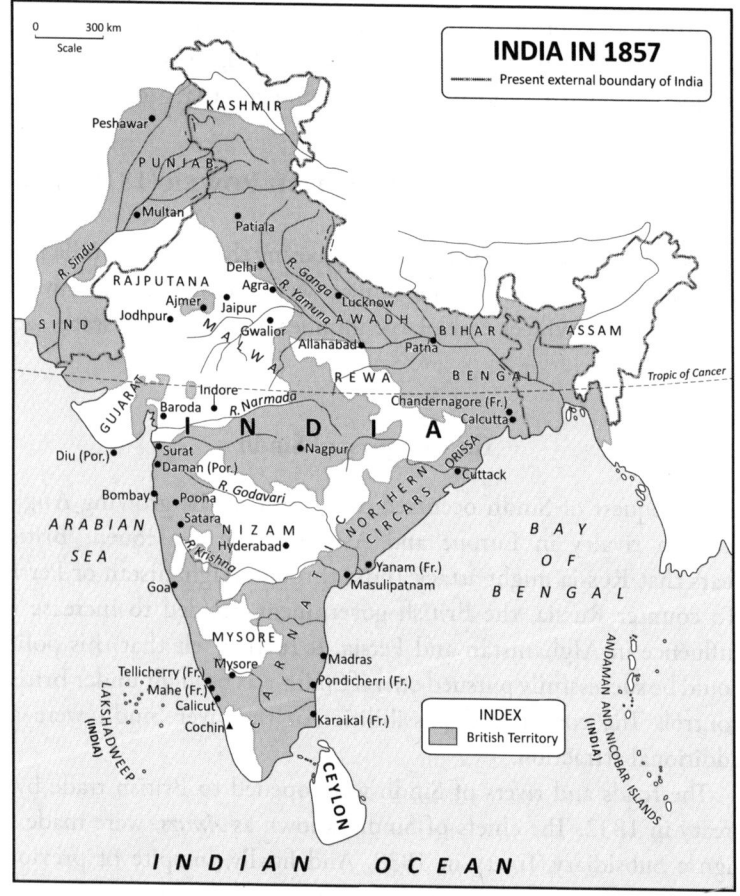

The Conquest of the Punjab

The death of Maharaja Ranjit Singh in June 1839 was followed by political instability and rapid changes of government in the Punjab. Selfish and corrupt leaders came to the fore. Ultimately, power fell into the hands of the brave and patriotic, but utterly indisciplined army. This led the British to look greedily across the Sutlej upon the land of the five rivers, even though they had signed a treaty of perpetual friendship with Ranjit Singh in 1809.

The Punjab army let itself be provoked by the warlike actions of the British and their intrigues with the corrupt chiefs of the Punjab. In the autumn of 1845, news reached Punjab that boats designed to form bridges had been despatched from Bombay to Ferozepur on the Sutlej. Barracks for additional troops were built in the forward area and additional regiments began to be despatched to the frontier with the Punjab. The Punjab army, now convinced that the British were determined to occupy the Punjab, took counter-measures. When it heard in December that Lord Gough, the Commander-in-Chief, and Lord Hardinge, the Governor-General, were marching towards Ferozepur, it decided to strike. War between the two was thus declared on 13 December 1845. The danger from the foreigner immediately united the Hindus, the Muslims and the Sikhs. The Punjab army fought heroically and with exemplary courage. But some of its leaders had already turned traitors. The Prime Minister, Raja Lal Singh, and the Commander-in-Chief, Misar Tej Singh, were secretly corresponding with the enemy. The Punjab army was forced to concede defeat and to sign the humiliating Treaty of Lahore on 8 March 1846. The British annexed the Jullundhar Doab and handed over Jammu and Kashmir to Raja Gulab Singh Dogra for a cash payment of five million rupees. The Punjab army was reduced to 20,000 infantry and 12,000 cavalry and a strong British force was stationed at Lahore.

Later, on 16 December 1846, another treaty was signed giving the British Resident at Lahore full authority over all matters in every department of the state. Moreover, the British were permitted to station their troops in any part of the state. From now on, the British Resident became the real ruler of the Punjab, which lost its independence and became a vassal state.

But the aggressively imperialist sections of British officialdom in India were still unsatisfied, for they wanted to impose direct British rule over the Punjab. Their opportunity came in 1848 when the freedom-loving Punjabis rose up in numerous local revolts. Two of the prominent revolts were led by Mulraj at Multan and Chattar Singh Attariwala near Lahore. The Punjabis were once again decisively defeated. Lord Dalhousie seized this opportunity to annex the Punjab. Thus, the last independent state of India was absorbed in the British empire.

Dalhousie and the Policy of Annexation (1848–56)

Lord Dalhousie came out to India as the Governor-General in 1848. He was from the beginning determined to extend direct British rule over as large an area as possible. He had declared that "the extinction of all native states of India is just a question of time". The underlying motive of this policy was the expansion of British exports to India. Dalhousie, like other aggressive imperialists, believed that British exports to the native states of India were suffering because of the maladministration of these states by their Indian rulers. Moreover, they thought that their 'Indian allies' had already served the purpose of facilitating British conquest of India and could now be got rid of profitably.

The chief instrument through which Lord Dalhousie implemented his policy of annexation was the 'Doctrine of Lapse'. Under this Doctrine, when the ruler of a protected state died without a natural heir, his state was not to pass to an adopted heir, as sanctioned by the age-old tradition of the country. Instead, it was to be annexed to British India, unless the adoption had been clearly approved earlier by the British authorities. Many states, including Satara in 1848 and Nagpur and Jhansi in 1854, were annexed by applying this doctrine.

Dalhousie also refused to recognise the titles of many ex-rulers or pay their pensions. Thus, the titles of the Nawabs of Carnatic and of Surat, and of the Raja of Tanjore were cancelled. Similarly, after the death of the ex-Peshwa Baji Rao II, who had been made the Raja of Bithur, Dalhousie refused to extend his pay or pension to his adopted son, Nana Saheb.

Dalhousie was keen on annexing the kingdom of Awadh. But the task presented certain difficulties. For one, the Nawabs of Awadh had been British allies since the Battle of Buxar. Moreover, they had been most obedient to the British over the years. The Nawab of Awadh had many heirs and could not therefore be covered by the Doctrine of Lapse. Some other pretext had to be found to deprive him of his dominions. Finally, Lord Dalhousie hit upon the idea of alleviating the plight of the people of Awadh. Nawab Wajid Ali Shah was accused of having misgoverned his state and of refusing to introduce reforms. His state was therefore annexed in 1856.

Undoubtedly, the degeneration of the administration of Awadh was a painful reality for its people. The Nawabs of Awadh, like other princes of the day, were selfish rulers absorbed in self-indulgence, who cared little for good administration or for the welfare of the people. But the responsibility for this state of affairs was in part that of the British who had, at least since 1801, controlled and indirectly governed Awadh. In reality, it was the immense potential of Awadh as a market for Manchester goods which excited Dalhousie's greed and aroused his 'philanthropic' feelings. And for similar reasons, to satisfy Britain's growing demand for raw cotton, Dalhousie took away the cotton-producing province of Berar from the Nizam in 1853.

It needs to be clearly understood that the question of the maintenance or annexation of native states was of no great relevance at this time. In fact, there were no Indian states in existence at that time. The protected native states were as much a part of the British empire as the territories ruled directly by the Company. If the form of British control over some of these states was changed, it was to suit British convenience. The interests of their people had little to do with the change.

Four

The Structure of Government and the Economic Policies of the British Empire in India, 1757–1857

Having acquired the vast empire, India, the East India Company had to devise suitable methods of government to control and administer it. The administrative policy of the Company underwent frequent changes during the long period between 1757 and 1857. However, it never lost sight of its main objects, which were to increase the Company's profits, enhance the profitability of its Indian possessions to Britain, and maintain and strengthen the British hold over India; all other purposes were subordinated to these aims. The administrative machinery of the Government of India was designed and developed to serve these ends. The main emphasis in this respect was placed on the maintenance of law and order so that trade with India and the exploitation of its resources could be carried on undisturbed.

THE STRUCTURE OF GOVERNMENT

When the officials of the East India Company acquired control over Bengal in 1765, they had little intention of making any innovations in its administration. They only desired to carry on their profitable trade and collect taxes for remission to England. From 1765 to 1772, in the period of the Dual Government, Indian officials were allowed to function as before, but under the overall control of the British Governor and British officials. The Indian officials had responsibility but no power, while the Company's officials had power but no responsibility. Both sets of officials were venal and corrupt men. In 1772, the Company ended the Dual Government and undertook to administer Bengal directly through its own servants. But the evils inherent in the administration of a country by a purely commercial company soon came to the surface.

Structure of Government and Economic Policies

The East India Company was at this time a commercial body designed to trade with the East. Moreover, its higher authority was situated in England, many thousands of kilometres away from India. Yet, it had come to wield political power over millions of people. This anomalous state of affairs posed many problems for the British government. What was to be the relation of the East India Company and its possessions to the government in Britain? How were the Company's authorities in Britain to control the great multitude of officials and soldiers stationed in far away India? How was a single centre of control to be provided in India over the far-flung British possessions in Bengal, Madras and Bombay?

The first of these problems was the most pressing as well as the most important. It was also closely interwoven with party and parliamentary rivalries in Britain, the political ambitions of English statesmen, and the commercial greed of English merchants. The rich resources of Bengal had fallen into the hands of the Company, whose Directors immediately raised dividends to 10 per cent in 1767 and proposed in 1771 to raise the rate further to 12½ per cent. The Company's English servants took advantage of their position to make quick fortunes through illegal and unequal trade, and the forcible collection of bribes and 'gifts' from Indian chiefs and zamindars. Clive returned to England at the age of 34 with wealth and property yielding £40,000 a year.

The Company's high dividends and the fabulous wealth brought home by its officials excited the jealousy of other sections of British society. Merchants kept out of the East by the monopoly of the Company, the growing class of manufacturers and, in general, the rising forces of free enterprise in Britain wanted to share in the profitable Indian trade and the riches of India, which the Company and its servants alone were enjoying. They therefore worked hard to destroy the Company's trade monopoly and, in order to achieve this, they attacked the Company's administration of Bengal. They also made the officials of the Company who returned from India their special target. These officials were given the derisive title of 'nabobs', and were ridiculed in the press and on the stage. They were boycotted by the aristocracy and condemned as the exploiters and oppressors of the Indian people. Their two main targets were

Clive and Warren Hastings. By condemning the 'nabobs', the opponents of the Company hoped to make the Company unpopular and then to displace it. Many ministers and other Members of Parliament were keen to benefit from the acquisition of Bengal. They sought to win popular support by forcing the Company to pay tribute to the British government so that Indian revenues could be used to reduce taxation or the public debt of England. In 1767, the Parliament passed an act obliging the Company to pay to the British treasury £400,000 per year. Many political thinkers and statesmen of Britain wanted to control the activities of the Company and its officials because they were afraid that the powerful Company and its rich officials would completely debauch the English nation and its politics. The parliamentary politics of Britain during the latter half of the eighteenth century was corrupt in the extreme. The Company, as well as its retired officials, bought seats in the House of Commons for their agents. Many English statesmen were worried that the Company and its officials, backed by Indian plunder, might gain a preponderant influence in the government of Britain. The Company and its vast empire in India had to be controlled or the Company, as master of India, would soon come to control British administration and be in a position to destroy the liberties of the British people.

The exclusive privileges of the Company were also attacked by the rising school of economists representing free-trade manufacturing capitalism. In his celebrated work, *The Wealth of Nations,* Adam Smith, the founder of classical economics, condemned the exclusive companies:

> Such exclusive companies, therefore, are nuisances in many respect; always more or less inconvenient to the countries in which they are established and destructive to those which have the misfortune to fall under their government.

Thus, reorganisation of the relations between the British state and the Company's authorities became necessary and the occasion arose when the Company had to ask the government for a loan of £1,000,000. But while the Company's enemies were many and powerful, it was not without powerful friends in Parliament;

moreover, the king, George III, was its patron. The Company, therefore, fought back. In the end, the Parliament worked out a compromise by which the interests of the Company and of the various influential sections of British society were delicately balanced. It was decided that the British government would control the basic policies of the Company's Indian administration so that British rule in India was carried on in the interests of the British upper classes as a whole. At the same time, the Company would retain its monopoly over Eastern trade and the valuable right to appoint its officials in India. The details of Indian admnistration were also left to the directors of the Company.

The first important parliamentary act regarding the Company's affairs was the Regulating Act of 1773. This Act made changes in the constitution of the Court of Directors of the Company and subjected their actions to the supervision of the British government. The Regulating Act soon broke down in practice. It had not given the British government effective and decisive control over the Company. The Act had also failed to resolve the conflict between the Company and its opponents in England, who were daily growing stronger and more vocal. Moreover, the Company remained extremely vulnerable to the attacks of its enemies as the administration of its Indian possessions continued to be corrupt, oppressive, and economically disastrous.

The defects of the Regulating Act and the exigencies of British politics necessitated the passing in 1784 of another important act, known as the Pitt's India Act. This Act gave the British government supreme control over the company's affairs and its administration in India. It established six commissioners for the affairs of India, popularly known as the Board of Control, including two Cabinet Ministers. The Board of Control was to guide and control the work of the Court of Directors and the Government of India. The Act placed the Government of India in the hands of the Governor-General and a Council of three, so that if the Governor-General could get the support of even one member, he could have his way. The Act clearly subordinated the Bombay and Madras Presidencies to Bengal in all questions of war, diplomacy, and revenues. With this Act began a new phase of the British conquest of India. While the East India Company became the instrument of British national policy, India was to be made to serve the interests of all sections of the ruling classes of Britain. The Company, having saved its monopoly over Indian and Chinese trade, was satisfied. Its directors retained the profitable right of appointing and dismissing its British officials in India. Moreover, the Government of India was to be carried on through their agency.

While the Pitt's India Act laid down the general framework in which the Government of India was to be carried on till 1857, later enactments brought about several important changes which gradually diminished the powers and privileges of the Company. In 1786, the Governor-General was given the authority to overrule his Council in matters of importance affecting safety, peace, or the interests of the empire in India.

By the Charter Act of 1813, the trade monopoly of the Company in India was ended and trade with India was thrown open to all British subjects. But trade in tea and trade with China were still exclusive to the Company. The government and the revenues of India continued to be in the hands of the Company. The Company also continued to appoint its officials in India. The Charter Act of 1833 brought the Company's monopoly of tea trade and trade with China to an end. At the same time, the debts of the Company were taken over by the Government of India, which was also to pay its share-holders a 10½ per cent dividend on their capital. The Government of India continued to be run by the Company, under the strict control of the Board of Control.

Thus, the various acts of Parliament discussed above completely subordinated the Company and its Indian administration to the British government. At the same time, it was recognised that the day-to-day administration of India could not be run or even superintended from a distance of 6,000 miles. Supreme authority in India was, therefore, delegated to the Governor-General-in-Council. The Governor-General, having the authority to overrule his Council on important questions, became in fact the real, effective ruler of India, functioning under the superintendence, control and direction of the British government.

The British created a new system of administration in India to serve their purposes. But before we discuss the salient features of this system, it would be better if we first examine the purposes which it was designed to serve, for the main function of the administrative system of a country is to accomplish the aims and objectives of its rulers. The chief aim of the British was to enable them to exploit India economically to the maximum advantage of various British interests, ranging from the Company to the Lancashire manufacturers. In 1793, Lord Cornwallis, the Governor-General, defined two primary objectives for the Bengal government. It must 'ensure its political safety and it must render the possession of the country as advantageous as possible to the East India Company and the British nation'. At the same time, India was to be made to bear the full cost of its own conquest as well as of foreign rule. An examination of the economic policies of the British in India is, therefore, of prime importance.

BRITISH ECONOMIC POLICIES IN INDIA (1757–1857)

Commercial Policy

From 1600 to 1757, the East India Company's role in India was that of a trading corporation which brought goods or precious metals into India and exchanged them for Indian goods like textiles and spices, which it then sold abroad. Its profits came primarily from the sale of Indian goods abroad. Naturally, it tried constantly to open new markets for Indian goods in Britain and other countries. Thereby, it increased the export of Indian manufacturers and thus encouraged their production. This is why Indian rulers tolerated and even encouraged the establishment of the Company's factories in India.

But from the very beginning, British manufacturers were jealous of the popularity that Indian textiles enjoyed in Britain. All of a sudden, dress fashions changed and light cotton textiles began to replace the coarse woollens of the English. Earlier, the author of the famous novel, *Robinson Crusoe*, had complained that Indian cloth had "crept into our houses, our closets and bed chambers; curtains, cushions, chairs, and at last beds themselves were nothing but calicos or India stuffs". The British manufacturers put pressure on their government to restrict and prohibit the sale of Indian goods in England. By 1720, laws had been passed forbidding the wear or use of printed or dyed cotton cloth. In 1760 a lady had to pay a fine of £200 for possessing an imported handkerchief! Moreover, heavy duties were imposed on the import of plain cloth. Other European countries, except Holland, also either prohibited the import of Indian cloth or imposed heavy import duties. In spite of these laws, however, Indian silk and cotton textiles still held their own in foreign markets, until the middle of the eighteenth century when the English textile industry began to develop on the basis of new and advanced technology.

After the Battle of Plassey in 1757, the pattern of the Company's commercial relations with India underwent a qualitative change. Now the Company could use its political control over Bengal to acquire monopolistic control over Indian trade and production and push its Indian trade. Moreover, it utilised the revenues of Bengal to finance its export of Indian goods. The activity of the Company should have encouraged Indian manufacturers, for Indian exports to Britain went up from £1.5 million in 1750–51 to £5.8 million in 1797–98, but this was not so. The Company used its political power to dictate terms to the weavers of Bengal, who were forced to sell their products at a cheaper and dictated price, even at a loss. Moreover, their labour was no longer free. Many of them were compelled to work for the Company for low wages and forbidden to work for Indian merchants. The Company eliminated its rival traders, both Indian and foreign, and prevented them from offering higher wages or prices to the Bengal handicraftsmen. The servants of the Company monopolised the sale of raw cotton and made the Bengal weaver pay exorbitant prices for it. Thus, the weaver lost both ways, as a buyer as well as a seller. At the same time, Indian textiles had to pay heavy duties on entering England. The British government was determined to protect its rising machine industry, whose products could still not compete with the cheaper and better Indian goods. Even so, Indian products held some of their ground. The real blow to Indian handicrafts fell after 1813, when they lost not only their foreign markets but, what was of much greater importance, their market in India itself.

The Industrial Revolution in Britain completely transformed Britain's economy and its economic relations with India. During the

Structure of Government and Economic Policies 93

second half of the eighteenth century and the first few decades of the nineteenth, Britain underwent profound social and economic transformation, and British industry developed and expanded rapidly on the basis of modern machines, the factory system, and capitalism. This development was aided by several factors.

British overseas trade had been expanding rapidly in the previous centuries. Britain had come to capture and monopolise many foreign markets by means of war and colonialism. These export markets enabled its export industries to expand production rapidly, utilising the latest techniques in production and organisation. Africa, the West Indies, Latin America, Canada, Australia, China and, above all, India provided unlimited opportunities for export. This was particularly true of the cotton textile industry, which served as the main vehicle of the Industrial Revolution in Britain. Britain had already evolved the colonial pattern of trade that helped the Industrial Revolution which, in turn, strengthened this pattern: the colonies and underdeveloped countries exported agricultural and mineral raw materials to Britain, while the latter sold them its manufactures.

Second, there was sufficient capital accumulated in the country for investment in new machinery and the factory system. Moreover, this capital was concentrated, not in the hands of the feudal class which would waste it in luxurious living, but in the hands of merchants and industrialists who were keen to invest it in trade and industry. Here again, the immense wealth drawn from Africa, Asia, the West Indies, and Latin America, including that drawn from India by the East India Company and its servants after the Battle of Plassey, played an important role in financing industrial expansion.

Third, the rapid increase in population met the need of the growing industries for more and cheaper labour. The population of Britain increased rapidly after 1740; it doubled in 50 years after 1780.

Fourth, Britain had a government which was under the influence of commercial and manufacturing interests and which, therefore, fought other countries determinedly for markets and colonies.

Fifth, the demands for increased production were met by developments in technology. Britain's rising industry could base itself on the inventions of Hargreaves, Watt, Crompton, Cartwright, and many others. Many of the inventions now utilised had been available for centuries. In order to take full advantage of these inventions and steam-power, production was now increasingly concentrated in factories. It should be noted that it was not these inventions that produced the Industrial Revolution. Rather, it was the desire of manufacturers to increase production rapidly for the expanding markets and their capacity to invest the needed capital which led them to utilise the existing technology and to call forth new inventions. In fact, the new organisation of industry was to make technical change a permanent feature of human development. The Industrial Revolution has, in this sense, never come to an end, for modern industry and technology have continued to develop from one stage to another ever since the middle of the eighteenth century.

The Industrial Revolution transformed British society in a fundamental manner. It led to rapid economic development, which is the foundation of today's high standard of living in Britain as well as in Europe, the Soviet Union, the U.S.A., Canada, Australia, and Japan. In fact, until the beginning of the nineteenth century, the difference in the standards of living of what are today economically the advanced and the backward countries was not marked. It was the absence of the Industrial Revolution in the latter group of countries which has led to the immense income gap that we see in the world of today.

Britain became increasingly urbanised as a result of the Industrial Revolution. More and more people began to live in factory towns. In 1750, Britain had only two cities with more than 50,000 inhabitants; in 1851, the number was 29.

Two entirely new classes of society were born, the industrial capitalists who owned the factories, and workers who hired out their labour for daily wages. While the former class developed rapidly, enjoying unprecedented prosperity, the workers—the labouring poor—in the beginning reaped a harvest of sorrow. They were uprooted from their rural surroundings, and their traditional way of life was disrupted and destroyed. They now had to live in cities which were full of smoke and filth. Housing was utterly inadequate and insanitary. Most of them lived in dark, sunless slums which have been described so well in the novels of Charles Dickens. The working hours in the factories and mines were intolerably long—often going up to 14 or 16 hours a day. Wages were very low. Women and children had to work equally hard. Sometimes 4- or 5-year-old children were employed in factories and mines. In general, a worker's life was one of poverty, hard work, disease, and malnutrition. It was only after the middle of the nineteenth century that improvement in their incomes began to take place.

The rise of a powerful class of manufacturers had an important impact on Indian administration and its policies. The interest of this class in the Empire was very different from that of the East India Company. It did not gain from the monopolisation of the export of Indian handicrafts or the direct appropriation of Indian revenues. As this class grew in number and strength and political influence, it began to attack the trade monopoly of the Company. Since the profits of this class came from manufacturing and not from trading, it wanted to encourage, not imports of manufactures from India, but exports of its own products to India as well as imports of raw materials like raw cotton from India. In 1769, the British industrialists compelled the Company by law to export every year British manufactures amounting to over £380,000, even though it suffered a loss on the transaction. In 1793, they forced the Company to grant them the use of 3,000 tons of its shipping every year to carry their goods. Exports of British cotton goods to the East, mostly to India, increased from £156 in 1794 to nearly £110,000 in 1813, that is, by nearly 700 times. But this increase was not enough to satisfy the wild hopes of the Lancashire manufacturers, who began to actively search for ways and means of promoting the export of their products to India. As R.C. Dutt pointed out later in 1901 in his famous work, *The Economic History of India,* the effort of the Parliamentary Select Committee of 1812 was "to discover how they (Indian manufacturers) could be replaced by British manufacturers, and how British industries could be promoted at the expense of Indian industries".

The British manufacturers looked upon the East India Company, its monopoly of eastern trade, and its methods of exploitation of India through control of India's revenues and export trade, as the chief obstacles in the fulfilment of their dreams. Between 1793 and 1813, they launched a powerful campaign against the Company and its commercial privileges and finally succeeded in 1813 in abolishing its monopoly of Indian trade.

With this event, a new phase in Britain's economic relations with India began. Agricultural India was to be made an economic colony of industrial England.

The Government of India now followed a policy of free trade or unrestricted entry of British goods. Indian handicrafts were exposed to the fierce and unequal competition of the machine-made products of Britain and faced extinction. India had to admit British goods free or at nominal tariff rates. The Government of India also tried to increase the number of purchasers of British goods by following a policy of fresh conquests and direct occupation of protected states like Awadh. Many British officials, political leaders and businessmen advocated reduction in land revenue so that the Indian peasant might be in a better position to buy foreign manufactures. They also advocated the Westernisation of India so that more and more Indians might develop a taste for Western goods.

Indian hand-made goods were unable to compete against the much cheaper products of British mills, which had been rapidly improving their productive capacity by using inventions and a wider use of steam power. Any government wedded to Indian interests alone would have protected Indian industry through high tariff walls and used the time thus gained to import the new techniques of the West. Britain had done this in relation to its own industries in the eighteenth century; France, Germany and the U.S.A. were also doing so at the time; Japan and the Soviet Union were to do it many decades later; and free India is doing it today. However, not only were Indian industries not protected by the foreign rulers, but foreign goods were also given free entry. Foreign imports rose rapidly. Imports of British cotton goods alone increased from £1,100,000 in 1813 to £6,300,000 in 1856.

The free trade imposed on India was, however, one-sided. While the doors of India were thus thrown wide open to foreign goods, Indian products which could still compete with British products were subjected to heavy import duties upon entry into Britain. The British would not take in Indian goods on fair and equal terms even at this stage when their industries had achieved technological superiority over Indian handicrafts. Duties in Britain on several categories of Indian goods continued to be high till their export to Britain virtually ceased. For example, in 1824, a duty of 67½ per cent was levied on Indian calicos and a duty of 37½ per cent on Indian muslins. Indian sugar had to pay on entry into Britain a duty that was over three times its cost price. In some cases, duties in England went up as high as 400 per cent. As a result of such prohibitive import duties and development of machine industries, Indian exports to foreign countries fell rapidly. The unfairness of British commercial policy has been summed up by the British historian, H.H. Wilson, in the following words:

> It was stated in evidence, that the cotton and silk goods of India up to this period could be sold for a profit in the British market, at a price from 50 to 60 per cent lower than those fabricated in England. It consequently became necessary to protect the latter by duties of 70 to 80 per cent on their value, or by positive prohibition. Had this not been the case, had not such prohibitory duties and decrees existed, the mills of Paisley and of Manchester would have been stopped in their outset and could scarcely have been again set in motion, even by the power of steam. They were created by the sacrifice of the Indian manufacture. Had India been independent, she would have retaliated, would have imposed preventive duties upon British goods, and would thus have preserved her own productive industry from annihilation. This act of self-defence was not permitted her; she was at the mercy of the stranger. British goods were forced upon her without paying any duty; and the foreign manufacturer employed the arm of political injustice to keep down and ultimately strangle a competitor with whom he could not have contended on equal terms.

Instead of exporting manufactures, India was now forced to export raw materials like raw cotton and raw silk which British industries needed urgently, or plantation products like indigo and tea, or foodgrains which were in short supply in Britain. In 1856, India exported £4,300,000 worth of raw cotton, only £810,000 worth of cotton manufactures, £2,900,000 worth of foodgrains, £1,730,000 worth of indigo, and £770,000 worth of raw silk. The British also promoted the sale of Indian opium in China, even though the Chinese placed a ban on it because of its poisonous and other harmful effects. But the trade yielded large profits to British merchants and fat revenues to the Company-controlled administration of India. Interestingly enough, the import of opium into Britain was strictly banned. By the end of the nineteenth century, Indian exports consisted primarily of raw cotton, jute and silk, oilseeds, wheat, hides and skins, indigo and tea.

Thus, the commercial policy of the East India Company after 1813 was guided by the needs of British industry. Its main aim was to transform India into a consumer of British manufactures and a supplier of raw materials.

The Drain of Wealth

The British exported to Britain part of India's wealth and resources for which India got no adequate economic or material return. This 'economic drain' was peculiar to British rule. Even the worst of previous Indian governments had spent the revenue they extracted from the people inside the country. Whether they spent it on irrigation canals and trunk roads, or on palaces, temples and mosques, or on wars and conquests, or even on personal luxury, it ultimately encouraged Indian trade and industry or gave employment to Indians. This was so because even foreign conquerors, like the Mughals, soon settled in India and made it their home. But the British remained perpetual foreigners. Englishmen working and trading in India nearly always planned to go back to Britain, and the Indian government was controlled by a foreign company of merchants and the government of Britain. The British, consequently, spent a large part of the taxes and income they derived from the Indian people not in India but in Britain, their home country.

The drain of wealth from Bengal began in 1757 when the Company's servants began to carry home immense fortunes extorted from Indian rulers, zamindars, merchants and the common people. They sent home nearly £6 million between 1758 and 1765. This amount was more than four times the total land revenue collection of the Nawab of Bengal in 1765. This amount of drain did not include the trading profits of the Company, which were often no less illegally derived. In 1765, the Company acquired the *Diwani* of Bengal and thus gained control over its revenues. The Company, even more than its servants, soon directly organised the drain. It began to purchase Indian goods out of the revenue of Bengal and to export them. These purchases were known as 'Investments'. Thus, through 'Investments', Bengal's revenue was sent to England. For example, from 1765 to 1770, the Company sent out nearly £4 million worth of goods or about 33 per cent of the net revenue of Bengal. By the end of the eighteenth century, the drain constituted nearly 9 per cent of India's national income. The actual drain was even more, as a large part of the salaries and other incomes of English officials and the trading fortunes of English merchants also found their way into England.

The drain took the form of an excess of India's exports over its imports, for which India got no return. While the exact amount of the annual drain has not been calculated so far and historians differ on its quantum, the fact of the drain, at least from 1757 to 1857, was widely accepted by British officials. Thus, for example, Lord Ellenborough, Chairman of the Select Committee of the House of Lords, and later Governor-General of India, admitted in 1840 that India was "required to transmit annually to this country (Britain), without any return except in the small value of military stores, a sum amounting to between two and three million sterling". And John Sullivan, President of the Board of Revenue, Madras, remarked: "Our system acts very much like a sponge, drawing up all the good things from the banks of the Ganges, and squeezing them down on the banks of the Thames."

The drain continued to increase after 1858, though the British administrators and imperialist writers now began to deny its existence. By the end of the nineteenth century, it constituted nearly 6 per cent of India's national income and one-third of its national savings. The wealth drained out of India played an important part in financing Britain's capitalist development, especially during the eighteenth century and the beginning of the nineteenth century, that is, during the period of Britain's early industrialisation. It has been estimated that it constituted nearly 2 per cent of Britain's national income during that period. The figure assumes importance if it is kept in view that Britain was at that time investing in industry and agriculture about 7 per cent of its national income.

Development of Means of Transport and Communication

Up to the middle of the nineteenth century, the means of transport in India were backward. They were confined to the bullock-cart and packhorse. The British rulers soon realised that a cheap and easy system of transport was a necessity if British manufactures were to flow into India on a large scale and her raw materials secured for British industries. They introduced steamships on the rivers and set about improving the roads. Work on the Grand Trunk Road from

Calcutta to Delhi was begun in 1839 and completed in the 1850s. Efforts were also made to link by road the major cities, ports and markets of the country. But real improvement in transport only came with the advent of the railways.

The first railway engine designed by George Stephenson was put on the rails in England in 1814. Railways developed rapidly in that country during the 1830s and 1840s. Pressure soon mounted for their speedy construction in India. The British manufacturers hoped thereby to open the vast and hitherto untapped market in the interior of the country and to facilitate the export of Indian raw materials and foodstuffs to feed their hungry machines and operatives. The British bankers and investors looked upon railway development in India as a channel for the safe investment of their surplus capital. The British steel manufacturers regarded it as an outlet for their products like rails, engines, wagons, and other plant and machinery. The Government of India soon fell in step with these views and found additional merit in the railways: they would enable it to administer the country more effectively and efficiently and to protect their regime from internal rebellion or external aggression by enabling rapid mobilisation and movement of troops.

The earliest suggestion to build a railway in India was made in Madras in 1831. But the wagons of this railway were to be drawn by horses. Construction of steam-driven railways in India was first proposed in 1834 in England. It was given strong political support by England's railway promoters, financiers, mercantile houses trading with India, and textile manufacturers. It was decided that the Indian railways were to be constructed and operated by private companies, who were guaranteed a minimum of 5 per cent return on their capital by the Government of India. The first railway line running from Bombay to Thana was opened to traffic in 1853.

Lord Dalhousie, who became Governor-General of India in 1849, was an ardent advocate of rapid railway construction. In a famous note written in 1853, he laid down an extensive programme of railway development. He proposed a network of four main trunk lines which would link the interior of the country with the big ports and interconnect the different parts of the country.

By the end of 1869, more than 6,000 kilometres of railways had been built by the guaranteed companies; but this system proved very costly and slow, and so in 1869 the Government of India decided to build new railways as state enterprises. But the speed of railway extension still did not satisfy officials in India and businessmen in Britain. After 1880, railways were built through private enterprise as well as through state agency. By 1905, nearly 45,000 km of railways had been built. Three important aspects of the development of Indian railways should be kept in view. First, nearly the entire amount of over 350 crores of rupees invested in them was provided by British investors, Indian capital contributing only a negligible share to it. Second, they were for the first fifty years financially losing concerns which were unable to pay interest on the capital invested in them. This loss was made good in the case of privately built railways by the Government of India, which guaranteed a fixed return on the capital invested. While the interest rate in Britain in the 1850s was about 3 per cent, the guaranteed return was an attractive 5 per cent. Third, in their planning, construction and management, the economic and political development of India and her people was not kept in the forefront. On the contrary, the primary consideration was to serve the economic, political and military interests of British imperialism in India. The railway lines were laid primarily with a view to linking India's raw material producing areas in the interior with the ports of export. The needs of Indian industries regarding their markets and their sources of raw materials were neglected. Further, the railway rates were fixed in a manner so as to favour imports and exports and to discriminate against the internal movement of goods. Several railway lines in Burma and north-western India were built at high cost to serve British imperial interests.

The British also established an efficient and modern postal system and introduced the telegraph. The first telegraph line from Calcutta to Agra was opened in 1853. Lord Dalhousie introduced postage stamps. Previously, cash payment had to be made when a letter was posted. He also cut down postal rates and charged a uniform rate of half an anna for a letter all over the land. Before his reforms, the postage on a letter depended on the distance it was to travel; in some cases, the postage on a letter was the equivalent of as much as four days' wages of a skilled Indian worker!

Land Revenue Policy

The Company needed Indian revenues to pay for its purchase of Indian handicrafts and other goods for export, meet the cost of the conquest of the whole of India and the consolidation of British rule, pay for the employment of thousands of Englishmen in superior administrative and military positions at salaries that were fabulous by contemporary standards, and to meet the costs of economic and administrative charges needed to enable colonialism to fully penetrate Indian villages and the far-flung areas. This meant a steep rise in the burden of taxation on the India peasant. In fact, nearly all the major changes in the administration and judicial system till 1813 were geared towards the collection of land revenues. The main burden of providing money for the trade and profits of the Company, the cost of administration, and the wars of British expansion in India had to be borne by the Indian peasant or *ryot*. In fact, the British could not have conquered such a vast country as India if they had not taxed the peasant heavily.

The Indian state had, since time immemorial, taken a part of the agricultural produce as land revenue. It had done so either directly through its servants or indirectly through intermediaries, such as zamindars, revenue farmers, etc., who collected the land revenue from the cultivator and kept a part of it as their commission. These intermediaries were primarily collectors of land revenue, although they did sometimes own some land in the area from which they collected revenue.

The Permanent Settlement

We have seen that in 1765, the East India Company acquired the *Diwani*, or control over the revenues, of Bengal, Bihar and Orissa. Initially, it made an attempt to continue the old system of revenue collection, though it increased the amount to be collected from Rs 14,290,000 in 1722 and Rs 18,180,000 in 1764 to Rs 23,400,000 in 1771. In 1773, it decided to manage the land revenues directly. Warren Hastings auctioned the right to collect revenue to the highest bidders. But his experiment did not succeed. Though the amount of land revenue was pushed high by zamindars and other speculators bidding against each other, the actual collection varied from year to year and seldom came up to official expectations. This introduced instability in the Company's revenues at a time when the Company was hard pressed for money. Moreover, neither the *ryot* nor the zamindar would do anything to improve cultivation when they did not know what the next year's assessment would be, or who the next year's revenue collector would be.

It was at this stage that the idea first emerged of fixing the land revenue at a permanent amount. Finally, after prolonged discussion and debate, the Permanent Settlement was introduced in Bengal and Bihar in 1793 by Lord Cornwallis. It had two special features. First, the zamindars and revenue collectors were converted into so many landlords. They were not only to act as agents of the government in collecting land revenue from the *ryot*, but also to become the owners of the entire land in their zamindaris. Their right of ownership was made hereditary and transferable. On the other hand, the cultivators were reduced to the low status of mere tenants and were deprived of long-standing rights to the soil and other customary rights. The use of the pasture and forest lands, irrigation canals, fisheries, and homestead plots and protection against enhancement of rent were some of the rights which were sacrificed. In fact, the tenantry of Bengal and Bihar was left entirely at the mercy of the zamindars. This was done so that the zamindars might be able to pay in time the exorbitant land revenue demand of the Company. Second, the zamindars were to give 10/11th of the rental they derived from the peasantry to the state, keeping only 1/11th for themselves. But the sums to be paid by them as land revenue were fixed in perpetuity. If the rental of a zamindar's estate increased owing to extension of cultivation and improvement in agriculture, or his capacity to extract more from his tenants, or any other reason, he would keep the entire amount of the increase. The state would not make any further demand upon him. At the same time, the zamindar had to pay his revenue rigidly on the due date even if the crop had failed for some reason; otherwise his lands were to be sold.

The initial fixation of revenue was made arbitrarily and without any consultation with the zamindars. The attempt of the officials was to secure the maximum amount. As a result, the rates of revenue were fixed very high. Between 1765–66 and 1793, the land revenue demand nearly doubled. John Shore, the man who planned the Permanent Settlement and later succeeded Cornwallis as Governor-General, calculated that if the gross produce of Bengal be taken as 100, the government claimed 45, zamindars and other intermediaries below them received 15, and only 40 remained with the actual cultivator. One result of this high and impossible land revenue demand was that nearly half the zamindari lands were put up for sale between 1794 and 1807.

It was later generally admitted by officials and non-officials alike that before 1793, the zamindars of Bengal and Bihar did not enjoy proprietary rights over most of the land. The question then arises: why did the British recognise them as such? One explanation is that this was in part the result of a misunderstanding. In England, the central figure in agriculture at the time was the landlord and the British officials made the mistake of thinking that the zamindar was his Indian counterpart. It is, however, to be noted that in one crucial respect the British officials clearly differentiated between the positions of the two. The landlord in Britain was the owner of land not only in relation to the tenant, but also in relation to the state. But in Bengal, while the zamindar was landlord over the tenant, he was himself subordinated to the state. In fact, he was reduced virtually to the status of a tenant of the East India Company. In contrast to the British landlord, who paid a small share of his income as land tax, he had to pay as tax 10/11th of his income from the land of which he was supposed to be the owner; and he could be turned out of the land unceremoniously and his estate sold if he failed to pay the revenue in time.

Other historians think that the decision to recognise the zamindars as the proprietors of land was basically determined by political, financial and administrative expediency. Here, the guiding factors were three. The first arose out of clever statecraft: the need to create political allies. The British officials realised that as they were foreigners in India, their rule would be unstable unless they acquired local supporters who would act as a buffer between them and the people of India. This argument had immediate importance as there were a large number of popular revolts in Bengal during the last quarter of the eighteenth century. So they brought into existence a wealthy and privileged class of zamindars which owed its existence to British rule and which would, therefore, be compelled by its own basic interests to support it. This expectation was, in fact, fully justified later when the zamindars as a class supported the foreign government in opposition to the rising movement for freedom. Second, and perhaps the predominant motive, was that of financial security. Before 1793, the Company was troubled by fluctuations in its chief source of income, the land revenue. The Company was faced with a constant financial crisis as Bengal revenue had to finance its army engaged in wars of expansion, the civil establishment in Bengal, Madras and Bombay, and the purchase of manufactures for export. The Permanent Settlement guaranteed stability of income. The newly created property of the zamindars acted as a security for this. Moreover, the Permanent Settlement enabled the Company to maximise its income as land revenue was now fixed higher than it had ever been in the past. Collection of revenue through a small number of zamindars seemed to be much simpler and cheaper than the process of dealing with lakhs of cultivators. Third, the Permanent Settlement was expected to increase agricultural production. Since the land revenue would not be increased in future even if the zamindar's income went up, the latter would be inspired to extend cultivation and improve agricultural productivity, as was being done in Britain by its landlords.

The Permanent Zamindari Settlement was later extended to Orissa, the Northern Districts of Madras, and the District of Varanasi.

In parts of Central India and Awadh, the British introduced a temporary zamindari settlement under which the zamindars were made owners of land, but the revenue they had to pay was revised periodically. Another group of landlords was created all over India when the government started the practice of giving land to persons who had rendered faithful service to the foreign rulers.

The Ryotwari Settlement

The establishment of British rule in south and south-western India brought new problems of land settlement. The officials believed that in these regions, there were no zamindars with large estates with whom settlement of land revenue could be made, and that the introduction of the zamindari system would upset the existing state of affairs. Many Madras officials led by Reed and Munro recommended that settlement should, therefore, be made directly with the actual cultivators. They also pointed out that under the Permanent Settlement, the Company was a financial loser as it had to share the revenues with the zamindars and could not claim a share of the growing income from land. Moreover, the cultivator was left at the mercy of the zamindar, who could oppress him at will. Under the system they proposed, which is known as the Ryotwari Settlement, the cultivator was to be recognised as the owner of his plot of land, subject to the payment of land revenue. The supporters of the Ryotwari system claimed that it was a continuation of the state of affairs that had existed in the past. Munro said: "It is the system which has always prevailed in India." The Ryotwari Settlement was in the end introduced in parts of the Madras and Bombay Presidencies in the beginning of the nineteenth century. The settlement under the Ryotwari system was not made permanent. It was revised periodically after 20 to 30 years when the revenue demand was usually raised.

The Ryotwari Settlement did not bring into existence a system of peasant ownership. The peasant soon discovered that the large number of zamindars had been replaced by one giant zamindar— the state— and that they were mere government tenants whose land was sold if they failed to punctually pay land revenue. In fact, the government later openly claimed that land revenue was rent and not a tax. The ryot's rights of ownership of his land were also negated by three other factors:

1. In most areas, the land revenue fixed was exorbitant; the ryot was hardly left with bare maintenance even in the best of seasons. For instance, in Madras the government claim was fixed as high as 45 to 55 per cent of gross production in the settlement. The situation was nearly as bad in Bombay.
2. The government retained the right to enhance land revenue at will.
3. The *ryot* had to pay revenue even when his produce was partially or wholly destroyed by drought or floods.

The Mahalwari System

A modified version of the zamindari settlement, introduced in the Ganga valley, the North-West Provinces, parts of central India, and the Punjab, was known as the Mahalwari System. The revenue settlement was to be made village by village or estate (mahal) by estate, with landlords or heads of families who collectively claimed to be the landlords of the village or the estate. In the Punjab, a modified Mahalwari System known as the village system was introduced. In Mahalwari areas also, the land revenue was periodically revised.

Both the Zamindari and the Ryotwari systems departed fundamentally from the traditional land systems of the country. The British created a new form of private property in land in such a way that the benefit of the innovation did not go to the cultivators. All over the country, land was now made saleable, mortgageable, and alienable. This was done primarily to protect the government's revenue. If land had not been made transferable or saleable, the government would find it very difficult to realise revenue from a cultivator who had no savings or possessions out of which to pay it. Now he could borrow money on the security of this land or even sell part of it and pay his land revenue. If he refused to do so, the government could and often did auction his land and realise the amount. Another reason for introducing private ownership of land was provided by the belief that only the right of ownership would make the landlord or the *ryot* exert himself in making improvements.

The British, by making land a commodity which could be freely bought and sold, introduced a fundamental change in the existing land systems of the country. The stability and the continuity of the Indian villages were shaken. In fact, the entire structure of rural society began to break up.

Five

Administrative Organisation and Social and Cultural Policy

We have seen in the previous chapter that by 1784, the East India Company's administration of India had been brought under the control of the British government and that its economic policies were being determined by the needs of the British economy. We will now discuss the organisation through which the Company administered its recently acquired dominion.

In the beginning, the Company left the administration of its possessions in India in Indian hands, confining its activities to supervision. But it soon found that British aims were not adequately served by following old methods of administration. Consequently, the Company took some aspects of administration into its own hands. Under Warren Hastings and Cornwallis, the administration at the top was overhauled and the foundations of a new system based on the English pattern laid. The spread of British power to new areas, new problems, new needs, new experiences and new ideas led in the nineteenth century to more fundamental changes in the system of administration. But the overall objectives of imperialism were never forgotten.

The British administration in India was based on three pillars: the Civil Service, the Army, and the Police. This was so for two reasons. For one, the chief aim of British Indian administration was the maintenance of law and order and the perpetuation of British rule. Without law and order, British merchants and British manufacturers could not hope to sell their goods in every nook and corner of India. Again, the British, being foreigners, could not hope to win the affections of the Indian people; they, therefore, relied on superior force rather than on public support for the maintenance of their control over India. The Duke of Wellington, who had served in India under his brother, Lord Wellesley, remarked after his return to Europe:

Administrative Organisation and Social and Cultural Policy

The system of Government in India, the foundation of authority, and the modes of supporting it and of carrying on the operations of government are entirely different from the systems and modes adopted in Europe for the same purpose.... The foundation and the instrument of all power there is the sword.

CIVIL SERVICES

The Civil Service was brought into existence by Lord Cornwallis. As we have seen in an earlier chapter, the East India Company had from the beginning carried on its trade in the East through servants who were paid low wages, but who were permitted to trade privately. Later, when the Company became a territorial power, the same servants assumed administrative functions. They now became extremely corrupt. By oppressing local weavers and artisans, merchants and zamindars, by extorting bribes and 'gifts' from rajas and nawabs, by indulging in illegal private trade, they amassed untold wealth with which they retired to England. Clive and Warren Hastings made attempts to put an end to their corruption, but were only partially successful.

Cornwallis, who came to India as Governor-General in 1786, was determined to purify the administration, but he realised that the Company's servants would not give honest and efficient service so long as they were not paid adequate salaries. He therefore enforced the rules against private trade and acceptance of presents and bribes by officials with strictness. At the same time, he raised the salaries of the Company's servants. For example, the Collector of a district was to be paid Rs 1,500 a month and 1 per cent commission on the revenue collection of his district. In fact, the Company's Civil Service became the highest paid service in the world. Cornwallis also laid down that promotion in the Civil Service would be by seniority, so that its members would remain independent of outside influence.

In 1800, Lord Wellesley established the College of Fort William at Calcutta for the education of young recruits to the Civil Service. The directors of the Company disapproved of his action and in 1806 replaced it by their own East Indian College at Haileybury in England.

Till 1853, all appointments to the Civil Service were made by the directors of the East India Company, who placated the members of the Board of Control by letting them make some of the nominations. The directors fought hard to retain this lucrative and prized privilege and refused to surrender it even when their other economic and political privileges were taken away by Parliament. They lost it finally in 1853 when the Charter Act decreed that all recruits to the Civil Service were to be selected through a competitive examination.

A special feature of the Indian Civil Service since the days of Cornwallis was the rigid and complete exclusion of Indians from it. It was laid down officially in 1793 that all higher posts in administration worth more than £500 a year in salary were to be held by Englishmen. This policy was also applied to other branches of government, such as the army, police, judiciary, engineering. In the words of John Shore, who succeeded Cornwallis:

> The fundamental principle of the English had been to make the whole Indian nation subservient, in every possible way, to the interests and benefits of ourselves. The Indians have been excluded from every honour, dignity, or office, which the lowest Englishmen could be prevailed to accept.

Why did the British follow such a policy? Many factors combined to produce it. For one, they were convinced that an administration based on British ideas, institutions, and practices could be firmly established only by English personnel. And, then, they did not trust the ability and integrity of the Indians. For example, Charles Grant, Chairman of the Court of Directors, condemned the people of India as "a race of men lamentably degenerate and base; retaining but a feeble sense of moral obligation; ... and sunk in misery by their vices". Similarly, Cornwallis believed that "Every native of Hindustan is corrupt." It may be noted that this criticism did apply to some extent to a small class of Indian officials and zamindars of the time. But, then, it was equally if not more true of British officials in India. In fact, Cornwallis had proposed to give them high salaries in order to help them resist temptations and to become honest and obedient. But he never thought of applying the same remedy of adequate salaries to eradicate corruption among Indian officials.

In reality, the exclusion of Indians from higher grades of the services was a deliberate policy. These services were required at the time to establish and consolidate British rule in India. Obviously the task could not be left to Indians, who did not possess the same instinctive sympathy for, and understanding of, British interests as Englishmen. Moreover, the influential classes of British society were keen to preserve the monopoly of lucrative appointments in the Indian Civil Service and other services for their sons. In fact, they fought tooth and nail among themselves over these appointments. The right to make them was a perpetual bone of contention between the directors of the Company and the members of the British Cabinet. How could the English then agree to let Indians occupy these posts? Indians were, however, recruited in large numbers to fill subordinate posts as they were cheaper and much more readily available than Englishmen.

The Indian Civil Service gradually developed into one of the most efficient and powerful civil services in the world. Its members exercised vast power and often participated in the making of policy. They developed certain traditions of independence, integrity and hard work, though these qualities obviously served British and not Indian interests. They came to believe that they had an almost divine right to rule India. The Indian Civil Service has often been called the 'steel-frame' which reared and sustained British rule in India. In course of time, it became the chief opponent of all that was progressive and advanced in Indian life and one of the main targets of attacks by the rising Indian national movement.

ARMY

The second important pillar of the British regime in India was the army. It fulfilled four important functions. It was the instrument through which the Indian powers were conquered; it defended the British empire in India from foreign rivals; it safeguarded British supremacy from the ever-present threat of internal revolt; and it was the chief instrument for extending and defending the British empire in Asia and Africa.

The bulk of the Company's army consisted of Indian soldiers, recruited chiefly from the area at present included in U.P. and Bihar.

For instance, in 1857, the strength of the army in India was 311,400, of whom 265,900 were Indians. Its officers were, however, exclusively British, at least since the days of Cornwallis. In 1856, only three Indians in the army received a salary of Rs 300 per month and the highest Indian officer was a *subedar*. A large number of Indian troops had to be employed, as British troops were far too expensive. Moreover, the population of Britain was perhaps too small to provide the large soldiery needed for the conquest of India. As a counterweight, the army was officered entirely by British officials and a certain number of British troops were maintained to keep the Indian soldiers under control. Even so, it appears surprising today that a handful of foreigners could conquer and control India with a predominantly Indian army. This was possible because of two factors. On the one hand, there was an absence of modern nationalism in the country at the time. A soldier from Bihar or Awadh did not think, and could not have thought, that in helping the Company defeat the Marathas or the Punjabis, he was being anti-Indian. On the other hand, the Indian soldier had a long tradition of loyalty to the salt. In other words, the Indian soldier was a good mercenary, and the Company on its part was a good paymaster. It paid its soldiers regularly and well, something that the Indian rulers and chieftains were no longer doing.

Police

The third pillar of British rule was the police, whose creator was once again Cornwallis. He relieved the zamindars of their police functions and established a regular police force to maintain law and order. In this respect, he went back to, and modernised, the old Indian system of *thanas*. This put India ahead of Britain, where a system of police had not developed yet. Cornwallis established a system of circles or *thanas* headed by a *daroga*, who was an Indian. Later, the post of the District Superintendent of Police was created to head the police organisation in a district. Once again, Indians were excluded from all superior posts. In the villages, the duties of the police continued to be performed by village-watchmen, who were maintained by the villagers. The police gradually succeeded in reducing major crimes such as dacoity. The police also prevented the organisation of a large-scale conspiracy against foreign control, and when the national movement arose, the police was used to suppress it. In its dealings with the people, the Indian police adopted an unsympathetic attitude. A Committee of Parliament reported in 1813 that the police committed "depredations on the peaceable inhabitants, of the same nature as those practised by the dacoits whom they were employed to suppress". And William Bentinck, the Governor-General, wrote in 1832:

> As for the police, so far from being a protection to the people, I cannot better illustrate the public feeling regarding it, than by the following fact, that nothing can exceed the popularity of a recent regulation by which, if a robbery has been committed, the police are *prevented* from making any enquiry into it, except upon the requisition of the persons robbed: that is to say, the shepherd is a more ravenous beast of prey than the wolf.

JUDICIAL ORGANISATION

The British laid the foundations of a new system of dispensing justice through a hierarchy of civil and criminal courts. Although it was started by Warren Hastings, the system was stabilised by Cornwallis in 1793. In each district was established a Diwani Adalat or civil court, presided over by the District Judge who belonged to the Civil Service. Cornwallis thus separated the posts of the Civil Judge and the Collector. Appeal from the District Court lay first to four Provincial Courts of Civil Appeal and then, finally, to the Sadar Diwani Adalat. Below the District Court were Registrars' Courts, headed by Europeans, and a number of subordinate courts headed by Indian judges known as *munsifs* and *amins*. To deal with criminal cases, Cornwallis divided the Presidency of Bengal into four divisions, in each of which a Court of Circuit presided over by the civil servants was established. Below these courts came a large number of Indian magistrates to try petty cases. Appeals from the Courts of Circuit lay with the Sadar Nizamat Adalat. The criminal courts applied Muslim Criminal Law in a modified and less harsh form so that the tearing apart of limbs and such other punishments were prohibited. The civil courts applied the customary law that had prevailed in any area or among a section of the people since time immemorial. In 1831, William Bentinck abolished the Provincial Courts of Appeal and Circuit. Their work was assigned first to Commissions and later to District Judges and District Collectors. Bentinck also raised the status and powers of Indians in the judicial service and appointed them as Deputy Magistrates, Subordinate Judges and Principal Sadar Amins. In 1865, High Courts were established at Calcutta, Madras and Bombay to replace the Sadar Courts of Diwani and Nizamat.

The British also established a new system of laws through the processes of enactment and codification of old laws. The traditional system of justice in India had been largely based on customary law which arose from long tradition and practice, though many laws were based on the *shastras* and *shariat* as well as on imperial authority. Though they continued to observe customary law in general, the British gradually evolved a new system of laws. They introduced regulations, codified the existing laws, and often systematised and modernised them through judicial interpretation. The Charter Act of 1833 conferred all law-making power on the Governor-General-in-Council. All this meant that Indians were now to live increasingly under man-made laws, which might be good or bad but which had to be obeyed blindly, and which could not be questioned as they were supposed to be divine and therefore sacred.

In 1833, the government appointed a Law Commission headed by Lord Macaulay to codify Indian laws. Its labours eventually resulted in the Indian Penal Code, the Western-derived Codes of Civil and Criminal Procedure and other codes of laws. The same laws now prevailed all over the country and they were enforced by a uniform system of courts. Thus, it may be said that India was judicially unified.

The Rule of Law

The British introduced the modern concept of the rule of law. This meant that their administration was to be carried out, at least in theory, in obedience to laws, which clearly defined the rights, privileges and obligations of the subjects, and not according to the caprice or personal discretion of the ruler. In practice, of course, the bureaucracy and the police enjoyed arbitrary powers and interfered with the rights and liberties of the people. The rule of law was to some extent a guarantee of the personal liberty of a person. It is true that previous rulers of India had been in general bound by tradition and custom. But they always had the legal right to take any administrative steps they wanted and there existed no other authority before whom their acts could be questioned. The Indian rulers and chiefs sometimes exercised this power to do as they wanted. Under British rule, on the other hand, administration was largely carried on according to laws as interpreted by the courts, though the laws themselves were often defective, were made not by the people through a democratic process but autocratically by the foreign rulers, and left a great deal of power in the hands of the civil servants and the police. But that was perhaps inevitable in a foreign regime that could not in the very nature of things be democratic or libertarian.

EQUALITY BEFORE LAW

The Indian legal system under the British was based on the concept of equality before law. This meant that in the eyes of the law, all men were equal. The same law applied to all persons irrespective of their caste, religion, or class. Previously, the judicial system had paid heed to caste distinctions and had differentiated between the so-called high-born and low-born. For the same crime, lighter punishment was awarded to a brahmin than to a non-brahmin. Similarly, in practice zamindars and nobles were not judged as harshly as the commoner. In fact, very often they could not be brought to justice at all for their actions. Now the humble could also move the machinery of justice.

There was, however, one exception to this excellent principle of equality before law. The Europeans and their descendants had separate courts and even laws. In criminal cases, they could be tried only by European judges. Many English officials, military officers, planters and merchants behaved with Indians in a haughty, harsh, and even brutal manner. When efforts were made to bring them to justice, they were given indirect and undue protection, and consequently light or no punishment, by many of the European judges before whom alone they could be tried. Consequently, there was frequent miscarriage of justice.

In practice, there emerged another type of legal inequality. Justice became quite expensive as court fees had to be paid, lawyers engaged, and the expenses of witnesses met. Courts were often situated in distant towns. Lawsuits dragged on for years. The complicated laws were beyond the grasp of the illiterate and ignorant peasants. Invariably, the rich could turn and twist the laws and courts to operate in their own favour. The mere threat to take a poor person through the long process of justice from the lower court to the highest court of appeal, and thus to face him with complete ruin, often sufficed to bring him to heel. Moreover, the widespread prevalence of corruption in the ranks of the police and the rest of the administrative machinery led to the denial of justice. Officials often favoured the rich. The zamindars oppressed the *ryots* without fear of official action. In contrast, the system of justice that had prevailed in pre-British times was comparatively informal, speedy and inexpensive. Thus, while the new judicial system marked a great step forward insofar as it was based on the laudable principles of the rule of law and equality before the law, and on rational and humane man-made laws, it was a retrograde step in some other respects: it was now costlier and involved long delays.

Social and Cultural Policy

We have seen that British authorities reorganised and regulated India's economy in the interests of British trade and industry and organised a modern administrative system to guarantee order and security. Till 1813, they also followed a policy of non-interference in the religious, social and cultural life of the country, but after 1813 they took active steps to transform Indian society and culture. This followed the rise of new interests and new ideas in Britain during the nineteenth century. The Industrial Revolution, which had begun in the middle of the eighteenth century, and the consequent growth of industrial capitalsm, were fast changing all aspects of British society. The rising industrial interests wanted to turn India into a big market for their goods. This could not be accomplished merely by adhering to the policy of keeping peace, and required the partial transformation and modernisation of Indian society. And so, in the words of the historians Thompson and Garratt, "the mood and methods of the old brigandage were changing into those of modern industrialism and capitalism."

Science and technology also opened new vistas of human progress. The eighteenth and nineteenth centuries witnessed a great ferment of new ideas in Britain and Europe, which influenced the British outlook towards Indian problems. All over Europe, "new attitudes of mind, manners, and morals were appearing". The great French Revolution of 1789, with its message of liberty, equality, and fraternity, generated powerful democratic sentiments and unleashed the force of modern nationalism. In the realm of thought, the new trend was represented by Bacon, Locke, Voltaire, Rousseau, Kant, Adam Smith and Bentham; in the realm of literature by Wordsworth, Byron, Shelley and Charles Dickens. The impact of the new thought—the product of the intellectual revolution of the eighteenth century, the French Revolution, and the Industrial Revolution—was naturally felt in India and, to some extent, affected the official notions of government.

The three outstanding characteristics of the new thought were rationalism or faith in reason and science, humanism or love of man, and confidence in the capacity of man to progress. The rational and scientific attitude indicated that only that which was in conformity with human reason and capable of being tested in practice was true. The scientific progress of the seventeenth, eighteenth and nineteenth centuries and the tremendous powers of production released by the application of science to industry were visible proofs of the power of human reason. Humanism was based on the belief that every human being was an end in himself and should be respected and prized as such. No man had the right to look upon another human being as a mere agent of his own happiness. The humanistic outlook gave birth to the doctrines of individualism, liberalism, and socialism. According to the doctrine of progress, all societies must change with time: nothing was or could be static. Moreover, man had the capacity to remodel nature and society on rational and just lines.

The new currents of thought in Europe came into conflict with the old outlook and produced a clash of attitudes among those who determined Indian policy or ran the Indian administration. The older attitude, known as the conservative or traditional attitude, believed in making as few changes in India as possible. The early representatives of this attitude were Warren Hastings and Edmund Burke, the famous writer and parliamentarian, and the later ones included the famous officials Munro, Malcolm, Elphinstone and Metcalfe. The conservatives maintained that Indian civilisation was different from European civilisation, but was not necessarily inferior to it. Many of them respected and admired Indian philosophy and culture. Realising that it might be necessary to introduce some Western ideas and practices, they proposed to introduce them very cautiously and gradually. Favouring social stability above all, they opposed any programme of rapid change. Sweeping or hasty innovations, they felt, would produce a violent reaction in the country. The conservative outlook remained influential in England as well as in India up to the very end of British rule. In fact, the majority of British officials in India were generally of conservative persuasion.

By 1800, the conservative attitude was fast giving way to a new attitude which was sharply critical of Indian society and culture. Indian civilisation was condemned as static; it was looked down upon with contempt. Indian customs were considered uncivilised, Indian institutions corrupt and decadent, and Indian thought narrow and unscientific. This critical approach was used by most officials and writers and statesmen of Britain to justify the political and economic enslavement of India and to proclaim that it was incapable of improvement and must therefore remain permanently under British tutelage. However, a few Englishmen, known as Radicals, went beyond this narrow criticism and imperialistic outlook and applied the advanced humanistic and rational thought of the West to the Indian situation as they saw it. The doctrine of reason led them to believe that India need not always be a fallen country, for all societies had the capacity to improve by following the dictates of reason and science. The doctrine of humanism led them to desire the improvement of Indian people. The doctrine of progress led them to the conviction that Indians were bound to improve. And so the Radicals, though few but representing the better elements of British society, desired to make India a part of the modern progressive world of science and humanism. To them, the answer to India's ills appeared to lie in the introduction of modern Western sciences, philosophy and literature—in fact, in all out and rapid change along modern lines. Some of the officials who came to India in the 1820s and after were deeply influenced by the Radical outlook.

It must, however, be emphasised at this stage that such honest and philanthropic Englishmen were few and that their influence was never decisive so far as the British administration of India was concerned. The ruling elements in British-Indian administration continued to be imperialistic and exploitative. They would accept new ideas and adopt reformist measures only if, and to the extent that, they did not come into conflict with the commercial interest and profit motives, and enabled the economic penetration of India and the consolidation of British rule. Modernisation of India had to occur within the broad limits imposed by the needs of easier and a more thorough exploitation of its resources. Thus, the modernisation of India was accepted by many English officials, businessmen and statesmen because it was expected to make Indians better customers for British goods and reconcile them to the alien rule. In fact, many of the Radicals themselves no longer remained true to their own beliefs when they discussed Indian policy. Instead of working for a democratic government, as they did in Britain, they demanded a more authoritarian regime, which they described as paternalistic. In this respect, they were at one with the conservatives, who were also ardent champions of a paternalism that would treat the Indian people as children and keep them out of the administration. The basic dilemma before the British administrators in India was that while British interests in India could not be served without some modernisation, full modernisation would generate forces which would go against their interests and would, in the long run, endanger British supremacy in the country. They had, therefore, to follow a delicately balanced policy of partial modernisation, that is, a policy of introducing modernisation in some respects and blocking and preventing it in others. In other words, the modernisation of India was to be colonial modernisation, carried out within the parameters of, and with a view to promoting, colonialism.

The policy of modernising Indian society and culture was also encouraged by Christian missionaries and religious-minded persons such as William Wilberforce and Charles Grant, the Chairman of the Court of Directors of the East India Company, who wanted to spread Christianity in India. They, too, adopted a critical attitude towards Indian society, but on religious grounds. They passionately believed that Christianity alone was the true religion and that all other religions were false. They supported a programme of Westernisation in the hope that it would eventually lead to the country's conversion to Christianity. They thought that the light of Western knowledge would destroy people's faith in their own religions and lead them to welcome and embrace Christianity. They therefore opened modern schools, colleges and hospitals in the country. The missionaries were, however, often the most unwilling allies of the rationalist Radicals, whose scientific approach undermined not only Hindu or Muslim mythology, but Christian mythology as well. As Professor H.H. Dodwell has pointed out: "Taught to question the validity of their own gods, they [the Westernised Indians] questioned also the validity of the Bible and the truth of its narrative." The missionaries also supported the paternalistic imperialistic policies since they looked upon law and order and British supremacy as essential for their work of religious propaganda. They also sought the support of British merchants and manufacturers by holding out the hope that Christian converts would be better customers for their goods.

The Radicals were given strong support by Raja Rammohun Roy and other like-minded Indians, who were conscious of the low state to which their country and society had sunk, who were sick of caste prejudices and other social evils, and who believed that the salvation of India lay in science and humanism. We will discuss the outlook and activities of these Indians at length in the next chapter.

Another reason why the Government of India followed a policy of cautious and gradual innovation and not that of all-out modernisation was the continuous prevalence of the conservative outlook among British officials in India, and the belief that interference in Indian religious beliefs and social customs might lead to rebellion among the Indian people. Even the most ardent Radicals paid heed to this warning for, along with the other members of the British governing classes, they too desired most of all the safety and perpetuation of British rule in India. Every other consideration was of secondary importance. As a matter of fact, the policy of hesitant and weak modernisation was gradually abandoned after 1858 as Indians proved apt pupils, shifted rapidly towards modernisation of their society and assertion of their culture, and demanded to be ruled in accordance with the modern principles of liberty, equality and nationality. The British increasingly withdrew their support from the reformers and gradually came to side with the socially orthodox and conservative elements of society. They also encouraged casteism and communalism.

HUMANITARIAN MEASURES

Official British efforts at reforming Indian society of its abuses were on the whole very meagre and, therefore, bore little fruit. Their biggest achievement was the outlawing of the practice of *sati* in 1829, when William Bentinck made it a crime to associate in any way with the burning of a widow on her husband's pyre. Earlier, the British rulers had been apathetic and afraid of arousing the anger of the orthodox Indians. It was only after Rammohun Roy and other enlightened Indians and missionaries agitated persistently for the abolition of this monstrous custom that the government agreed to take this humanitarian step. Many Indian rulers in the past, including Akbar and Aurangzeb, the Peshwas, and Jai Singh of Jaipur, had made unsuccessful attempts to suppress this evil practice. In any case, Bentinck deserves praise for having acted resolutely in outlawing a practice which had taken a toll of 800 lives in Bengal alone between 1815 and 1818, and for refusing to bow before the opposition of the orthodox supporters of the practice of *sati*.

Female infanticide, or the practice of killing female children at the time of their birth, had prevailed among some of the Rajput clans and other castes because of the paucity of young men who died in large numbers in warfare, and because of the difficulties of earning a livelihood in unfertile areas, and in parts of Western and Central India because of the prevalence of the evil custom of dowry in a virulent form. Regulations prohibiting infanticide had been passed in 1795 and 1802, but they were sternly enforced only by Bentinck and Hardinge. In 1856, the Government of India passed an Act enabling Hindu widows to remarry. The government acted after Pandit Ishwar Chandra Vidyasagar and other reformers carried on a prolonged agitation in favour of the measure. The immediate effects of this Act were negligible.

All these official reforms touched no more than the fringes of the Indian social system and did not affect the lives of the vast majority of the people. It was perhaps not possible for a foreign government to do more.

Spread of Modern Education

The British were more successful in the introduction of modern education. Of course, the spread of modern education was not solely the work of the government: the Christian missionaries and a large number of enlightened Indians also played an important part.

For the first 60 years of its dominion in India, the East India Company—a trading, profit-making concern—took little interest in the education of its subjects. There were, however, two very minor exceptions to this policy. In 1781, Warren Hastings set up the Calcutta Madrassa for the study and teaching of Muslim law and related subjects; and in 1791, Jonathan Duncan started a Sanskrit College at Varanasi, where he was the Resident, for the study of Hindu law and philosophy. Both these institutions were designed to provide a regular supply of qualified Indians to help the administration of law in the courts of the Company.

Missionaries and their supporters and many humanitarians soon began to exert pressure on the Company to encourage and promote modern, secular, Westernised education in India. While the humanitarians, including many Indians, believed that modern knowledge would be the best remedy for the social, economic and political ills of the country, the missionaries believed that modern education would destroy the faith of the people in their own religions and lead them to adopt Christianity. A humble beginning was made in 1813 when the Charter Act incorporated the principle of encouraging learned Indians and promoting the knowledge of modern sciences in the country. The Act directed the Company to spend the sum of one lakh of rupees for the purpose. But even this petty amount was not made available by Company authorities till 1823.

For years, a great controversy raged in the country on the question of the direction that this expenditure should take. While one section of opinion wanted it to be spent exclusively for the promotion of modern Western studies, others desired that, while Western sciences and literature should be taught to prepare students to take up jobs, emphasis should be placed on the expansion of traditional Indian learning. Even among those who wanted to spread Western learning, differences arose on the question of the medium of instruction to be adopted in modern schools and colleges. Some recommended the use of Indian languages, called vernaculars at the time, for the purpose, while others advocated the use of English. Unfortunately, there was a great deal of confusion on this question. Many people failed to distinguish between English as a medium and English as a subject for study, and between Indian languages as media and traditional Indian learning as the main object of study.

The two controversies were settled in 1835 when the Government of India decided to devote the limited resources it was willing to spare to the teaching of Western sciences and literature through the medium of English language alone. Lord Macaulay, who was the Law Member of the Governor-General's Council, argued in a famous minute that Indian languages were not sufficiently developed to serve the purpose, and that "Oriental learning was completely inferior to European learning". It is to be noted that, while Macaulay's views betrayed prejudice against and ignorance of India's past achievements in the realms of science and thought, he was on solid ground when he held European knowledge in the fields of physical and social sciences to be superior to the existing Indian knowledge which, though advanced at one time, had stagnated too long and lost touch with reality. That is why the most advanced Indians of the time, led by Raja Rammohun Roy, fervently advocated the study of Western knowledge, which was seen by them as "the key to the treasures of scientific and democratic thought of the modern West". They also realised that traditional education had bred superstition, fear and authoritarianism. In other words, they realised that the salvation of the country lay in going forward and not in looking backwards. In fact, no prominent Indian of the nineteenth and twentieth centuries deviated from this approach.

Moreover, throughout the period of modern history, the pressure exerted by Indians anxious to imbibe Western knowledge played an important part in persuading the government to expand its educational activities on modern lines.

The Government of India acted quickly, particularly in Bengal, on the decision of 1835 and made English the medium of instruction in its schools and colleges. It opened a few English schools and colleges instead of a large number of elementary schools. This policy was later sharply criticised for neglecting the education of the masses. In fact, the emphasis on the opening of institutes of modern and higher education was not wrong. If for nothing else, a large number of schools and colleges were needed to educate and train teachers for elementary schools. But along with the spread of higher education, the education of the masses should have been taken in hand. This the government would not do as it was not willing to spend more than an insignificant sum on education. To make up for the paucity of expenditure on education, the officials took recourse to the so-called "downward filtration theory". Since the allocated funds could educate only a handful of Indians, it was decided to spend the money in educating a few persons from the upper and middle classes, who were expected to assume the task of educating the masses and spreading modern ideas among them. Education and modern ideas were thus supposed to filter or radiate downwards from the upper classes. This policy continued until the very end of the British rule. It may also be pointed out here that even though education did not percolate downwards, modern ideas did to a large extent, though not in the form desired by the rulers. Through political parties, the press, pamphlets, literature and the public platform, though not through schools and textbooks, the educated Indians, or the intellectuals, spread ideas of democracy, nationalism, anti-imperialism, and social and economic equality and justice among the rural and urban masses. If the educational system acted as the carrier of these ideas, it did so indirectly by making available to its recipients some of the basic literature in the physical and social sciences and the humanities, thus stimulating their capacity to make social analysis. Otherwise, its structure and pattern, aims, methods, curricula and content were all designed to serve colonialism.

The Wood's Dispatch (the document dispatched from the Court

of Directors and popularly named after Sir Charles Wood, President of the Board of Control) of 1854 was another important step in the development of education in India. The Dispatch asked the Government of India to assume responsibility for the education of the masses. It thus repudiated the "downward filtration" theory, at least on paper. In practice, the government did little to spread education and spent very little on it. As a result of the directions given by the Dispatch, Departments of Education were instituted in all provinces and affiliating universities were set up in 1857 at Calcutta, Bombay and Madras. Bankim Chandra Chatterjee, the famous Bengali novelist, became in 1858 one of the first two graduates of Calcutta University.

For all the loud claims that it made, the Government of India under the Company, and later under the Crown, did not really take serious interest in spreading Western learning, or any other learning, in India. Even the limited effort that was made was the result of factors which had little to do with philanthropic motives. Of some importance in this respect was the agitation in favour of modern education by progressive Indians, foreign Christian missionaries, and humanitarian officials and other Englishmen. But the most important reason was the government's anxiety to economise on the cost of administration by getting a cheap supply of educated Indians to man the large and increasing number of subordinate posts in administration and British business concerns. It was manifestly too costly and perhaps not even possible to import enough Englishmen for the purpose. This emphasis on a cheap supply of clerks explains why the schools and colleges had to impart modern education, which fitted its recipients for their jobs in the Westernised administration of the Company, and why these institutions had to emphasise English, which was the language of the masters as well as the language of administration. Another motive behind the educational policy of the British sprang from the belief that educated Indians would help to expand the market for British manufactures in India. Lastly, Western education was expected to reconcile the people of India to British rule, particularly as it glorified the British conquerors of India and their administration. Macaulay, for example, laid down:

We must at present do our best to form a class who may be interpreters between us and the millions whom we govern; a class of persons, Indians in blood and colour, but English in taste, in opinions, in morals, and in intellect.

The British thus wanted to use modern education to strengthen the foundation of their political authority in the country.

The traditional Indian system of education gradually withered away for lack of official support, and even more because of the official announcement in 1844 that applicants for government employment should possess knowledge of English. This declaration made English-medium schools very popular and compelled more and more students to abandon the traditional schools.

A major weakness of the educational system was the neglect of mass education, with the result that mass literacy in India was hardly better in 1921 than in 1821. As many as 94 per cent of Indians were illiterate in 1911 and 92 per cent in 1921. The emphasis on English as the medium of instruction in place of the Indian languages also prevented the spread of education to the masses. It further tended to create a wide linguistic and cultural gulf between educated persons and the masses. Moreover, because students had to pay fees in schools and colleges, education was quite costly and became a virtual monopoly of the richer classes and the city-dwellers. For nearly 100 years, it was so very limited that it failed even to compensate for the ruin of the traditional educational system.

A major lacuna in the early educational policy was the almost total neglect of the education of girls, for which no funds were allotted. This was partly due to the government's anxiety not to hurt the susceptibilities of orthodox Indians. Even more, it was because female education lacked immediate usefulness in the eyes of the foreign officials since women could not be employed as clerks in the government. The result was that as late as 1921, only two out of 100 Indian women were able to read and write; and in 1919, only 490 girls were studying in the four top forms of high schools in the Bengal Presidency.

The Company's administration also neglected scientific and technical education. By 1857, there were only three medical colleges in the country, at Calcutta, Bombay and Madras. There was only one good engineering college at Roorkee to impart higher technical education, and even this was open only to Europeans and Eurasians.

At the root of many of these weaknesses lay the problem of finance. The government was never willing to spend more than a scanty sum on education. As late as 1886, it devoted only about one crore of rupees to education, out of its total net revenue of nearly Rs 47 crore.

Six

Social and Cultural Awakening in the First Half of the Nineteenth Century

Immense intellectual and cultural stirrings characterised nineteenth-century India. The impact of modern Western culture and consciousness of defeat by a foreign power gave birth to a new awakening. There was an awareness that a vast country like India had been colonised by a handful of foreigners because of the internal weaknesses of Indian social structure and culture. Thoughtful Indians began to look for the strengths and weaknesses of their society and for ways and means of removing the weaknesses. While a large number of Indians refused to come to terms with the West and still put their faith in traditional Indian ideas and institutions, others gradually came to hold that elements of modern Western thought had to be imbibed for the regeneration of their society. They were impressed in particular by modern science and the doctrines of reason and humanism. While differing on the nature and extent of reforms, nearly all nineteenth-century intellectuals shared the conviction that social and religious reform was urgently needed.

RAMMOHUN ROY

The central figure in this awakening was Rammohun Roy, who is rightly regarded as the first great leader of modern India. Rammohun Roy was moved by deep love for his people and country and worked hard all his life for their social, religious, intellectual and political regeneration. He was pained by the stagnation and corruption of contemporary Indian society, which was at that time dominated by caste and convention. Popular religion was full of superstitions and was exploited by ignorant and corrupt priests. The upper classes were selfish and often sacrificed social interest to their own narrow interests. Rammohun Roy possessed great love and respect for the traditional philosophic systems of the East; but, at the same time, he believed that modern culture alone would help to regenerate Indian society. In particular, he wanted his countrymen to accept the rational and scientific approach and the principle of human dignity and social equality of all men and women. He also wanted the introduction of modern capitalism and industry in the country.

Rammohun Roy represented a synthesis of the thought of East and West. He was a scholar who knew over a dozen languages, including Sanskrit, Persian, Arabic, English, French, Latin, Greek and Hebrew. As a young man, he had studied Sanskrit literature and Hindu philosophy at Varanasi and the *Quran* and Persian and Arabic literature at Patna. He was also well-acquainted with Jainism and other religious movements and sects of India. Later, he made an intensive study of Western thought and culture. To study the *Bible* in the original, he learnt Greek and Hebrew. In 1809, he wrote in Persian his famous work, *Gift to Monotheists,* in which he put forward weighty arguments against the belief in many gods and for the worship of a single God.

He settled in Calcutta in 1814 and soon attracted a band of young men, with whose cooperation he started the Atmiya Sabha. From now on, he carried on a persistent struggle against the religious and social evils widely prevalent among the Hindus in Bengal. In particular, he vigorously opposed their worship of idols, the rigidity of caste, and the prevalence of meaningless religious rituals. He condemned the priestly class for encouraging these practices. He held that all the principal ancient texts of the Hindus preached monotheism or worship of one God. He published the Bengali translation of the Vedas and of five of the principal Upanishads to prove his point. He also wrote a series of tracts and pamphlets in defence of monotheism.

While citing ancient authority for his philosophical views, Rammohun Roy relied ultimately on the power of human reason, which was in his view the final touchstone of the truth of any doctrine, Eastern or Western. He believed that the philosophy of Vedanta was based on this principle of reason. In any case, one should not hesitate to depart from holy books, scriptures and inherited traditions if human reason so dictates, and if such traditions are proving harmful to society. But Rammohun Roy did not confine his application of the rational approach to Indian religions and traditions alone. In this, he disappointed his many missionary friends who had hoped that his rational critique of Hinduism would lead him to embrace Christianity. Rammohun Roy insisted on applying rationalism to Christianity too, particularly to the elements of blind faith in it. In 1820, he published his *Precepts of Jesus,* in which he tried to separate the moral and philosophic message of the New Testament, which he praised, from its miracle stories. He wanted the high moral message of Christ to be incorporated in Hinduism. This earned for him the hostility of the missionaries.

Thus, as far as Rammohun was concerned, there was to be no blind reliance on India's own past or blind aping of the West. On the other hand, he put forward the idea that the new India, guided by reason, should acquire and treasure all that was best in the East and the West. Thus, he wanted India to learn from the West; but this learning was to be an intellectual and creative process through which Indian culture and thought were to be renovated; it was not to be an imposition of Western culture on India. He, therefore, stood for the reform of Hinduism and opposed its supersession by Christianity. He vigorously defended Hindu religion and philosophy from the ignorant attacks of the missionaries. At the same time, he adopted an extremely friendly attitude towards other religions. He believed that basically all religions preach a common message and that their followers are all brothers under the skin.

All his life, Rammohun Roy paid heavily for his daring religious outlook. The orthodox condemned him for criticising idolatry and for his philosophic admiration of Christianity and Islam. They organised a social boycott against him, in which even his mother joined. He was branded a heretic and an outcaste.

In 1828, he founded a new religious society, the Brahma Sabha, later known as the Brahmo Samaj, whose purpose was to purify Hinduism and to preach monotheism or belief in one God. The new society was to be based on the twin pillars of reason, and the Vedas and Upanishads. It was also to incorporate the teachings of other religions. The Brahmo Samaj laid emphasis on human dignity, opposed idolatry, and criticised such social evils as the practice of *sati*.

Rammohun Roy was a great thinker. He was also a man of action. There was hardly any aspect of nation-building that he left untouched. In fact, just as he began the reform of Hindu religion from within, he also laid the foundations for the reform of Indian society. The best example of his life-long crusade against social evils was the historic agitation he organised against the inhuman custom of women becoming *sati*. Beginning in 1818, he set out to rouse public opinion on the question. On the one hand he showed, by citing the authority of the oldest sacred books, that Hindu religion at its best was opposed to the practice; on the other, he appealed to the reason, humanity and compassion of the people. He visited the burning ghats at Calcutta to try to persuade the relatives of widows to give up their plan of self-immolation. He organised groups of like-minded people to keep a strict check on such performances and to prevent any attempt to force the widows to become *sati*. When the orthodox Hindus petitioned Parliament to withhold its approval of Bentinck's action to ban the rite of *sati*, he organised a counterpetition of enlightened Hindus in favour of Bentinck's action.

He was a stout champion of women's rights. He condemned the subjugation of women and opposed the prevailing idea that women were inferior to men in intellect or in a moral sense. He attacked polygamy and the degraded state to which widows were often reduced. To raise the status of women, he demanded that they be given the right of inheritance and property.

Rammohun Roy was one of the earliest propagators of modern education, which he looked upon as a major instrument for the spread of modern ideas in the country. In 1817, David Hare, who had come out to India in 1800 as a watchmaker but who spent his entire life promoting modern education in the country, founded the famous Hindu College. Rammohun Roy provided the most enthusiastic assistance to Hare, in this and other educational projects. In addition, he maintained, at his own cost, an English school in Calcutta from 1817 in which, among other subjects, mechanics and the philosophy of Voltaire were taught. In 1825, he established a Vedanta College in which courses in both Indian learning and Western social and physical sciences were offered.

Rammohun Roy was equally keen on making Bengali the vehicle of intellectual intercourse in Bengal. He compiled a Bengali grammar.

Through his translations, pamphlets and journals, he helped to evolve a modern and elegant prose style for that language.

Rammohun represented the first glimmerings of the rise of national consciousness in India. The vision of an independent and resurgent India guided his thoughts and actions. He believed that by trying to weed out corrupt elements from Indian religions and society and by preaching the Vedantic message of worship of one God he was laying the foundations for the unity of Indian society, which was divided into divergent groups. In particular, he opposed the rigidities of the caste system which, he declared, "has been source of want of unity among us". He believed that the caste system was doubly evil: it created inequality and it divided people and "deprived them of patriotic feeling". Thus, according to him, one of the aims of religious reform was political uplift.

Rammohun Roy was a pioneer of Indian journalism. He brought out journals in Bengali, Persian, Hindi and English to spread scientific, literary and political knowledge among the people, to educate public opinion on topics of current interest, and to represent popular demands and grievances before the government.

He was also the initiator of public agitation on political questions in the country. He condemned the oppressive practices of the Bengal zamindars, which had reduced the peasants to a miserable condition. He demanded that the maximum rents paid by the actual cultivators of land be permanently fixed so that they too could enjoy the benefits of the Permanent Settlement of 1793. He also protested against attempts to impose taxes on tax-free lands. He demanded the abolition of the Company's trading rights and the removal of heavy export duties on Indian goods. He also raised demands for the Indianisation of the superior services, separation of the executive and the judiciary, trial by jury, and judicial equality between Indians and Europeans.

Rammohun was a firm believer in internationalism and in free cooperation between nations. The poet Rabindranath Tagore has rightly remarked: "Rammohun was the only person in his time, in the whole world of man, to realise completely the significance of the Modern Age. He knew that the ideal of human civilisation does not lie in the isolation of independence, but in the brotherhood of interdependence of individuals as well as nations in all spheres of thought and activity." Rammohun Roy took a keen interest in international events and everywhere he supported the cause of liberty, democracy, and nationalism and opposed injustice, oppression and tyranny in every form. The news of the failure of the Revolution in Naples in 1821 made him so sad that he cancelled all his social engagements. On the other hand, he celebrated the success of the Revolution in Spanish America in 1823 by giving a public dinner. He condemned the miserable condition of Ireland under the oppressive regime of absentee English landlordism. He publicly declared that he would emigrate from the British empire if Parliament failed to pass the Reform Bill.

Rammohun was as fearless as a lion. He did not hesitate to support a just cause. All his life, he fought against social injustice and inequality, even at great personal loss and hardship. In his life of service to society, he often clashed with his family, with rich zamindars and powerful missionaries, and with high officials and foreign authorities. Yet he never showed fear nor shrank from his chosen course.

Rammohun was the brightest star in the Indian sky during the first half of the nineteenth century, but he was not a lone star. He had many distinguished associates, followers and successors. In the field of education, he was greatly helped by the Dutch watchmaker David Hare and the Scottish missionary Alexander Duff. Dwarkanath Tagore was the foremost among his Indian associates. His other prominent followers were Prasanna Kumar Tagore, Chandrashekhar Deb, and Tarachand Chakravarti, the first secretary of the Brahma Sabha.

DEROZIO AND YOUNG BENGAL

A radical trend arose among Bengali intellectuals during the late 1820s and 1830s. This trend was more modern than even Rammohun Roy's and was known as the Young Bengal movement. Its leader and inspirer was the young Anglo-Indian Henry Vivian Derozio, who was born in 1809 and who taught at Hindu College from 1826 to 1831. Derozio possessed a dazzling intellect and followed the most radical views of the time, drawing his inspiration from the great French Revolution. He was a brilliant teacher who, in spite of his youth, attached to himself a host of bright and adoring students. He inspired these students to think rationally and freely, to question all authority, to love liberty, equality and freedom, and to worship truth. Derozio and his famous followers, known as the Derozians and Young Bengal, were fiery patriots. Derozio was perhaps the first nationalist poet of modern India. For example, he wrote in 1827:

> My country! in the days of glory past
> A beauteous halo circled round thy brow,
> and worshipped as a deity thou wast,
> Where is that glory, where that reverence now?
> Thy eagle pinion is chained down at last,
> And grovelling in the lowly dust art thou,
> Thy minstrel hath no wreath to weave for thee
> save the sad story of thy misery!

And one of his pupils, Kashi Prasad Ghosh, wrote in 1861:

> Land of the Gods and lofty name;
> Land of the fair and beauty's spell;
> Land of the bards of mighty fame,
> My native land! for e'er farewell! (1830)
> But woe me! I never shall live to
> behold, That day of thy triumph, when firmly and bold,
> Thou shalt mount on the wings of an eagle on high,
> To the region of knowledge and blest liberty.

Derozio was removed from Hindu College in 1831 because of his radicalism and died of cholera soon after at the young age of 22. The Derozians attacked old and decadent customs, rites and traditions. They were passionate advocates of women's rights and demanded education for them. They did not, however, succeed in creating a movement because social conditions were not yet ripe for their ideas to flourish. They did not take up the peasant's cause and there was no other class or group in Indian society at the time which could support their advanced ideas. Moreover, they forgot to maintain their links with the people. In fact, their radicalism was bookish; they failed to come to grips with the Indian reality. Even so, the

Derozians carried forward Rammohun's tradition of educating the people in social, economic and political questions through newspapers, pamphlets and public associations. They carried on public agitation on questions such as the revision of the Company's Charter, the freedom of the Press, better treatment for Indian labour in British colonies abroad, trial by jury, protection of the *ryots* from oppressive zamindars, and employment of Indians in the higher grades of government services. Surendranath Banerjea, the famous leader of the nationalist movement, described the Derozians as "the pioneers of the modern civilization of Bengal, the conscript fathers of our race whose virtues will excite veneration and whose failings will be treated with gentlest consideration".

DEBENDRANATH TAGORE AND ISHWAR CHANDRA VIDYASAGAR

The Brahmo Samaj had in the meanwhile continued to exist, but without much life till Debendranath Tagore, father of Rabindranath Tagore, revitalised it. Debendranath was a product of the best in traditional Indian learning and the new thought of the West. In 1839, he founded the Tatvabodhini Sabha to propagate Rammohun Roy's ideas. In time, it came to include most of the prominent followers of Rammohun and Derozio and other independent thinkers like Ishwar Chandra Vidyasagar and Akshay Kumar Dutt. The Tatvabodhini Sabha and its organ, the *Tatvabodhini Patrika,* promoted a systematic study of India's past in the Bengali language. It also helped to spread a rational outlook among the intellectuals of Bengal. In 1843, Debendranath Tagore reorganised the Brahmo Samaj and breathed new life into it. The Samaj actively supported the movement for widow remarriage, abolition of polygamy, women's education, improvement of the *ryot's* condition and temperance.

The next towering personality to appear on the Indian scene was Pandit Ishwar Chandra Vidyasagar, the great scholar and reformer. Vidyasagar dedicated his entire life to the cause of social reform. Born in 1820 in a very poor family, he struggled through hardship to educate himself and in the end, rose in 1851 to the position of Principal of Sanskrit College. Though he was a great Sanskrit scholar, his mind was open to the best in Western thought, and he came to represent a happy blend of Indian and Western culture. His greatness lay above all in his sterling character and shining intellect. Possessed of immense courage and a fearless mind, he practised what he believed. There was no lag between his beliefs and his action, between his thought and his practice. He was simple in dress and habits and direct in his manner. He was a great humanist who possessed immense sympathy for the poor, the unfortunate and the oppressed.

In Bengal, innumerable stories regarding his high character, moral qualities and deep humanism are related till this day. He resigned from government service for he would not tolerate undue official interference. His generosity to the poor was fabulous. He seldom possessed a warm coat, for he invariably gave it to the first naked beggar he met on the street.

Vidyasagar's contribution to the making of modern India is many-sided. He evolved a new methodology of teaching Sanskrit. He wrote a Bengali primer, which is used to this day. His writings helped in the evolution of a modern prose style in Bengali. He opened the gates of Sanskrit College to non-brahmin students, for he was opposed to the monopoly of Sanskrit studies that the priestly caste was enjoying at the time. He was determined to break the priestly monopoly over scriptural knowledge. To free Sanskrit studies from the harmful effects of self-imposed isolation, he introduced the study of Western thought in Sanskrit College. He also helped to found a college which is now named after him.

Above all, Vidyasagar is remembered gratefully by his countrymen for his contribution to the uplift of India's downtrodden womanhood. Here, he proved a worthy successor to Rammohun Roy. He waged a long struggle in favour of widow remarriage. His humanism was aroused to the full by the sufferings of the Hindu widows. To improve their lot, he gave his all and virtually ruined himself. In 1855, he raised his powerful voice, backed by the weight of immense traditional learning, in favour of widow remarriage. Soon a powerful movement in favour of widow remarriage was started, which continues to this day. Later in 1855, a large number of petitions from Bengal, Madras, Bombay, Nagpur and other cities of India were presented to the government, asking it to pass an act legalising the remarriage of widows. This agitation was successful and such a law was enacted.

The first lawful Hindu widow remarriage among the upper castes in our country was celebrated in Calcutta on 7 December 1856 under the inspiration and supervision of Vidyasagar. Widows of many other castes in different parts of the country already enjoyed this right under customary law. An observer has described the ceremony in the following words:

> I shall never forget the day. When Pandit Vidyasagar came with his friend, the bridegroom, at the head of a large procession, the crowd of spectators was so great that there was not an inch of moving space, and many fell into the big drains which were to be seen by the sides of Calcutta streets in those days. After the ceremony, it became the subject of discussion everywhere; in the bazars and the shops, in the streets, in the public squares, in students' lodging-houses, in gentlemen's drawing-rooms, in offices and in distant village homes, where even women earnestly discussed it among themselves. The weavers of Santipore issued a peculiar kind of women's sari which contained woven along its borders the first line of a newly composed song which went on to say 'May Vidyasagar live long'.

For his advocacy of widow remarriage, Vidyasagar had to face the bitter enmity of the orthodox Hindus. At times, even his life was threatened. But he fearlessly pursued his chosen course. Through his efforts, which included the grant of monetary help to needy couples, 25 widow-remarriages were performed between 1855 and 1860.

In 1850, Vidyasagar protested against child marriage. All his life, he campaigned against polygamy. He was also deeply interested in the education of women. As a Government Inspector of Schools, he organised 35 girls' schools, many of which he ran at his own expense. As Secretary to the Bethune School, he was one of the pioneers of higher education for women.

The Bethune School, founded in Calcutta in 1849, was the first fruit of the powerful movement for women's education that arose in the 1840s and 1850s. While the education of women was not unknown in India, a great deal of prejudice against it existed. Some even believed that educated women would lose their husbands! The first steps in giving a modern education to girls were taken by the missionaries in 1821, but these efforts were marred by the emphasis on Christian religious education. The Bethune School had great difficulty in securing students. The young students were shouted at and abused, and sometimes even their parents were subjected to social boycott. Many believed that girls who had received Western education would make slaves of their husbands.

Pioneers of Reform in Western India

The impact of Western ideas was felt much earlier in Bengal than in western India, which was brought under effective British control as late as 1818. Bal Shastri Jambekar was one of the first reformers in Bombay. He attacked Brahmanical orthodoxy and tried to reform popular Hinduism. In 1832, he started a weekly, *Darpan,* with the objective of "chasing away the mists of error and ignorance which clouded men's minds, and shedding over them the light of knowledge, in which the people of Europe have advanced so far before the other nations of the world". In 1849, the Paramahansa Mandali was founded in Maharashtra. Its founders believed in one God and were primarily interested in breaking caste rules. At its meetings, members took food cooked by low-caste people. They also believed in permitting widow remarriage and in the education of women. Branches of the Mandali were formed in Poona, Satara and other towns of Maharashtra. Referring to the Mandali's influence on young people, R.G. Bhandarkar, the famous historian, later recalled: "When we went for long walks in the evening, we talked about the evils of caste distinctions, how much damage was done by this division between high and low, and how true progress for this country could never be achieved without removing these distinctions." In 1848, several educated young men formed the Students' Literary and Scientific Society, which had two branches, the Gujarati and the Marathi Dnyan Prasarak Mandalis. The Society organised lectures on popular science and social questions. One of the aims of the society was to start schools for the education of women. In 1851, Jotiba Phule and his wife started a girl's school at Poona, and soon many other schools came up. Among the active promoters of these schools were Jagannath Shankar Seth and Bhau Daji. Phule was also a pioneer of the widow remarriage movement in Maharashtra. Vishnu Shastri Pundit founded the Widow Remarriage Association in the 1850s.

Another prominent worker in this field was Karsondas Mulji, who started the *Satya Prakash* in Gujarati in 1852 to advocate for widow remarriage.

An outstanding champion of new learning and social reform in Maharashtra was Gopal Hari Deshmukh, who became famous by the pen-name of 'Lokahitawadi'. He advocated the reorganisation of Indian society on rational principles and modern humanistic and secular values. Jotiba Phule, born in a low-caste Mali family, was also acutely aware of the socially degraded position of non-Brahmins and untouchables in Maharashtra. All his life, he carried on a campaign against upper-caste domination and brahmanical supremacy.

Dadabhai Naoroji was another leading social reformer of Bombay. He was one of the founders of an association to reform the Zoroastrian religion and the Parsi Law Association, which agitated for the grant of legal status to women and for uniform laws of inheritance and marriage for the Parsis.

From the very beginning, it was, in the main, through the Indian language press and literature that the reformers carried on their struggle. To enable Indian languages to play this role successfully, they undertook such humdrum tasks as the preparation of language primers, etc. For example, both Ishwar Chandra Vidyasagar and Rabindranath Tagore wrote Bengali primers, which are still being used. In fact, the spread of modern and reformist ideas among the mass of people occurred primarily through Indian languages.

We should also remember that the significance of the nineteenth-century reformers lay not in their numbers but in the fact that they were the trendsetters—it was their thought and activity that were to have a decisive impact on the making of a new India.

SEVEN

The Revolt of 1857

A mighty popular revolt broke out in northern and central India in 1857 and nearly swept away British rule. It began with a mutiny of the sepoys, or the Indian soldiers of the Company's army, but soon engulfed wide regions and involved the massses. Millions of peasants, artisans and soldiers fought heroically for over a year and by their exemplary courage and sacrifice wrote a glorious chapter in the history of the Indian people.

GENERAL CAUSES

The Revolt of 1857 was much more than a mere product of sepoy discontent. It was in reality a product of the character and policies of colonial rule, of the accumulated grievances of people against the Company's administration and of their dislike of the foreign regime. For over a century, as the British had been conquering the country bit by bit, popular discontent and hatred against foreign rule were gaining strength among different sections of Indian society. It was this discontent that burst forth into a mighty popular revolt.

Perhaps the most important cause of the popular discontent was the economic exploitation of the country by the British and the complete destruction of its traditional economic fabric; this both impoverished the vast mass of peasants, artisans and handicraftsmen, as also a large number of traditional zamindars and chiefs. We have traced the disastrous economic impact of early British rule in another chapter. Other general causes were British land and land revenue policies and the systems of law and administration. In particular, a large number of peasant proprietors, subjected to exorbitant land revenue demand, lost their lands to traders and moneylenders and found themselves hopelessly mired in debt. The new landlords, lacking the ties of tradition that had linked the old zamindars to peasants, pushed rents up to ruinous heights and evicted them in case of non-payment. The economic decline of the peasantry found expression in 12 major and numerous minor famines from 1770 to 1857. Similarly, many zamindars were harassed by demands for higher land revenue and threatened with forfeiture of their zamindari lands and rights and loss of their status in the villages. They resented their loss even more when they were replaced by rank outsiders—officials, merchants and moneylenders. In addition, common people were hard hit by the prevalence of corruption at the lower levels of administration. The police, petty officials and lower law courts were notoriously corrupt. William Edwards, a British official, wrote in 1859 while discussing the causes of the Revolt that the police were "a scourge to the people" and that "their oppressions and exactions form one of the chief grounds of dissatisfaction with our government". The petty officials lost no opportunity to enrich themselves at the cost of the ryots and the zamindars. The complex judicial system enabled the rich to oppress the poor. Flogging, torture and jailing of the cultivators for arrears of rent or land revenue or interest on debt were quite common. Thus, the growing poverty of the people made them desperate and led them to join a general revolt in the hope of improving their lot.

The middle and upper classes of Indian society, particularly in the north, were hard hit by their exclusion from well-paid higher posts in the administration. The gradual disappearance of Indian states deprived those Indians who were employed in them in high administrative and judicial posts of their means of livelihood. British supremacy also led to the ruin of persons who made a living by following cultural pursuits. The Indian rulers had been partrons of art and literature and had supported scholars, and religious preachers. The displacement of these rulers by the East India Company meant the sudden withdrawal of this patronage and the impoverishment of those who had depended on it. Religious preachers, pandits and maulavis, who felt that their entire future was threatened, were to play an important role in spreading hatred against foreign rule.

Another basic cause of the unpopularity of British rule was its very foreignness. The British remained perpetual foreigners in the country. For one, there was no social link or communication between them and the Indians. Unlike foreign conquerors before them, they did not mix socially even with the upper classes of Indians; instead, they were filled with racial superiority and treated Indians with contempt and arrogance. As Sayyid Ahmad Khan wrote later: "Even natives of the highest rank never came into the presence of officials but with an inward fear and trembling." Most of all, the British did not come to settle in India and to make it their home. Their main aim was to enrich themselves and then go back to Britain along with their wealth. The people of India were aware of this basically foreign character of the new rulers. They refused to recognise the British as their benefactors and looked upon every act of theirs with suspicion. They had thus a vague anti-British feeling, which found expression even earlier than the Revolt in numerous popular uprisings against the British.

The period of the growth of discontent among the people coincided with certain events which shattered the general belief in the invincibility of British arms and encouraged the people to believe that the days of the British regime were numbered. The British army suffered major reversals in the First Afghan War (1838–42), in the Punjab Wars (1845–49), and in the Crimean War (1854–56). In 1855–56, the Santhal tribesmen of Bihar and Bengal rose up, armed with axes and bows and arrows, and revealed the potential of a popular uprising by temporarily sweeping away British rule from their area. Though the British ultimately won these wars and suppressed the Santhal uprising, the disasters they suffered in major battles revealed that the British army could be defeated by determined fighting, even by an Asian army. In fact, the Indians made a serious error of political judgement by underestimating British strength. This error was to cost the rebels of 1857 dear. At the same time, the historical significance of this factor should not be missed. People do not revolt simply because they have the desire to overthrow their rulers; they must, in addition, possess the confidence that they can do so successfully.

The annexation of Awadh by Lord Dalhousie in 1856 was widely resented in India in general and in Awadh in particular. More specifically, it created an atmosphere of rebellion in Awadh and in the

Company's army. Dalhousie's action angered the Company's sepoys, 75,000 of whom came from Awadh. Lacking an all-India feeling, these sepoys had helped the British conquer the rest of India. But they did possess regional and local patriotism and did not want their homelands to come under the foreigner's sway. Moreover, the annexation of Awadh adversely affected the sepoy's purse. He had to pay higher taxes on the land his family held in Awadh.

The excuse that Dalhousie had advanced for annexing Awadh was that he wanted to free the people from the Nawab's mismanagement and *taluqdars'* oppression, but, in practice, the people got no relief. Indeed, the common man had now to pay higher land revenue and additional taxes on articles of food, houses, ferries, opium, and justice. The dissolution of the Nawab's administration and army threw out of jobs thousands of nobles, gentlemen and officials, together with their retainers and officers and soldiers, and created unemployment in almost every peasant's home. Similarly, merchants, shopkeepers, and handicraftsmen who had catered to the Awadh Court and nobles lost their livelihood. Moreover, the British confiscated the estates of a majority of the *taluqdars* or zamindars. These dispossessed *taluqdars*, numbering nearly 21,000, anxious to regain their lost estates and position, became the most dangerous opponents of British rule.

The annexation of Awadh, along with the other annexations of Dalhousie, created panic among rulers of the native states. They now discovered that even their most grovelling loyalty had failed to satisfy the British greed for territory. What is of even greater importance, the political prestige of the British suffered a great deal because of the manner in which they had repeatedly broken their written and oral pledges and treaties with the Indian powers and annexed them or reduced them to subordination and imposed their own nominees on their thrones. This policy of annexation and subordination was, for example, directly responsible for making Nana Sahib, the Rani of Jhansi and Bahadur Shah their staunch enemies. Nana Sahib was the adopted son of Baji Rao II, the last Peshwa. The British refused to grant Nana Sahib the pension they were paying to Baji Rao II, and forced him to live at Kanpur, far away from his family seat at Poona. Similarly, the British insistence on the annexation of Jhansi incensed the proud Rani Lakshmibai, who wanted her adopted son to succeed her deceased husband. The house of the Mughals was humbled when Dalhousie announced in 1849 that the successor to Bahadur Shah would have to abandon the historic Red Fort and move to a humbler residence at the Qutab on the outskirts of Delhi. And, in 1856, Canning announced that after Bahadur Shah's death, the Mughals would lose the title of kings and would be known as mere princes.

An important factor in turning the people against British rule was their fear that it endangered their religion. This fear was largely due to the activities of the Christian missionaries who were "to be seen everywhere—in the schools, in the hospitals, in the prisons and at the market places". These missionaries tried to convert people and made violent and vulgar public attacks on Hinduism and Islam. They openly ridiculed and denounced the long-cherished customs and traditions of the people. They were, moreover, provided police protection. The actual conversions made by them appeared to the people as living proof of the threat to their religion. Popular suspicion that the alien government supported the activities of the missionaries was strengthened by certain acts of the government and the actions of some of its officials. In 1850, the government enacted a law which enabled a convert to Christianity to inherit his ancestral property. Moreover, the government maintained at its cost chaplains or Christian priests in the army. Many officials, civil as well as military, considered it their religious duty to encourage missionary propaganda and to provide instruction in Christianity in government schools and even in jails.

The conservative religious and social sentiments of many people were also hurt by some of the humanitarian measures which the government had undertaken on the advice of Indian reformers. They believed that an alien Christian government had no right to interfere in their religion and customs. The abolition of the custom of *sati*, the legalisation of widow remarriage, and the opening of Western education to girls appeared to them as examples of such undue interference. Religious sentiments were also hurt by the official policy of taxing lands belonging to temples and mosques and to their priests or the charitable institutions which had been exempted from taxation by previous Indian rulers. Moreover, the many brahman and Muslim families dependent on these lands were aroused to fury, and they began to propagate that the British were trying to undermine the religions of India.

The Revolt of 1857 started with the mutiny of the Company's sepoys. We have therefore to examine why the sepoys, who had by their devoted service enabled the Company to conquer India, and who enjoyed high prestige and economic security, suddenly became rebellious. Here, the first fact to be kept in view is that the sepoys were after all a part of Indian society and, therefore, felt and suffered to some extent what other Indians did. The hopes, desires, and despairs of the other sections of society, especially the peasantry, were reflected in them. The sepoy was, in fact, a 'peasant in uniform'. If their near and dear ones suffered from the destructive economic consequences of British rule, they, in turn, felt this suffering. They were also duly affected by the general belief that the British were interfering in their religions and were determined to convert Indians to Christianity. Their own experience predisposed them to such a belief. They knew that the army was maintaining chaplains at state cost. Moreover, some of the British officers in their religious ardour carried on Christian propaganda among the sepoys. The sepoys also had religious or caste grievances of their own. The Indians of those days were very strict in observing caste rules, etc. The military authorities forbade the sepoys to wear caste and sectarian marks, beards or turbans. In 1856, an Act was passed under which every new recruit undertook to serve even overseas, if required. This hurt the sepoys' sentiments as, according to the current religious beliefs of the Hindus, travel across the sea was forbidden and led to loss of caste.

The sepoys also had numerous other grievances. A wide gulf had come into existence between the officers and the sepoys, who were often treated with contempt by their British officers. A contemporary English observer noted that "the officers and men have not been friends but strangers to one another. The sepoy is esteemed an inferior creature. He is sworn at. He is treated roughly. He is spoken of as a 'nigger'. He is addressed as a '*suar*' or pig. ... The younger men ... treat him as an inferior animal." Even though a sepoy was as good a soldier as his British counterpart, he was paid much less and lodged and fed in a far worse manner than the latter. Moreover, he had little prospect of a rise; no Indian could rise higher than a subedar, drawing 60 to 70 rupees a month. In fact, the sepoy's life was quite hard. Naturally, the sepoy resented this artificial and enforced position of inferiority. As the British historian T.R. Holmes has put it:

> Though he might give signs of the military genius of a Hyder, he knew that he could never attain the pay of an English subaltern and that the rank to which he might attain, after some 30 years of faithful service, would not protect him from the insolent dictation of an ensign fresh from England.

A more immediate cause of the sepoys' dissatisfaction was the recent order that they would not be given the foreign service allowance *(batta)* when serving in Sindh or in the Punjab. This order resulted in a big cut in the salaries of a large number of them. The annexation of Awadh, the home of many sepoys, further inflamed their feelings.

The dissatisfaction of the sepoys had in fact a long history. A sepoy mutiny had broken out in Bengal as early as 1764. The authorities had suppressed it by blowing away 30 sepoys from the mouths of guns. In 1806 the sepoys at Vellore mutinied, but were crushed with terrible violence, with several hundred men dying in battle. In 1824, the 47th Regiment of sepoys at Barrackpore refused to go to Burma by the sea-route. The Regiment was disbanded, its unarmed men were fired upon by artillery, and the leaders of the sepoys were hanged. In 1844, seven battalions revolted on the question of salaries and *batta*. Similarly, the sepoys in Afghanistan were on the verge of revolt during the Afghan War. Two subedars, a Muslim and a Hindu, were shot dead for giving expression to the discontent in the army. Dissatisfaction was so widespread among the sepoys that Fredrick Halliday, Lieutenant-Governor of Bengal in 1858, was led to remark that the Bengal army was "more or less mutinous, always on the verge of revolt and certain to have mutinied at one time or another as soon as provocation might combine with opportunity".

Thus, widespread and intense dislike and even hatred of foreign rule prevailed among large numbers of Indian people and soldiers of the Company's army. This feeling was later summed up by Saiyid Ahmad Khan in his *Causes of the Indian Mutiny* as follows:

At length, the Indians fell into the habit of thinking that all laws were passed with a view to degrade and ruin them and to deprive them and their compatriots of their religion. ... At last came the time when all men looked upon the English government as slow poison, a rope of sand, a treacherous flame of fire. They began to believe that if today they escaped from the clutches of the government, tomorrow they would fall into them or that even if they escaped the morrow, the third day would see their ruin. ... The people wished for a change in the government, and rejoiced heartily at the idea of British rule being superseded by another.

Similarly, a proclamation issued by the rebels in Delhi complained:

First, in Hindustan they have exacted as revenue Rupees 300 where only 200 were due, and Rupees 500 where but 400 were demandable and still they are solicitous to raise their demands. The people must therefore be ruined and beggared. Second, they have doubted and quadrupled and raised tenfold the Chowkeedaree Tax and have wished to ruin the people. Third, the occupation of all respectable and learned men is gone, and millions are destitute of the necessaries of life. When any one in search of employment determines on proceeding from one Zillah to another, every soul is charged six pie as toll on roads, and has to pay from 4 to 8 annas for each cart. Those only who pay are permitted to travel on the public roads. How far can we detail the oppression of the Tyrants! Gradually matters arrived at such a pitch that the government had determined to subvert everyone's religion.

The Revolt of 1857 came as a culmination of popular discontent with British policies and imperialist exploitation. But it was no sudden occurrence. For nearly a century, there had been fierce popular resistance to British domination all over India. Armed rebellions began as British rule was established in Bengal and Bihar, and they occurred in area after area as it was conquered. There was hardly a year without armed opposition or a decade without a major rebellion in one part of the country or the other. From 1763 to 1856, there were more than 40 major rebellions and hundreds of minor ones. These rebellions had been often led by rajas, nawabs, zamindars, landlords and poligars, but their fighting forces had been provided by peasants, artisans and ex-soldiers of the deposed Indian rulers and dispossessed and disarmed zamindars and poligars. These almost continuous rebellions were massive in their totality, but were wholly local in their spread and isolated from each other. They were also localised in their effects.

The Immediate Cause

By 1857, the material for a mass upheaval was ready, only a spark was needed to set it afire. The episode of the greased cartridges provided this spark for the sepoys and their mutiny gave the general populace the occasion to revolt.

The new Enfield rifle had been first introduced in the army. Its cartridges had a greased paper cover whose end had to be bitten off before the cartridge was loaded into the rifle. The grease was in some instances composed of beef and pig fat. The sepoys, Hindu as well as Muslim, were enraged. The use of the greased cartridges would endanger their religion. Many of them believed that the government was deliberately trying to destroy their religion and convert them to Christianity. The time to rebel had come.

The Beginning and Course of the Revolt

Was the Revolt of 1857 spontaneous and unplanned or the result of careful and secret organisation? It is not easy to answer this question with certainty. A peculiar aspect of the study of the history of the Revolt of 1857 is that it has to be based almost entirely on British records. The rebels have left behind no records. As they worked illegally, they perhaps kept no records. Moreover, they were defeated and suppressed and their version of events died with them. Lastly, for years afterwards, the British suppressed any favourable mention of the Revolt, and took strong action against anyone who tried to present the rebels' side of the story.

One group of historians and writers has asserted that the Revolt was the result of a widespread and well-organised conspiracy. They point to the circulation of *chappattis* and red lotuses, propaganda by wandering *sanyasis, faqirs* and *madaris*. Other writers equally forcefully deny that any careful planning went into the making of the Revolt. They point out that not a scrap of paper was discovered before or after the Revolt indicating an organised conspiracy, nor did a single witness come forward to make such a claim.

The Revolt began at Meerut, 58 km from Delhi, on 10 May 1857 and then, gathering force rapidly, it cut across northern India as if

The Revolt of 1857

like a sword. It soon embraced a vast area from the Punjab in the north and the Narmada in the south to Bihar in the east and Rajputana in the west.

Even before the outbreak at Meerut, Mangal Pande had become a martyr at Barrackpore. Mangal Pande, a young soldier, was hanged on 29 March 1857 for revolting single-handed and attacking his superior officers. This and many similar incidents were a sign that discontent and rebellion were brewing among the sepoys. And then came the explosion at Meerut. On 24 April, 90 men of the 3rd Native Cavalry refused to accept the greased cartridges. On 9 May, 85 of them were dismissed, sentenced to 10 years' imprisonment and put into fetters. This sparked off a general mutiny among the Indian soldiers stationed at Meerut. The very next day, on 10 May, they released their imprisoned comrades, killed their officers, and unfurled the banner of revolt. As if drawn by a magnet, they set off for Delhi after sunset. When the Meerut soldiers appeared in Delhi the next morning, the local infantry joined them, killed their own European officers, and seized the city. The rebellious soldiers now proclaimed the aged and powerless Bahadur Shah, the Emperor of India. Delhi was soon to become the centre of the Great Revolt and Bahadur Shah its great symbol. This spontaneous raising of the last Mughal king to the leadership of the country was recognition of the fact that the long reign of the Mughal dynasty had made it the traditional symbol of India's political unity. With this single act, the sepoys had transformed a mutiny of soldiers into a revolutionary war. This is why rebellious sepoys from all over the country automatically turned their steps towards Delhi and all Indian chiefs who took part in the Revolt tended to proclaim their loyalty to the Mughal emperor. Bahadur Shah, in turn, under the instigation and perhaps the pressure of the sepoys, and after initial vacillation, wrote letters to all the chiefs and rulers of India urging them to organise a confederacy of Indian states to fight and replace the British regime.

The entire Bengal army soon rose in revolt, which spread quickly. Awadh, Rohilkhand, the Doab, the Bundelkhand, central India, large parts of Bihar, and the East Punjab all shook off British authority. In many of the princely states, rulers remained loyal to their British overlord but the soldiers revolted or remained on the brink of revolt.

Many of Indore's troops rebelled and joined the sepoys. Similarly, over 20,000 of Gwalior's troops went over to Tantia Tope and the Rani of Jhansi. Many small chiefs of Rajasthan and Maharashtra revolted with the support of the people who were quite hostile to the British. Local rebellions also occurred in Hyderabad and Bengal.

The tremendous sweep and breadth of the Revolt was matched by its depth. Everywhere in northern and central India, the mutiny of the sepoys triggered popular revolts among the civilian population. After the sepoys had destroyed British authority, the common people rose up in arms, often fighting with spears and axes, bows and arrows, lathis and sickles, and crude muskets. In many places, however, the people revolted even before the sepoys did or even when no sepoy regiments were present. It is the wide participation in the Revolt by the peasantry, the artisans, shopkeepers, day labourers, and zamindars which gave it real strength as well as the character of a popular revolt, especially in the areas at present included in Uttar Pradesh and Bihar. Here, the peasants and zamindars gave free expression to their grievances by attacking the moneylenders and new zamindars who had displaced them from the land. They took advantage of the Revolt to destroy the moneylenders' account books and records of debts. They also attacked the British-established law courts, revenue offices *(tehsils)* and revenue records, and *thanas*. It is of some importance to note that in many of the battles, commoners far surpassed the sepoys in numbers. According to one estimate, of the total number of about 150,000 men who died fighting the English in Awadh, over 100,000 were civilians.

It should also be noted that even where people did not rise up in revolt, they showed strong sympathy for the rebels. They rejoiced in the successes of the rebels and organised a social boycott of those sepoys who remained loyal to the British. They showed active hostility to British forces, refused to give them help or information, and even misled them with wrong information. W. H. Russel, who toured India in 1858 and 1859 as the correspondent of the *London Times,* wrote that:

> In no instance is a friendly glance directed to the white man's carriage.... Oh! that language of the eye! Who can doubt? Who can misinterpret it? It is by it alone that I have learnt our race is not even feared at times by many and that by all it is disliked.

The popular character of the Revolt of 1857 also became evident when the British tried to crush it. They had to wage a vigorous and ruthless war not only against the rebellious sepoys, but also against the people of Delhi, Awadh, North-Western Provinces and Agra, central India, and western Bihar, burning entire villages and massacring villagers and urban people. They had to fight and reconquer many parts of northern India, village by village. They had to cow down people with public hangings and executions without trial, thus revealing how deep the revolt was in these parts.

Much of the strength of the Revolt of 1857 lay in Hindu-Muslim unity. Among the soldiers and the people as well as among the leaders, there was complete cooperation, as between Hindus and Muslims. All the rebels recognised Bahadur Shah, a Muslim, as their emperor. Also, the first thoughts of the Hindu sepoys at Meerut was to march straight to Delhi. The Hindu and the Muslim rebels and sepoys respected each other's sentiments. For example, wherever the Revolt was successful, orders were immediately issued banning cow-slaughter out of respect for Hindu sentiments. Moreover, Hindus and Muslims were equally well-represented at all levels of the leadership. The role of Hindu-Muslim unity in the Revolt was indirectly acknowledged later by Aitchison, a senior British official, when he bitterly complained: "In this instance we could not play off the Mohammedans against the Hindus." In fact, the events of 1857 clearly bring out that the people and politics of India were basically not communal in medieval times and before 1858.

The storm-centres of the Revolt of 1857 were at Delhi, Kanpur, Lucknow, Bareilly, Jhansi, and Arrah in Bihar. At Delhi, the nominal and symbolic leadership belonged to the Emperor Bahadur Shah, but the real command lay with a Court of Soldiers headed by General Bakht Khan, who had led the revolt of the Bareilly troops and brought them to Delhi. In the British army, he had been an ordinary subedar of artillery. Bakht Khan represented the popular and plebeian element at the headquarters of the Revolt. The Emperor Bahadur Shah was perhaps the weakest link in the chain of leadership of the Revolt. His weak personality, old age and lack of qualities of leadership created political weakness at the nerve centre of the Revolt and did incalculable damage to it.

At Kanpur, the Revolt was led by Nana Sahib, the adopted son of Baji Rao II, the last Peshwa. Nana Sahib expelled the English from Kanpur with the help of the sepoys and proclaimed himself the Peshwa. At the same time, he acknowledged Bahadur Shah as the emperor of India and declared himself his Governor. The chief burden of fighting on behalf of Nana Sahib fell on the shoulders of Tantia Tope, one of his most loyal servants. Tantia Tope has won immortal fame by his patriotism, determined fighting and skilful guerrilla operations. Azimullah was another loyal servant of Nana Sahib. He was an expert in political propaganda. Unfortunately, Nana Sahib tarnished his brave record by deceitfully killing the British garrison at Kanpur after he had agreed to give them safe conduct.

The revolt at Lucknow was led by Hazrat Mahal, the Begum of Awadh, who had proclaimed her young son, Birjis Kadr, as the Nawab of Awadh. Helped by the sepoys at Lucknow, and by the zamindars and peasants of Awadh, the Begum organised an all-out attack on the British. Compelled to give up the city, the latter entrenched themselves in the Residency building. In the end, the seige of the Residency failed, as the small British garrison fought back with exemplary fortitude and valour.

One of the great leaders of the Revolt of 1857, and perhaps one of the greatest heroines of Indian history, was the young Rani Lakshmibai of Jhansi. The young Rani joined the rebels when the British refused to acknowledge her right to adopt an heir to the Jhansi *gaddi,* annexed her state, and threatened to treat her as an instigator of the rebellion of the sepoys at Jhansi. The Rani vacillated for some time. But once she decided to throw in her lot with the rebels, she fought valiantly at the head of her troops. Tales of her bravery and courage and military skill have inspired her countrymen ever since. Driven out of Jhansi by the British forces after a fierce battle in which "even women were seen working the batteries and distributing ammunition", she administered the oath to her followers that "with our own hands we shall not our *Azadshahi* [independent rule] bury". She captured Gwalior with the help of Tantia Tope and her trusted Afghan guards. Maharaja Sindhia, loyal to the British, made an attempt to fight the Rani, but most of his troops deserted to her. Sindhia sought refuge with the English at Agra. The brave Rani died fighting on 17 June 1858, clad in the battle dress of a soldier and mounted on a charger. Beside her fell her life-long friend and companion, a Muslim girl.

Kunwar Singh, a ruined and discontented zamindar of Jagdishpur near Arrah, was the chief organiser of the Revolt in Bihar. Though nearly 80 years old, he was perhaps the most outstanding military leader and strategist of the Revolt. Maulavi Ahmadullah of Faizabad was another outstanding leader of the Revolt. He was a native of Madras, where he had started preaching armed rebellion. In January 1857, he moved towards the north to Faizabad where he fought a large-scale battle against a company of British troops sent to stop him from preaching sedition. When the general revolt broke out in May, he emerged as one of its acknowledged leaders in Awadh.

The greatest heroes of the Revolt were, however, the sepoys, many of whom displayed great courage in the field of battle and thousands of whom unselfishly laid down their lives. More than anything else, it was their determination and sacrifice that nearly led to the expulsion of the British from India. In this patriotic struggle, they sacrificed even their deep religious prejudices. They had revolted on the question of the greased cartridges but now, to expel the hated foreigner, they freely used the same cartridges in their battles.

THE WEAKNESSES OF THE REVOLT AND ITS SUPPRESSION

Even though it was spread over a vast territory and was widely popular among the people, the Revolt of 1857 could not embrace the entire country or all the groups and classes of Indian society. It did not spread to south India and most of eastern and western India because these regions had repeatedly rebelled earlier. Most rulers of the Indian states and the big zamindars, selfish to the core and fearful of British might, refused to join in. On the contrary, the Sindhia of Gwalior, the Holkar of Indore, the Nizam of Hyderabad, the Raja of Jodhpur and other Rajput rulers, the Nawab of Bhopal, the rulers of Patiala, Nabha, Jind, and other Sikh chieftains of Punjab, the Maharaja of Kashmir, the Ranas of Nepal, and many other ruling chiefs, and a large number of big zamindars gave active help to the British in suppressing the Revolt. In fact, no more than 1 per cent of the chiefs of India joined the Revolt. Governor-General Canning later remarked that these rulers and chiefs "acted as the breakwaters to the storm which would have otherwise swept us in one great wave". Madras, Bombay, Bengal and the western Punjab remained undisturbed, even though the popular feeling in these provinces favoured the rebels. Moreover, except for the discontented and the dispossessed zamindars, the middle and upper classes were mostly critical of the rebels; most of the propertied classes were either cool towards them or actively hostile to them. Even many of the *taluqdars* (big zamindars) of Awadh, who had joined the Revolt, abandoned it once the government gave them an assurance that their estates would be returned to them. This made it very difficult for the peasants and soldiers of Awadh to sustain a prolonged guerrilla campaign.

The moneylenders were the chief targets of the villagers' attacks. They were, therefore, naturally hostile to the Revolt. The merchants, too, gradually became unfriendly. The rebels were compelled to impose heavy taxation on them in order to finance the war or to seize their stocks of foodstuffs to feed the army. The merchants often hid their wealth and goods and refused to give free supplies to the rebels. The zamindars of Bengal also remained loyal to the British. They were, after all, a creation of the British. Moreover, the hostility of Bihar peasants towards their zamindars frightened the Bengal zamindars. Similarly, the big merchants of Bombay, Calcutta and Madras supported the British because their main profits came from foreign trade and economic connections with the British merchants.

The modern educated Indians also did not support the Revolt. They were repelled by the rebels' appeals to superstitions and their opposition to progressive social measures. As we have seen, the educated Indians wanted to end the backwardness of their country. They mistakenly believed that British rule would help them accomplish these tasks of modernisation while the rebels, led by zamindars, old rulers and chieftains and other feudal elements, would take the country backward. Only later did the educated Indians learn from experience that foreign rule was incapable of modernising the country and that it would instead impoverish it and keep it backward. The revolutionaries of 1857 proved to be more far-sighted in this respect; they had a better, instinctive understanding of the evils of foreign rule and of the necessity to get rid of it. On the other hand, they did not realise, as did the educated intelligentsia, that the country had fallen prey to foreigners precisely because it had stuck to rotten and outmoded customs, traditions and institutions. They failed to see that national salvation lay not in going back to feudal monarchy, but in going forward to a modern society, a modern economy, scientific education and modern political institutions. In any case, it cannot be said that the educated Indians were anti-national or loyal to a foreign regime. As events after 1858 were to show, they were soon to lead a powerful and modern national movement against British rule.

Whatever the reasons for the disunity of Indians, it was to prove fatal to the Revolt. But this was not the only weakness from which the cause of the rebels suffered. They were short of modern weapons and other materials of war. Most of them fought with such ancient weapons as pikes and swords. They were also poorly organised. The sepoys were brave and selfless, but they were also ill-disciplined. Sometimes they behaved more like a riotous mob than a disciplined army. The rebel units did not have common plans of military action, or authoritative heads, or centralised leadership. The uprisings in different parts of the country were completely uncoordinated. The leaders were joined together by a common feeling of hatred for the alien rule, but by nothing else. Once they overthrew British power from an area, they did not know what sort of political power or institutions to create in its place. They were suspicious and jealous of one another and often indulged in suicidal quarrels. Similarly, the peasantry, having destroyed revenue records and moneylenders' books, and overthrown the new zamindars, became passive, not knowing what to do next.

In fact, the weakness of the Revolt went deeper than the failings of individuals. The movement had little understanding of colonialism, which had overpowered India, or of the modern world. It lacked a forward looking programme, a coherent ideology, a political perspective or a vision of the future society and economy. The Revolt represented no societal alternative to be implemented after the capture of power. The diverse elements which took part in the Revolt were united only by their hatred of British rule, but each of them had different grievances and differing conceptions of the politics of free India. This absence of a modern and progressive programme enabled the reactionary princes and zamindars to seize the levers of power of the revolutionary movement. But the feudal character of the Revolt should not be stressed over too much. Gradually, the soldiers and the people were beginning to evolve a different type of leadership. The very effort to make the Revolt a success was compelling them to create new types of organisation. For example, at Delhi, a court of administrators consisting of 10 members, six armymen and four civilians, was established. All its decisions were taken by a majority vote. The court took all military and administrative decisions in the name of the emperor. Similar efforts to create new organisational structures were made in other centres of the rebellion. As Benjamin Disraeli warned the British government at the time, if they did not suppress the Revolt in time, they would "find other characters on the stage, with whom to contend, besides the princes of India".

The lack of unity among Indians was perhaps unavoidable at this stage of Indian history. Modern nationalism was yet unknown in India. Patriotism meant love of one's small locality or region, or at most one's state. All-India interests and the consciousness that these interests bound all Indians together were yet to come. In fact, the Revolt of 1857 played an important role in bringing the Indian people together and imparting to them the consciousness of belonging to one country.

In the end, British imperialism, with a developing capitalist economy and at the height of its power the world over, and supported by most of the Indian princes and chiefs, proved militarily too strong for the rebels. The British government poured immense supplies of men, money and arms into the country, though Indians had later to repay the entire cost of their own suppression. The Revolt was suppressed. Sheer courage could not win against a powerful and determined enemy who planned their every step. The rebels were dealt an early blow when the British captured Delhi on 20 September 1857 after prolonged and bitter fighting. The aged Emperor Bahadur Shah was taken prisoner. The Royal Princes were captured and butchered on the spot. The emperor was tried and exiled to Rangoon where he died in 1862, bitterly lamenting the fate which had buried him far away from the city of his birth. Thus the great House of the Mughals was finally and completely extinguished.

With the fall of Delhi, the focal point of the Revolt disappeared. The other leaders of the Revolt carried on the brave but unequal struggle, with the British mounting a powerful offensive against them. John Lawrence, Outram, Havelock, Neil, Campbell, and Hugh Rose were some of the British commanders who earned military fame in the course of this campaign. One by one, all the great leaders of the Revolt fell. Nana Sahib was defeated at Kanpur. Defiant to the very end and refusing to surrender, he escaped to Nepal early in 1859, never to be heard of again. Tantia Tope escaped into the jungles of central India where he carried on bitter and brilliant guerrilla warfare until April 1859, when he was betrayed by a zamindar friend and captured while asleep. He was put to death after a hurried trial on 15 April 1859. The Rani of Jhansi had died on the field of battle earlier on 17 June 1858. By 1859, Kunwar Singh, Bakht Khan, Khan Bahadur Khan of Bareilly, Rao Sahib, brother of Nana Sahib, and Maulavi Ahmadullah were all dead, while the Begum of Awadh was compelled to hide in Nepal.

By the end of 1859, British authority over India was fully re-established, but the Revolt had not been in vain. It is a glorious landmark in our history. Though it was a desperate effort to save India in the old way and under traditional leadership, it was the first great struggle of the Indian people for freedom from British imperialism. It paved the way for the rise of the modern national movement. The heroic and patriotic struggle of 1857, and the series of rebellions preceding it, left an unforgettable impression on the minds of the Indian people, established valuable local traditions of resistance to British rule, and served as a perennial source of inspiration in their later struggle for freedom. The heroes of the Revolt soon became household names in the country, even though the very mention of their names was frowned upon by the rulers.

Eight

Administrative Changes after 1858

The Revolt of 1857 gave a severe jolt to the British administration in India and made its reorganisation inevitable. The Government of India's structure and policies underwent significant changes in the decades following the Revolt. But more important for changes in the Indian economy and government was the inauguration of a new stage of colonialism in India.

The second half of the nineteenth century witnessed the spread and intensification of the Industrial Revolution. Gradually, other countries of Europe, the USA and Japan underwent industrialisation, and the manufacturing and financial supremacy of Britain in world economy came to an end. Intense world-wide competition for markets, sources of raw materials and outlets for capital investment now began. The competition for colonies and semi-colonies became increasingly intense and bitter as areas open to fresh colonial domination became scarce. Facing a challenge to its dominant position in world capitalism from newcomers, Britain began a vigorous effort to consolidate its control over its existing empire and to extend it further.

Moreover, after 1850, a very large amount of British capital was invested in railways, loans to the Government of India, and to a smaller extent in tea plantations, coal mining, jute mills, shipping, trade and banking. It was necessary that, to render this British capital secure from economic and political dangers, British rule in India be clamped down even more firmly. Consequently, there was a renewed upsurge of imperial control and imperialist ideology, which was reflected in the reactionary policies of the viceroyalties of Lytton, Dufferin, Lansdowne, Elgin and, above all, Curzon.

ADMINISTRATION

An Act of Parliament in 1858 transferred the power to govern from the East India Company to the British Crown. While authority over

Administrative Changes after 1858

India had previously been wielded by the directors of the Company and the Board of Control, now this power was to be exercised by a Secretary of State for India, aided by a Council. The Secretary of State was a member of the British Cabinet and as such was responsible to Parliament. Thus, the ultimate power over India remained with Parliament.

Under the Act, government was to be carried on as before by the Governor-General, who was also given the title of Viceroy or Crown's personal representative. With the passage of time, the Viceroy was increasingly reduced to a subordinate status in relation to the British government in matters of policy as well as execution of policy. The Secretary of State controlled the minutest details of administration. Thus the authority that exercised final and detailed control and direction over Indian affairs came to reside in London, thousands of miles away from India. Under such conditions, Indian opinion had even less impact on government policy than before. On the other hand, British industrialists, merchants and bankers increased their influence over the Government of India. This made the Indian administration even more reactionary than it was before 1858, for now even the pretence of liberalism was gradually given up.

In India, the Act of 1858 provided that the Governor-General would have an Executive Council whose members were to act as heads of different departments and as his official advisers. The Council discussed all important matters and decided them by a majority vote; but the Governor-General had the power to override any important decision of the Council.

The Indian Councils Act of 1861 enlarged the Governor-General's Council for the purpose of making laws, in which capacity it was known as the Imperial Legislative Council. The Governor-General was authorised to add to his Executive Council between six and 12 members, of whom at least half had to be non-officials who could be Indian or English. The Imperial Legislative Council possessed no real powers and should not be seen as a sort of elementary or weak parliament. It was merely an advisory body. It could not discuss any important measures, and no financial measures at all, without the previous approval of the government. It had no control over the budget. It could not discuss the actions of the administration; the members could not even ask questions about them. In other words, the Legislative Council had no control over the executive. Moreover, no bill passed by it could become an Act till it was approved by the Governor-General. On top of all this, the Secretary of State could disallow any of its Acts. Thus, the only important function of the Legislative Council was to ditto official measures and give them the appearance of having been passed by a legislative body. In theory, the non-official Indian members were added to the Council to represent Indian views. But the Indian members of the Legislative Council were few in number and were not elected by the Indian people but nominated by the Governor-General, whose choice invariably fell on princes and their ministers, big zamindars, big merchants, or retired senior government officials. They were thoroughly unrepresentative of the Indian people or of the growing nationalist opinion. The Government of India remained, as before 1858, an alien despot. This was no accident, but a conscious policy. Charles Wood, the Secretary of State for India, while moving the Indian Councils Bill of 1861, said: "All experience teaches us that where a dominant race rules another, the mildest form of government is a despotism."

Provincial Administration

The British had divided India for administrative convenience into provinces, three of which—Bengal, Madras and Bombay—were known as Presidencies. The Presidencies were administered by a Governor and his Executive Council of three, who were appointed by the Crown. The Presidency governments possessed more rights and powers than governments of other provinces, which were administered by Lieutenant Governors and Chief Commissioners appointed by the Governor-General.

The provincial governments enjoyed a great deal of autonomy before 1833, when their power to pass laws was taken away and their expenditure subjected to strict central control. But experience soon showed that a vast country like India could not be efficiently administered on the principle of strict centralisation.

The evil of extreme centralisation was most obvious in the field of finance. The revenues from all over the country and from different sources were gathered at the centre and then distributed by it to the provincial governments. The central government exercised strict control over the smallest details of provincial expenditure. But this system proved quite wasteful in practice. It was not possible for the central government to supervise the efficient collection of revenues by a provincial government or to keep adequate check over its expenditure. The authorities therefore decided to decentralise public finance.

The first step in the direction of separating central and provincial finances was taken in 1870 by Lord Mayo. The provincial governments were granted fixed sums out of central revenues for the administration of certain services like police, jails, education, medical services, and roads, and were asked to administer them as they wished. Lord Mayo's scheme was enlarged in 1877 by Lord Lytton, who transferred to the provinces certain other heads of expenditure like land revenue, excise, general administration, and law and justice. To meet the additional expenditure, a provincial government was to get a fixed share of the income realised from that province from certain sources like stamps, excise taxes, and income tax. Further changes in these arrangements were made in 1882. The system of giving fixed grants to the provinces was ended and, instead, a province was to get the entire income from certain sources or revenue within it and a fixed share of the income from other sources. Thus, all sources of revenue were now divided into three—general, provincial, and those to be divided between the centre and the provinces.

The different measures of financial decentralisation discussed above did not really mean the beginning of genuine provincial autonomy or of Indian participation in provincial administration. They were much more in the nature of administrative reorganisation, whose chief aims were to keep down expenditure and increase income. In theory as well as in practice, the central government remained supreme and continued to exercise effective and detailed control over the provincial governments. This was inevitable, for both the central government and the provincial governments were completely subordinated to the Secretary of State and the British government.

Local Bodies

Financial difficulties led the government to further decentralise administration by promoting local government through municipalities and district boards. The Industrial Revolution gradually transformed European economy and society in the nineteenth century. India's increasing contact with Europe and new modes of imperialism and economic exploitation made it necessary that some of the European advances in economy, sanitation, and education should be transplanted in India. Moreover, the rising Indian nationalist movement demanded the introduction of modern improvements in civic life. Thus the need for education of the masses, sanitation, water supply, better roads, and other civic amenities was increasingly felt. The government could no longer afford to ignore it. But its finances were already in disorder due to heavy expenditure on the army and the railways. It could not increase its income through new taxes, as the burden of the existing taxation was already very heavy on the poor and a further addition to it was likely to create discontent against the government. On the other hand, the government did not want to tax the upper classes, especially the British civil servants, planters and traders. But the authorities felt that the people would not mind paying new taxes if they knew that their proceeds would be spent on their own welfare. It was therefore decided to transfer local services like education, health, sanitation and water supply to local bodies, who would finance them through local taxes. Many Englishmen had pressed for the formation of local bodies on another ground as well. They believed that associating Indians with the administration in some capacity or the other would prevent their becoming politically disaffected. This association could take place at the level of local bodies without in any way endangering British monopoly of power in India.

Local bodies were first formed between 1864 and 1868, but almost in every case they consisted of nominated members and were presided over by District Magistrates. They did not, therefore, represent local self-government at all. Nor did intelligent Indians accept them as such. They looked upon them as instruments for the extraction of additional taxes from the people.

A step forward, though a very hesitant and inadequate one, was taken in 1882 by Lord Ripon's government. A government resolution laid down the policy of administering local affairs largely through rural and urban local bodies, a majority of whose members would be non-officials. These non-official members would be elected by the people wherever and whenever officials felt that it was possible to introduce elections. The resolution also permitted the election of a non-official as chairperson of a local body. But the elected members were in a minority in all the district boards and in many of the municipalities. They were, moreover, elected by a small number of voters, since the right to vote was severely restricted. District officials continued to act as presidents of district boards, though non-officials gradually became chairpersons of municipal committees. The government also retained the right to exercise strict control over the activities of the local bodies and suspend and supersede them at its own discretion. The result was that except in the Presidency cities of Calcutta, Madras and Bombay, the local bodies functioned just like departments of the government and were in no way good examples of local self-government. All the same, the politically conscious Indians welcomed Ripon's resolution and worked actively in these local bodies in the hope that in time, they could be transformed into effective organs of local self-government.

CHANGES IN THE ARMY

The Indian army was carefully reorganised after 1858, most of all to prevent the recurrence of another revolt. The rulers had seen that their bayonets were the only secure foundation of their rule. Several steps were taken to minimise, if not completely eliminate, the capacity of Indian soldiers to revolt. First, the domination of the army by its European branch was carefully guaranteed. The proportion of Europeans to Indians in the army was raised and fixed at one to two in the Bengal army and two to five in the Madras and Bombay armies. Further, the European troops were kept in key geographical and military positions. The crucial branches of the army like artillery and, later in the twentieth century, tanks and armoured corps were put exclusively in European hands. The older policy of excluding Indians from the officer corps was strictly maintained. Till 1914, no Indian could rise higher than the rank of a subedar. Second, the organisation of the Indian section of the army was based on the policy of 'balance and counterpoise' or 'divide and rule' so as to prevent any chance of uniting again in an anti-British uprising. Discrimination on the basis of caste, region and religion was practised in recruitment to the army. A fiction was created that Indians consisted of 'martial' and 'non-martial' classes. Soldiers from Awadh, Bihar, central India, and south India, who had first helped the British conquer India but had later taken part in the Revolt of 1857, were declared to be non-martial. They were no longer taken in the army on a large scale. On the other hand, Punjabis, Gurkhas, and Pathans, who had assisted in the suppression of the Revolt, were declared to be martial and were recruited in large numbers. By 1875, half the British Indian army was being recruited from Punjab. In addition, Indian regiments were made up of a mixture of various castes and groups, which were so placed as to balance each other. Communal, caste, tribal and regional loyalties were encouraged among the soldiers so that the sentiment of nationalism would not grow among them. For example, caste and communal companies were introduced in most regiments. Charles Wood, Secretary of State for India, wrote to Viceroy Canning in 1861:

> I never wish to see again a great army, very much the same in its feelings and prejudices and connections, confident in its strength, and so disposed to rise in rebellion together. If one regiment mutinies, I should like to have the next regiment so alien that it would be ready to fire into it.

Thus, the Indian army remained a purely mercenary force. Moreover, every effort was made to keep it separate from the life and thoughts of the rest of the population. It was isolated from nationalist ideas by every possible means. Newspapers, journals and nationalist publications were prevented from reaching the soldiers. But, as we shall see later, all such efforts failed in the long run and sections of the Indian army played an important role in India's struggle for freedom.

The Indian army became in time a very costly military machine. In 1904, it absorbed nearly 52 per cent of the Indian revenues. This was because it served more than one purpose. India, being the most prized colonial possession of the time, had to be constantly defended from the competing imperialisms of Russia, France and Germany. This led to a big increase in the size of the Indian army. Second, the Indian troops were not maintained for India's defence alone. The Indian army was the chief instrument for the expansion and consolidation of British power and possessions in Asia and Africa. Lastly, the British section of the army served as an army of occupation. It was the ultimate guarantee of the British hold over the country. Its cost had, however, to be met by Indian revenues; it was in fact a very heavy burden on them.

Public Services

We have seen that Indians had little control over the Government of India. They were not permitted to play any part in the making of laws or in determining administrative policies. In addition, they were excluded from the bureaucracy, which put these policies into practice. All positions of power and responsibility in the administration were occupied by members of the Indian Civil Service who were recruited through an annual open competitive examination, held in London. Indians could also appear for this examination. Satyendranath Tagore, brother of Rabindranath Tagore, was the first Indian to do so successfully in 1863. Almost every year thereafter, one or two Indians joined the coveted ranks of the Civil Service, but their number was negligible compared with that of the English entrants. In practice, the doors of the Civil Service remained barred to Indians for they suffered from numerous handicaps. The competitive examination was held in faraway London. It was conducted through the medium of the alien English language. It was based on Classical Greek and Latin learning, which could be acquired only after a prolonged and costly course of studies in England. In addition, the maximum age for entry into the Civil Service was gradually reduced from 23 in 1859 to 19 in 1878. If a young Indian of 23 found it difficult to succeed in the Civil Service competition, the Indian aged 19 found it almost impossible to do so.

In other departments of administration—police, public works, medicine, post and telegraphs, forests, engineering, customs and, later, railways—the superior and highly paid posts were likewise reserved for British citizens.

This preponderance of Europeans in all strategic posts was not accidental. The rulers of India believed it to be an essential condition for the maintenance of British supremacy in India. Thus Lord Kimberley, Secretary of State, laid down in 1893 that "it is indispensable that an adequate number of the members of the Civil Service shall always be Europeans"; and the Viceroy, Lord Lansdowne, stressed "the absolute necessity of keeping the government of this widespread empire in European hands, if that empire is to be maintained."

Under Indian pressure, the different administrative services were gradually Indianised after 1918; but the positions of control and authority were still kept in British hands. Also, the people soon discovered that Indianisation of these services had not put any part of political power in their hands. The Indians in these services functioned as agents of British rule and loyally served Britain's imperial purposes.

Relations with the Princely States

The Revolt of 1857 led the British to reverse their policy towards the Indian states. Before 1857, they had availed themselves of every opportunity to annex princely states. This policy was now abandoned. Most of the Indian princes had not only remained loyal to the British, but had also actively aided the latter in suppressing the Revolt. As Lord Canning, the Viceroy, put it, they had acted as "breakwaters in the storm". Their loyalty was now rewarded with the announcement that their right to adopt heirs would be respected and the integrity of their territories guaranteed against future annexation. Moreover, the experience of the Revolt had convinced the British authorities that the princely states could serve as useful allies and supporters in case of popular opposition or revolt.

Canning wrote in 1860:

> It was long ago said by Sir John Malcolm that if we made All India into Zillahs (districts), it was not in the nature of things that our Empire should last 50 years: but that if we could keep up a number of Native States without political power, but as royal instruments, we should exist in India as long as our naval supremacy was maintained. Of the substantial truth of this opinion I have no doubt; and the recent events have made it more deserving of our attention than ever.

It was, therefore, decided to use the princely states as firm props of British rule in India. As the British historian P.E. Roberts remarked: "to preserve them as a bulwark of the empire has ever since been a principle of British policy."

Their perpetuation was, however, only one aspect of the British policy towards princely states. The other was their complete subordination to the British authorities. While even before the Revolt of 1857 the British had in practice interfered in the internal affairs of these states, in theory they had been considered subsidiary but sovereign powers. This position was now entirely changed. As the price of their continued existence, the princes were made to acknowledge Britain as the paramount power. In 1876, Queen Victoria assumed the title of the Empress of India to emphasise British sovereignty over the entire Indian subcontinent. Lord Curzon later made it clear that the princes ruled their states merely as agents of the British Crown. The princes accepted this subordinate position and willingly became junior partners in the empire because they were assured of their continued existence as rulers of their states.

As the paramount power, the British claimed the right to supervise the internal government of the princely states. They not only interfered in the day-to-day administration through the Residents, but also insisted on appointing and dismissing ministers and other high officials. Sometimes the rulers themselves were removed or deprived of their powers. One motive for such interference as provided by the British was their desire to give these states a modern administration so that their integration with British India would be complete. This integration and the consequent interference were also encouraged by the development of all-India railways, postal and telegraph systems, currency, and a common economic life. Another motive for interference was provided by the growth of popular democratic and nationalist movements in many of the states. On the one hand, the British authorities helped the rulers suppress these movements; on the other, they tried to eliminate the most serious of administrative abuses in these states.

Administrative Policies

British attitude towards India and, consequently, their policies in the subcontinent changed for the worse after the Revolt of 1857. While before 1857 they had tried, however half-heartedly and hesitantly, to modernise India, they now consciously began to follow reactionary policies. As the historian Percival Spear has put it, "the Indian Government's honeymoon with progress was over."

We have seen above how the organs of administrative control in India and in England, the Indian army and the civil service were reorganised to exclude Indians from an effective share in administration. Previously, at least lip-service had been paid to the idea that the British were 'training' and 'preparing' the Indians for self-government and that they would eventually transfer political power into their hands. The view was now openly put forward that because of their inherent social and cultural defects, the Indians were unfit to rule themselves and must be ruled by Britain for an indefinite period. This reactionary policy was reflected in many fields.

Divide and Rule: The British had conquered India by taking advantage of the disunity among the Indian powers and by playing them against one another. After 1858, they continued to follow this policy of divide and rule by turning the princes against the people, province against province, caste against caste, group against group and, above all, Hindus against Muslims.

The unity displayed by Hindus and Muslims during the Revolt of 1857 had disturbed the foreign rulers. They were determined to break this unity so as to weaken the rising nationalist movement. In fact, they missed no opportunity to do so. Immediately after the Revolt, they repressed Muslims, confiscated their lands and property on a large scale, and declared Hindus to be their favourites. After 1870, this policy was reversed and an attempt was made to turn upper-class and middle-class Muslims against the nationalist movement.

The government cleverly used the attractions of government service to create a split along religious lines among the educated Indians. Because of industrial and commercial backwardness and the near-absence of social services, educated Indians depended almost entirely on government service for employment. There were few other openings for them. This led to keen competition among them for the available government posts. The government utilised this competition to fan provincial and communal rivalry and hatred. It promised official favours on a communal basis in return for loyalty, and so played educated Muslims against educated Hindus.

Hostility towards Educated Indians: The Government of India had actively encouraged modern education after 1833. The Universities of Calcutta, Bombay and Madras were started in 1857 and higher education spread rapidly thereafter. Many British officials commended the refusal of educated Indians to participate in the Revolt of 1857. But this favourable official attitude towards educated Indians soon changed because some of them had begun to use their recently acquired modern knowledge to analyse the imperialistic character of British rule and to put forward demands for Indian participation in administration. The officials became actively hostile to higher education and to educated Indians when the latter began to organise a nationalist movement among the people and founded the Indian National Congress in 1885. The officials now took active steps to curtail higher education. They sneered at the educated Indians, whom they commonly referred to as *babus*.

Thus, the British turned against that group of Indians who had imbibed modern Western knowledge and who stood for progress along modern lines. Such progress was, however, opposed to the basic interests and policies of British imperialism in India. The official opposition to educated Indians and higher education shows that British rule in India had already exhausted whatever potential for progress it originally possessed.

Attitude towards the Zamindars: While being hostile to the forward-looking educated Indians, the British now turned for friendship to the most reactionary group of Indians, the princes, zamindars and landlords. We have already examined above the changed policy towards the princes and the official attempt to use them as a dam against the rise of popular and nationalist movements. The zamindars and landlords too were placated in the same manner. For example, the lands of most of the talukdars of Awadh were restored to them. The zamindars and landlords were now hailed as the traditional and 'natural' leaders of the Indian people. Their interests and privileges were protected. They were secured in the possession of their land at the cost of the peasants and were utilised as counterweights against the nationalist-minded intelligentsia. The Viceroy Lord Lytton openly declared in 1876 that "the Crown of England should henceforth be identified with the hopes, the aspirations, the sympathies and interests of a powerful native aristocracy." The zamindars and landlords in return recognised that their position was closely bound up with the maintenance of British rule and became its firm supporters.

Attitude towards Social Reforms: As a part of the policy of alliance with the conservative classes, the British abandoned their previous policy of helping the social reformers. They believed that their measures of social reform, such as the abolition of the custom of *sati* and permission to widows to remarry, had been a major cause of the Revolt of 1857. They therefore gradually began to side with orthodox opinion and stopped their support to the reformers.

Thus, as Jawaharlal Nehru put it in *Discovery of India*, "Because of this natural alliance of the British power with the reactionaries in India, it became the guardian and upholder of many an evil custom and practice, which it otherwise condemned." In fact, the British were in this respect on the horns of a dilemma. If they favoured social reform and passed laws to this effect, the orthodox Indians opposed them and declared that a government of foreigners had no right to interfere in the internal social affairs of Indians. On the other hand, if they did not pass such laws, they helped to perpetuate social evils and were condemned by socially-progressive Indians. It may, however, be noted that the British did not always remain neutral on social questions. By supporting the status quo, they indirectly gave protection to existing social evils. Moreover, by encouraging casteism and communalism for political purposes, they actively encouraged social fragmentation and backwardness.

Extreme Backwardness of Social Services: While social services like education, sanitation and public health, water supply, and rural roads made rapid progress in Europe during the nineteenth century, in India they remained at an extremely backward level. The Government of India spent most of its large income on the army and wars and the administrative services, and starved the social services. For example, in 1886, of its total net revenue of nearly Rs 47 crore, the Government of India spent nearly Rs 19.41 crore on the army and Rs 17 crore on civil administration, but less than Rs 2 crore on education, medicine, and public health and only Rs 65 lakh on irrigation. The few halting steps that were taken in the direction of providing services like sanitation, water supply and public health were usually confined to urban areas, and that too to the so-called civil lines or British or modern parts of the cities. They mainly served the Europeans and a handful of upper-class Indians who lived in the European part of the cities.

Labour Legislation: The condition of workers in modern factories and plantations in the nineteenth century was miserable. They had to work between 12 and 16 hours a day and there was no weekly day of rest. Women and children worked the same long hours as men. The wages were extremely low, ranging from Rs 4 to Rs 20 per month. The factories were overcrowded, badly lit and aired, and completely unhygienic. Work on machines was hazardous, and accidents very common.

The Government of India, which was generally pro-capitalist, took some half-hearted and totally inadequate steps to mitigate the sorry state of affairs in the modern factories, many of which were owned by Indians. In this, it was only in part moved by humanitarian considerations. The manufacturers of Britain put constant pressure on it to pass factory laws. They were afraid that cheap labour would enable Indian manufacturers to outsell them in the Indian market. The first Indian Factory Act was passed in 1881. The Act dealt primarily with the problem of child labour. It laid down that children between seven years and 12 years of age would not work for more than nine hours a day. Children would also get four holidays in a month. The Act also provided for the proper fencing off of dangerous machinery. The second Indian Factories Act was passed in 1891. It provided for a weekly holiday for all workers. Working hours for women were fixed at 11 hours per day, whereas daily hours of work for children were reduced to seven. Hours of work for men were still left unregulated.

Neither of these two Acts applied to British-owned tea and coffee plantations. On the contrary, the government gave every help to the foreign planters to exploit their workers in a most ruthless manner.

Most of the tea plantations were situated in Assam, which was very thinly populated and had an unhealthy climate. Labour to work in these plantations had therefore to be brought from outside. The planters would not attract workers from outside by paying high wages. Instead, they used coercion and fraud to recruit them and then keep them as virtual slaves on the plantations. The Government of India gave planters full help and passed penal laws in 1863, 1865, 1870, 1873 and 1882 to enable them to do so. Once a labourer had signed a contract to go and work in a plantation, he could not refuse to do so. Any breach of contract by a labourer was a criminal offence, the planter also having the power to arrest him.

Better labour laws were, however, passed in the twentieth century under pressure from the rising trade union movement. Still, the condition of the Indian working class remained extremely depressed and deplorable. The average worker lived below the margin of subsistence. Summing up the condition of the Indian workers under British rule, Professor Jurgen Kuczynski, the well-known German economic historian, wrote in 1938: "Underfed, housed like animals, without light and air and water, the Indian industrial worker is one of the most exploited of all in the world of industrial capitalism."

Restrictions on the Press: The British had introduced the printing press in India and thus initiated the development of the modern press. The educated Indians had immediately recognised that the press could play a great role in educating public opinion and in influencing government policies through criticism and censure. Rammohun Roy, Vidyasagar, Dadabhai Naoroji, Justice Ranade, Surendranath Banerjea, Lokamanya Tilak, G. Subramaniya Iyer, C. Karunakara Menon, Madan Mohan Malaviya, Lala Lajpat Rai, Bipin Chandra Pal, and other Indian leaders played an important part in starting newspapers and making them a powerful political force. The press gradually became a major weapon of the nationalist movement.

The Indian press was freed of restrictions by Charles Metcalfe in 1835. This step was welcomed enthusiastically by educated Indians. It was one of the reasons why they had for sometime supported British rule in India. But the nationalists gradually began to use the press to arouse national consciousness among the people and to sharply criticise the reactionary policies of the government. This turned the officials against the Indian press and they decided to curb its freedom. This was attempted by passing the Vernacular Press Act in 1878. This Act placed serious restrictions on the freedom of the Indian-language newspapers. Indian public opinion was now fully aroused and it protested loudly against the passage of this Act. This protest had immediate effect and the Act was repealed in 1882. For nearly 25 years thereafter, the Indian press enjoyed considerable freedom. But the rise of the Swadeshi and Boycott movements after 1905 once again led to the enactment of repressive press laws in 1908 and 1910.

RACIAL ANTAGONISM

The British in India had always held aloof from the Indians, believing that social distance from Indians had to be maintained to preserve their authority over them. They also considered themselves racially superior. The Revolt of 1857 and the atrocities committed by both sides had further widened the gulf between the Indians and the British, who now began to openly assert the doctrine of racial supremacy and practise racial arrogance. Railway compartments, waiting rooms at railway stations, parks, hotels, swimming pools, clubs, etc., reserved for 'Europeans only' were visible manifestations of this racialism. The Indians felt humiliated. In the words of Jawaharlal Nehru:

> ... We in India have known racialism in all its forms ever since the commencement of British rule. The whole ideology of this rule was that of Herrenvolk and the Master Race, and the structure of government was based upon it; indeed the idea of a master race is inherent in imperialism. There was no subterfuge about it; it was proclaimed in unambiguous language by those in authority. More powerful than words was the practice that accompanied them, and generation after generation and year after year, India as a nation and Indians as individuals, were subjected to insult, humiliation and contemptuous treatment. The English were an imperial Race, we were told, with God-given right to govern us and keep us in subjection; if we protested we were reminded of the 'tiger qualities of an imperial race'.

Foreign Policy

Under British rule, India developed relations with its neighbours on a new basis. This was the result of two factors. The development of modern means of communication and the political and administrative consolidation of the country impelled the Government of India to reach out to the natural, geographical frontiers of India. This was essential both for defence and internal cohesion. Inevitably, this tended to lead to some border clashes. Unfortunately, sometimes the Government of India went beyond the natural and traditional frontiers. The other factor was the alien character of the Government of India. The foreign policy of a free country is basically different from the foreign policy of a country ruled by a foreign power. In the former case, it is based on the needs and interests of the people of the country; in the latter, it serves primarily the interests of the ruling country. In India's case, the foreign policy that the Government of India followed was dictated by the British government. The British government had two major aims in Asia and Africa: the protection of its invaluable Indian empire and the expansion of British commerce and other economic interests in Africa and Asia. Both these aims led to British expansion and territorial conquests outside India's natural frontiers. Moreover, these aims brought the British government into conflict with other imperialist nations of Europe, who also wanted to extend their territorial possessions and commerce in Afro-Asian lands.

The desire to defend their Indian empire, to promote British economic interests, and to keep the other European powers at arm's length from India often led the British Indian government to commit aggression on India's neighbours. In other words, during the period of British domination, India's relations with its neighbours were ultimately determined by the needs of British imperialism.

But, while Indian foreign policy served British imperialism, the cost of its implementation was borne by India. In pursuance of British interests, India had to wage many wars against its neighbours; Indian soldiers had to shed their blood and Indian taxpayers had to meet the heavy cost.

War with Nepal, 1814: The British desire to extend its Indian empire to its natural geographical frontier brought them into conflict, first of all, with the northern Kingdom of Nepal. In October 1814, a clash between the border police of the two countries led to open war. The British were far superior in men, money and materials. In the end, the Nepal government had to make peace on British terms. It accepted a British Resident. It ceded the districts of Garhwal and Kumaon and abandoned claims to the *Tarai* areas. It also withdrew from Sikkim. The agreement held many advantages for the British. Their Indian empire now reached the Himalayas. They gained greater facilities for trade with Central Asia. They also obtained sites for important hill-stations, such as Shimla, Mussoorie and Nainital. Moreover, the Gurkhas gave added strength to the British-Indian army by joining it in large numbers.

Conquest of Burma: Through three successive wars, the independent kingdom of Burma was conquered by the British during the nineteenth century. The conflict between Burma and British India was initiated by border clashes and fanned by expansionist urges. The British merchants cast covetous glances at the forest resources of Burma and were keen to promote the export of their manufactures among its people. The British authorities also wanted to check the spread of French commercial and political influence in Burma and the rest of Southeast Asia.

Burma and British India developed a common frontier at the close of the eighteenth century when both were expanding powers. After centuries of internal strife, Burma was united by King Alaungpaya between 1752–60. His successor, Bodawpaya, ruling from Ava on the river Irrawaddi, repeatedly invaded Siam, repelled many Chinese invasions, and conquered the border states of Arakan (1785) and Manipur (1813), bringing Burma's border up to that of British India. Continuing his westward expansion, he threatened Assam and the Brahmaputra valley. Finally, in 1822, the Burmese conquered Assam. The Burmese occupation of Arakan and Assam led to continuous friction along the ill-defined border between Bengal and Burma.

In 1824, the British-Indian authorities declared war on Burma. After an initial setback, the British forces drove the Burmese out of Assam, Cachar, Manipur and Arakan. The British expeditionary forces by sea occupied Rangoon in May 1824 and reached within 72 km of the capital at Ava. Peace came in February 1826 with the Treaty of Yandabo. The Government of Burma agreed to the following conditions: (1) to pay one crore of rupees as war compensation; (2) to cede its coastal provinces of Arakan and Tenasserim; (3) to abandon all claims to Assam, Cachar, and Jaintia; (4) to recognise Manipur as an independent state; (5) to negotiate a commercial treaty with Britain; and (6) to accept a British Resident at Ava while posting a Burmese envoy at Calcutta. By this treaty, the British deprived Burma of most of its coastline, and acquired a firm base in Burma for future expansion.

The Second Burmese War, which broke out in 1852, was almost wholly the result of British commercial greed. British timber firms had begun to take an interest in the timber resources of Upper Burma. Moreover, the large population of Burma appeared to the British as a vast market for the sale of British cotton goods and other manufactures. The British, already in occupation of Burma's two coastal provinces, now wanted to dominate commercial relations with the rest of the country. They also wanted to strengthen their hold over Burma by peace or by war before their trade competitors, the French or the Americans, could establish themselves there. A full British expedition was despatched to Burma in April 1852. This time, the war was much shorter than in 1824–26 and the British victory more decisive. The British annexed Pegu, the only remaining coastal province of Burma. There was, however, a great deal of popular guerrilla resistance for three years before Lower Burma was brought under effective control. The British now controlled the whole of Burma's coastline and its entire sea-trade. The brunt of fighting the war was borne by Indian soldiers and its expense was wholly met from Indian revenues.

Relations between Burma and the British remained peaceful for several years after the annexation of Pegu. The British, of course, continued their efforts to open up Upper Burma. In particular, the British merchants and industrialists were attracted by the possibility of trade with China through Burma. In 1885, King Thibaw signed a purely commercial treaty with France, providing for trade. The British were intensely jealous of the growing French influence in Burma. The British merchants feared that the rich Burmese market would be captured by their French and American rivals. The chambers of

Administrative Changes after 1858

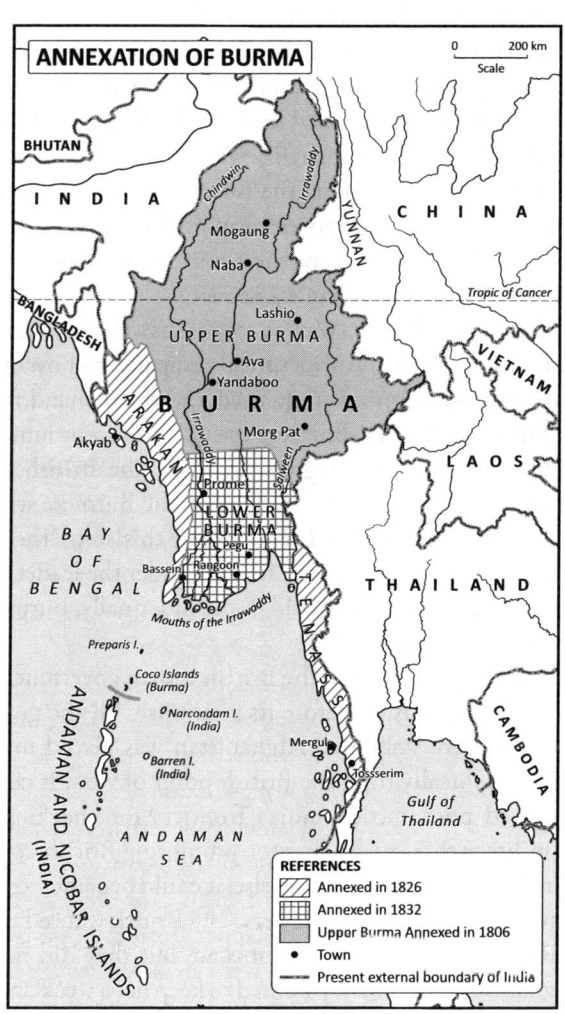

commerce in Britain and the British merchants in Rangoon now pressed the willing British government for the immediate annexation of Upper Burma. The British invaded Burma on 13 November 1885. King Thibaw surrendered on 28 November 1885 and his dominions were annexed to the Indian empire soon after.

The ease with which Burma had been conquered proved to be deceptive. The patriotic soldiers and officers of the Burmese army refused to surrender and vanished into the thick jungles. From there, they carried on widespread guerrilla warfare. The people of Lower Burma also rose up in rebellion. The British had to employ a 40,000 strong army for nearly five years to suppress the popular revolt. The expenses of the war as well as of the campaign of suppression were once again thrown on the Indian exchequer.

After the First World War, a vigorous modern nationalist movement arose in Burma. A widespread campaign to boycott British goods and administration was organised and the demand for Home Rule was put forward. The Burmese nationalists soon joined hands with the Indian National Congress. In 1935, the British separated Burma from India in the hope of weakening the Burmese struggle for freedom. The Burmese nationalists opposed this step. The Burmese nationalist movement reached new heights under the leadership of U. Aung San during the Second World War. And, finally, Burma won its independence on 4 January 1948.

Relations with Afghanistan: The British Indian government fought two wars with Afghanistan before its relations with the government of Afghanistan were stabilised. Afghanistan was placed in a crucial position geographically from the British point of view. It could serve as an advanced post outside India's frontiers for checking Russia's potential military threat as well as for promoting British commercial interests in Central Asia. If nothing else, it could become a convenient buffer between the two hostile powers. The British wanted to weaken and end Russian influence in Afghanistan, but they did not want a strong Afghanistan either. They wanted to keep her a weak and divided country which they could easily control.

The British decided to replace the independent ruler of Afghanistan, Dost Muhammed, with a 'friendly', i.e. subordinate, ruler. Their gaze fell on Shah Shuja, who had been deposed from the Afghan throne in 1809 and who had been living since then at

Ludhiana as a British pensioner, and they decided to put him back on the Afghan throne. Thus, without any reason or excuse, the British government decided to interfere in the internal affairs of Afghanistan and to commit aggression on this small neighbour. The British launched an attack on Afghanistan in February 1839. Most of the Afghan tribes had already been won over with bribes. Kabul fell to the English on 7 August 1839, and Shah Shuja was immediately placed on the throne. But Shah Shuja was detested and despised by the people of Afghanistan, especially as he had come back with the help of foreign bayonets. Many Afghan tribes rose in revolt. Then suddenly, on 2 November 1841, an uprising broke out at Kabul and the sturdy Afghans fell upon the British forces.

On 11 December 1841, the British were compelled to sign a treaty with the Afghan chiefs by which they agreed to evacuate Afghanistan and to restore Dost Muhammed. But the story did not end there. As the British forces withdrew, they were attacked all along the way. Out of 16,000 men, only one reached the frontier alive, while a few others survived as prisoners. Thus, the entire Afghan adventure ended in total failure. The British Indian government now organised a new expedition. Kabul was reoccupied on 16 September 1842. But it had learnt its lesson well. Having avenged its recent defeat and humiliation, it arrived at a settlement with Dost Muhammed, by which the British evacuated Kabul and recognised him as the independent ruler of Afghanistan.

The First Afghan War cost India over one and a half crores of rupees and its army nearly 20,000 men. The British now followed a policy of non-interference in Afghanistan's internal affairs. During the 1860s, as Russia again turned its attention to Central Asia after its defeat in the Crimean War, the British followed the policy of strengthening Afghanistan as a powerful buffer. They gave the Amir of Kabul aid and assistance to help him discipline his rivals internally and maintain his independence from foreign enemies. Thus, by a policy of non interference and occasional help, the Amir was prevented from aligning himself with Russia.

From 1870 onwards, there was a resurgence of imperialism all over the world. Anglo-Russian rivalry was also intensified. British statesmen once again thought of bringing Afghanistan under direct political control so that it could serve as a base for British expansion in Central Asia. To force British terms on Sher Ali, the Afghan ruler, a new attack on Afghanistan was launched in 1878. This is known as the Second Afghan War. Peace came in May 1879 when Sher Ali's son, Yakub Khan, signed the Treaty of Gandamak by which the British secured all they had desired. They secured certain border districts, the right to keep a Resident at Kabul, and control over Afghanistan's foreign policy.

The British success was short-lived. The national pride of the Afghans had been hurt and once again they rose to defend their independence. On 3 September 1879, the British Resident, Major Cavagnari, and his military escort were attacked and killed by rebellious Afghan troops. Afghanistan was again invaded and occupied. But the Afghans had made their point. The British reversed their policy and went back to the policy of non-interference in the internal affairs of a strong and friendly Afghanistan. Abdur Rahman, a grandson of Dost Muhammed, was recognised as the new ruler of Afghanistan. Abdur Rahman agreed not to maintain political relations with any power except the British. Thus, the Amir of Afghanistan lost control of his foreign policy and, to that extent, became a dependent ruler. At the same time, he retained complete control over his country's internal affairs.

The First World War and the Russian Revolution of 1917 created a new situation in Anglo-Afghan relations. The Afghans now demanded full independence from British control. Habibullah, who had succeeded Abdur Rahman in 1901 as Amir, was assassinated on 20 February 1919 and his son, Amanullah, the new Amir, declared open war on British India. Peace came in 1921 when, by a treaty, Afghanistan recovered its independence in foreign affairs.

Nine

The Economic Impact of British Rule

The British conquest had a pronounced and profound economic impact on India. There was hardly any aspect of the Indian economy that was not changed for better or for worse during the entire period of British rule down to 1947.

Disruption of the Traditional Economy

The economic policies followed by the British led to the rapid transformation of India's economy into a colonial economy whose nature and structure were determined by the needs of the British economy. In this respect, the British conquest of India differed from all previous foreign conquests. The previous conquerors had overthrown Indian political powers, but had made no basic changes in the country's economic structure; they had gradually become a part of Indian life, political as well as economic. The peasant, the artisan and the trader had continued to lead the same type of existence as before. The basic economic pattern, that of the self-sufficient rural economy, had been perpetuated. Change of rulers had merely meant a change in the personnel of those who appropriated the peasant's surplus. But the British conquerors were entirely different. They completely disrupted the traditional structure of the Indian economy. Moreover, they never became an integral part of Indian life. They always remained foreigners in the land, exploiting Indian resources and carrying away India's wealth as tribute.

The results of this subordination of the Indian economy to the interests of British trade and industry were many and varied.

Ruin of Artisans and Craftsmen

There was a sudden and quick collapse of the urban handicrafts industry, which had for centuries made India's name a byword in the markets of the entire civilised world. This collapse was caused largely by competition with the cheaper, imported machinemade goods from Britain. As we have seen earlier, the British imposed a policy of one-way free trade on India after 1813 and the invasion of British manufactures, in particular cotton textiles, immediately followed. Indian goods made with primitive techniques could not compete with goods produced on a mass scale by powerful steam-operated machines.

The ruin of Indian industries, particularly rural artisan industries, proceeded even more rapidly once the railways were built. The railways enabled British manufactures to reach and uproot the traditional industries in the remotest villages of the country. As the American writer, D.H. Buchanan, has put it, "The armour of the isolated self-sufficient village was pierced by the steel rail, and its life blood ebbed away."

The cotton-weaving and spinning industries were the worst hit. Silk and woollen textiles fared no better and a similar fate overtook the iron, pottery, glass, paper, metals, guns, shipping, oil-pressing, tanning and dyeing industries.

Apart from the influx of foreign goods, some other factors arising from British conquest also contributed to the ruin of Indian industries. The oppression practised by the East India Company and its servants on the craftsmen of Bengal during the second half of the eighteenth century, forcing them to sell their goods below the market price and to hire their services below the prevailing wage, compelled a large number of them to abandon their ancestral professions. In the normal course, Indian handicrafts would have benefited from the encouragement given by the Company to their export, but this oppression had an opposite effect.

The high import duties and other restrictions imposed on the import of Indian goods into Britain and Europe during the eighteenth and nineteenth centuries, combined with the development of modern manufacturing industries in Britain, led to the virtual closing of European markets to Indian manufacturers after 1820. The gradual disappearance of Indian rulers and their courts, who were the main customers of the handicrafts produced, also dealt a big blow to these industries. "For instance, the Indian states were completely dependent on the British in the production of military weapons." Moreover,

Indian rulers and nobles were replaced as the ruling class by British officials and military officers, who patronised their own home-products almost exclusively. This increased the cost of handicrafts and reduced their capacity to compete with foreign goods.

The ruin of Indian handicrafts was reflected in the ruin of the towns and cities famous for their manufacture. Cities which had withstood the ravages of war and plunder failed to survive British conquest. Dhaka, Surat, Murshidabad, and many other populous and flourishing industrial centres were depopulated and laid waste. By the end of the nineteenth century, the urban population formed barely 10 per cent of the total population. William Bentinck, the Governor-General, reported in 1834–35: "The misery hardly finds a parallel in the history of commerce. The bones of the cotton-weavers are bleaching the plains of India."

The tragedy was heightened by the fact that the decay of the traditional industries was not accompanied by the growth of modern machine industries, as was the case in Britain and Western Europe. Consequently, the ruined handicraftsmen and artisans failed to find alternative employment. The only choice open to them was to crowd into agriculture. Moreover, British rule also upset the balance of economic life in the villages. The gradual destruction of rural crafts broke up the union between agriculture and domestic industry in the countryside and thus contributed to the destruction of the self-sufficient rural economy. On the one hand, millions of peasants, who had supplemented their income by part-time spinning and weaving, now had to rely overwhelmingly on cultivation; on the other, millions of rural artisans lost their traditional livelihood and became agricultural labourers or petty tenants holding tiny plots. They added to the general pressure on land.

Thus, British conquest led to the de-industrialisation of the country and increased dependence of the people on agriculture. No figures for the earlier period are available but, according to Census Reports, between 1901 and 1941 alone the percentage of population dependent on agriculture increased from 63.7 per cent to 70 per cent. This increasing pressure on agriculture was one of the major causes of the extreme poverty in India under British rule.

In fact, India now became an agricultural colony of manufacturing Britain, which needed it as a source of raw materials for its industries. Nowhere was the change more glaring than in the cotton textile industry. While India had been for centuries the largest exporter of cotton goods in the world, it was now transformed into an importer of British cotton products and an exporter of raw cotton.

Impoverishment of the Peasantry

The peasant was also progressively impoverished under British rule. Although he was now free from internal wars, his material condition deteriorated and he steadily sank into poverty.

In the very beginning of British rule in Bengal, the policy of Clive and Warren Hastings of extracting the largest possible land revenue had led to such devastation that even Cornwallis complained that one-third of Bengal had been transformed into "a jungle inhabited only by wild beasts". Nor did improvement occur later. In both the Permanently and the Temporarily Settled Zamindari areas, the lot of the peasants remained unenviable. They were left to the mercies of the zamindars who raised rents to unbearable limits, compelled them to pay illegal dues and to perform forced labour or *begar*, and oppressed them in diverse other ways.

The condition of the cultivators in the Ryotwari and Mahalwari areas was no better. Here, the government took the place of the zamindars and levied excessive land revenue, which was in the beginning fixed as high as one-third to one-half of the produce. Heavy assessment of land was one of the main causes of the growth of poverty and the deterioration of agriculture in the nineteenth century. Many contemporary writers and officials noted this fact. For instance, Bishop Heber wrote in 1826:

> Neither Native nor European agriculturist, I think, can thrive at the present rate of taxation. Half of the gross produce of the soil is demanded by government. ... In Hindustan [Northern India] I found a general feeling among the King's officers ... that the peasantry in the Company's Provinces are on the whole worse off, poorer and more dispirited than the subjects of the Native Provinces; and here in Madras, where the soil is, generally speaking, poor, the difference is said to be still more marked. The fact is, no Native Prince demands the rent which we do.

Even though the land revenue demand went on increasing year after year—it increased from Rs 15.3 crore in 1857–58 to Rs 35.8 crore in 1936–37—the proportion of the total produce taken as land revenue tended to decline, especially in the twentieth century as the prices rose and production increased. No proportional increase in land revenue was made, as the disastrous consequences of demanding extortionate revenue became obvious. But by now, the population pressure on agriculture had increased to such an extent that the lesser revenue demand of later years weighed on the peasants as heavily as the higher revenue demand of the earlier years of the Company's administration. Moreover, by the twentieth century, the agrarian economy had been ruined and the landlords, moneylenders and merchants had made deep inroads into the village.

The evil of high revenue demand was made worse because the peasant got little economic return for his labour. The government spent very little on improving agriculture. It devoted almost its entire income to meeting the needs of the British-Indian administration, making the payments of direct and indirect tribute to England, and serving the interests of British trade and industry. Even the maintenance of law and order tended to benefit the merchant and the moneylender rather than the peasant.

The harmful effects of an excessive land revenue demand were further heightened by the rigid manner of its collection. Land revenue had to be paid promptly on the fixed dates, even if the harvest had been below normal or had failed completely. But in bad years, the peasant found it difficult to meet the revenue demand, even if he had been able to do so in good years.

Whenever the peasant failed to pay land revenue, the government put up his land on sale to collect the arrears of revenue. But in most cases the peasant himself took this step and sold part of his land to meet the government demand. In either case, he lost his land.

More often, the inability to pay revenue drove the peasant to borrow money at high rates of interest from the moneylender. He preferred getting into debt by mortgaging his land to a moneylender or to a rich peasant neighbour to losing it outright. He was also forced to go to the moneylender whenever he found it impossible to make both ends meet. But once in debt, he found it difficult to get out of it. The moneylender charged high rates of interest and through cunning and deceitful measures, such as false accounting, forged signatures and making the debtor sign for larger amounts than he had borrowed, got the peasant deeper and deeper into debt till he parted with his land.

The moneylender was greatly helped by the new legal system and the new revenue policy. In pre-British times, the moneylender was subordinated to the village community. He could not behave in a manner totally disliked by the rest of the village. For instance, he could not charge usurious rates of interest. In fact, the rates of interest were fixed by usage and public opinion. Moreover, he could not seize the land of the debtor; he could at most take possession of the debtor's personal effects like jewellery, or part of his standing crop. By introducing transferability of land, the British revenue system enabled the moneylender or the rich peasant to take possession of the land. Even the benefits of peace and security established by the British through their legal system and police were primarily reaped by the moneylender in whose hands the law placed enormous power; he also used the power of the purse to turn the expensive process of litigation in his favour and to make the police serve his purposes. Moreover, the literate and shrewd moneylender could easily take advantage of the ignorance and illiteracy of the peasant to twist the complicated processes of law to get favourable judicial decisions.

Gradually the cultivators in the Ryotwari and Mahalwari areas sank deeper and deeper into debt and more and more land passed into the hands of moneylenders, merchants, rich peasants and other moneyed classes. The process was repeated in the zamindari areas where the tenants lost their tenancy rights, and were ejected from the land or became subtenants of the moneylender.

The process of transfer of land from cultivators was intensified during periods of scarcity and famines. The Indian peasant hardly had any savings for critical times, and whenever crops failed, he fell back upon the moneylender not only to pay land revenue, but also to feed himself and his family.

By the end of the nineteenth century, the moneylender had become a major curse of the countryside and an important cause of the growing poverty of the rural people. In 1911, the total rural debt was estimated at Rs 300 crore. By 1937, it amounted to Rs 1800 crore. The entire process became a vicious circle. The pressure of taxation and growing poverty pushed the cultivators into debt, which in turn increased their poverty. In fact, the cultivators often failed to understand that the moneylender was an inevitable cog in the mechanism of imperialist exploitation and turned their anger against him as he appeared to be the visible cause of their impoverishment. For instance, during the Revolt of 1857, wherever the peasantry rose in revolt, quite often its first target of attack was the moneylender and his account books. Such peasant actions soon became a common occurrence.

The growing commercialisation of agriculture also helped the moneylender-cum-merchant to exploit the cultivator. The poor peasant was forced to sell his produce just after the harvest and at whatever price he could get as he had to meet in time the demands of the government, the landlord and the moneylender. This placed him at the mercy of the grain merchant, who was in a position to dictate terms and who purchased his produce at much less than the market price. Thus, a large share of the benefit of the growing trade in agricultural products was reaped by the merchant, who was very often also the village moneylender.

The loss and overcrowding of land caused by de-industrialisation and lack of modern industry compelled the landless peasants and ruined artisans and handicraftsmen to become either tenants of the moneylenders and zamindars by paying rack-rent or agricultural labourers at starvation wages. Thus, the peasantry was crushed under the triple burden of the government, the zamindar or landlord, and the moneylender. After these three had taken their share, not much was left for the cultivator and his family to subsist on. It has been calculated that in 1950–51, land rent and moneylenders' interest amounted to Rs 1400 crore or roughly equal to one-third of the total agricultural produce for the year. The result was that the impoverishment of the peasantry continued, along with an increase in the incidence of famines. People died in millions whenever droughts or floods caused the failure of crops and scarcity.

RUIN OF OLD ZAMINDARS AND RISE OF NEW LANDLORDISM

The first few decades of British rule witnessed the ruin of most of the old zamindars in Bengal and Madras. This was particularly so with Warren Hastings' policy of auctioning the rights of revenue collection to the highest bidders. The Permanent Settlement of 1793 also had a similar effect in the beginning. The heaviness of land revenue—the government claimed ten-elevenths of the rental—and the rigid law of collection, under which the zamindari estates were ruthlessly sold in case of delay in payment of revenue, wreaked havoc for the first few years. Many of the great zamindars of Bengal were utterly ruined and were forced to sell their zamindari rights. By 1815, nearly half of the landed property of Bengal had been transferred from the old zamindars, who had resided in the villages and who had traditionally shown some consideration to their tenants, to merchants and other moneyed classes, who usually lived in towns and who were quite ruthless in collecting to the last pie what was due from the tenant, irrespective of difficult circumstances. Being utterly unscrupulous and possessing little sympathy for the tenants, these new landlords began to subject the latter to rack-renting and ejectment.

The Permanent Settlement in north Madras and the Temporary Zamindari Settlement in Uttar Pradesh were equally harsh on the local zamindars.

But the condition of the zamindars soon improved radically. In order to enable the zamindars to pay the land revenue in time, the authorities increased their power over the tenants by extinguishing their traditional rights. The zamindars now set out to push up the rents to the utmost limit. Consequently, they rapidly grew in prosperity.

In the Ryotwari areas, too, the system of landlord-tenant relations spread gradually. As we have seen above, more and more land passed into the hands of moneylenders, merchants and rich peasants, who usually got the land cultivated by tenants. One reason why the Indian moneyed classes were keen to buy land and become landlords was the absence of effective outlets for investment of their capital in industry. Another process through which this landlordism spread was that of subletting. Many owner-cultivators and occupancy tenants, having a permanent right to hold land, found it more convenient to lease out land to land-hungry tenants at exorbitant rents than to cultivate it themselves. In time, landlordism became the main feature of agrarian relations not only in the zamindari areas, but also in the Ryotwari ones.

A remarkable feature of the spread of landlordism was the growth of subinfeudation or intermediaries. Since the cultivating tenants were generally unprotected and the overcrowding of land led the tenants to compete with one another to acquire land, the rent of land went on increasing. The zamindars and new landlords found it convenient to sublet their right to collect rent to other eager persons on profitable terms. But as rents increased, sub-leasers of land in their turn sublet their rights in land. Thus, by a chain-process, a large number of rent-receiving intermediaries between the actual cultivator and the government sprang up. In some cases in Bengal, their number went up to as high as 50! The condition of the helpless cultivating tenants who ultimately had to bear the burden of maintaining this horde of superior landlords was precarious beyond imagination. Many of them were little better than slaves.

An extremely harmful consequence of the rise and growth of zamindars and landlords was the political role they played during India's struggle for independence. Along with the princes of protected states, many of them became the chief political supporters of the foreign rulers and opposed the rising national movement. Realising that they owed their existence to British rule, they tried hard to maintain and perpetuate it.

STAGNATION AND DETERIORATION OF AGRICULTURE

As a result of overcrowding in agriculture, excessive land revenue demand, growth of landlordism, increasing indebtedness and the growing impoverishment of cultivators, Indian agriculture began to stagnate and even deteriorate, resulting in extremely low yields per acre. Overall agricultural production fell by 14 per cent between 1901 and 1939.

The overcrowding in agriculture and increase in subinfeudation led to subdivision and fragmentation of land into small holdings, most of which could not maintain their cultivators. The extreme poverty of the overwhelming majority of peasants left them without any resources with which to improve agriculture, by using better cattle and seeds, more manure and fertilisers, and improved techniques of production. Nor did the cultivator, rack-rented by both the government and the landlord, have any incentive to do so. After all, the land he cultivated was rarely his property and the bulk of the benefit which agricultural improvements would bring was likely to be reaped by the horde of absentee landlords and moneylenders. Subdivision and fragmentation of land also made it difficult to effect improvements.

In England and other European countries, the rich landlords often invested capital in their land to increase its productivity with a view to sharing in the increased income. But in India, the absentee landlords, both old and new, performed no useful function. They were mere rent-receivers who had often no roots in the land and who took no personal interest in it beyond collecting rent. They found it possible, and therefore preferred, to increase their income by further squeezing their tenants rather than by making productive investments in their lands.

The government could have helped in improving and modernising agriculture. But the government refused to recognise any such responsibility. A characteristic of the financial system of British India was that, while the main burden of taxation fell on the shoulders of the peasant, the government spent only a very small part of it on him. An example of this neglect of the peasant and agriculture was the stepmotherly treatment meted out to public works and agricultural improvement. While the Government of India had spent by 1905 over 360 crore of rupees on the railways, which was demanded by British business interests, it spent in the same period less than 50 crores of rupees on irrigation, which would have benefited millions of Indian cultivators. Even so, irrigation was the only field in which the government took some steps forward.

At a time when agriculture all over the world was being modernised and revolutionised, Indian agriculture was technologically stagnating; hardly any modern machinery was used. What was worse was that even ordinary implements were centuries old. For example, in 1951, there were only 930,000 iron ploughs in use, while wooden ploughs numbered 31.8 million. The use of inorganic fertilisers was virtually unknown, whereas a large part of animal manure, i.e. cow-dung, night-soil and cattle bones, was wasted. In 1922–23, only 1.9 per cent of all cropped land was under improved seeds. By 1938–39, this percentage had gone up to only 11 per cent. Furthermore, agricultural education was completely neglected. In 1939, there were only six agricultural colleges with 1306 students. There was not a single agricultural college in Bengal, Bihar, Orissa and Sind. Nor could peasants make improvements through self-study. There was hardly any spread of primary education or even literacy in the rural areas.

Development of Modern Industries

An important development in the second half of the nineteenth century was the establishment of large-scale machine-based industries in India. The machine age in India began when cotton textile, jute and coal-mining industries were started in the 1850s. The first textile mill was started in Bombay by Cowasjee Nanabhoy in 1853, and the first jute mill in Rishra (Bengal) in 1855. These industries expanded slowly, but continuously. In 1879, there were 56 cotton textile mills in India employing nearly 43,000 persons. In 1882 there were 20 jute mills, most of them in Bengal, employing nearly 20,000 persons. By 1905, India had 206 cotton mills employing nearly 196,000 persons. In 1901, there were over 36 jute mills employing nearly 115,000 persons. The coal-mining industry employed nearly one lakh persons in 1906. Other mechanical industries, which developed during the second half of the nineteenth and the beginning of the twentieth centuries, were cotton gins and presses, rice, flour and timber mills, leather tanneries, woollen textiles, sugar mills, iron and steel works, and such mineral industries as salt, mica and saltpetre. Cement, paper, matches, sugar and glass industries developed during the 1930s. But all these industries had a very stunted growth.

Most of the modern Indian industries were owned or controlled by British capital. Foreign capitalists were attracted to Indian industry by the prospect of high profit. Labour was extremely cheap; raw materials were readily and cheaply available; and for many goods, India and its neighbours provided a ready market. For many Indian products, such as tea, jute and manganese, there was a ready demand the world over. On the other hand, profitable investment opportunities at home were getting fewer. At the same time, the colonial government and officials were willing to provide all help and show all favours.

Foreign capital easily overwhelmed Indian capital in many of the industries. Only in the cotton textile industry did Indians have a large share from the beginning, and in the 1930s, the sugar industry was developed by Indians. Indian capitalists also had to struggle from the beginning against the power of British managing agencies and British banks. To enter a field of enterprise, Indian businessmen had to bend before the British managing agencies dominating that field. In many cases, even Indian-owned companies were controlled by foreign-owned or controlled managing agencies. Indians also found it difficult to get credit from banks, most of which were dominated by British financiers. Even when they could get loans, they had to pay high interest rates, while foreigners could borrow on much easier terms. Of course, gradually Indians began to develop their own banks and insurance companies. In 1914, foreign banks held over 70 per cent of all bank deposits in India; by 1937, their share had decreased to 57 per cent.

British enterprises in India also took advantage of their close connection with British suppliers of machinery and equipment, shipping, insurance companies, marketing agencies, government officials and political leaders to maintain their dominant position in Indian economic life. Moreover, the government followed a conscious policy of favouring foreign capital over Indian capital.

The railway policy of the government also discriminated against Indian enterprise; railway freight rates encouraged foreign imports at the cost of trade in domestic products. It was more difficult and costlier to distribute Indian goods than to distribute imported goods.

Another serious weakness of the Indian industrial effort was the almost complete absence of heavy or capital goods industries, without which there can be no rapid and independent development of industries. India had no big plants to produce iron and steel, or to manufacture machinery. A few petty repair workshops represented engineering industries and a few iron and brass foundries represented metallurgical industries. The first steel in India was produced only in 1913. Thus, India lacked such basic industries as steel, metallurgy, machine, chemical and oil. India also lagged behind in the development of electric power.

Apart from machine-based industries, the nineteenth century also witnessed the growth of plantation industries such as indigo, tea and coffee. They were almost exclusively European in ownership. Indigo was used as a dye in textile manufacture. Indigo manufacture was introduced into India at the end of the eighteenth century and flourished in Bengal and Bihar. Indigo planters gained notoriety for their oppression over the peasants, who were compelled to cultivate indigo. This oppression was vividly portrayed by the famous Bengali writer Dinbandhu Mitra in his play *Neel Darpan* in 1860. The invention of a synthetic dye dealt a big blow to the indigo industry and it gradually declined. The tea industry developed in Assam, Bengal, south India and the hills of Himachal Pradesh after 1850. Being foreign-owned, it was helped by the government with grants of rent-free land and other facilities. In time, the use of tea spread all over India and it also became an important item of export. Coffee plantations developed during this period in south India.

The plantation and other foreign-owned industries were of hardly any advantage to the Indian people. Their profits went out of the country. A large part of their salary bill was spent on highly paid foreign staff. They purchased most of their equipment abroad. Most of their technical staff was foreign. Most of their products were sold in foreign markets and the foreign exchange so earned was utilised by Britain. The only advantage that Indians got out of these industries was the creation of unskilled jobs. Most of the workers in these enterprises were, however, extremely low paid, and they worked under extremely harsh conditions for very long hours. Moreover, conditions of near-slavery prevailed in the plantations.

On the whole, industrial progress in India was exceedingly slow and painful. It was mostly confined to cotton and jute industries and tea plantations in the nineteenth century, and to sugar and cement in the 1930s. As late as 1946, cotton and jute textiles accounted for 40 per cent of all workers employed in factories. In terms of production as well as employment, the modern industrial development of India was paltry compared with the economic development of other countries, or those with India's economic needs. It did not, in fact, compensate even for the displacement of the indigenous handicrafts; it had little effect on the problems of poverty and overcrowding of land. The paltry nature of Indian industrialisation is brought out by the fact that out of a population of 357 million in 1951, only about 2.3 million were employed in modern industrial enterprises. Furthermore, the decay and decline of the urban and rural handicraft industries continued unabated after 1858. The Indian Planning Commission has calculated that the number of persons engaged in processing and manufacturing fell from 10.3 million in 1901 to 8.8 million in 1951, even though the population increased by nearly 40 per cent. The government made no effort to protect, rehabilitate, reorganise and modernise these old indigenous industries.

Moreover, even the modern industries had to develop without government help and often in opposition to British policy. British manufacturers looked upon Indian textile and other industries as their rivals and put pressure on the Government of India not to encourage, but rather to actively discourage industrial development in India. Thus, British policy artificially restricted and slowed down the growth of Indian industries.

Furthermore, Indian industries, still in a period of infancy, needed protection. They developed at a time when Britain, France, Germany and the United States had already established powerful industries and could not therefore compete with them. In fact, all other countries, including Britain, had protected their infant industries by imposing heavy customs duties on the import of foreign manufacturers. But India was not a free country. Its policies were determined in Britain and in the interests of British industrialists who forced a policy of Free Trade upon their colony. For the same reason, the Government of India refused to give any financial or other help to the newly founded Indian industries, as was being done at the time by the governments of Europe and Japan for their own infant industries. It would not even make adequate arrangements for technical education, which remained extremely backward until 1951 and further contributed to industrial backwardness. In 1939, there were only seven engineering colleges with 2217 students in the country. Many Indian projects, for example, those concerning the construction of ships, locomotives, cars and aeroplanes, could not get started because of the government's refusal to give any help.

Finally, in the 1920s and 1930s, under pressure from the rising nationalist movement and the Indian capitalist class, the Government of India was forced to grant some tariff protection to Indian industries. But once again, the government discriminated against Indian-owned industries such as cement, iron and steel, and glass, which were denied protection or given inadequate protection. On the other hand, foreign dominated industries, such as the match industry, were given the protection they desired. Moreover, British imports were given special privileges under the system of 'imperial preferences', even though Indians protested vehemently.

Another feature of Indian industrial development was that it was extremely lopsided regionally. Indian industries were concentrated only in a few regions and cities of the country. Large parts of the country remained totally underdeveloped. This unequal regional economic development not only led to wide regional disparities in income, but also affected the level of national integration. It made the task of creating a unified Indian nation more difficult.

An important social consequence of even the limited industrial development of the country was the birth and growth of two new social classes in Indian society—the industrial capitalist class and the modern working class. These two classes were entirely new in Indian history because modern mines, industries and means of transport were new. Even though these classes formed a very small part of the Indian population, they represented new technology, a new system of economic organisation, new social relations, new ideas and a new outlook. They were not weighed down by the burden of old traditions, customs and styles of life. Most of all, they possessed an all-India outlook. Moreover, both new classes were vitally interested in the industrial development of the country. Their economic and political importance and roles were, therefore, out of all proportion to their numbers.

POVERTY AND FAMINES

A major characteristic of British rule in India, and the net result of British economic policies, was the prevalence of extreme poverty among its people. While historians disagree on the question of whether India was getting poorer under British rule, there is no disagreement on the fact that throughout the period of British rule, most Indians always lived on the verge of starvation. As time passed, they found it more and more difficult to find employment or make a living. British economic exploitation, the decay of indigenous industries, the failure of modern industries to replace them, high taxation, the drain of wealth to Britain, and a backward agrarian structure leading to the stagnation of agriculture and the exploitation of the poor peasants by the zamindars, landlords, princes, moneylenders, merchants and the state gradually reduced the Indian people to extreme poverty and prevented them from progressing. India's colonial economy stagnated at a low economic level.

The poverty of the people found its culmination in a series of famines which ravaged all parts of India in the second half of the nineteenth century. The first of these famines occurred in western Uttar Pradesh in 1860–61 and cost over 2 lakh lives. In 1865–66, a famine engulfed Orissa, Bengal, Bihar and Madras and took a toll of nearly 20 lakh lives, Orissa alone losing 10 lakh people. More than 14 lakh persons died in the famine of 1868–70 in western Uttar Pradesh, Bombay and Punjab. Many states in Rajputana, another affected area, lost one-fourth to one-third of their population.

Perhaps the worst famine in Indian histoy till then occurred in 1876–78 in Madras, Mysore, Hyderabad, Maharashtra, western Uttar Pradesh, and Punjab. Maharashtra lost eight lakh people, Madras nearly 35 lakh. Mysore lost nearly 20 per cent of its population and Uttar Pradesh over 12 lakh. Drought led to a country-wide famine in 1896–97 which affected over 9.5 crores of people, of whom nearly 45 lakh died. The famine of 1899–1900 followed quickly and caused widespread distress. In spite of official efforts to save lives through provision of famine relief, over 25 lakhs of people died. Apart from these major famines, many other local famines and scarcities occurred. William Digby, a British writer, has calculated that, in all, over 28,825,000 people died during famines from 1854 to 1901. Another famine in 1943 carried away nearly three million people in Bengal. These famines and the high losses of life caused by them indicate the extent to which poverty and starvation had taken root in India.

Many English officials in India recognised the grim reality of India's poverty during the nineteenth century. For example, Charles Elliott, a member of the Governor-General's Council, remarked: "I do not hesitate to say that half the agricultural population do not know from one year's end to another what it is to have a full meal."

William Hunter, the compiler of the Imperial Gazetteer, conceded that "forty million of the people of India habitually go through life on insufficient food." The situation became still worse in the twentieth century. The quantity of food available to an Indian declined by as much as 29 per cent in the 30 years between 1911 and 1941.

There were many other indications of India's economic backwardness and impoverishment. Colin Clark, a famous authority on national income, has calculated that during the period 1925–34, India and China had the lowest per capita incomes in the world. The income of an Englishman was five times that of an Indian. Similarly, the average life expectancy of an Indian during the 1930s was only 32 years, in spite of the tremendous progress that modern medical sciences and sanitation had made. In most of the West European and North American countries, the average age was already over 60 years.

India's economic backwardness and poverty were not due to the niggardliness of nature. They were man-made. The natural resources of India were abundant and capable of yielding, if properly utilised, a high degree of prosperity to the people. But, as a result of foreign rule and exploitation, and of a backward agrarian and industrial economic structure—in fact, as the total outcome of its historical and social development—India presented the paradox of a poor people living in a rich country.

The poverty of India was not a product of its geography or of the lack of natural resources or of some 'inherent' defect in the character and capabilities of the people. Nor was it a remnant of the Mughal period or of the pre-British past. It was mainly a product of the history of the last two centuries. Before that, India was no more backward than the countries of Western Europe. Nor were the differences in standards of living at the time very wide among the countries of the world. Precisely during the period that the countries of the West developed and prospered, India was subjected to modern colonialism and was prevented from developing. All the developed countries of today developed almost entirely over the period during which India was ruled by Britain, most of them doing so after 1850. It is interesting, in this connection, to note that the dates of the beginning of the Industrial Revolution in Britain and the British conquest of Bengal virtually coincide!

The basic fact is that the same social, political and economic processes that produced industrial development and social and cultural progress in Britain also produced and then maintained economic underdevelopment and social and cultural backwardness in India. The reason for this is obvious. Britain subordinated the Indian economy to its own economy and determined the basic social trends in India according to her own needs. The result was stagnation of India's agriculture and industries, exploitation of its peasants and workers by the zamindars, landlords, princes, moneylenders, merchants, capitalists, and the foreign government and its officials, and the spread of poverty, disease and semi-starvation.

Ten

The Nationalist Movement: 1858–1905

The second half of the nineteenth century witnessed the full flowering of national political consciousness and the growth of an organised national movement in India. In December 1885 was born the Indian National Congress under whose leadership Indians waged a prolonged and courageous struggle for independence from foreign rule, a struggle which India finally won on 15 August 1947.

Consequence of Foreign Domination

Basically, modern Indian nationalism arose to meet the challenge of foreign domination. The very conditions of British rule helped the growth of national sentiment among the Indian people. It was British rule and its direct and indirect consequences which provided the material, and the moral and intellectual conditions for the development of a national movement in India.

The root of the matter lay in the clash of interests of the Indian people with British interests in India. The British had conquered India to promote their own interests and they ruled it primarily with that purpose in view, often subordinating Indian welfare to British gain. The Indians gradually realised that their interests were being sacrificed to those of Lancashire manufacturers and other dominant British interests.

The foundations of the Indian nationalist movement lay in the fact that increasingly, British rule had become the major cause of India's economic backwardness. It became the major barrier to India's further economic, social, cultural, intellectual and political development. Moreover, this fact began to be recognised by an increasingly larger number of Indians.

Every class, every section of Indian society gradually discovered that its interests were suffering at the hands of the foreign rulers.

The peasant saw that the government took away a large part of his produce as land revenue; that the government and its machinery—the police, the courts, the officials—favoured and protected the zamindars and landlords, who rack-rented him, and the merchants and moneylenders, who cheated and exploited him in diverse ways and who took his land away from him. Whenever the peasant struggled against landlord and moneylender oppression, the police and the army suppressed him in the name of law and order.

The artisan or the handicraftsman saw that the foreign regime had helped foreign competition ruin him and had done nothing to rehabilitate him.

Later, in the twentieth century, the worker in modern factories, mines, and plantations found that, in spite of lip sympathy, the government sided with the capitalists, especially the foreign capitalists. Whenever he tried to organise trade unions to improve his lot through strikes, demonstrations, and other struggles, government machinery was freely used against him. Moreover, he soon realised that the growing unemployment could be checked only by rapid industrialisation, which only an independent government could bring about.

Other sections of Indian society were no less dissatisfied. The rising intelligentsia—the educated Indians—used their newly acquired modern knowledge to understand the sad economic and political condition of their country. Those who had earlier, as in 1857, supported British rule in the hope that, though alien, it would modernise and industrialise the country, were gradually disappointed. Economically, they had hoped that British capitalism would help to develop India's productive forces as it had done at home. Instead, they found that British policies in India, guided by British capitalists at home, were keeping the country economically backward or underdeveloped and checking the development of its productive forces.

Politically, educated Indians found that the British had abandoned all previous pretensions of guiding India towards self-government. Most of the British officials and political leaders openly declared that the British were in India to stay. Moreover, instead of increasing the freedom of speech, of the press, and of the individual, the government increasingly restricted them. British officials and writers declared Indians unfit for democracy or self-government. In the field of culture, the rulers were increasingly taking a negative and even hostile attitude towards higher education and the spread of modern ideas.

The rising Indian capitalist class was slow in developing a national political consciousness. But it too gradually saw that it was suffering at the hands of imperialism. Its growth was severely checked by the trade, tariff, taxation, and transport policies of the government. As a new and weak class, it needed active government help to counterbalance many of its weaknesses. But no such help was given. Instead, the government and its bureaucracy favoured foreign capitalists who came to India with their vast resources and appropriated the limited industrial field. Indian capitalists were particularly opposed to the strong competition from foreign capitalists. The Indian capitalists therefore also realised that there existed a contradiction between imperialism and their own independent growth, and that only a national government would create conditions for the rapid development of Indian trade and industries.

As we have seen in an earlier chapter, the zamindars, the landlords, and the princes were the only section of Indian society whose interests coincided with those of the foreign rulers and who, therefore, on the whole supported foreign rule until the end. But even from these classes, many individuals joined the national movement. In the prevailing nationalist atmosphere, patriotism appealed to many. Further, the policies of racial dominance and discrimination apalled and aroused every thinking and self-respecting Indian, to whichever class he might belong. Most of all, the foreign character of the British regime in itself produced a nationalist reaction, since foreign domination invariably generates patriotic sentiments in the hearts of a subject people.

To sum up, it was as a result of the intrinsic nature of foreign imperialism and its harmful impact on the lives of the Indian people that a powerful anti-imperialist movement gradually arose and developed in India. This was a national movement because it united people from different classes and sections of society, who put aside their mutual differences to unite against the common enemy.

Administrative and Economic Unification of the Country

Nationalist sentiments grew easily among the people because India was unified and welded into a nation during the nineteenth and twentieth centuries. The British had gradually introduced a uniform and modern system of government throughout the country and thus unified it administratively. The destruction of the rural and local self-sufficient economy and the introduction of modern trade and industries on an all-India scale had increasingly turned India's economic life into a single whole and interlinked the economic fate of people living in different parts of the country. For example, if famine or scarcity occurred in one part of India, prices and availability of foodstuffs were affected in all other parts of the country too. Furthermore, the introduction of the railways, telegraph and a unified postal system had brought the different parts of the country together and promoted mutual contact among the people, especially among the leaders.

Here again, the very existence of foreign rule that oppressed all the Indian people irrespective of their social class, caste, religion or region acted as a unifying factor. All over the country, people saw that they were suffering at the hands of a common enemy—British rule. On the one hand, the emergence of the Indian nation was a major factor in the rise of nationalism; on the other hand, the anti-imperialist struggle and the feeling of solidarity born in its course contributed powerfully to the making of the Indian nation.

Western Thought and Education

As a result of the spread of modern Western education and thought during the nineteenth century, a large number of Indians imbibed a modern rational, secular, democratic and nationalist political outlook. They also began to study, admire and emulate the contemporary nationalist movements of European nations. Rousseau, Paine, John Stuart Mill and other Western thinkers became their political guides, while Mazzini, Garibaldi and Irish nationalist leaders became their political heroes.

These educated Indians were the first to feel the humiliation of foreign subjection. By becoming modern in their thinking, they also acquired the ability to study the evil effects of foreign rule. They were inspired by the dream of a modern, strong, prosperous, and united India. In course of time, the best among them became the leaders and organisers of the national movement.

It should be clearly understood that it was not the modern educational system that created the national movement, which was the product of the conflict of interests between Britain and India. The system only enabled educated Indians to imbibe Western thought and thus to assume the leadership of the national movement and to give it a democratic and modern direction. In fact, in the schools and colleges, the authorities tried to inculcate notions of docility and servility to foreign rule. Nationalist ideas were a part of the general spread of modern ideas. In other Asian countries such as China and Indonesia, and all over Africa, modern and nationalist ideas spread, despite modern schools and colleges existing on a much smaller scale.

Modern education also created a certain uniformity and community of outlook and interests among the educated Indians. The English language played an important role in this respect. It became the medium for the spread of modern ideas. It also became the medium of communication and exchange of ideas between educated Indians from different linguistic regions of the country. But soon English also became a barrier to the spread of modern knowledge among the common people. It also acted as a wall separating the educated urban people from the common people, especially in the rural areas. This fact was fully recognised by Indian political leaders. From Dadabhai Naoroji, Sayyid Ahmed Khan and Justice Ranade to Tilak and Gandhiji, they agitated for a bigger role for the Indian languages in the educational system. In fact, so far as the common people were concerned, the spread of modern ideas occurred through the developing Indian languages, the growing literature in them, and most of all, the popular Indian language press.

The Role of the Press and Literature

The chief instrument through which nationalist-minded Indians spread the message of patriotism and modern economic, social and political ideas, and created an all-India consciousness was the press.

Large numbers of nationalist newspapers made their appearance during the second half of the nineteenth century. In their columns, the official policies were constantly criticised; the Indian point of view was put forward; people were asked to unite and work for national welfare, and ideas of self-government, democracy, industrialisation, etc., were popularised among the people. The press also enabled nationalist workers living in different parts of the country to exchange views with one another.

National literature in the form of novels, essays and patriotic poetry also played an important role in arousing national consciousness. Bankim Chandra Chatterjee and Rabindranath Tagore in Bengali, Lakshminath Bezbarua in Assamese, Vishnu Shastri Chiplunkar in Marathi, Subramanya Bharati in Tamil, Bharatendu Harishchandra in Hindi and Altaf Husain Hali in Urdu were some of the prominent nationalist writers of the period.

Rediscovery of India's Past

Many Indians had fallen so low that they had lost confidence in their own capacity for self-government. Also, many British officials and writers of the time constantly advanced the thesis that Indians had never been able to rule themselves in the past, that Hindus and Muslims had always fought one another, that Indians were destined to be ruled by foreigners, that their religion and social life were degraded and uncivilised, making them unfit for democracy or even self-government. Many of the nationalist leaders tried to arouse the self-confidence and self-respect of the people by countering this propaganda. They pointed to the cultural heritage of India with pride and referred the critics to the political achievements of rulers like Ashoka, Chandragupta Vikramaditya and Akbar. In this task, they were helped and encouraged by the work of European and Indian scholars in rediscovering India's national heritage in art, architecture, literature, philosophy, science and politics. Unfortunately, some of the nationalists went to the other extreme and began to glorify India's past uncritically, ignoring its weaknesses and backwardness. Great harm was done, in particular, by the tendency to look up only to the heritage of ancient India while ignoring the equally great achievements of the medieval period. This encouraged the growth of communal sentiments among the Hindus and the counter tendency among the Muslims of looking to the history of the Arabs and the Turks for cultural and historical inspiration. Morevoer, in meeting the challenge of cultural imperialism of the West, many Indians tended to ignore the fact that in many respects, the people of India were culturally backward. A false sense of pride and smugness was produced, which tended to prevent Indians from looking critically at their society. This weakened the struggle against social and cultural backwardness, and led many Indians to turn away from healthy and fresh tendencies and ideas from other parts of the world.

RACIAL ARROGANCE OF THE RULERS

An important, though secondary factor in the growth of national sentiments in India was the tone of racial superiority adopted by many Englishmen in their dealings with Indians. A particularly odious and frequent form taken by racial arrogance was the failure of justice whenever an Englishman was involved in a dispute with an Indian. As G.O. Trevelyan pointed out in 1864: "The testimony of a single one of our countrymen has more weight with the court than that of any number of Hindoos, a circumstance which puts a terrible instrument of power into the hands of an unscrupulous and grasping Englishman."

Racial arrogance branded all Indians, irrespective of their caste, religion, province, or class, with the badge of inferiority. They were kept out of exclusively European clubs and often not permitted to travel in the same compartment in a train with European passengers. This made them conscious of national humiliation, and led them to think of themselves as one people when facing Englishmen.

PREDECESSORS OF THE INDIAN NATIONAL CONGRESS

By the 1870s, it was evident that Indian nationalism had gathered enough momentum to appear as a major force on the Indian political scene. The Indian National Congress, founded in December 1885, was the first organised expression of the Indian national movement on an all-India scale. It had, however, many predecessors.

As we have seen in an earlier chapter, Raja Rammohun Roy was the first Indian leader to start an agitation for political reforms in

India. Many public associations were started in different parts of India after 1836. All these associations were dominated by wealthy and aristocratic elements—known in those days as 'prominent persons'— and were provincial or local in character. They worked for reform of administration, association of Indians with the administration, and spread of education, and sent long petitions, putting forward Indian demands, to the British Parliament.

The period after 1858 witnessed a gradual widening of the gulf between the educated Indians and the British Indian administration. As educated Indians studied the character of British rule and its consequences for India, they became more and more critical of British policies in India. The discontent gradually found expression in political activity. The existing associations no longer satisfied the politically conscious Indians.

In 1866, Dadabhai Naoroji organised the East India Association in London to discuss the Indian question and to influence British public officials to promote Indian welfare. Later, he organised branches of the Association in prominent Indian cities. Born in 1825, Dadabhai devoted his entire life to the national movement and soon came to be known as the 'Grand Old Man of India'. He was also India's first economic thinker. In his writings on economics, he showed that the basic cause of India's poverty lay in the British exploitation of India and the drain of its wealth. Dadabhai was honoured by being thrice elected president of the Indian National Congress. In fact, he was the first in the long line of popular nationalist leaders of India whose very name stirred the hearts of the people.

The most important of the pre-Congress nationalist organisations was the Indian Association of Calcutta. The younger nationalists of Bengal had been gradually becoming discontented with the conservative and pro-landlord policies of the British India Association. They wanted sustained political agitation on issues of wider public interest. They found a leader in Surendranath Banerjea, who was a brilliant writer and orator. He was unjustly turned out of the Indian Civil Service as his superiors could not tolerate the presence of an independent-minded Indian in the ranks of this service. He began his public career in 1875 by delivering brilliant addresses on nationalist topics to the students of Calcutta. Led by Surendranath and Ananda Mohan Bose, the younger nationalists of Bengal founded the Indian Association in July 1876. The Indian Association set before itself the aims of creating strong public opinion in the country on political questions and the unification of the Indian people under a common political programme. In order to attract large numbers of people to its banner, it fixed a low membership fee for the poorer classes. Many branches of the Association were opened in the towns and villages of Bengal and also in many towns outside Bengal.

The younger elements were also active in other parts of India. Justice Ranade and others organised the Poona Sarvajanik Sabha in 1870. M. Viraraghavachari, G. Subramaniya Iyer, Ananda Charlu and others formed the Madras Mahajan Sabha in 1884. Pherozeshah Mehta, K.T. Telang, Badruddin Tyabji and others formed the Bombay Presidency Association in 1885.

The time was now ripe for the formation of an all-India political organisation of nationalists who felt the need to unite politically against the common enemy—foreign rule and exploitation. The existing organisations had served a useful purpose, but they were narrow in their scope and functioning. They dealt mostly with local questions and their membership and leadership were confined to a few people belonging to a single city or province. Even the Indian Association had not succeeded in becoming an all-India body.

The Indian National Congress

Many Indians had been planning to form an all-India organisation of nationalist political workers. But the credit for giving the idea concrete and final shape goes to A.O. Hume, a retired English Civil Servant. He got in touch with prominent Indian leaders and organised with their cooperation the first Session of the Indian National Congress at Bombay in December 1885. It was presided over by W.C. Bonnerjee and attended by 72 delegates. The aims of the National Congress were declared to be the promotion of friendly relations between nationalist political workers from different parts of the country, development and consolidation of the feeling of national unity irrespective of caste, religion or province, formulation of popular demands and their presentation before the government, and most important of all, the training and organisation of public opinion in the country.

It has been said that Hume's main purpose in encouraging the foundation of the Congress was to provide a 'safety valve' or a safe outlet to the growing discontent among the educated Indians. He wanted to prevent the union of a discontented nationalist intelligentsia with a discontented peasantry.

The 'safety valve' theory is, however, a small part of the truth and is totally inadequate and misleading. More than anything else, the National Congress represented the urge of politically conscious Indians to set up a national organisation to work for their political and economic advancement. We have already seen above that a national movement was growing in the country as a result of the working of powerful forces. No one man or group of men can be given credit for creating this movement. Even Hume's motives were mixed ones. He was also moved by motives nobler than those of the 'safety valve'. He possessed a sincere love for India and its poor cultivators. In any case, the Indian leaders, who cooperated with Hume in starting this National Congress, were patriotic men of high character who willingly accepted Hume's help as they did not want to arouse official hostility towards their efforts at so early a stage of political activity, and they hoped that a retired Civil Servant's active presence would allay official suspicions. If Hume wanted to use the Congress as a 'safety valve', the early Congress leaders hoped to use him as a 'lightning conductor'.

Thus, with the foundation of the National Congress in 1885, the struggle for India's freedom from foreign rule was launched in a small but organised manner. The national movement was to grow and the country and its people were to know no rest till freedom was won. The Congress itself was to serve from the beginning not as a party, but as a movement. In 1886, delegates to the Congress, numbering 436, were elected by different local organisations and groups. Hereafter, the National Congress met every year in December, in a different part of the country each time. The number of its delegates soon increased to thousands. Its delegates consisted mostly of lawyers, journalists, traders, industrialists, teachers and landlords. In 1890, Kadambini Ganguli, the first woman graduate of Calcutta University, addressed the Congress session. This was symbolic of the fact that India's struggle for freedom would raise Indian women from the degraded position to which they had been reduced for centuries past.

The Nationalist Movement: 1858–1905

The Indian National Congress was not the only channel through which the stream of nationalism flowed. Provincial conferences, provincial and local associations, and nationalist newspapers were the other prominent organs of the growing nationalist movement. The press, in particular, was a powerful factor in developing nationalist opinion and the nationalist movement. Of course, most of the newspapers of the period were not carried on as business ventures but were consciously started as organs of nationalist activity. Some of the great presidents of the National Congress during its early years were Dadabhai Naoroji, Badruddin Tyabji, Pherozeshah Mehta, P. Ananda Charlu, Surendranath Banerjea, Romesh Chandra Dutt, Ananda Mohan Bose and Gopal Krishna Gokhale. Other prominent leaders of the Congress and the national movement during this period were Mahadev Govind Ranade, Bal Gangadhar Tilak, the brothers Sisir Kumar and Motilal Ghose, Madan Mohan Malaviya, G. Subramaniya Iyer, C. Vijayaraghava Chariar and Dinshaw E. Wacha.

The Programme and Activities of the Early Nationalists

Early nationalist leadership believed that a direct struggle for the political emancipation of the country was not yet on the agenda of history. What was on the agenda was the arousal of national feeling, consolidation of this feeling, the bringing of a large number of Indian people into the vortex of nationalist politics, and their training in politics and political agitation. The first important task in this respect was the creation of public interest in political questions and the organisation of public opinion in the country. Second, popular demands had to be formulated on a country-wide basis so that the emerging public opinion might have an all-India focus. Most important of all, national unity had to be created, in the first instance, among the politically conscious Indians and political workers and leaders. The early national leaders were fully aware of the fact that India had just entered the process of becoming a nation—in other words, India was a nation-in-the-making. Indian nationhood had to be carefully promoted. Indians had to be carefully welded into a nation. Politically conscious Indians had to constantly work for the development and consolidation of the feeling of national unity, irrespective of region, caste or religion. The economic and political demands of the early nationalists were formulated with a view to unifying the Indian people on the basis of a common economic and political programme.

Economic Critique of Imperialism

Perhaps the most important aspect of the early nationalists' political work was their economic critique of imperialism. They took note of all three forms of contemporary colonial economic exploitation, namely through trade, industry and finance. They clearly grasped that the essence of British economic imperialism lay in the subordination of the Indian economy to the British economy. They vehemently opposed the British attempt to develop in India the basic characteristics of a colonial economy, namely the transformation of India into a supplier of raw materials, a market for British manufactures, and a field of investment for foreign capital. They organised a powerful agitation against nearly all important official economic policies based on this colonial structure.

The early nationalists complained of India's growing poverty and economic backwardness and the failure of modern industry and agriculture to grow; and they put the blame on British economic exploitation of India. Thus, Dadabhai Naoroji declared as early as 1881 that British rule was "an everlasting, increasing, and every day increasing foreign invasion" that was "utterly, though gradually, destroying the country". The nationalists criticised the official economic policies for bringing about the ruin of India's traditional handicraft industries and for obstructing the development of modern industries. Most of them opposed the large-scale investment of foreign capital in the Indian railways, plantations and industries on the grounds that it would lead to the suppression of Indian capitalists and the further strengthening of British hold on India's economy and polity. They believed that the employment of foreign capital posed a serious economic and political danger not only to the present generation, but also for generations to come. The chief remedy they suggested for the removal of India's poverty was the rapid development of modern industries. They wanted the government to promote modern industries through tariff protection and direct government aid. They popularised the idea of *swadeshi* or the use of Indian goods, and the boycott of British goods as a means of promoting Indian industries. For example, students in Poona and in other towns of Maharashtra publicly burnt foreign clothes in 1896 as part of the larger *swadeshi* campaign.

The nationalists complained that India's wealth was being drained to England, and demanded that this drain be stopped. They carried on a persistent agitation for the reduction of land revenue in order to lighten the burden of taxation on the peasant. Some of them also criticised the semi-feudal agrarian relations that the British sought to maintain. The nationalists also agitated for improvement in the conditions of work of the plantation labourers. They declared high taxation to be one of the causes of India's poverty and demanded the abolition of the salt tax and the reduction of land revenue. They condemned the high military expenditure of the Government of India and demanded its reduction. As time passed, more and more nationalists came to the conclusion that economic exploitation, impoverishment of the country and the perpetuation of its economic backwardness by foreign imperialism more than outweighed some of the beneficial aspects of the alien rule. Thus, regarding the benefits of security of life and property, Dadabhai Naoroji remarked:

> The *romance* is that there is security of life and property in India; the reality is that there is no such thing. There is security of life and property in one sense or way—i.e. the people are secure from any violence from each other or from Native despots.... But from England's own grasp there is no security of property at all and, as a consequence, no security for life. India's property is not secure. What is secure, and well secure, is that England is perfectly safe and secure, and does so with perfect security, to carry a way from India, and to eat up in India, her property at the present rate of £30,000,000 or £40,000,000 a year.... I therefore venture to submit that India *does not* enjoy security of her property and life ... To millions in India life is simply 'half-feeding', or starvation, or famine and disease.

With regard to law and order, Dadabhai said:

> There is an Indian saying: 'Pray strike on the back, but don't strike on the belly'. Under the native despot the people keep and enjoy what they produce, though at times they suffer some violence on the back. Under the British Indian despot the man is at peace, there is no violence; his

substance is drained away, unseen, peaceably and subtly—he starves in peace and perishes in peace, with law and order!

Nationalist agitation on economic issues led to the growth of an all-India opinion that British rule was based on the exploitation of India; leading to India's impoverishment and producing economic backwardness and under-development. These disadvantages far outweighed any indirect advantages that might have followed British rule.

Constitutional Reforms

From the beginning, the early nationalists believed that India should eventually move towards democratic self-government. But they did not ask for the immediate fulfilment of their goal. Their immediate demands were extremely moderate. They hoped to win freedom through gradual steps. They were also extremely cautious, lest the government suppress their activities. From 1885 to 1892, they demanded the expansion and reform of the Legislative Councils.

The British government was forced by their agitation to pass the Indian Councils Act of 1892. By this Act, the number of members of the Imperial Legislative Council as well as the provincial councils was increased. Some of these members could be elected indirectly by Indians, but the officials' majority remained. The nationalists were totally dissatisfied with the Act of 1892 and declared it to be a hoax. They demanded a larger share for Indians in the councils, as also wider powers for them. In particular, they demanded Indian control over the public purse and raised the slogan that had earlier become the national cry of the American people during their War of Independence: 'No taxation without representation'. At the same time, they failed to broaden the base of their democratic demands; they did not demand the right to vote for the masses or for women.

By the beginning of the twentieth century, the nationalist leaders advanced further and put forward the claim for *swarajya* or self-government within the British empire on the model of self-governing colonies like Australia and Canada. This demand was made from the Congress platform by Gokhale in 1905 and by Dadabhai Naoroji in 1906.

Administrative and Other Reforms

The early nationalists were fearless critics of individual administrative measures and worked incessantly for the reform of an administrative system ridden with corruption, inefficiency and oppression. The most important administrative reform they desired was the Indianisation of the higher grades of the administrative services. They put forward this demand on economic, political and moral grounds. Economically, the European monopoly of the higher services was harmful on two grounds: Europeans were paid at very high rates and this made Indian administration very costly—Indians of similar qualifications could be employed at lower salaries; and Europeans sent out of India a large part of their salaries and their pensions were paid in England. This added to the drain of wealth from India. Politically, the nationalists hoped that the Indianisation of these services would make the administration more responsive to Indian needs. The moral aspect of the question was stated by Gopal Krishna Gokhale in 1897:

> The excessive costliness of the foreign agency is not, however, its only evil. There is a moral evil which, if anything, is even greater. A kind of dwarfing or stunting of the Indian race is going on under the present system. We must live all the days of our life in an atmosphere of inferiority, and the tallest of us must bend.... The full height of which our manhood is capable of rising can never be reached by us under the present system. The moral elevation which every self-governing people feel cannot be felt by us. Our administrative and military talents must gradually disappear, owing to sheer disuse, till at last our lot, as hewers of wood and drawers of water in our own country, is stereotyped.

The nationalists demanded the separation of the judicial from executive powers so that the people might get some protection from the arbitrary acts of the police and the bureaucracy. They agitated against the oppressive and tyrannical behaviour of the police and other government agents towards the common people. They criticised the delays of the law and the high cost of the judicial process. They opposed the aggressive foreign policy against India's neighbours. They protested against the annexation of Burma, the attack upon Afghanistan and the suppression of the tribal people in North-Western India.

They urged the government to undertake and develop welfare activities of the state. They laid a great deal of emphasis on the spread of primary education among the masses. They also demanded greater facilities for technical and higher education. They urged the development of agricultural banks to save the peasant from the clutches of the moneylender. They wanted the government to undertake a large-scale programme of extension of irrigation for the development of agriculture and to save the country from famines. They demanded the extension of medical and health facilities and improvement of the police system to make it honest, efficient and popular.

The nationalist leaders also spoke up in defence of Indian workers who had been compelled by poverty to migrate to foreign countries such as South Africa, Malaya, Mauritius, the West Indies and British Guyana in search of employment. In many of these foreign lands, they were subjected to severe oppression and racial discrimination. This was particularly true of South Africa, where Mohandas Karamchand Gandhi was leading a popular struggle in defence of the basic human rights of Indians.

Defence of Civil Rights

From the beginning, politically conscious Indians had been powerfully attracted not only to democracy but also to modern civil rights, namely the freedoms of speech, the press, thought and association. They put up a strong defence of these civil rights whenever the government tried to curtail them. It was during this period and as a result of nationalist political work that democratic ideas began to take root among the Indian people in general, and the intelligentsia in particular. In fact, the struggle for democratic freedoms became an integral part of the nationalist struggle for freedom. In 1897, the Bombay government arrested B.G. Tilak and several other leaders and newspaper editors and tried them, spreading disaffection against the government. They were sentenced to long terms of imprisonment. At the same time two Poona leaders, the Natu brothers, were deported without trial. The entire country protested against this attack on the liberties of the people. Tilak, hitherto known largely in Maharashtra, became overnight an all-India leader.

Methods of Political Work

The Indian national movement up to 1905 was dominated by leaders who have often been described as moderate nationalists or Moderates. The political methods of the Moderates can be summed up briefly as constitutional agitation within the four walls of the law, and slow, orderly political progress. They believed that if public opinion was created and organised and popular demands presented to the authorities through petitions, meetings, resolutions and speeches, the authorities would concede these demands gradually and step by step.

Their political work had, therefore, a two-pronged direction. First, to build up a strong public opinion in India to arouse the political consciousness and national spirit of the people, and to educate and unite them on political questions. Basically, even the resolutions and petitions of the National Congress were directed towards this goal. Though ostensibly their memorials and petitions were addressed to the government, their real aim was to educate the Indian people. For example, when in 1891 the young Gokhale expressed disappointment at the two-line reply of the government to a carefully proposed memorial by the Poona Sarvajanik Sabha, Justice Ranade replied:

> You don't realise our place in the history of our country. These memorials are nominally addressed to government. In reality they are addressed to the people, so that they may learn how to think in these matters. This work must be done for many years, without expecting any other results, because politics of this kind is altogether new in this land.

Second, the early nationalists wanted to persuade the British government and British public opinion to introduce reforms along directions laid down by the nationalists. The Moderate nationalists believed that the British people and Parliament wanted to be just to India, but that they did not know the true state of affairs there. Therefore, next to educating Indian public opinion, the Moderate nationalists worked to educate British public opinion. For this purpose, they carried on active propaganda in Britain. Deputations of leading Indians were sent to Britain to propagate the Indian view. In 1889, a British Committee of the Indian National Congress was founded. In 1890, this Committee started a journal called *India*. Dadabhai Naoroji spent a major part of his life and income in England popularising India's case among its people.

A student of the Indian national movement sometimes gets confused when he reads loud professions of loyalty to British rule by prominent Moderate leaders. These professions do not at all mean that they were not genuine patriots or that they were cowardly men. They genuinely believed that the continuation of India's political connection with Britain was in the interests of India at that stage of history. They therefore planned not to expel the British but transform British rule to approximate national rule. Later, when they took note of the evils of British rule and the failure of the government to accept nationalist demands for reform, many of them stopped talking of loyalty to British rule and started demanding self-government for India. Moreover, many of them were Moderates because they felt that the time was not yet ripe to throw a direct challenge to the foreign rulers.

Role of the Masses

The basic weakness of the early national movement lay in its narrow social base. It did not yet penetrate down to the masses. In fact, the leaders lacked political faith in the masses. Describing the difficulties in the way of the organisation of active political struggle, Gopal Krishna Gokhale pointed to "endless divisions and sub-divisions in the country, the bulk of the population ignorant and clinging with a tenacity to the old modes of thought and sentiment, which are averse to all changes and do not understand change". Thus, the Moderate leaders believed that aggressive mass struggle against colonial rule could be waged only after the heterogeneous elements of Indian society had been welded into a nation. But in fact, it was mainly in the course of such a struggle that the Indian nation could get formed. The result of this wrong approach towards the masses was that the latter were assigned a passive role in the early phase of the national movement. It also led to political moderation. Without the support of the masses, they could not adopt a more aggressive political position. As we shall see, the later nationalists were to differ from the Moderates in precisely this respect.

The narrow social base of the early national movement should not, however, lead to the conclusion that it fought for the narrow interests of the social groups which joined it. Its programme and

The Nationalist Movement: 1858–1905

policies championed the cause of all sections of the Indian people and represented the interests of the emerging Indian nation against colonial domination.

Attitude of the Government

The British authorities were from the beginning hostile to the rising nationalist movement and had become suspicious of the National Congress. Dufferin, the Viceroy, had tried to divert the national movement by suggesting to Hume that the Congress devote itself to social rather than political affairs. But the Congress leaders had refused to make the change. It soon became a tool in the hands of the authorities and it was gradually becoming a focus of Indian nationalism. British officials now began to openly criticise and condemn the National Congress and other nationalist spokesmen. British officials from Dufferin downwards began to brand the nationalist leaders as 'disloyal *babus*', 'seditious brahmins' and 'violent villains'. The Congress was described as 'a factory of sedition'. In 1887, Dufferin attacked the National Congress in a public speech and ridiculed it as representing only "a microscopic minority of the people". In 1900, Lord Curzon announced to the Secretary of State that "the Congress is tottering to its fall, and one of my great ambitions, while in India is to assist it to a peaceful demise." Realising that the growing unity of the Indian people posed a major threat to their rule, the British authorities also pushed further the policy of 'divide and rule'. They encouraged Sayyid Ahmad Khan, Raja Shiva Prasad of Benaras, and other pro-British individuals to start an anti-Congress movement. They also tried to drive a wedge between Hindus and Muslims. They followed a policy of minor concessions on the one hand and ruthless repression on the other to put down the growth of nationalism. Opposition by the authorities failed, however, in checking the growth of the national movement.

Evaluation of the Early National Movement

According to some critics, the nationalist movement and the National Congress did not achieve much success in their early phase. Very few of the reforms for which the nationalists agitated were introduced by the government.

There is a great deal of truth in this criticism. But the critics are not quite correct in declaring the early national movement a failure. Historically viewed, its record is quite bright if the immediate difficulties of the task they had undertaken are kept in view. It represented the most progressive force of the time. It succeeded in creating a wide national awakening, in arousing among the people the feeling that they belonged to one common nation—the Indian nation. It made the people of India conscious of the bonds of common political, economic, social and cultural interests and of the existence of a common enemy in imperialism, and thus helped to weld them in a common nationality. It trained people in the art of political work, popularised among them the ideas of democracy, civil liberties, secularism and nationalism, propagated among them a modern outlook and exposed before them the evils resulting from British rule. Most of all, the early nationalists did pioneering work in mercilessly exposing the true character of British imperialism in India. They linked nearly every important economic question with the politically dependent status of the country. Their powerful economic critique of imperialism was to serve as the main plank of nationalist agitation in the later years of active mass struggle against British imperialism. They had, by their economic agitation, undermined the moral foundations of British rule by exposing its cruel, exploitative character. The early national movement also evolved a common political and economic programme around which the Indian people could gather and wage political struggles later on. It established the political truth that India must be ruled in the interests of Indians. It made the issue of nationalism a dominant one in Indian life. Moreover, the political work of the Moderates was based on a concrete study and analysis of the hard reality of the life of the people, rather than on narrow appeals to religion, mere emotion or shallow sentiments. While the weaknesses of the early movement were to be removed by the succeeding generation, its achievements were to serve as a base for a more vigorous national movement in later years. It can, therefore, be said that in spite of their many weaknesses, the early nationalists laid strong foundations for the national movement to build on, and they deserve a high place among the makers of modern India.

Eleven

Religious and Social Reform after 1858

The rising tide of nationalism and democracy, which led to the struggle for freedom, also found expression in movements to reform and democratise the social institutions and religious outlook of the Indian people. Many Indians realised that social and religious reformation was an essential condition for the all-round development of the country on modern lines, and for the growth of national unity and solidarity. The growth of nationalist sentiments, the emergence of new economic forces, the spread of education, the impact of modern Western ideas and culture, and increased awareness of the world not only heightened awareness of the backwardness and degeneration of Indian society, but also further strengthened the resolve to reform. Keshub Chandra Sen, for example, said:

> What we see around us today is a fallen nation—a nation whose primitive greatness lies buried in ruins. Its national literature and science, its theology and philosophy, its industry and commerce, its social prosperity and domestic simplicity and sweetness, are almost numbered with the things that were. As we survey the mournful and dismal scene of desolation—spiritual, social and intellectual—which spreads around us, we in vain try to recognise therein the land of Kalidas—the land of poetry, of science, and of civilization.

Similarly, Swami Vivekananda described the condition of the Indian people in the following words:

> Moving about here and there emaciated figures of young and old in tattered rags, whose faces bear deep-cut lines of the despair and poverty of hundreds of years; cows, bullocks, buffaloes common everywhere—aye, the same melancholy look in their eyes, the same feeble physique, on the wayside, refuse and dirt;—this is our present day India! Worn-out huts by the very side of palaces, piles of refuse in the near proximity

of temples, the Sannyasin clad with only a little loin cloth, walking by the gorgeously dressed, the pitiful gaze of lustreless eyes of the hunger-stricken at the well-fed and the amply-provided;—this is our native land! Devastation by violent plague! and cholera; malaria eating into the very vitals of the nation; starvation and semi-starvation as second nature; death-like famine often dancing its tragic dance;... A conglomeration of three hundred million souls, resembling men only in apearance;—crushed out of life by being down-trodden by their own people and foreign nations ... without any hope, without any past, without any future—... of a malicious nature befitting a slave, to whom the property of their fellowman is unbearable;—... licking the dust of the feet of the strong, withal dealing a death-blow to those who are weak;—full of ugly, diabolical superstitions which come naturally to those who are weak, and hopeless of the future;—without any standard of morality as their backbone;—three hundred millions of souls such as these are swarming on the body of India, like so many worms on a rotten, stinking carcass;— this is the picture concerning us, which naturally presents itself to the English official.

Thus, after 1858, the earlier reforming tendency was broadened. The work of earlier reformers, like Raja Rammohun Roy and Pandit Vidyasagar, was carried further by major movements of religious and social reform.

Religious Reform

Filled with the desire to adapt their society to the requirements of the modern world of science, democracy and nationalism, and determined to let no obstacle stand in the way, thoughtful Indians set out to reform their traditional religions, for religion was in those times a basic part of people's life and there could be little social reform without religious reform. While trying to remain true to the foundations of their religions, they remodelled them to suit the new needs of the Indian people.

Brahmo Samaj

The Brahmo tradition of Raja Rammohun Roy was carried forward after 1843 by Devendranath Tagore, who also repudiated the doctrine that the Vedic scriptures were infallible, and after 1866 by Keshub

Chandra Sen. The Brahmo Samaj made an effort to reform Hindu religion by removing social ills and basing it on the worship of one God and on the teachings of the Vedas and Upanishads, even though it repudiated the doctrine of the infallibility of the Vedas. It also tried to incorporate the best aspects of modern Western thought. Most of all, it based itself on human reason, which was to be the ultimate criterion for deciding what was worthwhile and what was useless in the past or present religious principles and practices. For that reason, the Brahmo Samaj denied the need for a priestly class for interpreting religious writings. Every individual had the right and the capacity to decide with the help of his own intellect what was right and what was wrong in a religious book or principle. Thus, the Brahmos were basically opposed to idolatry and superstitious practices and rituals, in fact to the entire Brahmanical system. They could worship one God without the mediation of the priests.

The Brahmos were also great social reformers. They actively opposed the caste system and child-marriage and supported the general uplift of women, including widow remarriage, and the spread of modern education to men and women.

The Brahmo Samaj was weakened by internal dissensions in the second half of the nineteenth century. Moreover, its influence was confined mostly to urban educated groups. Yet it had a decisive influence on the intellectual, social, cultural and political life of Bengal, and the rest of India in the nineteenth and twentieth centuries.

Religious Reform in Maharashtra

Religious reform was begun in Bombay in 1840 by the Parmahans Mandali, which aimed to fight idolatry and the caste system. Perhaps the earliest religious reformer in western India was Gopal Hari Deshmukh, known popularly as 'Lokahit-wadi', who wrote in Marathi, made powerful rationalist attacks on Hindu orthodoxy, and preached religious and social equality. For example, he wrote in the 1840s:

> The priests are very unholy because they repeat things without understanding their meaning and profanely reduce knowledge to such

repetition. The Pandits are worse than priests; because they are more ignorant and also are haughty. ... Who are the *brahmins* and in what respects do they differ from us? Have they twenty hands and do we lack something in us? When such questions are now asked the *brahmins* should give up their foolish concepts; they must accept that all men are equal and every body has a right to acquire knowledge.

He also said that if religion did not sanction social reforms, then religion should be changed, for after all, religion was made by human beings and scriptures, written long ago, and might not remain relevant to later times. Later, the Prarthana Samaj was started with the aim of reforming Hindu religious thought and practice in the light of modern knowledge. It preached the worship of one God and tried to free religion of caste orthodoxy and priestly domination. Two of its great leaders were R.G. Bhandarkar, the famous Sanskrit scholar and historian, and Mahadev Govind Ranade (1842–1901). It was powerfully influenced by the Brahmo Samaj. Its activities also spread to south India as a result of the efforts of the Telugu reformer, Viresalingam. One of the greatest rationalist thinkers of modern India, Gopal Ganesh Agarkar, also lived and worked in Maharashtra at this time. Agarkar was an advocate of the power of human reason. He sharply criticised any blind dependence on tradition or the false glorification of India's past.

RAMAKRISHNA AND VIVEKANANDA

Ramakrishna Parmahamsa (1834–86) was a saintly person who sought religious salvation in the traditional ways of renunciation, meditation and devotion (bhakti). In his search for religious truth or the realisation of God, he lived with mystics of other faiths, Muslims and Christians. He again and again emphasised that there were many roads to God and salvation and that service of man was service of God, for man was the embodiment of God.

It was his great disciple, Swami Vivekananda (1863–1902), who popularised his religious message and who tried to put it in a form that would suit the needs of contemporary Indian society. Above all, Vivekananda stressed social action. Knowledge unaccompanied by action in the actual world in which we live was useless, he said. He, too, like his guru, proclaimed the essential oneness of all religions and condemned any narrowness in religious matters. Thus, he wrote in 1898: "For our own motherland a junction of the two great systems, Hinduism and Islam ... is the only hope". At the same time, he was convinced of the superior approach of the Indian philosophical tradition. He himself subscribed to *Vedanta*, which he declared to be a fully rational system.

Vivekananda criticised Indians for having lost touch with the rest of the world and become stagnant and mummified. He wrote: "The fact of our isolation from all other nations of the world is the cause of our degeneration and its only remedy is getting back into the current of the rest of the world. Motion is the sign of life."

Vivekananda condemned the caste system and the current Hindu emphasis on rituals and superstitions, and urged the people to imbibe the spirit of liberty, equality and free thought. Thus, he bitingly remarked:

> There is a danger of our religion getting into the kitchen. We are neither Vedantists, most of us now, nor Pauranics, nor Tantrics. We are just "don't touchists". Our religion is in the kitchen. Our God is in the cooking-pot, and our religion is "Don't touch me, I am holy". If this goes on for another century, everyone of us will be in a lunatic asylum.

Regarding liberty of thought, he said:

> Liberty in thought and action is the only condition of life, growth and well being: Where it does not exist, the man, the race, and the nation must go down.

Like his guru, Vivekananda was also a great humanist. Shocked by the poverty, misery and suffering of the common people of the country, he wrote:

> The only God in whom I believe, the sum total of all souls, and above all, my God the wicked, my God the afflicted, my God the poor of all races.

To the educated Indians, he said:

> So long as the millions live in hunger and ignorance, I hold everyman a traitor, who having been educated at their expense, pays not the least heed to them.

In 1897, Vivekananda founded the Ramakrishna Mission to carry on humanitarian relief and social work. The Mission had many branches in different parts of the country and carried on social service by opening schools, hospitals and dispensaries, orphanages, libraries, etc. It thus laid emphasis not on personal salvation, but on social good or social service.

Swami Dayanand and the Arya Samaj

The Arya Samaj undertook the task of reforming Hindu religion in north India. It was founded in 1875 by Swami Dayanand Saraswati (1824–83). Swami Dayanand believed that selfish and ignorant priests had perverted Hindu religion with the aid of the Puranas which, he said, were full of false teachings. For his own inspiration, Swami Dayanand went to the Vedas, which he regarded as infallible, being the inspired word of God, and as the fount of all knowledge. He rejected such later religious thought as conflicted with the Vedas. This total dependence on the Vedas and their infallibility gave his teachings an orthodox colouring, for infallibility meant that human reason was not to be the final deciding factor. However, his approach had a rationalist aspect, because the Vedas, though revealed, were to be rationally interpreted by himself and others, who were human beings. Thus, individual reason was the decisive factor.

He believed that every person had the right of direct access to God. Moreover, instead of supporting Hindu orthodoxy, he attacked it and led a revolt against it. The teachings he derived from his own interpretation of the Vedas were consequently similar to the religious and social reforms that other Indian reformers were advocating. He was opposed to idolatry, ritual and priesthood, and particularly to the prevalent caste practices and popular Hinduism as preached by brahmins. He also directed attention towards problems of men as they lived in this real world and away from the traditional belief in the other world. He also favoured the study of Western sciences. Interestingly enough, Swami Dayanand had met and had discussions with Keshub Chandra Sen, Vidyasagar, Justice Ranade, Gopal Hari Deshmukh, and other modern religious and social reformers. In fact, the ideas of the Arya Samaj with its Sunday meeting resembled the practices of the Brahmo Samaj and the Prarthana Samaj in this respect. Some of Swami Dayanand's followers later started a network of schools and colleges in the country to impart education on Western lines. Lala Hansraj played a leading part in this effort. On the other hand, in 1902, Swami Shradhananda started the Gurukul near Hardwar to propagate the more traditional ideals of education.

The Arya Samajists were vigorous advocates of social reform and worked actively to improve the condition of women, and to spread education among them. They fought untouchability and the rigidities of the hereditary caste system. They were thus advocates of social equality and promoted social solidarity and consolidation. They also inculcated a spirit of self-respect and self-reliance among the people. This promoted nationalism. At the same time, one of the Arya Samaj's objectives was to prevent the conversion of Hindus to other religions. This led it to start a crusade against other religions. This crusade became a contributory factor in the growth of communalism in India in the twentieth century. While the Arya Samaj's reformist work tended to remove social ills and to unite people, its religious work tended, though perhaps unconsciously, to divide the growing national unity among Hindus, Muslims, Parsis, Sikhs and Christians. It was not seen clearly that in India, national unity had to be secular and above religion so that it would embrace the people of all religions.

THE THEOSOPHICAL SOCIETY

The Theosophical Society was founded in the United States by Madam H.P. Blavatsky and Colonel H.S. Olcott, who later came to India and founded the headquarters of the Society at Adyar near Madras in 1886. The Theosophist movement soon grew in India as a result of the leadership given to it by Mrs. Annie Besant, who had come to India in 1893. The Theosophists advocated the revival and strengthening of the ancient religions of Hinduism, Zoroastrianism and Buddhism. They recognised the doctrine of the transmigration of the soul. They also preached the universal brotherhood of man. As religious revivalists, the Theosophists were not very successful. But they made a peculiar contribution to developments in modern

India. It was a movement led by Westerners who glorified Indian religious and philosophical traditions. This helped Indians to recover their self-confidence.

One of Mrs. Besant's many achievements in India was the establishment of the Central Hindu School at Benaras, which was later developed by Madan Mohan Malaviya into the Benaras Hindu University.

SAYYID AHMAD KHAN AND THE ALIGARH SCHOOL

Movements for religious reform were late in emerging among the Muslims. The Muslim upper classes had tended to avoid contact with Western education and culture, and it was mainly after the Revolt of 1857 that modern ideas of religious reform began to appear. A beginning in this direction was made when the Muhammedan Literary Society was founded at Calcutta in 1863. This Society promoted the discussion of religious, social and political questions in the light of modern ideas and encouraged upper and middle-class Muslims to take to Western education.

The most important reformer among the Muslims was Sayyid Ahmad Khan (1817–98). He was tremendously impressed by modern scientific thought and worked all his life to reconcile it with Islam. This he did, first of all, by declaring that the Quran alone was the authoritative work for Islam and all other Islamic writings were secondary. Even the Quran he interpreted in the light of contemporary rationalism and science. In his view, any interpretation of the Quran that conflicted with human reason, science or nature was in reality a misinterpretation. Nor were religious tenets immutable, he said. If religion did not change with time, it would become fossilised, as had happened in India. All his life he struggled against blind obedience to tradition, dependence on custom, ignorance and irrationalism. He urged the people to develop a critical approach and freedom of thought. "So long as freedom of thought is not developed, there can be no civilised life," he declared. He also warned against fanaticism, narrow-mindedness, and exclusiveness, and urged students and others to be broadminded and tolerant. A closed mind, he said, was the hallmark of social and intellectual backwardness. Praising the study of world classics, he remarked:

> The student will learn to appreciate the temper with which great minds approach the consideration of great questions, he will discover that truth is many-sided, that it is not identical or merely coextensive with individual opinion and that world is a good deal wider than his own sect, society or class.

Sayyid Ahmad Khan believed that the religious and social life of the Muslims could be improved only by imbibing modern Western scientific knowledge and culture. Therefore, the promotion of modern education remained his first task throughout his life. As an official, he founded schools in many towns and had many Western books translated into Urdu. In 1875, he founded at Aligarh the Muhammedan Anglo-Oriental College as a centre for spreading Western sciences and culture. Later, this College grew into the Aligarh Muslim University.

Sayyid Ahmad Khan was a great believer in religious toleration. He believed that all religions had a certain underlying unity which could be called practical morality. Believing that a person's religion was his or her private affair, he roundly condemned any sign of religious bigotry in personal relations. He was also opposed to communal friction. Appealing to Hindus and Muslims to unite, he said in 1883:

> Now both of us live on the air of India, drink the holy waters of the Ganga and Jumna. We both feed upon the products of the Indian soil. We are together in life and death; living in India both of us have changed our blood, the colour of our bodies has become the same, our features have become similar; the Musalmans have adopted numerous Hindu customs, the Hindus have accepted many Muslim traits of conduct, we became so fused that we developed the new language of Urdu, which was neither our language nor that of the Hindus. Therefore, if we accept that part of our lives which belongs to God, then undoubtedly in consideration of the fact that we both belong to the same country, we are a nation, and the progress and welfare of the country, and both of us, depend on our unity, mutual sympathy, and love, while our mutual disagreement, obstinacy and opposition and ill-feeling are sure to destroy us.

Moreover, Hindus, Parsis and Christians had freely contributed to the funds of his college, whose doors were also open to all Indians. For example, in 1898, there were 64 Hindu and 285 Muslim students in the college. Out of the seven Indian teachers, two were Hindu, one of them being a professor of Sanskrit. However, towards the end of his life, he began to talk of Hindu domination to prevent his followers from joining the rising national movement. This was unfortunate, though basically he was not a communalist. He only wanted the backwardness of the Muslim middle and upper classes to go. His politics were the result of his firm belief that immediate political progress was not possible because the British Government could not be easily dislodged. On the other hand, any hostility by the officials might prove dangerous to the educational effort which he saw as the need of the hour. He believed that only when Indians had become as modern in their thinking and actions as the English were, could they hope to successfully challenge foreign rule. He therefore advised all Indians, and particularly the educationally backward Muslims, to remain aloof from politics for some time to come. The time for politics, he said, had not yet come. In fact, he had become so committed to his college and the cause of education that he was willing to sacrifice all other interests to them. Consequently, to prevent orthodox Muslims from opposing his college, he virtually gave up his agitation in favour of religious reform. For the same reason, he would not do anything to offend the government and, on the other hand, encouraged communalism and separatism. This was, of course, a serious political error, which was to have harmful consequences in later years. Moreover, some of his followers deviated from his broad-mindedness and tended later to glorify Islam and its past while criticising other religions.

Sayyid Ahmad's reformist zeal also embraced the social sphere. He urged Muslims to give up medieval customs and ways of thought and behaviour. In particular, he wrote in favour of raising women's status in society and advocated the removal of purdah and the spread of education among women. He also condemned the customs of polygamy and easy divorce.

Sayyid Ahmad Khan was helped by a band of loyal followers who are collectively described as the Aligarh School. Chiragh Ali, the Urdu poet Altaf Husain Hali, Nazir Ahmad and Maulana Shibli Nomani were some of the other distinguished leaders of the Aligarh School.

Muhammad Iqbal

One of the greatest poets of modern India, Muhammad Iqbal (1876–1938) also profoundly influenced, through his poetry, the philosophical and religious outlook of the younger generation of Muslims as well as of Hindus. Like Swami Vivekananda, he emphasised the need for constant change and ceaseless activity and condemned resignation, contemplation, and quiet contentment. He urged the adoption of a dynamic outlook that would help change the world. He was basically a humanist. In fact, he raised human action to the status of a prime virtue. Man should not submit to nature or the powers that be, he said, but should control this world through constant activity. Nothing was more sinful in his eyes than the passive acceptance of things as they were. Condemning ritualism and an other-wordly attitude, he urged men to work for and achieve happiness in this world of the living. In his earlier poetry, he extolled patriotism, though later he encouraged Muslim separatism.

Religious Reform among the Parsis

Religious reform began among the Parsis in Bombay in the middle of the nineteenth century. In 1851, the Rehnumai Mazdayasan Sabha or Religious Reform Association was started by Naoroji Furdonji, Dadabhai Naoroji, S.S. Bengalee, and others. It campaigned against the entrenched orthodoxy in the religious field and initiated the modernisation of Parsi social customs regarding the education of women, marriage and the social position of women in general. In course of time, the Parsis became socially the most Westernised section of Indian society.

Religious Reform among the Sikhs

Religious reform among the Sikhs was begun at the end of the nineteenth century when the Khalsa College was started at Amritsar. But the reform effort gained momentum after 1920 when the Akali Movement rose in the Punjab. The main aim of the Akalis was to purify the management of the gurudwaras or Sikh shrines. These gurudwaras had been heavily endowed with land and money by devout Sikhs. But they had come to be managed autocratically by corrupt and selfish mahants. In 1921, the Sikh masses led by the Akalis started a powerful satyagraha against the mahants and the government which aided them.

The Akalis soon forced the government to pass a new Gurudwara Act in 1922, which was later amended in 1925. Sometimes with the aid of the Act, but often through direct action, the Sikhs gradually turned out of the gurudwaras the corrupt mahants, even though hundreds of lives had to be sacrificed in the process.

Apart from the reform movements and individual reformers discussed above, there were numerous other similar movements and individuals during the nineteenth and twentieth centuries.

The religious reform movements of modern times had an underlying unity—most of them were based on the twin doctrines of reason (rationalism) and humanism, though they also sometimes tended to appeal to faith and ancient authority to bolster their appeal. Moreover, it was to the rising middle classes and the modern educated intellectuals that they appealed the most. They tried to free from anti-intellectual religious dogmas and blind faith the human intellect's capacity to think and reason. They opposed the ritualistic, superstitious, irrational and obscurantist elements in Indian religions. Many of them abandoned, though to varying degrees, the principle of authority in religion and evaluated truth in any religion or its holy books by its conformity to logic, reason, or science. Swami Vivekananda said:

> Is religion to justify itself by the discoveries of reason through which every science justifies itself? Are the same methods of investigation which apply to the sciences and knowledge outside, to be applied to the science of religion? In my opinion, this must be so, and I am also of opinion that the sooner this is done the better.

Some of these religious reformers appealed to tradition and claimed that they were merely reviving the pure doctrines, beliefs and practices of the past. But, in fact, the past could not be revived. Often there was no agreed picture of the past. The problems that an appeal to the past often created were posed by Justice Ranade, who had himself often asked the people to revive the best traditions of the past, in the following words:

> What shall we revive? Shall we revive the old habits of our people when the most sacred of our castes indulged in all the abominations, as we now understand them, of animal food and intoxicating drink? Shall we revive the twelve forms of sons, or eight forms of marriage, which included capture, and recognised mixed and illegitimate intercourse? ... Shall we revive the hacatombs of animals sacrificed from year's end to year's end, in which even human beings were not spared as propitiatory offering to God? ... Shall we revive the *sati*, and infanticide customs?

And he came to the conclusion that society as a living organism is constantly changing and can never go back to the past. "The dead and the buried or burnt are dead, buried, and burnt once for all, and the dead past cannot, therefore, be revived," he wrote. Every reformer who appealed to the past so interpreted it as to make it appear to agree with the reforms he was suggesting. Often the reforms and the outlook were new, only their justification was based on an appeal to the past. Many of the ideas which conflicted with modern scientific knowledge were usually declared to be a later accretion or misinterpretation. And since the orthodox could not accept this view, the religious reformers came into conflict with the orthodox sections and became, at least in the beginning, religious and social rebels. For example, this is what Lala Lajpat Rai writes regarding the orthodox opposition to Swami Dayanand:

> The amount of obloquy and persecution to which Swami Dayanand was exposed in his lifetime may be gathered from the fact that numerous attempts were made on his life by the orthodox Hindus; assassins were hired to kill him, missiles were thrown at him during his lectures and disputation; he was called a hired emissary of the Christians, an apostate, an atheist, and so on.

Similarly, Sayyid Ahmad Khan aroused the anger of the traditionalists. They abused him, issued *fatwas* (religious decrees) against him and even threatened his life.

The humanist aspect of the religious reform movements was expressed in the general attack on the priesthood and rituals, and the emphasis on the individual's right to interpret religious scriptures in the light of human reason and human welfare. A significant feature of humanism was expressed in a new humanitarian morality which included the notion that humanity can progress and has progressed and that moral values are, ultimately, those which favour human progress. The social reform movements were an embodiment of this new humanitarian morality.

Though the reformers tried to reform their religions, their general outlook was universalistic. Rammohun Roy saw different religions as particular expressions of a universal God and religious truth. Sayyid Ahmad Khan said that prophets had the same faith or *din* and every people had been sent prophets by God. Keshub Chandra Sen expressed the same idea as follows: "Our position is not that truths are to be found in all religions, but all established religions are true".

Apart from purely religious considerations, these religious reform movements fostered among Indians greater self-respect, self-confidence, and pride in their country. By interpreting their religious past in modern rational terms and by weeding out many of the corrupting and irrational elements from nineteenth-century religious beliefs and practices, the reformers enabled their followers to meet the official taunt that their religions and society were decadent and inferior. As Jawaharlal Nehru has put it:

> The rising middle classes were politically inclined and were not so much in search of a religion; but they wanted some cultural roots to cling on to, something that gave them assurance of their own worth, something that would reduce the sense of frustration and humiliation that foreign conquest and rule had produced.

The religious reform movements helped many Indians to come to terms with the modern world. In fact, they arose to recast the old religions into a new modern mould to suit the needs of new social groups of society. Thus, pride in the past did not prevent Indians from accepting the essential superiority of the modern world in general, and modern science in particular. Of course, some people insisted that they were merely going back to the original, most ancient scriptures which were suitably interpreted. As a result of the reformed outlook, many Indians began to acquire a modern, this-worldly, secular and national outlook in place of a narrow outlook dominated by considerations of caste and religion, though the latter tendency was by no means at an end. Also, more and more people began to think in terms of promoting their physical and cultural welfare in this world in place of passively accepting their lot and waiting for improvement in life after death. These movements also, to some extent, ended India's cultural and intellectual isolation from the rest of the world and enabled Indians to share in the stream of world ideas. At the same time, they were no longer bewitched by everything in the West; those who copied the West blindly were increasingly looked down upon. In fact, while adopting a critical attitude towards backward elements of traditional religions and culture and welcoming positive elements of modern culture, most religious reformers also opposed a blind imitation of the West and waged an ideological struggle against the colonialisation of Indian culture and thought. The problem here was to maintain a balance between the two aspects. Some went too far in modernisation and tended to encourage colonialisation of culture; others defended traditional thought, culture and institutions to the extent of glorifying them and opposing any introduction of modern ideas and culture. The best of reformers argued that modern ideas and culture could be best imbibed by integrating them into Indian cultural streams.

Two negative aspects of the religious reform movements may also be noted. First, all of them catered to the needs of a small percentage of the population—the urban middle and upper classes. None of them could reach the vast masses of the peasantry and the urban poor, who continued by and large to lead their lives in traditional, custom-ridden ways. This was because they basically gave voice to the urges of the educated and urban strata of Indian society.

The second limitation, which later became a major negative factor, was the tendency to look backward, appeal to past greatness, and to rely on scriptural authority. These tended to go against the positive teachings of the reform movements themselves. They undermined to some extent the supremacy of human reason and scientific outlook. They encouraged mysticism in new garbs, and fostered pseudo-scientific thinking. Appeals to past greatness created false pride and smugness, while the habit of finding a 'Golden Age' in the past acted as a check on the full acceptance of modern science and hampered the effort to improve the present. But, most of all, these tendencies divided Hindus, Muslims, Sikhs, and Parsis, as also high-caste Hindus from low-caste Hindus. Any over-emphasis on religion in a country containing many religions was bound to have a divisive effect. Moreover, the reformers placed a one-sided emphasis on the religious and philosophical aspects of the cultural heritage. These aspects were, moreover, not a common heritage of all people. On the other hand, art and architecture, literature, music, science and technology, etc., in which all sections of people had played an equal role, were not sufficiently emphasised. In addition, Hindu reformers invariably confined their praise of the Indian past to its ancient period. Even a broad-minded man like Swami Vivekananda talked of the Indian spirit or India's past achievements in this sense alone. These reformers looked upon the medieval period of Indian history as essentially an era of decadence. This was not only unhistorical, but also socially and politically harmful. It tended to create the notion of two separate peoples. Similarly, an uncritical praise of the ancient period and religions could not be fully acceptable to persons coming from lower castes, who had for centuries suffered under the most destructive caste oppression which had developed precisely during the ancient period. The result of all these factors was that instead of all Indians taking an equal pride in their past material and cultural achievements and deriving inspiration from them, the past became a heritage of the few.

Moreover, the past itself tended to be torn into compartments on a partisan basis. Many in the Muslim middle classes went to the extent of turning to the history of West Asia for their traditions and moments of pride. Increasingly, Hindus, Muslims, Sikhs and Parsis, and later on lower-caste Hindus who had been influenced by the reform movements, tended to be different from one another. On the other hand, the Hindu and Muslim masses who followed traditional ways untouched by the reform movements still lived in harmony, practising their different religious rituals. To some extent, the process of the evolution of a composite culture that had been going on for centuries was arrested; though in other spheres, national unification of the Indian people was accelerated. The evil aspects of this phenomenon became apparent when it was found that, along with a rapid rise in national consciousness, another consciousness—communal consciousness—had begun to rise among the middle classes. Many other factors were certainly responsible for the birth of communalism in modern times; but, undoubtedly, the *social reform* nature of the religious reform movements also contributed to it.

Social Reform

The major effect of national awakening in the nineteenth century was seen in the field of social reform. The newly educated persons increasingly revolted against rigid social conventions and outdated customs. They could no longer tolerate irrational and dehumanising social practices. In their revolt, they were inspired by the humanistic ideals of social equality and the equal worth of all individuals.

Nearly all the religious reformers contributed to the social reform movement. This was because the backward features of Indian society, such as the caste system or inequality of the sexes, had religious sanctions in the past. In addition, certain other organisations like the Social Conference, Servants of India Society, and the Christian missionaries worked actively for social reform. Many prominent persons—Jyotiba Govind Phule, Gopal Hari Deshmukh, Justice Ranade, K.T. Telang, B.M. Malabari, D.K. Karve, Sasipada Banerjee, B.C. Pal, Viresalingam, Sri Narayan Guru, E.V. Ramaswami Naicker and B.R. Ambedkar, and many others—also played an important role. In the twentieth century, and especially after 1919, the national movement became the main propagator of social reform. Increasingly, the reformers took recourse to propaganda in the Indian language to reach the masses. They also used novels, dramas, poetry, short stories, the Press and, in the 1930s, the cinema to spread their views.

While social reform was linked with religious reform in some cases during the nineteenth century, in later years it was increasingly secular in approach. Moreover, many people who were orthodox in their religious approach participated in it. Similarly, in the beginning social reform had largely been the effort of newly educated Indians belonging to higher castes to adjust their social behaviour to the requirements of modern Western culture and values. But gradually it penetrated down to the lower strata of society and began to revolutionise and reconstruct the social sphere. In time, the ideas and ideals of the reformers won almost universal acceptance and are today enshrined in the Indian Constitution.

The social reform movements tried in the main to achieve two objectives: the emancipation of women and extension of equal rights to them; and the removal of caste rigidities and in particular the abolition of untouchability.

Emancipation of Women

For countless centuries, women in India had been subordinated to men and socially oppressed. The various religions practised in India as well as the personal laws based on them consigned women to a status inferior to men. The condition of upper-class women was in this respect worse than that of peasant women. Since the latter worked actively in the fields alongside men, they enjoyed relatively greater freedom of movement and, in some respects, a better status in the family than upper-class women. For example, they seldom observed purdah and many of them had the right to remarry. The traditional view often praised the role of women as wives and mothers, but as individuals, they were assigned a very lowly social position. They were supposed to have no personality of their own apart from their ties to their husbands. They could not find any other expression to their inborn talents or desires except as housewives. In fact, they were seen as mere adjuncts to men. For example, while a woman could marry only once among Hindus, a man was permitted to have more than one wife. Among Muslims, too, this custom of polygamy prevailed. In large parts of the country, women had to live behind the purdah. The custom of early marriage prevailed, and even children of eight or nine were married. Widows could not remarry and had to lead an ascetic and restricted life. In many parts of the country, the horrifying custom of sati or self-immolation of widows prevailed. Hindu women had no right to inherit property, nor did they enjoy the right to terminate an undesirable marriage. Muslim women could inherit property, but only half as much as a man could; and in the matter of divorce, even theoretically there was no equality between husband and wife. In fact, Muslim women dreaded divorce. The social position of Hindu and Muslim women as well as their values were similar.

Moreover, in both cases they were economically and socially totally dependent on men. Lastly, the benefit of education was denied to most of them. In addition, women were taught to accept their subjection and even to welcome it as a badge of honour. It is true that occasionally women of the character and personality of Razia Sultana, Chand Bibi, or Ahilyabai Holkar arose in India. But they were exceptions to the general pattern, and did not in any way change the picture.

Moved by the humanitarian and egalitarian impulses of the nineteenth century, the social reformers started a powerful movement to improve the position of women. While some reformers appealed to ideals of individuality and equality, others declared that true Hinduism or Islam or Zoroastrianism did not sanction the inferior status of women and that true religion assigned them a high social position.

Numerous individuals, reform societies and religious organisations worked hard to spread education among women, to encourage widow remarriage, to improve the living conditions of widows, to prevent the marriage of young children, to bring women out of the purdah, to enforce monogamy and to enable middle-class women to take up professions or public employment. After the 1880s, when the Dufferin hospitals (named after Lady Dufferin, the wife of the Viceroy) were started, efforts were made to make modern medicine and child delivery techniques available to Indian women.

The movement for the liberation of women received a great stimulus from the rise of the national movement in the twentieth century. Women played an active and important role in the struggle for freedom. They participated in large numbers in the agitation against the partition of Bengal and in the Home Rule movement. After 1918, they marched in political processions, picketed shops selling foreign cloth and liquor, spun and propagated khadi, went to jail in the non-cooperation movements, faced lathis, tear gas and bullets during public demonstrations, participated actively in the revolutionary movement, and voted in elections to legislatures and even stood as candidates themselves. Sarojini Naidu, the famous poet, became president of the National Congress. Several women became ministers or parliamentary secretaries in the popular ministries of 1937. Hundreds of them became members of municipalities and other organs of local government. When the trade union and kisan movements arose in the 1920s, women were often found in their forefront. More than any other factor, participation in the national movement contributed to the awakening of Indian women and their emancipation: For how could those who had braved British jails and bullets be declared inferior! And how could they any longer be confined to the home and be satisfied with the life of 'a doll or a slave girl'? They were bound to assert their rights as human beings.

Another important development was the birth of a women's movement in the country. Up to the 1920s, enlightened men had worked for the uplift of women. Now aware and self-confident women undertook that task. They started many organisations and institutions for the purpose, the most outstanding of which was the All India Women's Conference, founded in 1927.

Women's struggle for equality took a big step forward with the coming of independence. Articles 14 and 15 of the Indian Constitution (1950) guaranteed the complete equality of men and women. The Hindu Succession Act of 1956 made the daughter an equal co-heir with the son. The Hindu Marriage Act of 1955 permitted dissolution of marriage on specific grounds. Monogamy was also made mandatory, for men as well as women. But the evil custom of dowry still continues, even though the demanding of dowry has been banned. The Constitution gives women the equal right to work and to get employment in state agencies. The Directive Principles of the Constitution lay down the principle of equal pay for equal work for both men and women. Of course, many visible and invisible obstacles still remain in putting the principle of the equality of sexes into practice. A proper social climate has still to be created. But the social reform movements, the freedom struggle, the women's movement and the Constitution of free India have made a big contribution in this direction.

STRUGGLE AGAINST CASTE

The caste system was another major target of attack for the social reform movement. The Hindus were at this time divided into numerous castes (jatis). The caste into which a man was born determined large areas of his life. It determined whom he would marry and with whom he would dine. It largely determined his profession, as also his social loyalties. Moreover, the castes were carefully graded into a hierarchy of status. At the bottom of the ladder came the untouchables, or Scheduled Castes as they came to be called later, who formed about 20 per cent of the Hindu population. The untouchables suffered from numerous severe disabilities and restrictions, which of course varied from place to place. Their touch was considered impure and was a source of pollution. In some parts of the country, particularly in the south, their very shadow was to be avoided, so that they had to move away if a brahmin was seen or heard coming. An untouchable's dress, food, place of residence, all were carefully regulated. He could not draw water from wells and tanks used by the higher castes; he could do so only from wells and tanks specially reserved for untouchables. Where no such well or tank existed, he had to drink dirty water from ponds and irrigation canals. He could not enter the Hindu temples or study the *shastras*. Often, his children could not attend a school in which the children of caste Hindus studied. Public services such as the police and the army were closed to him. The untouchables were forced to take up menial and other such jobs which were considered 'unclean,' for example, scavenging, shoe-making, removing dead bodies, skinning dead animals, tanning hides and skins. Usually denied ownership of land, many of them worked even as tenants-at-will and field labourers.

The caste system was an evil in another respect. Not only was it humiliating and inhuman and based on the anti-democratic principle of inequality by birth, it was also a cause of social disintegration. It splintered people into numerous groups. In modern times, it became a major obstacle in the growth of a united national feeling and the spread of democracy. It may also be noted that caste consciousness, particularly with regard to marriage, prevailed also among Muslims, Christians and Sikhs, who practised untouchability, though in a less virulent form.

British rule released many forces which gradually undermined the caste system. The introduction of modern industries, railways and buses, and growing urbanisation made it difficult to prevent mass contact among persons of different castes, especially in the cities.

Modern commerce and industry opened new fields of economic activity to all. For example, a brahmin or upper-caste merchant could hardly miss the opportunity to trade in skins or shoes, nor would he agree to deny himself the opportunity of becoming a doctor or a soldier. Free sale of land upset the caste balance in many villages. The close connection between caste and vocation could hardly continue in a modern industrial society in which the profit motive was increasingly becoming dominant.

In matters of administration, the British introduced equality before law, took away the judicial functions of caste panchayats and gradually opened the doors of administrative services to all castes. Moreover, the new educational system was wholly secular and therefore basically opposed to caste distinctions and the caste outlook.

As modern democratic and rationalist ideas spread among Indians, they began to raise their voice against the caste system. The Brahmo Samaj, the Prarthana Samaj, the Arya Samaj, the Ramakrishna Mission, the Theosophists, the Social Conference and nearly all the great reformers of the nineteenth century attacked it. Even though many of them defended the system of the four *varnas*, they were critical of the caste (jati) system. In particular, they condemned the inhuman practice of untouchability. They also realised that national unity and national progress in political, social and economic fields could not be achieved so long as millions were deprived of their right to live with dignity and honour.

The growth of the national movement played a significant role in weakening the caste system. The national movement was opposed to all those institutions which tended to divide the Indian people. Common participation in public demonstrations, giant public meetings and *satyagraha* struggles weakened caste consciousness. In any case, those who were fighting for freedom from foreign rule in the name of liberty and equality could hardly support the caste system, which was totally opposed to these principles. Thus, from the beginning, the Indian National Congress and, in fact, the entire national movement opposed caste privileges and fought for equal civic rights and equal freedom for the development of the individual without distinctions of caste, sex or religion.

All his life, Gandhiji kept the abolition of untouchability at the forefront of his public activities. In 1932, he founded the All India

Harijan Sangh for this purpose. His campaign for the "root and branch removal of untouchability" was based on the grounds of humanism and reason. He argued that there was no sanction for untouchability in the Hindu shastras. But, if any shastra approved of untouchability, it should be ignored for it would then be going against human dignity. Truth, he said, could not be confined within the covers of a book.

Since the middle of the nineteenth century, numerous individuals and organisations worked to spread education among the untouchables (or depressed classes and Scheduled Castes, as they came to be called later), to open the doors of schools and temples to them, to enable them to use public wells and tanks, and to remove other social disabilities and distinctions from which they suffered.

As education and awakening spread, the lower castes themselves began to stir. They became conscious of their basic human rights and began to rise in defence of these rights. They gradually built up a powerful movement against the traditional oppression by the higher castes. In Maharashtra, in the second half of the nineteenth century, Jyotiba Phule, born in a lower-caste family, led a lifelong movement against Brahmanical religious authority as part of his struggle against upper-caste domination. He regarded modern education as the most important weapon for the liberation of the lower castes. He was the first to open several schools for girls of the lower castes. Dr B.R. Ambedkar, who belonged to one of the Scheduled Castes, devoted his entire life to fighting against caste tyranny. He organised the All India Scheduled Castes Federation for the purpose. Several other Scheduled Caste leaders founded the All India Depressed Classes Association. In Kerala, Sri Narayan Guru organised a lifelong struggle against the caste system. He coined the famous slogan: "One religion, one caste and one God for mankind." In south India, the non-brahmins organised during the 1920s the Self-Respect Movement to fight the disabilities which brahmins had imposed upon them. Numerous satyagraha movements were organised all over India jointly by the upper and depressed castes against the ban on the latter's entry into temples and other such restrictions.

The struggle against untouchability could not, however, be fully successful under alien rule. The foreign government was afraid of arousing the hostility of the orthodox sections of society. Only the government of a free India could undertake a radical reform of society. Moreover, the problem of social uplift was closely related to the problem of political and economic uplift. For example, economic progress was essential for raising the social status of the depressed castes; so also were the spread of education and political rights. This was fully recognised by the Indian leaders. Dr Ambedkar, for example, said:

> Nobody can remove your grievance as well as you can and you cannot remove these unless you get political power into your hands. ... We must have a government in which men in power will not be afraid to amend the social and economic code of life which the dictates of justice and expediency so urgently call for. This role the British Government will never be able to play. It is only a government which is of the people, for the people and by the people, in other words, it is only the *Swaraj* Government that, will make it possible.

The Constitution of 1950 has provided the legal framework for the final abolition of untouchability. It has declared that "untouchability' is abolished and its practice in any form is forbidden. The endorsement of any disability arising out of 'untouchability' shall be an offence punishable in accordance with law." The Constitution further forbids any restrictions on the use of wells, tanks and bathing ghats, or on access to shops, restaurants, hotels and cinemas. Furthermore, one of the Directive Principles that it has laid down for the guidance of the government says: "The State shall strive to promote the welfare of the people by securing and protecting as effectively as it may a social order in which justice, social, economic and political, shall inform all the institutions of the national life." The struggle against the evils of the caste system, however, still remains an urgent task before the Indian people, especially in the rural areas.

TWELVE

The Nationalist Movement: 1905–18

Gradually, over the years, the trend of an aggressive form of nationalism had been growing in the country. It found expression in the movement against the partition of Bengal in 1905.

The Indian national movement, even in its early days, had increasingly made a large number of people conscious of the evils of foreign domination and of the need for fostering patriotism. It had imparted the necessary political training to the educated Indians. It had, in fact, changed the temper of the people and created a new life in the country.

At the same time, the failure of the British government to accept any of the important demands of the nationalists led to disillusionment among the politically conscious people with the principles and methods of the dominant moderate leadership. Instead of conciliating the moderate nationalists, the British rulers denigrated and looked down upon them. Consequently, there was a strong demand for more vigorous political action and methods than those of meetings, petitions, memorials and speeches in the legislative councils.

RECOGNITION OF THE TRUE NATURE OF BRITISH RULE

The politics of the moderate nationalists were founded on the belief that British rule could be reformed from within. But the spread of knowledge regarding political and economic questions gradually undermined this belief. The political agitation of the moderates was itself responsible for this to a large extent. The nationalist writers and agitators blamed the British rule for the poverty of the people. Politically conscious Indians were convinced that the purpose of British rule was to exploit India economically, that is, to enrich England at the cost of India. They realised that India could make little progress in the economic field unless British imperialism was replaced by a government controlled and run by the Indian people. In particular, the nationalists came to see that Indian industries could not flourish except under an Indian government, which could protect and promote them. The evil economic consequences of foreign rule were symbolised in the eyes of the people by the disastrous famines which ravaged India from 1896 to 1900 and took a toll of over 90 lakh lives.

The political events of the years 1892–1905 also disappointed the nationalists and made them think of more radical politics. The Indian Councils Act of 1892, discussed in Chapter 10, was a complete disappointment. On the other hand, even the existing political rights of the people were attacked. In 1898, a law was passed making it an offence to excite "feelings of disaffection" towards the foreign government. In 1899, the number of Indian members in the Calcutta Corporation was reduced. In 1904, the Indian Official Secrets Act was passed, restricting the freedom of the press. The Natu brothers were deported in 1897 without being tried; even the charges against them were not made public. In the same year, Lokamanya Tilak and other newspaper editors were sentenced to long terms of imprisonment for arousing the people against the foreign government. Thus, the people found that, instead of giving them wider political rights, the rulers were taking away even their few existing ones. The anti-Congress attitude of Lord Curzon convinced the people more and more that it was useless to expect any political and economic advancement as long as Britain ruled India. Even the moderate leader Gokhale complained that "the bureaucracy was growing frankly selfish and openly hostile to national aspirations."

Even socially and culturally, British rule was no longer progressive. Primary and technical education was not making any progress. At the same time, the officials were becoming suspicious of higher education and were even trying to discourage its spread in the country. The Indian Universities Act of 1904 was seen by the nationalists as an attempt to bring Indian universities under tighter official control and to check the growth of higher education.

Thus, an increasing number of Indians were becoming convinced that self-government was essential for the sake of the economic,

The Nationalist Movement: 1905-18

political and cultural progress of the country and that political enslavement meant stunting the growth of the Indian people.

GROWTH OF SELF-RESPECT AND SELF-CONFIDENCE

By the end of the nineteenth century, the Indian nationalists had grown in self-respect and self-confidence. They had acquired faith in their capacity to govern themselves and in the future development of their country. Leaders like Tilak, Aurobindo Ghose and Bipin Chandra Pal preached the message of self-respect and asked the nationalists to rely on the character and capacities of the Indian people. They taught the people that the remedy to their sad condition lay in their own hands and that they should therefore become fearless and strong. Swami Vivekananda, though not a political leader, again and again drove home this message. He declared:

> If there is a sin in the world it is weakness; avoid all weakness, weakness is sin, weakness is death. ... And here is the test of truth—anything that makes you weak physically, intellectually and spiritually, reject as poison, there is no life in it, it cannot be true.

He also urged the people to give up living on the glories of the past and manfully build the future. "When, O Lord," he wrote, "shall our land be free from this eternal dwelling upon the past?"

The belief in self-effort also created an urge for extending the national movement. No longer should the nationalist cause rely on a few upper-class, educated Indians. Instead, political consciousness of the masses was to be aroused. Thus, for example, Swami Vivekananda wrote: "The only hope of India is from the masses. The upper classes are physically and morally dead." There was the realisation that only the masses could make the immense sacrifices needed to win freedom.

GROWTH OF EDUCATION AND UNEMPLOYMENT

By the close of the nineteenth century, the number of educated Indians had increased perceptibly. Large numbers of them worked in the administration on extremely low salaries, while many others increasingly faced unemployment. Their economic plight made them look critically at the nature of British rule. Many of them were attracted by radical nationalist politics.

Even more important was the ideological aspect of the spread of education. The larger the number of educated Indians, the larger was the area of influence of Western ideas of democracy, nationalism and radicalism. The educated Indians became the best propagators and followers of a more aggressive nationalism both because they were low-paid or unemployed and because they were educated in modern thought and politics, and in European and world history.

INTERNATIONAL INFLUENCES

Several events abroad during this period tended to encourage the growth of aggressive nationalism in India. The rise of modern Japan after 1868 showed that a backward Asian country could develop itself without Western control. In a matter of a few decades, the Japanese leaders made their country a first-rate industrial and military power, introduced universal primary education and evolved an efficient, modern administration. The defeat of the Italian army by the Ethiopians in 1896 and of Russia by Japan in 1905 exploded the myth of European superiority. Everywhere in Asia, people heard with enthusiasm the news of the victory of a small Asian country over one of the biggest military powers of Europe.

The *Karachi Chronicle* of 18 June 1905 expressed the popular feeling as follows:

> What one Asiatic has done others can do. ... If Japan can drub Russia, India can drub England with equal ease. ... Let us drive the British into the sea and take our place side by side with Japan among the great powers of the world.

Revolutionary movements in Ireland, Russia, Egypt, Turkey and China, and the Boer War in South Africa convinced the Indians that a united people willing to make sacrifices could challenge even the most powerful of despotic governments. What was needed more than anything else was a spirit of patriotism and self-sacrifice.

EXISTENCE OF AN AGGRESSIVE NATIONALIST SCHOOL OF THOUGHT

From almost the beginning of the national movement, a school of a more aggressive nationalism had existed in the country. This school was represented by leaders like Rajnarain Bose and Ashwini Kumar Dutt in Bengal and Vishnu Shastri Chiplunkar in Maharashtra. The most outstanding representative of this school was Bal Gangadhar Tilak, later popularly known as Lokamanya Tilak. He was born in 1856. From the day of his graduation from Bombay University, he devoted his entire life to the service of his country. He helped to found during the 1880s the New English School, which later became the Fergusson College, and the newspapers the *Mahratta* (in English) and the *Kesari* (in Marathi). From 1889, he edited the *Kesari* and preached nationalism in its columns and taught people to become courageous, self-reliant and selfless fighters in the cause of India's independence. In 1893, he started using the traditional religious Ganpati festival to propagate nationalist ideas through songs and speeches, and in 1895, he started the Shivaji festival to stimulate nationalism among young Maharashtrians by holding up the example of Shivaji for emulation. During 1896–97, he initiated a no-tax campaign in Maharashtra. He asked the famine-stricken peasants of Maharashtra to withhold payment of land revenue if their crops had failed. He set a real example of boldness and sacrifice when the authorities arrested him in 1897 on the charge of spreading hatred and disaffection against the government. He refused to apologise to the government and was sentenced to 18 months' rigorous imprisonment. Thus, he became a living symbol of the new national spirit of self-sacrifice.

At the dawn of the twentieth century, this particular school of nationalist thought found a favourable political climate and its adherents came forward to lead the second stage of the national movement. The most outstanding leaders of this kind of nationalism, apart from Lokamanya Tilak, were Bipin Chandra Pal, Aurobindo Ghose and Lala Lajpat Rai. The distinctive political aspects of the programme of these nationalists were as follows.

They believed that Indians themselves must work out their own salvation and make the effort to rise from their degraded position. They declared that great sacrifices and sufferings were needed for this task. Their speeches, writings and political work were full of boldness and self-confidence, and they considered no personal sacrifice too great for the good of their country.

They did not believe that India could progress under the 'benevolent guidance' and control of the English. They deeply hated foreign rule, and declared in a clear-cut manner that *swaraj* or independence was the goal of the national movement.

They had deep faith in the strength of the masses and planned to achieve *swaraj* through mass action. They, therefore, pressed for political work among the masses and for direct political action by the masses.

A Trained Leadership

By 1905, India possessed a large number of leaders who had acquired during the previous period valuable experience in guiding political agitations and leading political struggles. Without a trained band of political workers, it would have been difficult to take the national movement to a higher political stage.

The Partition of Bengal

The conditions for the emergence of such an aggressive nationalism had thus developed when in 1905 the partition of Bengal was announced and the Indian national movement entered its second stage. On 20 July 1905, Lord Curzon issued an order dividing the province of Bengal into two parts: Eastern Bengal and Assam with a population of 31 million, and the rest of Bengal with a population of 54 million, of whom 18 million were Bengalis and 36 million Biharis and Oriyas. It was said that the existing province of Bengal was too big to be efficiently administered by a single provincial government. However, the officials who worked out the plan also had other political ends in view. They hoped to stem the rising tide of nationalism in Bengal, considered at the time the nerve centre of Indian nationalism. Risley, Home Secretary to the Government of India, wrote in an official note on 6 December 1904:

Bengal united is a power. Bengal divided will pull in several different ways. That is what the Congress leaders feel: their apprehensions are perfectly correct and they form one of the great merits of the scheme. ... One of our main objects is to split up and thereby to weaken a solid body of opponents to our rule.

The Indian National Congress and the nationalists of Bengal firmly opposed the partition. Within Bengal, different sections of the population—zamindars, merchants, lawyers, students, the city poor and even women—rose up in spontaneous opposition to the partition of their province.

The nationalists saw the act of partition as a challenge to Indian nationalism and not merely as an administrative measure. They saw that it was a deliberate attempt to divide the Bengalis territorially and on religious grounds—for in the Eastern part, Muslims would be a big majority and in the Western part, Hindus—and thus to disrupt and weaken nationalism in Bengal. It would also be a big blow to the growth of Bengali language and culture. They pointed out that administrative efficiency could have been better secured by separating the Hindi-speaking Bihar and the Oriya-speaking Orissa from the Bengali-speaking part of the province. Moreover, the official step had been taken in utter disregard of public opinion. Thus, the vehemence of Bengal's protest against the partition is explained by the fact that it was a blow to the sentiments of a very sensitive and courageous people.

THE ANTI-PARTITION MOVEMENT

The Anti-Partition Movement was the work of the entire national leadership of Bengal and not of any one section of the movement. Its most prominent leaders at the initial stage were moderate leaders like Surendranath Banerjea and Krishna Kumar Mitra; revolutionary nationalists took over in the later stages. In fact, both the moderate and revolutionary nationalists cooperated with one another during the course of the movement.

The Anti-Partition Movement was initiated on 7 August 1905. On that day, a massive demonstration against the partition was organised in the Town Hall in Calcutta. From this meeting, delegates dispersed to spread the movement to the rest of the province.

The partition took effect on 16 October 1905. The leaders of the protest movement declared it to be a day of national mourning throughout Bengal. It was observed as a day of fasting. There was a *hartal* in Calcutta. People walked barefoot and bathed in the Ganga in the early morning hours. Rabindranath Tagore composed the national song, 'Amar Sonar Bangla,' for the occasion, which was sung by huge crowds parading the streets. This song was adopted as its national anthem by Bangladesh in 1971 after liberation. The streets of Calcutta were full of the cries of 'Bande Mataram', which overnight became the national song of Bengal and which was soon to become the theme song of the national movement. The ceremony of *Raksha Bandhan* was utilised in a new way. Hindus and Muslims tied the rakhi on one another's wrists as a symbol of the unbreakable unity of the Bengalis and of the two halves of Bengal.

In the afternoon, there was a great demonstration when the veteran leader Ananda Mohan Bose laid the foundation of a Federation Hall to mark the indestructible unity of Bengal. He addressed a crowd of over 50,000.

THE SWADESHI AND BOYCOTT

The Bengal leaders felt that mere demonstrations, public meetings and resolutions were not likely to have much effect on the rulers. More positive action that would reveal the intensity of popular feelings and exhibit them at their best was needed. The answer was Swadeshi and Boycott. Mass meetings were held all over Bengal where Swadeshi, or the use of Indian goods, and the boycott of British goods were proclaimed and pledged. In many places, the public burning of foreign cloth was organised and shops selling foreign cloth were picketed. The Swadeshi Movement was an immense success. According to Surendranath Banerjea:

> Swadeshism during the days of its potency coloured the entire texture of our social and domestic life. Marriage presents that included foreign goods, the like of which could be manufactured at home, were returned.

Priests would often decline to officiate at ceremonies where foreign articles were offered as oblations to the gods. Guests would refuse to participate in festivities where foreign salt or foreign sugar was used.

An important aspect of the Swadeshi Movement was the emphasis placed on self-reliance or *Atmasakti*. Self-reliance meant assertion of national dignity, honour and self-confidence. In the economic field, it meant fostering indigenous industrial and other enterprises. Many textile mills, soap and match factories, handloom-weaving concerns, national banks and insurance companies were opened. Acharya P.C. Ray organised his famous Bengal Chemical Swadeshi Stores. Even the great poet Rabindranath Tagore helped to open a Swadeshi store.

The Swadeshi Movement had several consequences in the realm of culture. There was a flowering of nationalist poetry, prose and journalism. The patriotic songs written at the time by poets like Rabindranath Tagore, Rajani Kant Sen, Syed Abu Mohammed and Mukunda Das are sung in Bengal to this day. Another self-reliant, constructive activity undertaken at the time was that of National Education. National educational institutions where literary, technical or physical education was imparted were opened by nationalists who regarded the existing system of education as de-nationalising and, in any case, inadequate. On 15 August 1906, a National Council of Education was set up. A National College with Aurobindo Ghose as Principal was started in Calcutta.

The Role of Students, Women, Muslims and the Masses

A prominent part in the Swadeshi agitation was played by the students of Bengal. They practised and propagated Swadeshi and took the lead in organising picketing of shops selling foreign cloth. The government made every attempt to suppress the students. Orders were issued to penalise those schools and colleges whose students took an active part in the Swadeshi agitation; their grants-in-aid and other privileges were to be withdrawn, they were to be disaffiliated, their students were not to be permitted to compete for scholarships and were to be barred from all service under the government. Disciplinary action was taken against students found guilty of participating in the nationalist agitation. Many of them were fined, expelled from schools and colleges, arrested and sometimes beaten by the police with lathis. The students, however, refused to be cowed down.

A remarkable aspect of the Swadeshi agitation was the active participation of women in the movement. The traditionally home-centred women of the urban middle classes joined processions and picketing. From then onwards, they were to take an active part in the nationalist movement.

Many prominent Muslims joined the Swadeshi Movement, including Abdul Rasul, the famous barrister; Liaquat Hussain, the popular agitator; and Guznavi, the businessman. Maulana Abul Kalam Azad joined one of the revolutionary groups. Many other middle- and upper-class Muslims, however, remained neutral or, led by the Nawab of Dhaka (who was given a loan of Rs 14 lakh by the Government of India), even supported partition on the plea that East Bengal would have a Muslim majority. In this communal attitude, the Nawab of Dhaka and others were encouraged by the officials. In a speech at Dhaka, Lord Curzon declared that one of the reasons for the partition was "to invest the Mohammedans in Eastern Bengal with a unity which they have not enjoyed since the days of the old Mussalman Viceroys and Kings."

All-India Aspect of the Movement

The cry of Swadeshi and Swaraj was soon taken up by other provinces of India. Movements in support of Bengal's unity and boycott of foreign goods were organised in Bombay, Madras and northern India. The leading role in spreading the Swadeshi Movement to the rest of the country was played by Tilak. Tilak quickly saw that with the inauguration of this movement in Bengal, a new chapter in the history of Indian nationalism had opened. Here was a challenge and an opportunity to lead a popular struggle against the British Raj and to unite the entire country in one bond of common sympathy.

Growth of The Revolutionary Struggle

The leadership of the Anti-Partition Movement soon passed to revolutionary nationalists like Tilak, Bipin Chandra Pal and Aurobindo Ghose. This was due to many factors.

First, the early movement of protest led by the moderates failed to yield results. Even the liberal Secretary of State John Morley, from whom much was expected by the moderate nationalists, declared the partition to be a settled fact which would not be changed. Second, the governments of the two Bengals, particularly of East Bengal, made active efforts to divide Hindus and Muslims. Seeds of Hindu-Muslim disunity in Bengal politics were perhaps sown at this time. This embittered the nationalists. But, most of all, it was the repressive policy of the government which led people to aggressive revolutionary politics. The Government of East Bengal, in particular, tried to crush the nationalist movement. Official attempts at preventing student participation in the Swadeshi agitation have already been mentioned above. The singing of *Bande Mataram* in public streets in East Bengal was banned. Public meetings were restricted and sometimes forbidden. Laws controlling the press were enacted. Swadeshi workers were prosecuted and imprisoned for long periods. Many students were even awarded corporal punishment. From 1906 to 1909, more than 550 political cases came up before the Bengal courts. Prosecutions against a large number of nationalist newspapers were launched and freedom of the press was completely suppressed. Military police was stationed in many towns, where it clashed with the people. One of the most notorious examples of repression was the police assault on the peaceful delegates of the Bengal Provincial Conference at Barisal in April 1906. Many of the young volunteers were severely beaten up and the Conference itself was forcibly dispersed. In December 1908, nine Bengal leaders, including the venerable Krishna Kumar Mitra and Ashwini Kumar Dutt, were deported. Earlier, in 1907, Lala Lajpat Rai and Ajit Singh had been deported, following riots in the canal colonies of the Punjab. In 1908, the great Tilak was again arrested and given the savage sentence of six years' imprisonment. Chidambaram Pillai in Madras and Harisarvottam Rao and others in Andhra were put behind bars.

As the revolutionary nationalists came to the fore, they gave the call for passive resistance in addition to Swadeshi and Boycott. They asked the people to refuse to cooperate with the government and to boycott government service, the courts, government schools and colleges, and municipalities and legislative councils, and thus, as Aurobindo Ghose put it, "to make the administration under present conditions impossible." These aggressive nationalists tried to transform the Swadeshi and Anti-Partition agitation into a mass movement and gave the slogan of independence from foreign rule. Aurobindo Ghose openly declared: "Political freedom is the lifebreath of a nation." Thus, the question of the partition of Bengal became a secondary one and the question of India's freedom became the central question of Indian politics. The revolutionary nationalists also gave the call for self-sacrifice, without which no great aim could be achieved.

It should be remembered, however, that the revolutionary nationalists also failed in providing a positive lead to the people. They were not able to offer effective leadership or to create an effective organisation to guide their movement. They aroused the people, but did not know how to harness or utilise the newly-released energies of the people or to find new forms of political struggle. Passive resistance and non-cooperation remained mere ideas. They also failed to reach the real masses of the country, the peasants. Their movement remained confined to the urban lower and middle classes and zamindars. They had come to a political dead end by the beginning of 1908. Consequently, the government succeeded to a large extent in suppressing them. Their movement could not survive the arrest of their main leader Tilak, and the retirement from active politics of Bipin Chandra Pal and Aurobindo Ghose.

But the upsurge of nationalist sentiments could not die. People had been aroused from their slumber of centuries; they had learned to take a bold and fearless attitude in politics. They had acquired self-confidence and self-reliance and learnt to participate in new forms of mass mobilisation and political action. They now waited for a new movement to arise. Moreover, they were able to learn valuable lessons from their experience. Gandhiji wrote later that "after the Partition, people saw that petitions must be backed up by force, and that they must be capable of suffering." The Anti-Partition agitation in fact marked a great revolutionary leap forward for Indian nationalism. The later national movement was to draw heavily on its legacy.

GROWTH OF REVOLUTIONARY NATIONALISM

Government repression and frustration caused by the failure of the Indian leadership to provide a positive lead to the people ultimately resulted in revolutionary activism. The youth of Bengal found all avenues of peaceful protest and political action blocked, and out of desperation, they fell back upon individual heroic action and the cult of the bomb. They no longer believed that passive resistance could achieve nationalist aims. The British must, therefore, be physically expelled. As the *Yugantar* wrote on 22 April 1906 after the Barisal Conference: "The remedy lies with the people themselves. The 30 crores of people inhabiting India must raise their 60 crores of hands to stop this curse of oppression. Force must be stopped by force." But the revolutionary young men did not try to generate a mass revolution. Instead, they decided to copy the methods of the Irish terrorists and the Russian Nihilists, that is, to assassinate unpopular officials. A beginning had been made in this direction when, in 1897, the Chapekar brothers assassinated two unpopular British officials at Poona. In 1904, V.D. Savarkar had organised *the Abhinava Bharat,* a secret society of revolutionaries. After 1905, several newspapers had begun to advocate revolutionary activism. The *Sandhya* and the *Yugantar* in Bengal and the *Kal* in Maharashtra were the most prominent among them.

In December 1907, an attempt was made on the life of the Lieutenant-Governor of Bengal, and in April 1908, Khudiram Bose and Prafulla Chaki threw a bomb at a carriage which they believed was occupied by Kingsford, the unpopular Judge at Muzaffarpur. Prafulla Chaki shot himself dead while Khudiram Bose was tried and hanged. The era of revolutionary activism had begun. Many secret societies of revolutionary youth came into existence. The most famous of these were the Anushilan Samiti, whose Dhaka Section alone had 500 branches, and soon revolutionary societies became active in the rest of the country as well. They became so bold as to throw a bomb at the Viceroy Lord Hardinge while he was riding on an elephant in a state procession at Delhi. The Viceroy was wounded.

The revolutionaries also established centres of activity abroad. In, London, the lead was taken by Shyamaji Krishnavarma, V.D. Savarkar and Har Dayal, while in Europe, Madame Cama and Ajit Singh were the prominent leaders.

Extremism, too, gradually petered out. In fact, extremism as a political weapon was bound to fail. It could not mobilise the masses; in fact, it had no base among the people. But the revolutionaries did make a valuable contribution to the growth of nationalism in India. As a historian has put it, "they gave us back the pride of our manhood." Because of their heroism, the revolutionaries became immensely popular among their compatriots, even though most politically conscious people did not agree with their political approach.

The Indian National Congress (1905–1914)

The agitation against the partition of Bengal made a deep impact on the Indian National Congress. All sections of the National Congress united in opposing the Partition. At its session of 1905, Gokhale, the President of the Congress, roundly condemned the partition as well as the reactionary regime of Curzon. The National Congress also supported the Swadeshi and Boycott movement of Bengal.

There was much public debate and disagreement between the moderate and the revolutionary nationalists. The latter wanted to extend the Swadeshi and Boycott movement from Bengal to the rest of the country, and to extend the boycott to every form of association with the colonial government. The moderates wanted to confine the Boycott movement to Bengal and even there, to limit it to the boycott of foreign goods. There was a tussle between the two groups for the presidentship of the National Congress for that year (1906). In the end, Dadabhai Naoroji, respected by all nationalists as a great patriot, was chosen as a compromise. Dadabhai electrified the nationalist ranks by openly declaring in his presidential address that the goal of the Indian national movement was "'self-government' or Swaraj like that of the United Kingdom or the Colonies."

But the differences between the two wings of the nationalist movement could not be kept in check for long. Many of the moderate nationalists did not keep pace with events. They were not able to see that their outlook and methods, which had served a real purpose in the past, were no longer adequate. They had failed to advance to the new stage of the national movement. The revolutionary nationalists, on the other hand, were not willing to be held back. The split between the two came at the Surat session of the National Congress in December 1907. The moderate leaders, having captured the machinery of the Congress, excluded the more aggressive elements from it.

But, in the long run, the split did not prove useful to either party. The moderate leaders lost touch with the younger generation of nationalists. The British government played the game of 'divide and rule'. While suppressing the revolutionary nationalists, it tried to win over moderate nationalist opinion so that the former could be isolated and suppressed. To placate the moderate nationalists, it announced constitutional concessions through the Indian Councils Act of 1909, which are known as the Morley-Minto Reforms of 1909. In 1911, the government also announced the annulment of the Partition of Bengal. Western and Eastern Bengals were to be reunited, while a new province consisting of Bihar and Orissa was to be created. At the same time, the seat of the central government was shifted from Calcutta to Delhi.

The Morley-Minto Reforms increased the number of elected members in the Imperial Legislative Council and the provincial councils. But most of the elected members were elected indirectly, by the provincial councils in the case of the Imperial Council and by municipal committees and district boards in the case of the provincial councils. Some of the elected seats were reserved for landlords and British capitalists in India. For instance, of the 68 members of the Imperial Legislative Council, 36 were officials and five were nominated non-officials. Of the 27 elected members, six were to represent the big landlords and two the British capitalists. Moreover, the reformed councils still enjoyed no real power, being merely advisory bodies. The reforms in no way changed the undemocratic and foreign character of British rule, or the fact of foreign economic exploitation of the country. They were, in fact, not designed to democratise Indian administration. Morley openly declared at the time: "If it could be said that this chapter of reforms led directly or necessarily to the establishment of a parliamentary system in India, I for one would have nothing at all to do with it." His successor as the Secretary of State, Lord Crewe, further clarified the position in 1912: "There is a certain section in India which looks forward to a measure of self-government approaching that which has been granted in the dominions. I see no future for India on those lines." The real purpose of the Reforms of 1909 was to confuse the moderate nationalists, to divide the nationalist ranks and to check the growth of unity among Indians.

The Reforms also introduced the system of separate electorates under which all Muslims were grouped in separate constituencies from which Muslims alone could be elected. This was done in the name of protecting the Muslim minority. But, in reality, this was a part of the policy of dividing Hindus and Muslims, and thus maintaining British supremacy in India. The system of separate electorates was based on the notion that the political and economic interests of Hindus and Muslims were separate. This notion was unscientific because religions cannot be the basis of political and economic interests or of political groupings. What is even more important, this system proved extremely harmful in practice. It checked the progress of India's unification, which had been a continuous historical process. It became a potent factor in the growth of communalism—both Muslim and Hindu—in the country. Instead of removing the educational and economic backwardness of the middle-class Muslims and thus integrating them into the mainstream of Indian nationalism, the system of separate electorates tended to perpetuate their isolation from the developing nationalist movement. It encouraged separatist tendencies. It prevented people from concentrating on economic and political problems common to all Indians, Hindu or Muslim.

The moderate nationalists did not fully support the Morley-Minto Reforms. They soon realised that the Reforms had not really granted much. But they decided to cooperate with the government in working out the Reforms. This cooperation with the government and their opposition to the programme of the more aggressive nationalists proved very costly to them. They gradually lost the respect and support of the public and were reduced to a small political group.

The Growth of Communalism

Along with the rise of nationalism, communalism too made its appearance around the end of the nineteenth century and posed the biggest threat to the unity of the Indian people and the national movement. Before we discuss the emergence and growth of communalism, it is perhaps necessary to define the term.

Communalism is basically an ideology. Communal riots are only one consequence of the spread of this ideology. Communalism is the belief that because a group of people follow a particular religion, they have as a result common secular, that is, social, political and economic interests. It is the belief that in India, religious groups like Hindus, Muslims, Sikhs and Christians form different and distinct communities; that all the followers of a religion share not only a commonality of religious interests, but also common secular interests; that there is, and can be, no such thing as an Indian nation, but only a Hindu nation, or a Muslim nation, and so on; that India can, therefore, only be a mere confederation of religious communities. Inherent in communalism is the second notion that the social, cultural, economic and political interests of the followers of one religion are dissimilar and divergent from the interests of the followers of another religion. The third stage of communalism is reached when the interests of the followers of different religions or of different religious 'communities' are seen to be mutually incompatible, antagonistic and hostile. Thus, at this stage, the communalists assert that Hindus and Muslims cannot have common secular interests, and that their secular interests are bound to be opposed.

It is not true that communalism was a remnant of, or survival from, the medieval period. Though religion was an important part of people's lives and they did sometimes quarrel over religion, there was hardly any communal ideology or communal politics before the 1870s. Communalism is a modern phenomenon. It had its roots in the modern colonial socio-economic political structure.

Communalism emerged as a result of the emergence of new, modern politics based on the people and on popular participation and mobilisation. It made it necessary to have wider links and loyalties among the people and to form new identities. This process was bound to be difficult, gradual and complex. This process required the birth and spread of modern ideas of nation, class and cultural-linguistic identity. These identities, being new and unfamiliar, arose and grew slowly and in a zig-zag fashion. Quite often, people used the old, familiar pre-modern identity of caste, locality, sect and religion to grasp the new reality, to make wider connections and to evolve new identities. This has happened all over the world. But gradually the new, modern and historically-necessary identities of nation, nationality and class have prevailed. Unfortunately, in India this process has remained incomplete for decades, for, as pointed out earlier, India has been for the last 150 years or more a nation-in-the-making. In particular, religious consciousness was transformed into communal consciousness in some parts of the country and among some sections of the people. The question is, why did this happen?

In particular, modern political consciousness was late in developing among the Muslims. As nationalism spread among the Hindus and Parsis of the lower-middle class, it failed to grow equally rapidly among the Muslims of the same class.

As we have seen earlier, Hindus and Muslims had fought shoulder to shoulder during the Revolt of 1857. In fact, after the suppression of the Revolt, British officials had taken a particularly vindictive attitude towards the Muslims, hanging 27,000 Muslims in Delhi alone. From now on, the Muslims were in general looked upon with suspicion But this attitude changed in the 1870s. With the rise of the nationalist movement, British statesmen grew apprehensive about the safety and stability of their empire in India. To check the growth of a united national feeling in the country, they decided to follow more actively the policy of 'divide and rule' and to divide the people along religious lines; in other words, to encourage communal and separatist tendencies in Indian politics. For this purpose, they decided to come out as 'champions' of the Muslims and to win over to their side Muslim zamindars, landlords and the newly educated. They also fostered other divisions in Indian society. They promoted provincialism by talking of Bengali domination. They tried to utilise the caste structure to turn non-brahmins against brahmins and the lower castes against the higher castes. In Uttar Pradesh and Bihar, where Hindus and Muslims had always lived in peace, they actively encouraged the movement to replace Urdu as the court language by Hindi. In other words, they tried to use even the legitimate demands of different sections of Indian society to create divisions among the Indian people. The colonial government treated Hindus, Muslims and Sikhs as separate communities. It readily accepted communal leaders as authentic representatives of all their co-religionists. It permitted the propagation of virulent communal ideas and communal hatred through the press, pamphlets, posters, literature and other public platforms. This was in sharp contrast to its frequent suppression of the nationalist newspapers, writers, etc.

In the rise of the separatist tendency along communal lines, Sayyid Ahmad Khan played an important role. Though a great educationist and social reformer, Sayyid Ahmad Khan became towards the end of his life a conservative in politics. In the 1880s, he gave up his earlier views and declared that the political interests of Hindus and Muslims were different, and even divergent. He also preached complete obedience to British rule. When the Indian National Congress was founded in 1885, he decided to oppose it and tried to organise along with Raja Shiva Prasad of Varanasi a movement of loyalty to the British rule. He also began to preach that, since the Hindus formed the larger part of the Indian population, they would dominate the Muslims in case of the weakening or withdrawal of British rule. He urged the Muslims not to listen to Badruddin Tyabji's appeal to them to join the National Congress.

These views were, of course, unscientific and without any basis in reality. Even though Hindus and Muslims followed different religions, their economic and political interests were not different for that reason. Hindus were divided from fellow Hindus, and Muslims from fellow Muslims, by language, culture, caste, class, social status, food and dress habits, social practices and so on. Even socially and culturally, the Hindu and the Muslim masses had developed common ways of life. A Bengali Muslim and a Bengali Hindu had much more in common than a Bengali Muslim and a Punjabi Muslim had. Moreover, Hindus and Muslims were being equally and jointly oppressed and exploited by British imperialism. Even Sayyid Ahmad Khan had said in 1884:

> Do you not inhabit the same land? Are you not burned and buried on the same soil? Do you not tread the same ground and live upon the same soil? Remember that the words Hindu and Mohammedan are only meant for religious distinction— otherwise all persons, whether Hindu or Mohammedan, even the Christians who reside in this country, are all in this particular respect belonging to one and the same nation. When all these different sects can be described as one nation, they must each and all unite for the good of the country which is common to all.

The question then arises: how could the communal and separatist trend of thinking grow among the Muslims?

This was to some extent due to the relative backwardness of the Muslims in education and in trade and industry. Muslim upper classes consisted mostly of zamindars and aristocrats. Because the upper-class Muslims during the first 70 years of the nineteenth century were very anti-British, conservative and hostile to modern education, the number of educated Muslims in the country remained very small. Consequently, modern Western thought with its emphasis on science, democracy and nationalism did not spread among Muslim intellectuals, who remained traditional and backward. Later, as a result of the efforts of Sayyid Ahmad Khan, Nawab Abdul Latif, Badruddin Tyabji and others, modern education spread among Muslims. But the proportion of the educated was far lower among Muslims than among Hindus, Parsis or Christians. Similarly, the Muslims had also taken little part in the growth of trade and industry. The small number of educated persons and men of trade and industry among the Muslims made it possible for the reactionary big landlords to maintain their influence over the Muslim masses. As we have seen earlier, landlords and zamindars, whether Hindu or Muslim, supported the British rule out of self-interest. But, among the Hindus, the modern intellectuals and the rising commercial and industrialist class had pushed out the landlords from leadership. Unfortunately, the opposite remained the case with the Muslims.

The educational backwardness of the Muslims had another harmful consequence. Since modern education was essential for entry into government service or the professions, the Muslims had also lagged behind non-Muslims in this respect. Moreover, the government had consciously discriminated against the Muslims after 1858, holding them largely responsible for the Revolt of 1857. When modern education did spread among the Muslims, the educated Muslim found few opportunities in business or the professions. He inevitably looked for government employment. And, in any case, India being a backward colony, there were very few opportunities of employment for its people. In these circumstances, it was easy for the British officials and the loyalist Muslim leaders to incite the educated Muslims against the educated Hindus. Sayyid Ahmad Khan and others raised the demand for special treatment for Muslims in the matter of government service. They declared that if the educated Muslims remained loyal to the British, the latter would reward them with government jobs and other special favours. Some loyalist Hindus and Parsis too tried to argue in this manner, but they remained a small minority. The result was that while in the country as a whole, independent and nationalist lawyers, journalists, students, merchants and industrialists were becoming political leaders, among the Muslims, loyalist landlords and retired government servants still influenced political opinion. Bombay was the only province where the Muslims had taken to commerce and education quite early; and there the National Congress included in its ranks such brilliant Muslims as Badruddin Tyabji, R.M. Sayani, A. Bhimji, and the young barrister, Muhammad Ali Jinnah. We can sum up this aspect of the problem with a quotation from Jawaharlal Nehru's *The Discovery of India*:

> There has been a difference of a generation or more in the development of the Hindu and the Muslim middle classes, and that difference continues to show itself in many directions, political, economic, and other. It is this lag which produces a psychology of fear among the Muslims.

As students of history, we should also know that the manner in which Indian history was taught in schools and colleges in those days also contributed to the growth of communalist feelings among the educated Hindus and Muslims. British historians and, following them, Indian historians described the medieval period of Indian history as the Muslim period. The rule of Turk, Afghan and Mughal rulers was called Muslim rule. Even though the Muslim masses were as poor and oppressed by taxes as the Hindu masses, and even though both were looked down upon by the rulers, nobles, chiefs and zamindars, whether Hindu or Muslim, with contempt and regarded as low creatures, yet these writers declared that all Muslims were rulers in medieval India and all non-Muslims were the ruled. They failed to bring out the fact that ancient and medieval politics in India, as politics everywhere else, were based on economic and political interests and not on religious considerations. Rulers as well as rebels used religious appeals as an outer colouring to disguise the play of material interests and ambitions. Moreover, the British and communal historians attacked the notion of a composite culture in India.

The Hindu communal view of history also relied on the myth that Indian society and culture had reached great, ideal heights in the ancient period, from which they fell into permanent and continuous decay during the medieval period because of 'Muslim' rule and domination. The basic contribution of the medieval period to the development of Indian economy and technology, religion and philosophy, arts and literature, culture and society, and fruits, vegetables and dress was denied.

All this was seen by many contemporary observers. Gandhiji, for example, wrote: "Communal harmony could not be permanently established in our country so long as highly distorted versions of history were taught in her schools and colleges, through the history textbooks." In addition, the communal view of history was spread widely through poetry, drama, historical novels and short stories, newspapers and popular magazines, children's magazines, pamphlets and, above all, orally through the public platform, classroom teaching, socialisation through the family and private conversation.

The founding fathers of Indian nationalism fully realised that the welding of Indians into a single nation would be a gradual and hard task, requiring prolonged political education of the people. They, therefore, set out to convince the minorities that the nationalist movement would carefully protect their religious and social rights while uniting all Indians in their common national, economic and political interests. In his presidential address to the National Congress of 1886, Dadabhai Naoroji had given the clear assurance that the Congress would take up only national questions and would not deal with religious and social matters. In 1889, the Congress adopted the principle that it would not take up any proposal which was considered harmful to the Muslims by a majority of the Muslim delegates to the Congress. Many Muslims joined the Congress in its early years. In other words, the early nationalists tried to modernise the political outlook of the people by teaching that politics should not be based on religion and community.

While revolutionary nationalism was a great step forward in every other respect, it was to some extent a step back in respect of the growth of national unity. The speeches and writings of some of the aggressive nationalits had a strong religious tinge. They emphasised ancient Indian culture to the exclusion of medieval Indian culture. They identified Indian culture and the Indian nation with a particular religion. They tried to abandon elements of a composite culture. For example, Tilak's propagation of the Shivaji and Ganapati festivals, Aurobindo Ghose's semi-mystical concept of India as mother and nationalism as a religion, the revolutionaries' oaths before the goddess Kali and the initiation of the Anti-Partition agitation with dips in the Ganga could hardly appeal to the Muslims. In fact, such actions were against the spirit of their religion, and they could not be expected as Muslims to associate with these and other similar activities. Nor could Muslims be expected to respond with full enthusiasm when they saw Shivaji or Pratap being hailed not merely for their historical roles but also as 'national' leaders who fought against the 'foreigners'. Akbar or Aurangzeb could hardly be declared a foreigner; and in reality, the struggle between Pratap and Akbar, or Shivaji and Aurangzeb had to be viewed as a political struggle in its particular historical setting. To declare Akbar or Aurangzeb a 'foreigner' and Pratap or Shivaji a 'national' hero was to project into past history the communal outlook of twentieth-century India. This served as a blow to national unity.

This does not mean that revolutionary nationalists were anti-Muslim or even wholly communal. Most of them, including Tilak, favoured Hindu-Muslim unity. To most of them, the motherland, or *Bharatmata*, was a modern notion, being in no way linked with religion. Most were modern in their political thinking and not backward looking. Economic boycott, their chief political weapon, was indeed very modern, as was their political organisation. Tilak, for example, declared in 1916: "He who does what is beneficial to the people of this country, be he a Muhammedan or an Englishman, is not alien. 'Alienness' has to do with interests. Alienness is certainly not concerned with white or black skin or religion." Even the revolutionaries were in reality inspired by European revolutionary movements, for example, those of Ireland, Russia and Italy, rather than by Kali or Bhawani cults. But, as pointed out earlier, there was a certain Hindu tinge in the political work and ideas of the revolutionary nationalists. This proved to be particularly harmful as clever British and pro-British propagandists took advantage of the Hindu colouring to poison the minds of the Muslims. The result was that a large number of educated Muslims either remained aloof from the rising nationalist movement or became hostile to it, thus falling an easy prey to a separatist outlook. This also made it difficult for the nationalist movement to eliminate Hindu communal, political and ideological elements from within its own ranks. Even so, quite a large number of advanced Muslim intellectuals such as the barrister Abdul Rasul and Hasrat Mohani joined the Swadeshi movement, Maulana Azad joined the revolutionary nationalists and Muhammad Ali Jinnah became one of the leading younger leaders of the National Congress. This was because the national movement remained basically secular in its approach and ideology. This secularism became sturdier when leaders like Gandhiji, C.R. Das, Motilal Nehru, Jawaharlal Nehru, Maulana Abul Kalam Azad, M.A. Ansari, Hakim Ajmal Khan, Khan Abdul Ghaffar Khan, Subhas Bose, Sardar Patel, Rajendra Prasad and C. Rajagopalachari came to the helm.

The economic backwardness of the country, the consequence of colonial underdevelopment, also contributed to the rise of communalism. Due to the lack of modern industrial development, unemployment was an acute problem in India, especially for the educated. There was, as a consequence, an intense competition for existing jobs. Far-sighted Indians diagnosed the disease and worked for an economic and political system in which the country would develop economically and in which, therefore, employment would be plentiful. However, many others thought of such short-sighted and short-term remedies as communal, provincial or caste reservation in jobs. They aroused communal and religious and, later, caste and provincial passions in an attempt to get a larger share of the existing, limited employment opportunities. To those looking desperately for employment, such a narrow appeal had a certain immediate attraction. In this situation, Hindu and Muslim communal leaders, caste leaders and officials following the policy of 'divide and rule' were able to achieve some success. Many Hindus began to talk of Hindu nationalism and many Muslims of Muslim nationalism. The politically immature people failed to realise that their economic, educational and cultural difficulties were the result of common subjection to foreign rule and of economic backwardness, and that only through common effort could they free their country, develop it economically, and thus solve the underlying common problems, such as unemployment.

Some believe that a major factor in the growth of communalism was the existence of several religions in India. This is not so. It is not true that communalism must arise inevitably in a multi-religious society. Here, we must distinguish between religion as a belief system, which people follow as a part of their personal belief, and the ideology of a religion-based socio-political identity that is communalism. Religion is not the cause of communalism, nor is communalism inspired by religion. Religion comes into communalism to the extent that it serves politics arising in non-religious spheres. Communalism has been rightly described as political trade in religion. Religion was used, after 1937, as a mobilising factor by the communalists. Secularism is not, therefore, opposed to religion. It only means confining religion to the private life of the individual and dissociating it from politics and the state. As Gandhiji repeatedly declared: "Religion is the personal affair of each individual. It must not be mixed up with politics or national affairs."

The separatist and loyalist tendencies among a section of the educated Muslims and the big Muslim nawabs and landlords reached a climax in 1906 when the All India Muslim League was founded under the leadership of Aga Khan, the Nawab of Dhaka, and Nawab Mohsin-ul-Mulk. Founded as a loyalist, communal and conservative political organisation, the Muslim League made no critique of colonialism, supported the partition of Bengal and demanded special safeguards for the Muslims in government services. Later, with the help of Lord Minto, the Viceroy, it put forward and secured the acceptance of the demand for separate electorates. Thus, while the National Congress was taking up anti-imperialist economic and political issues, the Muslim League and its reactionary leaders preached that the interests of Muslims were different from those of Hindus. The Muslim League's political activities were directed not against the foreign rulers, but against Hindus and the National Congress. Hereafter, the League began to oppose every nationalist and democratic demand of the Congress. It thus played into the hands of the British, who announced that they would protect the 'special interests' of the Muslims. The League soon became one of the main instruments with which the British hoped to fight the rising nationalist movement and to keep the emerging intelligentsia among Muslims from joining the national movement.

To increase its usefulness, the British also encouraged the Muslim League to approach the Muslim masses and assume their leadership. It is true that the nationalist movement was also dominated at this time by educated town-dwellers but, in its anti-imperialism, it was representing the interests of all Indians—rich or poor, Hindu or Muslim. On the other hand, the Muslim League and its upper-class leaders had little in common with the interests of the Muslim masses, who were suffering as much as the Hindu masses at the hands of foreign imperialism.

This basic weakness of the League came to be increasingly recognised by patriotic Muslims. The educated Muslim young men were, in particular, attracted by radical nationalist ideas. The aggressively nationalist *Ahrar* movement was founded at this time under the leadership of Maulana Mohamed Ali, Hakim Ajmal Khan, Hasan Imam, Maulana Zafar Ali Khan and Mazhar-ul-Haq. These young men disliked the loyalist politics of the Aligarh School and the big nawabs and zamindars. Moved by modern ideas of self-government, they advocated active participation in the revolutionary nationalist movement.

Similar nationalist sentiments were arising among a section of traditional Muslim scholars led by the Deoband School. The most prominent of these scholars was the young Maulana Abul Kalam Azad, who propagated his rationalist and nationalist ideas in his newspaper *Al Hilal,* which he brought out in 1912 at the age of 24. Maulana Mohamed Ali, Azad and other young men preached a message of courage and fearlessness and said that there was no conflict between Islam and nationalism.

In 1911, war broke out between the Ottoman empire (Turkey) and Italy, and during 1912 and 1913, Turkey had to fight the Balkan powers. The Turkish ruler claimed at this time to be also the *Caliph* or religious head of all Muslims; moreover, nearly all of the Muslim holy places were situated within the Turkish empire. A wave of sympathy for Turkey swept India. A medical mission, headed by Dr M.A. Ansari, was sent to help Turkey. Since Britain's policy during the Balkan War and after was not sympathetic to Turkey, the pro-

Turkey and pro-Caliph or *Khilafat* sentiments tended to become anti-imperialist. In fact, for several years—from 1912 to 1924—the loyalists among the Muslim League were completely overshadowed by nationalist young men.

Unfortunately, with the exception of a few persons like Azad who were rationalists in their thinking, most of the revolutionary nationalists among Muslim young men also did not fully accept the modern secular approach to politics. The result was that the most important issue they took up was not political independence, but protection of holy places and of the Turkish empire. Instead of understanding and opposing the economic and political consequences of imperialism, they fought imperialism on the ground that it threatened the Caliph and the holy places of Islam. Even their sympathy for Turkey was on religious grounds. Their political appeal was to religious sentiments. Moreover, the heroes and myths and cultural traditions they appealed to belonged not to ancient or medieval Indian history, but to West Asian history. It is true that this approach did not immediately clash with Indian nationalism. Rather, it made its adherents and supporters anti-imperialist and encouraged the nationalist trend among urban Muslims. But in the long run, this approach too proved harmful, as it encouraged the habit of looking at political questions from a religious viewpoint. In any case, such political activity did not promote among the Muslim masses a modern, secular approach towards political and economic questions.

Simultaneously, Hindu communalism was also being born and Hindu communal ideas were arising. Many Hindu writers and political workers echoed the ideas and programme of Muslim communalism and the Muslim League. From the 1870s, a section of Hindu zamindars, moneylenders and middle-class professionals began to arouse anti-Muslim sentiments. Fully accepting the colonial view of Indian history, they talked and wrote about the 'tyrannical' Muslim rule in the medieval period and the 'liberating' role of the British in 'saving' Hindus from 'Muslim oppression'. In Uttar Pradesh and Bihar, they took up, correctly, the question of Hindi, but gave it a communal twist, declaring, totally unhistorically, that Urdu was the language of Muslims and Hindi of Hindus. All over India, anti-cow slaughter propaganda was undertaken in the early 1890s. The campaign was, however, primarily directed not against the British but against Muslims; the British cantonments, for example, were left free to carry on cow slaughter on a large scale.

The Punjab Hindu Sabha was founded in 1909. Its leaders attacked the National Congress for trying to unite Indians into a single nation. They opposed the Congress' anti-imperialist politics. Instead, they argued that Hindus should placate the foreign government in their fight against Muslims. One of its leaders, Lal Chand, declared that a Hindu should believe that he was "a Hindu first and an Indian later". The first session of the All-India Hindu Mahasabha was held in April 1915 under the presidentship of the Maharaja of Kasim Bazar. But it remained for years a rather weak organisation. One reason was the greater weight and influence of the modern secular intelligentsia and middle class among Hindus. Among Muslims, on the other hand, landlords, bureaucrats and traditional religious leaders still exercised dominant influence. Moreover, the colonial government gave Hindu communalism few concessions and little support, for it relied heavily on Muslim communalism and could not easily simultaneously placate both these forms of communalism.

The Nationalists and the First World War

In June 1914, the First World War broke out between Great Britain, France, Russia and Japan on one side (joined later by Italy and USA), and Germany, Austria-Hungary and Turkey on the other. In India, the years of the War marked the maturing of nationalism.

In the beginning, the Indian nationalist leaders, including Lokamanya Tilak, who had been released in June 1914, decided to support the war effort of the government in the mistaken belief that grateful Britain would repay India's loyalty with gratitude and enable India to take a long step forward on the road to self-government. They did not realise fully that the different powers were fighting the First World War precisely to safeguard their existing colonies.

THE HOME RULE LEAGUES

At the same time, many Indian leaders saw clearly that the government was not likely to give any real concessions unless popular pressure was brought to bear upon it. Hence, a real mass political movement was necessary. Some other factors were leading the nationalist movement in the same direction. The World War, involving mutual struggle between the imperialist powers of Europe, destroyed the myth of the racial superiority of Western nations over the Asian peoples. Moreover, the War led to increased misery among the poorer classes of Indians. For them, the War had meant heavy taxation and soaring prices of the daily necessities of life. They were getting ready to join any revolutionary movement of protest. Consequently, the war years were years of intense nationalist political agitation. But this mass agitation could not be carried out under the leadership of the Indian National Congress, which had become, under moderate leadership, a passive and inert political organisation with no political work among the people to its credit. Therefore, two Home Rule Leagues were started in 1915–16, one under the leadership of Lokamanya Tilak and the other under the leadership of Annie Besant, an English admirer of Indian culture and the Indian people, and S. Subramaniya Iyer. The two Home Rule Leagues worked in cooperation and carried out intense propaganda all over the country in favour of the demand for the grant of Home Rule or self-government to India after the War. It was during this agitation that Tilak gave the popular slogan: "Home Rule is my birthright, and I will have it." The two Leagues made rapid progress and the cry of Home Rule resounded throughout the length and breadth of India. Many moderate nationalists, who were dissatisfied with the Congress inactivity, joined the Home Rule agitation. The Home Rule Leagues soon attracted the government's anger. In June 1917, Annie Besant was arrested. Popular protest forced the government to release her in September 1917.

The war period also witnessed the growth of the revolutionary movement. The revolutionary groups spread from Bengal and Maharashtra to the whole of northern India. Moreover, many Indians began to plan a violent rebellion to overthrow British rule. Indian revolutionaries in the United States of America and Canada had established the Ghadar (Rebellion) Party in 1913. Most of the members of the party were Punjabi Sikh peasants and ex-soldiers, who had migrated there in search of livelihood, and who faced the full brunt of racial and economic discrimination. Lala Har Dayal,

Mohammed Barkatullah, Bhagwan Singh, Ram Chandra and Sohan Singh Bhakna were some of the prominent leaders of the Ghadar Party. The party was built around the weekly paper the *Ghadar*, which carried the caption on the masthead: *Angrezi Raj Ka Dushman* (An Enemy of British Rule). "Wanted brave soldiers", the *Ghadar* declared, "to stir up Rebellion in India. Pay—death; Price—martyrdom; Pension—liberty; Field of Battle—India." The ideology of the party was strongly secular. In the words of Sohan Singh Bhakna, who later became a major peasant leader of Punjab: "We were not Sikhs or Punjabis. Our religion was patriotism." "The party had active members in other countries such as Mexico, Japan, China, Philippines, Malaya, Singapore, Thailand, Indo-China, and East and South Africa."

The Ghadar Party was pledged to wage revolutionary war against the British in India. As soon as the First World War broke out in 1914, the Ghadarites decided to send arms and men to India to start an uprising with the help of soldiers and local revolutionaries. Several thousand men volunteered to go back to India. Millions of dollars were contributed to pay for their expenses. Many gave their lifelong savings and sold lands and other property. The Ghadarites also contacted Indian soldiers in the Far East, Southeast Asia and all over India and persuaded several regiments to rebel. Finally, 21 February 1915 was fixed as the date for an armed revolt in the Punjab. Unfortunately, the authorities came to know of these plans and took immediate action. The rebellious regiments were disbanded and their leaders were either imprisoned or hanged. For example, 12 men of the 23rd Cavalry were executed. The leaders and members of the Ghadar Party in the Punjab were arrested on a mass scale and tried. Forty-two of them were hanged, 114 were transported for life and 93 were sentenced to long terms of imprisonment. Many of them, after their release, founded the Kirti and Communist movements in the Punjab. Some of the prominent Ghadar leaders were: Baba Gurmukh Singh, Kartar Singh Saraba, Sohan Singh Bhakna, Rahmat Ali Shah, Bhai Parmanand and Mohammad Barkatullah.

Inspired by the Ghadar Party, 700 men of the 5th Light Infantry at Singapore revolted under the leadership of Jamadar Chisti Khan and Subedar Dundey Khan. They were crushed after a bitter battle in which many died. Thirty-seven others were publicly executed, while 41 were transported for life.

Other revolutionaries were active in India and abroad. In 1915, during an unsuccessful revolutionary attempt, Jatin Mukerjea, popularly known as 'Bagha Jatin', gave his life fighting with the police at Balasore. Rash Bihari Bose, Raja Mahendra Pratap, Lala Hardayal, Abdul Rahim, Maulana Obaidullah Sindhi, Champakaraman Pillai, Sardar Singh Rana and Madame Cama were some of the prominent Indians who carried on revolutionary activities and propaganda outside India, where they gathered the support of socialists and other anti-imperialists.

LUCKNOW SESSION OF THE CONGRESS (1916)

The nationalists soon saw that disunity in their ranks was injuring their cause and that they must put up a united front before the government. The growing nationalist feeling in the country and the urge for national unity produced two historic developments at the Lucknow session of the Indian National Congress in 1916. First, the two wings of the Congress were reunited. The old controversies had lost their meaning and the split in the Congress had led to political inactivity. Tilak, released from jail in 1914, immediately saw the change in the situation and set out to unify the two streams of Congressmen. To conciliate the moderate nationalists, he declared:

> I may state once for all that we are trying in India, as the Irish Home-rulers have been all along doing in Ireland, for a reform of the system of administration and not for the overthrow of government; and I have no hesitation in saying that the acts of violence which have been committed in the different parts of India are not only repugnant to me, but have, in my opinion, only unfortunately retarded to a great extent, the pace of our political progress.

On the other hand, the rising tide of nationalism compelled the old leaders to welcome back into the Congress Lokamanya Tilak and other revolutionary nationalists. The Lucknow Congress was the first united Congress since 1907. It demanded further constitutional reforms as a step towards self-government.

Second, at Lucknow, the Congress and the All India Muslim League sank their old differences and put up common political demands before the government. While the War and the two Home Rule Leagues were creating a new sentiment in the country and changing the character of the Congress, the Muslim League had also been undergoing gradual changes. We have already noted earlier that the younger section of the educated Muslims was turning to bolder nationalist politics. The War period witnessed further developments in that direction. Consequently, in 1914, the government suppressed the publication of the *Al Hilal* of Abul Kalam Azad and the *Comrade* of Maulana Mohamed Ali. It also interned the Ali Brothers— Maularias Mohamed Ali and Shaukat Ali—and Hasrat Mohani and Abul Kalam Azad. The League reflected, at least partially, the political aggression of its younger members. It gradually began to outgrow the limited political outlook of the Aligarh school of thought and moved closer to the policies of the Congress.

The unity between the Congress and the League was brought about by the signing of the Congress-League Pact, known popularly as the Lucknow Pact. An important role in bringing the two together was played by Lokamanya Tilak and Mohammad Ali Jinnah, because the two believed that India could win self-government only through Hindu-Muslim unity. Tilak declared at the time:

> It has been said, gentlemen, by some that we Hindus have yielded too much to our Mohammedan brethren. I am sure I represent the sense of the Hindu community all over India when I say that we could not have yielded too much. I would not care if the rights of self-government are granted to the Mohammedan community only. ... I would not care if they are granted to the lower and the lowest classes of the Hindu population. ... When we have to fight against a third party, it is a very important thing that we stand on this platform united, united in race, united in religion, as regard all different shades of political creed.

The two organisations passed the same resolutions at their sessions, put forward a joint scheme of political reforms based on separate electorates and demanded that the British government should make a declaration that it would confer self-government on India at an early date. The Lucknow Pact marked an important step forward in

Hindu-Muslim unity. Unfortunately, it did not involve the Hindu and Muslim masses and it accepted the pernicious principle of separate electorates. It was based on the notion of bringing together the educated Hindus and Muslims as separate political entities; in other words, without secularisation of their political outlook, which would make them realise that in politics, they had no separate interests as Hindus or Muslims. The Lucknow Pact, therefore, left the way open to the future resurgence of communalism in Indian politics.

But the immediate effect of the developments at Lucknow was tremendous. The unity between the moderate nationalists and the more aggressive nationalists, and between the National Congress and the Muslim League aroused great political enthusiasm in the country. Even the British government felt it necessary to placate the nationalists. Hitherto, it had relied heavily on repression to quieten the nationalist agitation. Large numbers of radical nationalists and revolutionaries had been jailed or interned under the notorious Defence of India Act and other similar regulations. The government now decided to appease nationalist opinion and announced on 20 August 1917 that its policy in India was "the gradual development of self-governing institutions with a view to the progressive realisation of Responsible Government of India as an integral part of the British empire." And in July 1918, the Montague-Chelmsford Reforms were announced. But Indian nationalism was not appeased. In fact, the Indian national movement was soon to enter its third and last phase—the era of mass struggle, or the Gandhian Era.

Thirteen

The Struggle for Swaraj: 1919-27

The third and the last phase of the national movement began in 1919 when the era of popular mass movements was initiated. The Indian people waged perhaps the greatest mass struggle in world history and India's national revolution was victorious.

As we have seen in the previous chapter, a new political situation was maturing during the War years, 1914-18. Nationalism had gathered its forces and the nationalists were expecting major political gains after the war; and they were willing to fight back if their expectations were thwarted. The economic situation in the post-War years had taken a turn for the worse. There was first a rise in prices and then a depression in economic activity. Indian industries, which had prospered during the War because foreign imports of manufactured goods had ceased, now faced losses and closure. Moreover, foreign capital now began to be invested in India on a large scale. The Indian industrialists wanted protection of their industries through imposition of high customs duties and grant of government aid; they realised that a strong nationalist movement and an independent Indian government alone could secure these. The workers and artisans, facing unemployment and high prices, also turned actively towards the nationalist movement. Indian soldiers, who returned from their triumphs in Africa, Asia and Europe, imparted some of their confidence and their knowledge of the wide world to the rural areas. The peasantry, groaning under deepening poverty and high taxation, was waiting for a lead. The urban, educated Indians faced increasing unemployment. Thus, all sections of Indian society were suffering economic hardships, compounded by droughts, high prices and epidemics.

The international situation was also favourable to the resurgence of nationalism. The First World War gave a tremendous impetus to nationalism all over Asia and Africa. In order to win popular support for their War effort, the Allied nations—Britain, the United States,

France, Italy and Japan—promised a new era of democracy and national self-determination to all the peoples of the world. But after their victory, they showed little willingness to end the colonial system. On the contrary, at the Paris Peace Conference and in the different peace settlements, all the wartime promises were forgotten and, in fact, betrayed. The ex-colonies of the defeated powers, Germany and Turkey, in Africa, West Asia and East Asia, were divided among the victorious powers. A militant nationalism, born out of a strong sense of disillusionment, began to arise everywhere in Asia and Africa. In India, while the British government made a half-hearted attempt at constitutional reform, it also made it clear that it had no intention of parting with political power or even sharing it with Indians.

Another major consequence of the World War was the erosion of the White man's prestige. The European powers had from the beginning of their imperialism utilised the notion of racial and cultural superiority to maintain their supremacy. But during the War, both sides carried on intense propaganda against each other, exposing the opponent's brutal and uncivilised colonial record. Naturally, the people of the colonies tended to believe both sides and to lose their awe of the White man's superiority.

A major impetus to the national movements in the colonies was given by the impact of the Russian Revolution. On 7 November 1917, the Bolshevik (Communist) Party, led by V.I. Lenin, overthrew the Czarist regime in Russia and declared the formation of the first socialist state, the Soviet Union, in the history of the world. The new Soviet regime electrified the colonial world by unilaterally renouncing its imperialist rights in China and other parts of Asia, by granting the right of self-determination to the former Czarist colonies in Asia, and by giving an equal status to the Asian nationalities within its border, which had been oppressed as inferior and conquered peoples by the previous regime. The Russian Revolution put heart into the colonial people. It brought home to the colonial people the important lesson that immense strength and energy resided in the common people. If the unarmed peasants and workers could carry out a revolution against their domestic tyrants, then the people of the subject nations too could fight for their independence, provided they were equally well-united, organised and determined to fight for freedom.

The nationalist movement in India was also affected by the fact that the rest of the Afro-Asian world was also convulsed by nationalist agitations after the War. Nationalism surged forward not only in India, but also in Ireland, Turkey, Egypt and other Arab countries of Northern Africa, and West Asia, Iran, Aghanistan, Burma, Malaya, Indonesia, Indo-China, the Philippines, China and Korea.

The government, aware of the rising tide of nationalist and anti-government sentiments, once again decided to follow the policy of the 'carrot and the stick', in other words, of concessions and repression. The carrot was represented by the Montagu-Chelmsford Reforms.

THE MONTAGU-CHELMSFORD REFORMS

In 1918, Edwin Montagu, the Secretary of State, and Lord Chelmsford, the Viceroy, produced their scheme of constitutional reforms which led to the enactment of the Government of India Act of 1919. The Provincial Legislative Councils were enlarged and the majority of their members were to be elected. The provincial governments were given more powers under the system of Dyarchy. Under this system some subjects, such as finance and law and order, were called 'reserved' subjects and remained under the direct control of the Governor; others, such as education, public health and local self-government, were called 'transferred' subjects and were to be controlled by ministers responsible to the legislatures. This also meant that while some of the spending departments were transferred, the Governor retained complete control over the finances. The Governor could, moreover, overrule the ministers on any grounds that he considered special. At the centre, there were to be two houses of legislature. The lower house, the Legislative Assembly, was to have 41 nominated members out of a total strength of 144. The upper house, the Council of State, was to have 26 nominated and 34 elected members. The legislature had virtually no control over the Governor-General and his Executive Council. On the other hand, the central government had unrestricted control over the provincial governments. Moreover, the right to vote was severely restricted. In 1920, the total number of voters was 909,874 for the lower house and 17,364 for the upper house.

Indian nationalists had, however, advanced far beyond such halting concessions. They were no longer willing to be satisfied with the shadow of political power. The Indian National Congress met in a special session at Bombay in August 1918 under the presidentship of Hasan Imam to consider the reform proposals. It condemned them as "disappointing and unsatisfactory" and demanded effective self-government instead. Some of the veteran Congress leaders led by Surendranath Banerjea were in favour of accepting the government proposals. They left the Congress at this time and founded the Indian Liberal Federation. They came to be known as Liberals and played a minor role in Indian politics hereafter.

THE ROWLATT ACT

While trying to appease Indians, the Government of India was ready with repression. Throughout the war, repression of nationalists had continued. The aggressive revolutionaries had been hunted down, hanged and imprisoned. Many other nationalists, such as Abul Kalam Azad, had also been kept behind bars. The government now decided to arm itself with more far-reaching powers, which went against the accepted principles of rule of law, to be able to suppress those nationalists who would refuse to be satisfied with the official reforms. In March 1919 it passed the Rowlatt Act, even though every single Indian member of the Central Legislative Council opposed it. This Act authorised the government to imprison any person without trial and conviction in a court of law. The Act would thus also enable the government to suspend the right of Habeas Corpus, which had been the foundation of civil liberties in Britain.

Mahatma Gandhi assumes Leadership

The Rowlatt Act came like a sudden blow. To the people of India, who had been promised an extension of democracy during the War, the government step appeared to be a cruel joke. It was like a hungry man, expecting bread, being offered stones. Instead of democratic progress had come further restriction of civil liberties. Unrest spread in the country and a powerful agitation against the Act arose. During this agitation, a new leader, Mohandas Karamchand Gandhi, took command of the nationalist movement. The new leader made good one of the basic weaknesses of the previous leadership. In his struggle against racism in South Africa, he had evolved a new form of struggle—non-cooperation—and a new technique of struggle—satyagraha—which could be put into practice against the British in India. He had, moreover, a basic sympathy for and understanding of the problems and psychology of the Indian peasantry. He was, therefore, able to appeal to it and bring it into the mainstream of the national movement. He was thus able to arouse and unite all sections of the Indian people in a mass national movement.

Gandhiji And His Ideas

M.K. Gandhi was born on 2 October 1869 at Porbandar in Gujarat. After getting his legal education in Britian, he went to South Africa to practise law. Imbued with a high sense of justice, he was revolted by the racial injustice, discrimination and degradation to which Indians had to submit in the South African colonies. Indian labourers who had gone to South Africa, and the merchants who followed were denied the right to vote. They had to register and pay a poll-tax. They could not reside except in prescribed locations, which were insanitary and congested. In some of the South African colonies, the Asians, as also the Africans, could not stay out of doors after 9 p.m.; nor could they use public footpaths. Gandhi soon became the leader of the struggle against these conditions and during 1893–1914, was engaged in a heroic though unequal struggle against the racist authorities of South Africa. It was during this long struggle lasting nearly two decades that he evolved the technique of satyagraha based on truth and non-violence. The ideal satyagrahi was to be truthful and perfectly peaceful, but at the same time he would refuse to submit to what he considered wrong. He would accept suffering willingly in the course of struggle against the wrong-doer. This struggle was to be part of his love of truth. But even while resisting evil, he would love the evil-doer. Hatred would be alien to the nature of a true satyagrahi. He would, moreover, be utterly fearless. He would never bow down before evil, whatever the consequences. In Gandhi's eyes, non-violence was not a weapon of the weak and the cowardly. Only the strong and the brave could practise it. Even violence was preferable to cowardice. In a famous article in his weekly journal, *Young India,* he wrote in 1920 that "Non-violence is the law of our species, as violence is the law of the brute," but that "where there is only a choice between cowardice and violence, I would advise violence. ... I would rather have India resort to arms in order to defend her honour, than that she should, in a cowardly manner, become or remain a helpless witness to her own dishonour." He once summed up his entire philosophy of life as follows:

> The only virtue I want to claim is truth and non-violence. I lay no claim to super-human powers: I want none.

Another important aspect of Gandhi's outlook was that he would not separate thought and practice, belief and action. His truth and non-violence were meant for daily living and not merely for high-sounding speeches and writings.

Gandhiji, moreover, had an immense faith in the capacity of the common people to fight. For example, in 1915, referring to the common people who fought along with him in South Africa, in the course of his reply to an address of welcome at Madras, he said:

> You have said that I inspired these great men and women, but I cannot accept that proposition. It was they, the simple-minded folk, who worked away in faith, never expecting the slightest reward, who inspired me, who kept me to the proper level, and who compelled me by their sacrifice, by their great faith, by their great trust in the great God to do the work that I was able to do.

Similarly, in 1942, when asked how he expected "to resist the might of the empire," he replied: "with the might of the dumb millions."

Gandhiji returned to India in 1915 at the age of 46. He spent an entire year travelling all over India, understanding Indian conditions and the Indian people and then, in 1916, founded the Sabarmati Ashram at Ahmedabad where his friends and followers were to learn and practise the ideas of truth and non-violence. He also set out to experiment with his new method of struggle.

Champaran Satyagraha (1917)

Gandhi's first great experiment in satyagraha came in 1917 in Champaran, a district in Bihar. The peasantry on the indigo plantations in the district was excessively oppressed by European planters. They were compelled to grow indigo on at least 3/20th of their land and to sell it at prices fixed by the planters. Similar conditions had prevailed earlier in Bengal, but as a result of a major uprising during 1859–61 the peasants there had won their freedom from the indigo planters.

Having heard of Gandhi's campaigns in South Africa, several peasants of Champaran invited him to come and help them. Accompanied by Babu Rajendra Prasad, Mazhar-ul-Huq, J.B. Kripalani, Narhari Parekh and Mahadev Desai, Gandhiji reached Champaran in 1917 and began to conduct a detailed inquiry into the condition of the peasantry. The infuriated district officials ordered him to leave Champaran, but he defied the order and was willing to face trial and imprisonment. This forced the government to cancel its earlier order and to appoint a committee of inquiry on which Gandhiji served as a member. Ultimately, the disabilities from which the peasantry was suffering were reduced and Gandhiji won his first battle of civil disobedience in India. He also had a glimpse into the naked poverty in which the peasants of India lived.

Ahmedabad Mill Strike

In 1918, Mahatma Gandhi intervened in a dispute between the workers and mill-owners of Ahmedabad. He advised the workers to go on strike and to demand a 35 per cent increase in wages. But he insisted that the workers should not use violence against the employers during the strike. He undertook a fast unto death to strengthen the workers' resolve to continue the strike. But his fast also put pressure on the mill-owners, who relented on the fourth day and agreed to give the workers a 35 per cent increase in wages.

In 1918, crops failed in the Kheda District in Gujarat, but the government refused to remit land revenue and insisted on its full collection. Gandhiji supported the peasants and advised them to withhold payment of revenue till their demand for its remission was met. The struggle was withdrawn when it was learnt that the government had issued instructions that revenue should be recovered only from those peasants who could afford to pay. Sardar Vallabhbhai Patel was one of the many young persons who became Gandhiji's followers during the Kheda peasant struggle.

These experiences brought Gandhiji in close contact with the masses whose interests he actively espoused all his life. In fact, he was the first Indian nationalist leader who identified his life and his manner of living with the life of the common people. In time, he became the symbol of poor India, nationalist India and rebellious India. Three other causes were very dear to Gandhi's heart. The first was Hindu-Muslim unity; the second, the fight against untouchability; and the third, the raising of the social status of women in the country. He once summed up his aims as follows:

> I shall work for an India in which the poorest shall feel that it is their country, in whose making they have an effective voice, an India in which there shall be no high class and low class of people, an India in which all communities shall live in perfect harmony. ... There can be no room in such an India for the curse of untouchability. ... Women will enjoy the same rights as men.... This is the India of my dreams.

Though a devout Hindu, Gandhi's cultural and religious outlook was universalist and not narrow. "Indian culture," he wrote, "is neither Hindu, Islamic, nor any other, wholly. It is a fusion of all." He wanted Indians to have deep roots in their own culture, but at the same time to acquire the best that other world cultures had to offer. He said:

> I want the culture of all lands to be blown about my house as freely as possible. But I refuse to be blown off my feet by any. I refuse to live in other peoples' houses as an interloper, a beggar or a slave.

Satyagraha Against the Rowlatt Act

Along with other nationalists, Gandhiji was also aroused by the Rowlatt Act. In February 1919, he founded the Satyagraha Sabha, whose members took a pledge to disobey the Act and thus to court arrest and imprisonment. Here was a new method of struggle. The nationalist movement, whether under moderate or extremist leadership, had hitherto confined its struggle to agitation. Big meetings and demonstrations, refusal to cooperate with the government, boycott of foreign cloth and schools, or individual acts of violence were the only forms of political work known to the nationalists. Satyagraha immediately raised the movement to a new, higher level. Nationalists could now act, instead of merely agitating and giving only verbal expression to their dissatisfaction and anger.

The movement, moreover, was to rely increasingly on the political support of the peasants, artisans and the urban poor. Gandhiji asked the nationalist workers to go to the villages. That is where India lives, he said. He increasingly turned the face of nationalism towards the common man and the symbol of this transformation was to be khadi, or hand-spun and hand-woven cloth, which soon became the uniform of the nationalists. He spun daily to emphasise the dignity of labour and the value of self-reliance. India's salvation would come, he said, when the masses were wakened from their sleep and became active in politics. And the people responded magnificently to Gandhi's call. March and April 1919 witnessed a remarkable political awakening in India. Almost the entire country came to life. There were *hartals*, strikes, processions and demonstrations. The slogans of Hindu-Muslim unity filled the air. The entire country was electrified. The Indian people were no longer willing to submit to the degradation of foreign rule.

JALLIANWALA BAGH MASSACRE

The government was determined to suppress the mass agitation. It repeatedly lathi-charged and fired upon unarmed demonstrators at Bombay, Ahmedabad, Calcutta, Delhi and other cities. Gandhiji gave a call for a mighty *hartal* on 6 April 1919. The people responded with unprecedented enthusiasm. The government decided to meet the popular protest with repression, particularly in the Punjab. At this time was perpetrated one of the worst political crimes in modern history. A large but unarmed crowd had gathered on 13 April 1919 at

Amritsar (in the Punjab) in the Jallianwala Bagh to protest against the arrest of their popular leaders, Dr Saifuddin Kitchlew and Dr Satyapal. General Dyer, the military commander of Amritsar, decided to terrorise the people of Amritsar into complete submission. Jallianwala Bagh was a large open space which was enclosed on three sides by buildings and had only one exit. He surrounded the Bagh (garden) with his army unit, closed the exit with his troops and then ordered his men to shoot into the trapped crowd with rifles and machine-guns. They fired till their ammunition was exhausted. Thousands were killed and wounded. After this massacre, martial law was proclaimed throughout the Punjab and the people were submitted to the most uncivilised atrocities. A liberal lawyer, Sivaswamy Aiyer, who had received a knighthood from the government, wrote as follows on the Punjab atrocities:

> The wholesale slaughter of hundreds of unarmed men of Jallianwala Bagh without giving the crowd an opportunity to disperse, the indifferences of General Dyer to the condition of hundreds of people who were wounded in the firing, the firing of machine-guns into crowds who had dispersed and taken to their heels, the flogging of men in public, the order compelling thousands of students to walk 16 miles a day for roll-calls, the arrest and detention of 500 students and professors, the compelling of school children of 5 to 7 to attend on parade to salute the flag ... the flogging of a marriage party, the censorship of mails, the closure of the Badshahi mosque for six weeks, the arrest and detention of people without any substantial reasons ... the flogging of six of the biggest boys in the Islamiah school simply because they happened to be school boys and to be big boys, the construction of an open cage for the confinement of arrested persons, the invention of novel punishments like the crawling order, the skipping order and others unknown to any system of law, civil or military, the handcuffing and roping together of persons and keeping them in open trucks for fifteen hours, the use of aeroplanes and Lewis guns and the latest paraphernalia of scientific warfare against unarmed citizens, the taking of hostages and the confiscation and destruction of property for the purposes of securing the attendance of absentees, the handcuffing of Hindus and Muhammedans in pairs with the object of demonstrating the consequences of Hindu-Muslim unity, the cutting off of electric and water supplies from Indians' houses, the removal of fans from Indian houses and giving them for use by Europeans, the commandeering of all vehicles owned by Indians and giving them to Europeans for use. ... These are some of the many incidents of the

administration of martial law, which created a reign of terror in the Punjab and have shocked the public.

A wave of horror ran through the country as the knowledge of the Punjab happenings spread. People saw, as if in a flash, the ugliness and brutality that lay behind the facade of civilisation that imperialism and foreign rule professed. Popular shock was expressed by the great poet and humanist Rabindranath Tagore, who renounced his knighthood in protest and declared:

> The time has come when badges of honour make our shame glaring in their incongruous context of humiliation, and I for my part wish to stand shorn of all special distinctions, by the side of my countrymen who, for their so-called insignificance, are liable to suffer degradation not fit for human beings.

The Khilafat and Non-Cooperation Movement (1919–22)

A new stream came into the nationalist movement with the Khilafat movement. We have seen earlier that the younger generation of educated Muslims and a section of traditional divines and theologians had been growing more and more radical and nationalist. The ground for common political action by Hindus and Muslims had already been prepared by the Lucknow Pact. The nationalist agitation against the Rowlatt Act had touched all the Indian people alike and brought Hindus and Muslims together in political agitation.

For example, as if to declare before the world the principle of Hindu-Muslim unity in political action, Swami Shradhanand, a staunch Arya Samaj leader, was asked by the Muslims to preach from the pulpit of the Jama Masjid at Delhi while Dr Kitchlew, a Muslim, was given the keys of the Golden Temple, the Sikh shrine at Amritsar. At Amritsar, such political unity had been brought about by governmental repression. Hindus and Muslims were handcuffed together, made to crawl together and drink water together, when ordinarily a Hindu would not drink water from the hands of a Muslim. In this atmosphere, the nationalist trend among the Muslims took the form of the Khilafat agitation. The politically-conscious Muslims were critical of the treatment meted out to the Ottoman (or

Turkish) empire by Britain and its allies who had partitioned it and taken away Thrace from Turkey proper. This was in violation of the earlier pledge of the British Premier Lloyd George, who had declared: "Nor are we fighting to deprive Turkey of the rich and renowned lands of Asia Minor and Thrace which are predominantly Turkish in race." The Muslims also felt that the power of the Sultan of Turkey, who was also regarded by many as the Caliph or the religious head of the Muslims, over the religious places of Islam should not be undermined. A Khilafat Committee was soon formed under the leadership of the Ali Brothers, Maulana Azad, Hakim Ajmal Khan and Hasrat Mohani, and a country-wide agitation was organised.

The All-India Khilafat Conference held at Delhi in November 1919 decided to withdraw all cooperation from the government if their demands were not met. The Muslim League, now under the leadership of nationalists, gave full support to the National Congress and its agitation on political issues. On their part, the Congress leaders, including Lokamanya Tilak and Mahatma Gandhi, viewed the Khilafat agitation as a golden opportunity for cementing Hindu-Muslim unity and bringing the Muslim masses into the national movement. They realised that different sections of the people— Hindus, Muslims, Sikhs and Christians, capitalists and workers, peasants and artisans, women and youth, tribal people and people of different regions—would come into the national movement through the experience of fighting for their own different demands and seeing that the alien regime stood in opposition to them. Gandhiji looked upon the Khilafat agitation as "an opportunity of uniting Hindus and Mohammedans as would not arise in a hundred years." Early in 1920, he declared that the Khilafat question overshadowed that of the constitutional reforms and the Punjab wrongs and announced that he would lead a movement of non-cooperation if the terms of peace with Turkey did not satisfy the Indian Muslims. In fact, very soon Gandhi became one of the leaders of the Khilafat movement.

Meanwhile, the government had refused to annul the Rowlatt Act, make amends for the atrocities in the Punjab or satisfy the nationalist urge for self-government. In June 1920, an all-party conference met at Allahabad and approved a programme of boycott of schools, colleges and law courts. The Khilafat Committee launched a Non-Cooperation Movement on 31 August 1920.

The Congress met at a special session in September 1920 at Calcutta. Only a few weeks earlier it had suffered a grievous loss—Lokamanya Tilak had passed away on 1 August at the age of 64. But his place was soon taken by Gandhiji, C.R. Das and Motilal Nehru. The Congress supported Gandhi's plan for non-cooperation with the government till the Punjab and Khilafat wrongs were removed and swaraj established. The people were asked to boycott government educational institutions, law courts and legislatures; to give up foreign cloth; to surrender officially-conferred titles and honours; and to practise hand-spinning and hand-weaving for producing khadi. Later, the programme would include resignation from government service and mass civil disobedience, including refusal to pay taxes. Congressmen immediately withdrew from elections, and the voters too largely boycotted them. This decision to defy in a most peaceful manner the government and its laws was endorsed at the annual session of the Congress held at Nagpur in December 1920. "The British people will have to beware," declared Gandhiji at Nagpur, "that if they do not want to do justice, it will be the bounden duty of every Indian to destroy the empire." The Nagpur session also made changes in the constitution of the Congress. Provincial Congress Committees were reorganised on the basis of linguistic areas. The Congress was now to be led by a Working Committee of 15 members, including the president and the secretaries. This would enable the Congress to function as a continuous political organisation and would provide it with the machinery for implementing its resolutions. The Congress organisation was to reach down to the villages, small towns and *mohallas*, and its membership fee was reduced to 4 annas (25 paise of today) per year to enable the rural and urban poor to become members.

The Congress now changed its character. It became the organiser and leader of the masses in their national struggle for freedom from foreign rule. There was a general feeling of exhilaration. Political freedom might come years later, but the people had begun to shake off their slavish mentality. It was as if the very air that India breathed had changed. The joy and enthusiasm of those days was something special, for the sleeping giant was beginning to wake up. Moreover, Hindus and Muslims were marching together shoulder to shoulder. At the same time, some of the older leaders now left the Congress.

The Struggle for Swaraj: 1919–27

They did not like the new turn that the national movement had taken. They still believed in the traditional methods of agitation and political work, which were strictly confined within the four walls of the law. They opposed the organisation of the masses, *hartals*, strikes, satyagraha, breaking of laws, courting of imprisonment and other forms of violent struggle. Muhammad Ali Jinnah, G.S. Khaparde, Bipin Chandra Pal and Annie Besant were among the prominent leaders who left the Congress during this period.

The years 1921 and 1922 were to witness an unprecedented movement of the Indian people. Thousands of students left government schools and colleges and joined national schools and colleges. It was at this time that the Jamia Millia Islamia (National Muslim University) of Aligarh, the Bihar Vidyapith, the Kashi Vidyapith and the Gujarat Vidyapith came into existence. The Jamia Millia later shifted to Delhi. Acharya Narendra Dev, Dr Zakir Husain and Lala Lajpat Rai were among the many distinguished teachers at these national colleges and universities. Hundreds of lawyers, including Chittaranjan Das, popularly known as Deshbandhu, Motilal Nehru, Rajendra Prasad, Saifuddin Kitchlew, C. Rajagopalachari, Sardar Patel, T. Prakasam and Asaf Ali gave up their lucrative legal practice. The Tilak Swarajya Fund was started to finance the non-cooperation movement and within six months, over a crore of rupees were subscribed. Women showed great enthusiasm and freely offered their jewellery. Boycott of foreign cloth became a mass movement. Huge bonfires of foreign cloth were organised all over the land. Khadi soon became a symbol of freedom. In July 1921, the All-India Khilafat Committee passed a resolution declaring that no Muslim should serve in the British-Indian army. In September, the Ali brothers were arrested for 'sedition'. Immediately, Gandhiji gave a call for repetition of this resolution at hundreds of meetings. Fifty members of the All-India Congress Committee issued a similar declaration that no Indian should serve a government which degraded India socially, economically and politically. The Congress Working Committee issued a similar statement.

The Congress now decided to raise the movement to a higher level. It permitted the Congress Committee of a province to start civil disobedience or disobedience of British laws, including non-payment of taxes, if in its opinion the people were ready for it.

The government again took recourse to repression. The activities of the Congress and Khilafat volunteers, who had begun to drill together and thus unite Hindu and Muslim political workers at lower levels, were declared illegal. By the end of 1921, all important nationalist leaders, except Gandhiji, were behind bars, along with 3000 others. In November 1921, huge demonstrations greeted the Prince of Wales, heir to the British throne, during his tour of India. He had been asked by the government to come to India to encourage loyalty among the people and the princes. In Bombay, the government tried to suppress the demonstration, killing 53 persons and wounding about 400 more. The annual session of the Congress, meeting at Ahmedabad in December 1921, passed a resolution affirming "the fixed determination of the Congress to continue the programme of non-violent non-cooperation with greater vigour than hitherto ... till the Punjab and Khilafat wrongs were redressed and Swarajya is established." The resolution urged all Indians, and in particular students, "quietly and without any demonstration to offer themselves for arrest by belonging to the volunteer organisations." All such satyagrahis were to take a pledge to "remain non-violent in word and deed," to promote unity among Hindus, Muslims, Sikhs, Parsis, Christians and Jews, and to practise swadeshi and wear only khadi. A Hindu volunteer was also to undertake to fight actively against untouchability. The resolution also called upon the people to organise, whenever possible, individual or mass civil disobedience along non-violent lines.

The people now waited impatiently for the call for further struggle. The movement had, moreover, spread deep among the masses. Thousands of peasants in Uttar Pradesh and Bengal had responded to the call of non-cooperation. In parts of Uttar Pradesh, tenants refused to pay illegal dues to the zamindars. In the Punjab, the Sikhs were leading a non-violent movement, known as the Akali movement, to remove corrupt *mahants* from the Gurudwaras, their places of worship. In Assam, tea-plantation labourers went on strike. The peasants of Midnapore refused to pay Union Board taxes. A powerful agitation led by Duggirala Gopalakrishnayya developed in Guntur district. The whole population of Chirala, a town in that district, refused to pay municipal taxes and moved out of town. All village officers resigned in Peddanadipadu. In Malabar (northern Kerala) the *Moplahs,* or Muslim peasants, created a powerful anti-zamindar movement. The Viceroy wrote to the Secretary of State in February 1919 that "The lower classes in the towns have been seriously affected by the Non-Cooperation Movement. ... In certain areas the peasantry have been affected, particularly in parts of Assam valley, United Provinces, Bihar and Orissa, and Bengal." On 1 February 1922, Mahatma Gandhi announced that he would start mass civil disobedience, including non-payment of taxes, unless within seven days the political prisoners were released and the press freed from government control.

This mood of struggle was soon transformed into retreat. On 5 February, a Congress procession of 3000 peasants at Chauri Chaura, a village in the Gorakhpur District of Uttar Pradesh, was fired upon by the police. The angry crowd attacked and burnt the police station, causing the death of 22 policemen. Other incidents of violence by crowds had occurred earlier in different parts of the country. Gandhiji was afraid that in this moment of popular ferment and excitement, the movement might easily take a violent turn. He was convinced that the nationalist workers had not yet properly understood nor learnt the practice of non-violence without which, he was convinced, civil disobedience could not be a success. Apart from the fact that he would have nothing to do with violence, he also perhaps believed that the British would be able to easily crush a violent movement, for people had not yet built up enough strength and stamina to resist massive government repression. He therefore decided to suspend the nationalist campaign. The Congress Working Committee met at Bardoli in Gujarat on 12 February and passed a resolution stopping all activities which would lead to breaking of laws. It urged Congressmen to donate their time to the constructive programme—popularisation of the charkha, national schools, temperance, removal of untouchability and promotion of Hindu-Muslim unity.

The Bardoli resolution stunned the country and had a mixed reception among the bewildered nationalists. While some had implicit faith in Gandhiji and believed that the retreat was a part of the Gandhian strategy of struggle, others, especially the younger nationalists, resented this decision to retreat. Subhas Bose, one of the popular and younger leaders of the Congress, has written in his autobiography, *The Indian Struggle*:

To sound the order of retreat just when public enthusiasm was reaching the boiling-point was nothing short of a national calamity. The principal lieutenants of the Mahatma, Deshbandhu Das, Pandit Motilal Nehru and Lala Lajpat Rai, who were all in prison, shared the popular resentment. I was with the Deshbandhu at the time and I could see that he was beside himself with anger and sorrow at the way Mahatma Gandhi was repeatedly bungling.

Many other young leaders such as Jawaharlal Nehru had a similar reaction. But both the people and the leaders had faith in Gandhiji and did not want to publicly disobey him. They accepted his decision without open opposition. The first Non-Cooperation and Civil Disobedience Movement virtually came to an end.

The last act of the drama was played when the government decided to take full advantage of the situation and to strike hard. It arrested Mahatma Gandhi on 10 March 1922 and charged him with spreading disaffection against the government. Gandhiji was sentenced to six years' imprisonment after a trial, which was made historic by the statement that he made before the court. Pleading guilty to the prosecution's charge, he invited the court to award him "the highest penalty that can be inflicted upon me for what in law is a deliberate crime, and what appears to me to be the highest duty of a citizen." He traced at length his own political evolution from a supporter of the British rule to its sharpest critic and said:

> I came reluctantly to the conclusion that the British connection had made India more helpless than she ever was before, politically and economically. A disarmed India has no power of resistance against any aggression. ... She has become so poor that she has little power of resisting famines. ... Little do town dwellers know how the semi-starved masses of India are slowly sinking to lifelessness. Little do they know that their miserable comfort represents the brokerage they get for the work they do for the foreign exploiter, that the profits and the brokerage are sucked from the masses. Little do they realise that the government established by law in British India is carried on for the exploitation of the masses. No sophistry, no jugglery in figures, can explain away the evidence that the skeletons in many villages present to the naked eye. ... In my opinion, administration of the law is thus prostituted, consciously or unconsciously, for the benefit of the exploiter. The greater misfortune is that Englishmen and their Indian associates in the administration of the country do not know that

they are engaged in the crime I have attempted to describe. I am satisfied that many Englishmen and Indian officials honestly believe that they are administering one of the best systems devised in the world, and that India is making steady, though slow progress. They do not know that a subtle but effective system of terrorism and an organised display of force on the one hand, and the deprivation of all powers of retaliation or self-defence on the other, have emasculated the people and induced in them the habit of simulation.

In conclusion, Gandhiji expressed his belief that "non-cooperation with evil is as much a duty as is cooperation with good." The judge noted that he was passing on Gandhiji the same sentence as was passed on Lokamanya Tilak in 1908.

Very soon the Khilafat question also lost relevance. The people of Turkey rose up under the leadership of Mustafa Kamal Pasha and, in November 1922, deprived the Sultan of his political power. Kamal Pasha took many measures to modernise Turkey and to make it a secular state. He abolished the Caliphate (or the institution of the Caliph) and separated the state from religion by eliminating Islam from the Constitution. He nationalised education, granted women extensive rights, introduced legal codes based on European models, took steps to develop agriculture and to introduce modern industries. All these steps broke the back of the Khilafat agitation.

The Khilafat agitation had made an important contribution to the non-cooperation movement. It had brought urban Muslims into the nationalist movement and had been, thus, responsible in part for the feeling of nationalist enthusiasm and exhilaration that prevailed in the country in those days. Some historians have criticised it for mixing religion with politics. As a result, they say, religious consciousness spread to politics, and in the long run, the forces of communalism were strengthened. This is true to some extent. There was, of course, nothing wrong in the nationalist movement taking up a demand that affected Muslims only. It was inevitable that different sections of society would come to understand the need for freedom through their particular demands and experiences. The nationalist leadership, however, failed to some extent in raising the religious political consciousness of the Muslims to the higher plane of secular political consciousnesss. At the same time, it should also be kept in view that the Khilafat agitation represented much wider feelings of the Muslims than their concern for the Caliph. It was in reality an aspect of the general spread of anti-imperialist feelings among the Muslims. These feelings found concrete expression on the Khilafat question. After all, there was no protest in India when Kamal Pasha abolished the Caliphate in 1924.

It may be noted at this stage that even though the Non-Cooperation and Civil Disobedience Movement had ended in apparent failure, the national movement had been strengthened in more ways than one. Nationalist sentiments and the national movement had now reached the remotest corners of the land. Millions of peasants, artisans and the urban poor had been brought into the national movement. All strata of Indian society had been politicised. Women had been drawn into the movement. It is this politicisation and activisation of millions of men and women that imparted a revolutionary character to the Indian national movement.

British rule was based on the twin notions that the British ruled India for the good of the Indians, and that it was invincible and incapable of being overthrown. As we have seen earlier, the first notion was challenged by the moderate nationalists who developed a powerful economic critique of colonial rule. It was now, during the mass phase of the national movement, that this critique was disseminated among the common people by youthful agitators, through speeches, pamphlets, dramas, songs, *prabhat pheries* and newspapers.

The notion of invincibility of the British rule was challenged by satyagraha and mass struggle. As Jawaharlal Nehru wrote in *The Discovery of India*:

> The essence of his (Gandhiji's) teaching was fearlessness ... not merely body courage but the absence of fear from the mind. ... But the dominant impulse in India under British rule was that of fear, pervasive, oppressing, strangling fear; fear of the army, the police, the widespread secret service; fear of the official class; fear of laws meant to suppress and of prison; fear of landlord's agents; fear of the moneylender; fear of unemployment and starvation, which were always on the threshold. It was against this all-pervading fear that Gandhiji's quiet and determined voice was raised: Be not afraid.

A major result of the Non-Cooperation Movement was that the Indian people lost their sense of fear—the brute strength of British power in India no longer frightened them. They had gained tremendous self-confidence and self-esteem, which no defeats and retreats could shake. This was expressed by Gandhiji when he declared that "the fight that was commenced in 1920 is a fight to the finish, whether it lasts one month or one year or many months or many years."

The Swarajists

Major developments in Indian politics occurred during 1922–28. The withdrawal of the Non-Cooperation Movement led to demoralisation in the nationalist ranks. Moreover, serious differences arose among the leaders who had to decide how to prevent the movement from lapsing into passivity. One school of thought, headed by C.R. Das and Motilal Nehru, advocated a new line of political activity under the changed conditions. They said that nationalists should end the boycott of the Legislative Councils, enter them, obstruct their working according to official plans, expose their weaknesses, transform them into arenas of political struggle and thus use them to arouse public enthusiasm. Sardar Vallabhbhai Patel, Dr Ansari, Babu Rajendra Prasad and others, known as 'no-changers', opposed Council entry. They warned that legislative politics would lead to neglect of work among the masses, weaken nationalist fervour and create rivalries among the leaders. They, therefore, continued to emphasise the constructive programme of spinning, temperance, Hindu-Muslim unity, removal of untouchability and grassroots work in the villages and among the poor. This would, they said, gradually prepare the country for the new round of mass struggle. In December 1922, Das and Motilal Nehru formed the Congress-Khilafat Swarajya Party with C.R. Das as president and Motilal Nehru as one of the secretaries. The new party was to function as a group within the Congress. It accepted the Congress programme except in one respect—it would take part in Council elections.

The Swarajists and the 'no-changers' now engaged in fierce political controversy. Even Gandhiji, who had been released on 5 February 1924 on grounds of health, failed in his efforts to unite them. But both were determined to avoid the disastrous experience of the 1907 split at Surat. On the advice of Gandhiji, the two groups agreed to remain in the Congress, though they would work in their separate ways.

Even though the Swarajists had little time for preparations, they did very well in the election of November 1923. They won 42 seats out of the 101 elected seats in the Central Legislative Assembly. With the cooperation of other Indian groups, they repeatedly out-voted the government in the Central Assembly and in several of the Provincial Councils. They agitated through powerful speeches on questions of self-government, civil liberties and industrial development. In March 1925, they succeeded in electing Vithalbhai J. Patel, a leading nationalist leader, as the president (Speaker) of the Central Legislative Assembly. They filled the political void at a time when the national movement was recouping its strength. They also exposed the hollowness of the Reform Act of 1919. But they failed to change the policies of the authoritarian Government of India and found it necessary to walk out of the Central Assembly first in March 1926, and then in January 1930.

Meanwhile, the 'no-changers' carried on quiet, constructive work. Symbolic of this work were hundreds of ashrams that came up all over the country, where young men and women promoted charkha and khadi, and worked among the lower castes and tribal people. Hundreds of National schools and colleges came up, where young persons were trained in a non-colonial ideological framework. Moreover, constructive workers served as the backbone of the civil disobedience movements as their active organisers.

While the Swarajists and the 'no-changers' worked in their own separate ways, there was no basic difference between the two, and, because they kept on the best of terms and recognised each other's anti-imperialist character, they could readily unite later when the time was ripe for a new national struggle. Meanwhile, the nationalist movement and the Swarajists suffered another grievous blow in the death of C.R. Das in June 1925.

As the Non-Cooperation Movement petered out and the people felt frustrated, communalism reared its ugly head. The communal elements took advantage of the situation to propagate their views and after 1923, the country was repeatedly plunged into communal riots. The Muslim League and the Hindu Mahasabha, which was founded in December 1917, once again became active. The result was that the growing feeling that all people were Indians first received a setback. Even the Swarajist Party, whose main leaders, Motilal Nehru and Das, were staunch nationalists, was split by communalism. A group known as 'responsivists', including Madan Mohan Malaviya, Lala Lajpat Rai and N.C. Kelkar, offered cooperation to the government so that the so-called Hindu interests might be safeguarded. They accused Motilal Nehru of letting down the Hindus. The Muslim communalists were no less active in fighting for the loaves and fishes of office. Gandhiji, who had repeatedly asserted that "Hindu-Muslim unity must be our creed for all time and under all circumstances", tried to intervene and improve the situation. In September 1924, he went on a 21-day-fast at Delhi in Maulana Mohamed Ali's house to do penance for the inhumanity revealed in the communal riots. But his efforts were of little avail.

The situation in the country appeared to be dark indeed. There was general political apathy; Gandhi was living in retirement, the Swarajists were split, communalism was flourishing. Gandhiji wrote in May 1927: "My only hope lies in prayer and answer to prayer." But, behind the scenes, forces of national upsurge had been growing. When in November 1927 the announcement of the formation of the Simon Commission came, India again emerged from darkness and entered a new era of political struggle.

Fourteen

The Struggle for Swaraj: 1927–47

Emergence of New Forces

The year 1927 witnessed many portents of national recovery and the emergence of the new trend of socialism. Marxism and other socialist ideas spread rapidly. Politically, this force and energy found reflection in the rise of a new left wing in the Congress under the leadership of Jawaharlal Nehru and Subhas Chandra Bose. The left wing did not confine its attention to the struggle against imperialism. It simultaneously raised the question of internal class oppression by the capitalists and landlords.

Indian youth were becoming active. All over the country, youth leagues were being formed and student conferences held. The first All-Bengal Conference of Students was held in August 1928 and was presided over by Jawaharlal Nehru. After this, many other student associations were started in the country and hundreds of student and youth conferences held. Moreover, the young Indian nationalists began gradually to turn to socialism and to advocate radical solutions for the political, economic and social ills from which the country was suffering. They also put forward and popularised the programme of complete independence. Socialist and Communist groups came into existence in the 1920s. The example of the Russian Revolution had aroused interest among many young nationalists. Many of them were dissatisfied with Gandhian political ideas and programmes and turned to socialist ideology for guidance. M.N. Roy became the first Indian to be elected to the leadership of the Communist International. In 1924, the government arrested Muzaffar Ahmed and S.A. Dange, accused them of spreading Communist ideas, and tried them along with others in the Kanpur Conspiracy case. In 1925, the Communist Party came into existence. Moreover, many worker and peasant parties were founded in different parts of the country. These parties and groups propagated Marxist and communist ideas. At the same time, they remained integral parts of the national movement and the National Congress.

The peasants and workers were also once again stirring. In Uttar Pradesh, there was large-scale agitation among tenants for the revision of tenancy laws. The tenants wanted lower rents, protection from eviction and relief from indebtedness. In Gujarat, the peasants protested against official efforts to increase land revenue. The famous Bardoli Satyagraha occurred at this time. In 1928, under the leadership of Sardar Vallabhbhai Patel, the peasants organised a No Tax Campaign and in the end won their demand. There was a rapid growth of trade unionism under the leadership of the All-India Trade Union Congress. Many strikes occurred during 1928. There was a long strike lasting for two months in the railway workshop at Kharagpur. The South Indian Railway workers went on strike. Another strike was organised in the Tata Iron and Steel Works at Jamshedpur. Subhas Chandra Bose played an important role in the settlement of this strike. The most important strike of the period was in the Bombay textile mills. Nearly 150,000 workers went on strike for over five months. This strike was led by the communists. Over five lakh workers took part in strikes during 1928.

Another reflection of the new mood was the growing activity of the revolutionary movement, which was also beginning to take a socialist turn. The failure of the First Non-Cooperation Movement had led to the revival of the revolutionary movement. After an All India Conference, the Hindustan Republican Association was founded in October 1924 to organise an armed revolution. The government struck at it by arresting a large number of youth and trying them in the Kakori Conspiracy Case (1925). Seventeen were sentenced to long terms of imprisonment, four were transported for life, and four, including Ram Prasad Bismil and Ashfaqulla, were hanged. The revolutionaries soon came under the influence of socialist ideas, and in 1928, under the leadership of Chandra Shekhar Azad, changed the name of their organisation to the Hindustan Socialist Republican Association (HSRA).

They also gradually began to move away from individual heroic action and acts of violence. But the brutal lathi-charge on an anti-Simon Commission demonstration on 30 October 1928 led to a sudden change. The great Punjabi leader Lala Lajpat Rai died as a result of the lathi blows. This enraged the youth and on 17 December 1928 Bhagat Singh, Azad and Rajguru assassinated Saunders, the British police officer who had led the lathi charge.

The HSRA leadership also decided to let the people know about their changed political objectives and the need for a revolution by the masses. Consequently, Bhagat Singh and B.K. Dutt threw a bomb in the Central Legislative Assembly on 8 April 1929. The bomb did not harm anyone, for it had been deliberately made harmless. The aim was not to kill but, as their leaflet put it, "to make the deaf hear". Bhagat Singh and B.K. Dutt could have easily escaped after throwing the bomb but they deliberately chose to be arrested, for they wanted to make use of the court as a forum for revolutionary propaganda.

In Bengal, too, revolutionary activities were revived. In April 1930, a well-planned and large-scale armed raid was organised on the government armoury at Chittagong under the leadership of Surya Sen. This was the first of many attacks on unpopular government officials. A remarkable aspect of the revolutionary movement in Bengal was the participation of young women. The Chittagong revolutionaries marked a major advance. Theirs was not an individual action but a group action aimed at the organs of the colonial state.

The government struck hard at the revolutionaries. Many of them were arrested and tried in a series of famous cases. Bhagat Singh and a few others were also tried for the assassination of Saunders. The statements of the young revolutionaries in the courts and their fearless and defiant attitude won the sympathy of the people. Their defence was organised by Congress leaders who were otherwise votaries of non-violence. Particularly inspiring was the hunger strike they undertook as a protest against the horrible conditions in the prisons. As political prisoners, they demanded an honourable and decent treatment in jail. During the course of this hunger strike, Jatin Das, a frail young man, achieved martydom after a 63-day-long epic fast. Bhagat Singh, Sukhdev and Rajguru were executed on 23 March 1931, despite popular protest. In a letter to the Jail Superintendent written a few days before their execution, the three affirmed: "Very soon, the final battle will begin. Its outcome will be decisive. We took part in the struggle and we are proud of having done so."

In two of his last letters, the 23-year-old Bhagat Singh also affirmed his faith in socialism. He wrote: "The peasants have to liberate themselves not only from foreign yoke but also from the yoke of landlords and capitalists." In his last message of 3 March 1931, he declared that the struggle in India would continue so long as "a handful of exploiters go on exploiting the labour of the common people for their own ends. It matters little whether these exploiters are purely British capitalists, or British and Indians in alliance, or even purely Indian." Bhagat Singh defined socialism in a scientific manner—it meant the abolition of capitalism and class domination. He also made it clear that much before 1930, he and his comrades had abandoned violence. In his last political testament, written on 2 February 1931, he declared: "Apparently, I have acted like a terrorist. But I am not a terrorist. ... Let me announce with all the strength at my command that I am not a terrorist and I never was, except perhaps in the beginning of my revolutionary career. And I am convinced that we cannot gain anything through those methods."

Bhagat Singh was also fully and consciously secular. He often told his comrades that communalism was as big an enemy as colonialism and was to be as firmly opposed. In 1926, he had helped to establish the Punjab Naujawan Bharat Sabha and had become its first secretary. Two of the rules of the Sabha, drafted by Bhagat Singh, were: "To have nothing to do with communal bodies or other parties which disseminate communal ideas" and "to create the spirit of general toleration among the people considering religion as a matter of personal belief of man and to act upon the same fully."

The national revolutionary movement soon abated, though stray activities were carried on for several years more. Chandra Shekhar Azad was killed in a shooting encounter with the police in a public park, later renamed Azad Park, at Allahabad in February 1931. Surya Sen was arrested in February 1933 and hanged soon after. Hundreds of other revolutionaries were arrested and sentenced to varying terms of imprisonment, some being sent to the Cellular Jail in the Andamans.

Thus, a new political situation was beginning to arise by the end of the 1920s. Writing of these years, Lord Irwin, the Viceroy, recalled later that "some new force was working of which even those, whose knowledge of India went back for 20 or 30 years, had not yet learnt the full significance." The government was determined to suppress this new trend. As we have seen, the revolutionaries were suppressed with ferocity. The growing trade union movement and the communist movement were dealt with in the same manner. In March 1929, 31 prominent trade union and communist leaders (including three Englishmen) were arrested and, after a trial (Meerut Conspiracy Case) lasting four years, sentenced to long periods of imprisonment.

BOYCOTT OF THE SIMON COMMISSION

The catalyst to the new phase of the movement was provided when, in November 1927, the British government appointed the Indian Statutory Commission, known popularly after the name of its chairman as the Simon Commission, to go into the question of further constitutional reform. All the members of the Commission were Englishmen. This announcement was greeted with a chorus of protest from all Indians. What angered them most was the exclusion of Indians from the Commission and the basic notion behind this exclusion that foreigners would discuss and decide upon India's fitness for self-government. In other words, this British action was seen as a violation of the principle of self-determination and a deliberate insult to the self-respect of the Indians. At its Madras session in 1927, presided over by Dr Ansari, the National Congress decided to boycott the Commission "at every stage and in every form". The Muslim League and the Hindu Mahasabha decided to support the Congress decision. In fact, the Simon Commission united, at least temporarily, different groups and parties in the country. As a gesture of solidarity with the nationalists, the Muslim League even accepted the principle of joint electorates, provided seats were reserved for the Muslims.

All important Indian leaders and parties also tried to meet the challenge of the Simon Commission by getting together and trying to evolve an alternative scheme of constitutional reforms. Tens of conferences and joint meetings of leading political workers were held.

The end result was the Nehru Report, named after its chief architect, Motilal Nehru, and finalised in August 1928. Unfortunately, the All Party Convention, held at Calcutta in December 1928, failed to pass the Report. Objections were raised by some of the leaders belonging to the Muslim League, the Hindu Mahasabha and the Sikh League. Thus, the prospects of national unity were foiled by these groups and communalism began to grow steadily after this.

It should also be noted that there existed a basic difference between the politics of the nationalists and the politics of the communalists. The nationalists carried on a political struggle against the alien government to win political rights and freedom for the country. This was not the case with the communalists, Hindu or Muslim. Their demands were made on the nationalists; on the other hand, they usually looked to the foreign government for support and favours. They frequently struggled against the Congress and cooperated with the government.

Far more important than the proceedings of the All Parties Conference was the popular upsurge against the Simon Commission. The Commission's arrival in India led to a powerful protest movement in which nationalist enthusiasm and unity reached new heights.

On 3 February, the day the Commission reached Bombay, an all-India *hartal* was organised. Wherever the Commission went, it was greeted with *hartals* and black-flag demonstrations under the slogan, 'Simon Go Back'. The government used brutal suppression and police attacks to break the popular opposition.

The anti-Simon Commission movement did not immediately lead to wider political struggle because Gandhi, the unquestioned though undeclared leader of the national movement, was not yet convinced that the time for struggle had come. But popular enthusiasm could not be held back for long as the country was once again in a mood for struggle.

POORNA SWARAJ

The National Congress soon reflected this new mood. Gandhi came back to active politics and attended the Calcutta session of the Congress in December 1928. He now began to consolidate the nationalist ranks. The first step was to reconcile the militant left wing of the Congress. Jawaharlal Nehru was now made the President of the Congress at the historic Lahore session of 1929. This event had its romantic side too. Son had succeeded father (Motilal Nehru was the President of the Congress in 1928) as the official head of the national movement, marking a unique family triumph in the annals of modern history.

The Lahore session of the Congress gave voice to the new, revolutionary spirit. It passed a resolution declaring *Poorna Swaraj* (Complete Independence) to be the Congress objective. On 31 December 1929 was hoisted the newly adopted tri-colour flag of freedom. 26 January 1930 was fixed as the first Independence Day, which was to be so celebrated every year with the people taking the pledge that it was "a crime against man and God to submit any longer" to the British rule. The Congress session also announced the launching of a civil disobedience movement. But it did not draw up a programme of struggle. That was left to Mahatma Gandhi, the Congress organisation being placed at his disposal. Once again, the nationalist movement led by Gandhi faced the government. The country was again filled with hope and exhilaration and the determination to be free.

The Civil Disobedience Movement

The Civil Disobedience Movement was started by Gandhi on 12 March 1930 with his famous Dandi March. Together with 78 chosen followers, Gandhi walked nearly 375 km from Sabarmati Ashram to Dandi, a village on the Gujarat sea-coast. Day after day, newspapers reported his progress, his speeches and the impact on the people. Hundreds of village officials on his route resigned their jobs. On 6 April, Gandhiji reached Dandi, picked up a handful of salt and broke the salt law as a symbol of the Indian people's refusal to live under British-made laws, and therefore under British rule. Gandhiji declared:

> The British rule in India has brought about moral, material, cultural, and spiritual ruination of this great country. I regard this rule as a curse. I am out to destroy this system of Government. ... Sedition has become my religion. Ours is a non-violent battle. We are not to kill anybody but it is our *dharma* to see that the curse of this Government is blotted out.

The movement now spread rapidly. Violation of salt laws all over the country was soon followed by defiance of forest laws in Maharashtra, Karnataka and the Central Provinces, and refusal to pay the rural *chaukidari* tax in eastern India. Everywhere in the country, people joined *hartals*, demonstrations and the campaign to boycott foreign goods and to refuse to pay taxes. Lakhs of Indians offered satyagraha. In many parts of the country, the peasants refused to pay land revenue and rent and had their lands confiscated. A notable feature of the movement was the wide participation of women. Thousands of them left the seclusion of their homes and offered satyagraha. They took active part in picketing shops selling foreign cloth or liquor. They marched shoulder to shoulder with the men in processions.

The movement reached the extreme north-western corner of India and stirred the brave and hardy Pathans. Under the leadership of Khan Abdul Ghaffar Khan, popularly known as 'the Frontier Gandhi', the Pathans organised the society of Khudai Khidmatgars (or Servants of God), known popularly as Red Shirts. They were pledged to non-violence and the freedom struggle. Another noteworthy incident occurred in Peshawar at this time. Two platoons of Garhwali soldiers refused to open fire on non-violent mass demonstrators, even though it meant facing court martial and long terms of imprisonment. This episode showed that nationalism was beginning to penetrate the Indian army, the chief instrument of British rule.

Similarly, the movement found an echo in the eastern-most corner of India. The Manipuris took a brave part in it and Nagaland produced a brave heroine in Rani Gaidilieu, who at the age of 13 responded to the call of Gandhi and the Congress and raised the banner of rebellion against foreign rule. The young Rani was captured in 1932 and sentenced to life imprisonment. She wasted her bright youthful years in the dark cells of various Assam jails, to be released only in 1947 by the government of free India. Jawaharlal Nehru was to write of her in 1937: "A day will come when India also will remember her and cherish her."

The government's reply to the national struggle was the same as before—an effort to crush it through ruthless repression, lathi-charges and firing on unarmed crowds of men and women. Over 90,000 satyagrahis, including Gandhiji and other Congress leaders, were imprisoned. The Congress was declared illegal. The nationalist press

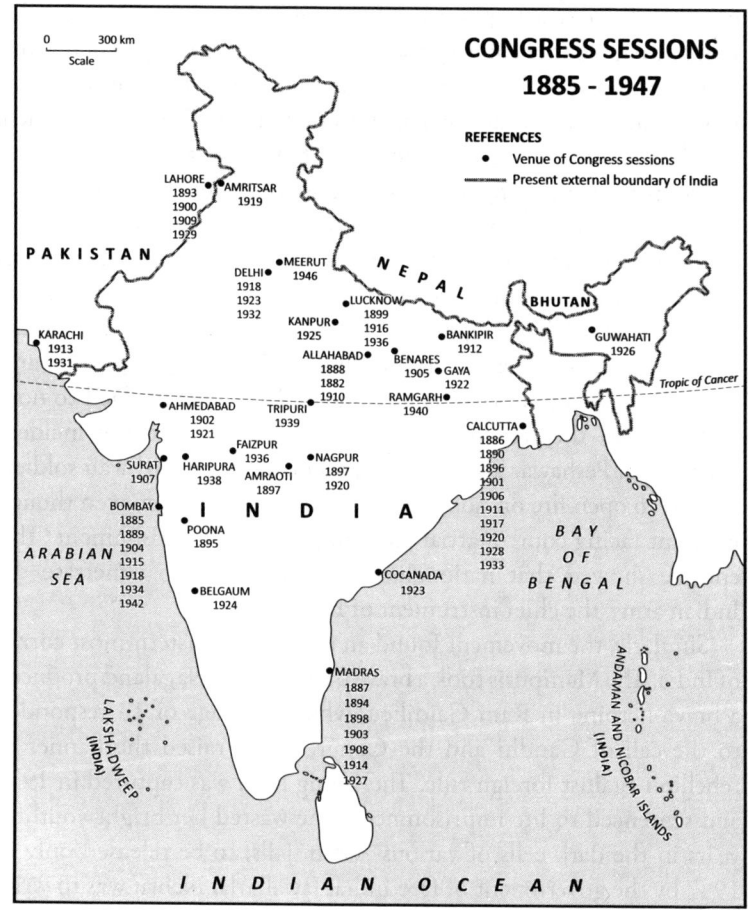

was gagged through strict censorship of news. According to official figures, over 110 persons were killed and over 300 wounded in police firings. Unofficial estimates place the number of dead far higher. Moreover, thousands of persons had their heads and bones broken in lathi-charges. South India in particular experienced repression in its most severe form. The police often beat up men just for wearing khadi or Gandhi caps.

Meanwhile, the British government summoned in London in 1930 the first Round Table Conference of Indian leaders and spokesmen of the British government to discuss the Simon Commission Report. But the National Congress boycotted the Conference and its proceedings proved abortive; for a conference on Indian affairs without the Congress was like staging Ramlila without Rama.

The government now made attempts to negotiate an agreement with the Congress so that it would attend the Round Table Conference. Finally, Lord Irwin and Gandhiji negotiated a settlement in March 1931. The government agreed to release those political prisoners who had remained non-violent and conceded the right to make salt for consumption, as also the right to peaceful picketing of liquor and foreign cloth shops; the Congress suspended the Civil Disobedience Movement and agreed to take part in the Second Round Table Conference. Many of the Congress leaders, particularly the younger, left-wing section, were opposed to the Gandhi-Irwin Pact, for the government had not accepted even one of the major nationalist demands. It had not agreed even to the demand that the death sentence on Bhagat Singh and his two comrades be commuted to life imprisonment. But Gandhiji was convinced that Lord Irwin and the British were sincere in their desire to negotiate on Indian demands. His concept of satyagraha included the need to give the opponent every chance to show a change of heart. His strategy was based on the understanding that a mass movement must necessarily be of short duration and could not go on for ever, for the people's capacity to sacrifice was not endless. Consequently, a phase of extra-legal mass struggle must be followed by a more passive phase when political struggle was carried on within the four walls of the law. Gandhiji had moreover negotiated with the Viceroy on equal terms and, thus, at one stroke enhanced the prestige of the Congress as the equal of the government. He prevailed upon the Karachi session of the Congress to approve the agreement.

Gandhiji went to England in September 1931 to attend the Second Round Table Conference. But in spite of his powerful advocacy, the British government refused to concede the basic nationalist demand for freedom on the basis of the immediate grant of Dominion Status.

In the meantime, peasant unrest had developed in several parts of the country as peasants found that the fall in the prices of agricultural products because of world depression had made the burden of land revenue and rent unbearable. In Uttar Pradesh, the Congress agitated for reduction of rent and prevention of eviction of tenants. In December 1931, the Congress started a no-rent, no-tax campaign. The government's response was to arrest Jawaharlal Nehru on 26 December. In the North-West Frontier Province, the Khudai Khidmatgars were leading a peasant movement against the government's land revenue policy. On 24 December, their leader Khan Abdul Ghaffar Khan was arrested. Peasant struggles were also developing in Bihar, Andhra, Uttar Pradesh, Bengal and Punjab. On his return to India, Gandhiji had no choice but to resume the Civil Disobedience Movement.

The government, now headed by the new Viceroy Lord Willingdon, who believed that a major error had been made in signing a truce with the Congress, was this time fully determined and prepared to crush the Congress. In fact, the bureaucracy in India had never relented. Just after the signing of the Gandhi-Irwin Pact, a crowd had been fired upon in East Godavari in Andhra, and four persons were killed simply because the people had put up Gandhi's portrait. On 4 January 1932, Gandhiji and other leaders of the Congress were again arrested and the Congress declared illegal. The normal working of laws was suspended and the administration carried on through special ordinances. The police indulged in naked terror and committed innumerable atrocities on the freedom fighters. Over a lakh of satyagrahis were arrested; the lands, houses and other property of thousands was confiscated. Nationalist literature was banned, while the nationalist newspapers were again placed under censorship.

Government repression succeeded in the end, helped as it was by the differences among Indian leaders on communal and other questions. The Civil Disobedience Movement gradually waned. The

Congress officially suspended the movement in May 1933 and withdrew it in May 1934. Gandhiji once again withdrew from active politics. Once again, many political activists felt despair. As early as 1933, Subhas Bose and Vithalbhai Patel had declared that "the Mahatma as a political leader has failed." Willingdon, the Viceroy, had also declared: "The Congress is in a definitely less favourable position than in 1930, and has lost its hold on the public." But in reality, this was not so. True, the movement had not succeeded in winning freedom, but it had succeeded in further politicising the people, and in further deepening the social roots of the freedom struggle. As H.N. Brailsford, the British journalist, put it: as a result of the recent struggle, Indians "had freed their own minds, they had won independence in their hearts." A true measure of the real outcome, the real impact, of the Civil Disobedience Movement was the heroes' welcome given to political prisoners on their release in 1934.

NATIONALIST POLITICS, 1935–1939

The Government of India Act, 1935

While the Congress was in the thick of battle, the Third Round Table Conference met in London in November 1932, once again without the leaders of the Congress. Its discussions eventually led to the passing of the Government of India Act of 1935. The Act provided for the establishment of an All India Federation and a new system of government for the provinces on the basis of provincial autonomy. The federation was to be based on a union of the provinces of British India and the princely states. There was to be a bicameral federal legislature in which the states were given disproportionate weightage. Moreover, the representatives of the states were not to be elected by the people, but appointed directly by the rulers. Only 14 per cent of the total population in British India was given the right to vote. Even this legislature, in which the princes were once again to be used to check and counter the nationalist elements, was denied any real power. Defence and foreign affairs remained outside its control, while the Governor-General retained special control over the other subjects.

The Governor-General and the Governors were to be appointed by the British government and were to be responsible to it. In the provinces, local power was increased. Ministers responsible to the provincial assemblies were to control all departments of provincial administration. But the Governors were given special powers. They could veto legislative action and legislate on their own. Moreover, they retained full control over the civil service and the police. The Act could not satisfy the nationalist aspirations, for both political and economic power continued to be concentrated in the hands of the British government. Foreign rule was to continue as before; only a few popularly elected ministers were to be added to the structure of British administration in India. The Congress condemned the Act as "totally disappointing".

The federal part of the Act was never introduced, but the provincial part was soon put into operation. Bitterly opposed to the Act though the Congress was, it decided to contest the elections under the new Act of 1935, though with the declared aim of showing how unpopular the Act was. The whirlwind election campaign of the Congress met with massive popular response, even though Gandhiji did not address a single election meeting. The elections, held in February 1937, conclusively demonstrated that a large majority of Indian people supported the Congress, which swept the polls in most of the provinces. Congress ministries were formed in July 1937 in seven out of 11 provinces. Later, Congress formed coalition governments in two others. Only Bengal and Punjab had non-Congress ministries. Punjab was ruled by the Unionist Party and Bengal by a coalition of the Krishak Praja Party and the Muslim League.

The Congress Ministries

The Congress ministries could obviously not change the basically imperialist character of British administration in India and they failed to introduce a radical era. But they did try to improve the condition of the people within the narrow limits of the powers given to them under the Act of 1935. The Congress ministers reduced their own salaries drastically to Rs 500 per month. Most of them travelled second or third class on the railways. They set up new standards of honesty and public service. They undertook positive measures in several fields.

They promoted civil liberties, repealed restrictions on the press and radical organisations, permitted trade unions and *kisan* (peasant) organisations to function and grow, curbed the powers of the police and released political prisoners, including a large number of revolutionaries. They passed agrarian legislation dealing with tenancy rights, security of tenure, rent reduction and relief, and protection to the peasant-debtors. Trade unions felt freer and were able to win wage increases for workers. The Congress governments also introduced prohibition in selected areas, undertook Harijan uplift and paid greater attention to primary, higher and technical education and public health. Support was given to khadi and other village industries. Modern industries too were encouraged. One of the major achievements of the Congress ministries was their firm handling of communal riots. The largest gain was psychological. People felt as if they were breathing the air of victory and self-government, for was it not a great achievement that men who were in prison till the other day were now ruling in the secretariat?

The period between 1935 and 1939 witnessed several other important political developments which, in a way, marked a new turn in the nationalist movement and the Congress.

Growth of Socialist Ideas

The 1930s witnessed the rapid growth of socialist ideas within and outside the Congress. In 1929, there was a great economic slump or depression in the United States which gradually spread to the rest of the world. Everywhere in the capitalist countries there was a steep decline in production and foreign trade, resulting in economic distress and large-scale unemployment. At one time, the number of unemployed was 3 million in Britain, 6 million in Germany and 12 million in the United States. On the other hand, the economic situation in the Soviet Union was just the opposite. Not only was there no slump, but the years between 1929 and 1936 also witnessed the successful completion of the first two Five-Year Plans, which pushed up the Soviet industrial production by more than four times. The world depression, thus, brought the capitalist system into disrepute and drew attention towards Marxism, socialism and economic planning. Consequently, socialist ideas began to attract more and more people, especially the young, the workers and the peasants.

From its early days, the national movement had adopted a pro-poor orientation. This orientation was immensely strengthened with the impact of the Russian Revolution of 1917, the emergence of Gandhiji on the political stage and the growth of powerful left-wing groups during the 1920s and 1930s. It was Jawaharlal Nehru who played the most important part in popularising the vision of a socialist India, both within the national movement and in the country at large. Within the Congress, the left-wing tendency found reflection in the election of Jawaharlal Nehru as president for 1929, 1936 and 1937, and of Subhas Chandra Bose for 1938 and 1939. Nehru argued that political freedom must mean the economic emancipation of the masses, especially of the toiling peasants from feudal exploitation.

In his presidential address to the Lucknow Congress in 1936, Nehru urged the Congress to accept socialism as its goal and to bring itself closer to the peasantry and the working class. This was also, he felt, the best way of weaning away the Muslim masses from the influence of their reactionary communal leaders. He said:

> I am convinced that the only key to the solution of the world's problems and of India's problems lies in socialism, and, when I use this word, I do so not in a vague humanitarian way but in the scientific, economic sense. ... That involves vast and revolutionary changes in our political and social structure, the ending of vested interests in land and industry, as well as the feudal and autocratic Indian states system. That means the ending of private property, except in a restricted sense, and the replacement of the present profit system by a higher ideal of cooperative service. It means ultimately a change in our instincts and habits and desires. In short, it means a new civilisation, radically different from the present capitalist order.

The growth of radical forces in the country was soon reflected in the programme and policies of the Congress. A major point of departure was the resolution on Fundamental Rights and Economic Policy passed by the Karachi session of the Congress on the urging of Jawaharlal Nehru. The resolution declared: "In order to end the exploitation of the masses, political freedom must include real economic freedom of the starving millions." The resolution guaranteed the basic civil rights of the people, equality before law irrespective of caste, creed or sex, elections on the basis of universal adult franchise, and free and compulsory primary education. It promised substantial reduction in rent and revenue, exemption from rent in case of uneconomic holdings and relief from agricultural indebtedness and control of moneylending; better conditions for workers, including a living wage, limited hours of work and protection of women workers; the right to organise and form unions by workers and peasants; and state ownership or control of key industries, mines and means of transport.

Radicalism in the Congress was further reflected in the Faizpur Congress resolutions and the Election Manifesto of 1936, which promised radical transformation of the agrarian system, substantial reduction in rent and revenue, scaling down of rural debts and provision of cheap credit, abolition of feudal levies, security of tenure for tenants, a living wage for agricultural labourers, and the right to form trade unions and peasant unions and the right to strike. In 1945, the Congress Working Committee adopted a resolution recommending the abolition of landlordism.

During 1938, when Subhas Chandra Bose was its president, the Congress committed itself to economic planning and set up a National Planning Committee under the Chairmanship of Jawaharlal Nehru. Nehru and other leftists and Gandhi also argued for the public sector in large-scale industries as a means of preventing the concentration of wealth in a few hands. In fact, a major development of the 1930s was the increasing acceptance of radical economic policies by Gandhiji. In 1933, he agreed with Nehru that "without a material revision of vested interests the condition of the masses can never be improved." He also accepted the principle of land to the tiller. He declared in 1942 that "the land belongs to those who will work on it and to no one else."

Outside the Congress, the socialist tendency led to the growth of the Communist Party after 1935 under the leadership of P.C. Joshi and the foundation of the Congress Socialist Party in 1934 under the leadership of Acharya Narendra Dev and Jai Prakash Narayan. In 1939, Subhas Chandra Bose had been re-elected president of the Congress, even though Gandhiji had opposed him. But the opposition of Gandhiji and his supporters in the Congress Working Committee compelled Bose to resign from the presidentship of the

Congress in April 1939. He and many of his left-wing followers now founded the Forward Bloc. By 1939, within the Congress the left was able to command influence over one-third votes on important issues. Moreover, socialism became the accepted creed of most of the politicised youth of India during the 1930s and 1940s. The 1930s also witnessed the foundation of the All India Students Federation and the All India Progressive Writers Association.

The Peasants' and Workers' Movements

The 1930s witnessed the nation-wide awakening and organisation of the peasants and workers in India. The two nationalist mass movements of 1920–22 and 1930–34 had politicised the peasants and workers on a large scale. The economic depression that hit India and the world after 1929 also worsened the conditions of the peasants and workers in India. The prices of agricultural products dropped by over 50 per cent by the end of 1932. Employers tried to reduce wages. The peasants all over the country began to demand land reforms, reduction of land revenue and rent, and relief from indebtedness. Workers in factories and plantations increasingly demanded better conditions of work and recognition of their trade union rights.

The Civil Disobedience Movement and the rise of the left parties and groups produced a new generation of political workers who devoted themselves to the organisation of peasants and workers. Consequently, there was rapid growth of trade unions in the cities and kisan sabhas (peasants' unions) all over the country, particularly in Uttar Pradesh, Bihar, Tamil Nadu, Andhra Pradesh, Kerala and Punjab. The first all-India peasant organisation, the All-India Kisan Sabha, was formed in 1936 under the presidentship of Swami Sahajanand Saraswati.

Congress and World Affairs

The third major development of the period 1935–39 was the increasing interest the Congress took in world affairs. The Congress had from its inception in 1885 opposed the use of the Indian army and of India's resources to serve British interests in Africa and Asia. It had gradually developed a foreign policy based on opposition to the spread of imperialism. In February 1927, Jawaharlal Nehru on behalf of the National Congress attended the Congress of Oppressed Nationalities at Brussels organised by political exiles and revolutionaries from the countries of Asia, Africa and Latin America suffering from economic or political imperialism. The Congress was called to coordinate and plan their common struggle against imperialism. Many left-wing intellectuals and political leaders of Europe also joined the Congress. In his address to the Congress, Nehru said:

> We realise that there is much in common in the struggle which various subject and semi-subject and oppressed peoples are carrying on today. Their opponents are often the same, although they sometimes appear in different guises and the means employed for their subjection are often similar.

Nehru was elected to the Executive Council of the League Against Imperialism that was born at this Congress. In 1927, the Madras session of the National Congress warned the government that the people of India would not support Britain in any war undertaken to further its imperialist aims.

In the 1930s, the Congress took a firm stand against imperialism in any part of the world and supported national movements in Asia and Africa. It condemned fascism, which had arisen at the time in Italy, Germany and Japan as the most extreme form of imperialism and racialism, and gave full support to the people of Ethiopia, Spain, Czechoslovakia and China in their fight against aggression by the fascist powers. In 1937, when Japan launched an attack on China, the National Congress passed a resolution calling upon the Indian people "to refrain from the use of Japanese goods as a mark of their sympathy with the people of China." And in 1938, it sent a medical mission, headed by Dr M. Atal, to work with the Chinese armed forces.

The National Congress fully recognised that the future of India was closely interlinked with the coming struggle between fascism and the forces of freedom, socialism and democracy. The emerging Congress approach to world problems and the awareness of India's position in the world were clearly enunciated in Jawaharlal Nehru's presidential address to the Lucknow Congress in 1936:

> Our struggle was but part of a far wider struggle for freedom, and the forces that moved us were moving millions of people all over the world and driving them into action. Capitalism, in its difficulties, took to fascism. ... It became, even in some of its homelands, what its imperialist counterpart had long been in the subject colonial countries. Fascism and imperialism thus stood out as the two faces of the now decaying capitalism. ... Socialism in the West and the rising nationalism of the Eastern and other dependent countries opposed this combination of fascism and imperialism.

While stressing the Congress opposition to any participation of the Indian government in a war between imperialist powers, he offered full cooperation "to the progressive forces of the world, to those who stood for freedom and the breaking of political and social bonds," for "in their struggle against imperialism and fascist reaction, we realise that our struggle is a common one."

People's Struggle in the Princely States

The fourth major development during this period was the spread of the national movement to the princely states. Appalling economic, political and social conditions prevailed in most of them. Peasants were oppressed, land revenue and taxation were excessive and unbearable, education was retarded, health and other social services were extremely backward, and freedom of the press and other civil rights hardly existed. The bulk of the state revenues were spent on the luxuries of the princes. In several states serfdom, slavery and forced labour flourished. Throughout history, a corrupt and decadent ruler was checked to some extent by the challenge of internal revolt or external aggression. British rule freed the princes of both these dangers, and they felt free to indulge in gross misgovernment.

Moreover, the British authorities began to use the princes to prevent the growth of national unity and to counter the rising national movement. The princes in turn depended for their self-preservation from popular revolt on the protection of the British power and adopted a hostile attitude to the national movement. In 1921, the Chamber of Princes was created to enable the princes to meet and discuss under British guidance matters of common interest. In the

Government of India Act of 1935, the proposed federal structure was so planned as to check the forces of nationalism. It was provided that the princes would get two-fifth of the seats in the Upper House and one-third of the seats in the Lower House.

People of many of the princely states now began to organise movements for democratic rights and popular governments. The All-India States People's Conference had already been founded in December 1927 to coordinate political activities in the different states. The Civil Disobedience Movement had a deep impact on the minds of the people of these states and stirred them into political activity. Popular struggles were waged in many of the states, particularly in Rajkot, Jaipur, Kashmir, Hyderabad and Travancore. The princes met these struggles with violent repression. Some of them also took recourse to communalism. The Nizam of Hyderabad declared that the popular agitation was anti-Muslim; the Maharaja of Kashmir branded it as anti-Hindu; while the Maharaja of Travancore claimed that Christians were behind the popular agitation.

The National Congress supported the States People's struggle and urged the princes to introduce democratic representative government and to grant fundamental civil rights. In 1938, when the Congress defined its goal of independence, it included the independence of the princely states. Next year, at the Tripuri session, it decided to take a more active part in the States People's movements. As if to emphasise the common national aims of the political struggles in British India and in the states, Jawaharlal Nehru became the President of the All-India States People's Conference in 1939. The States People's movement awakened national consciousness among the people of the states. It also spread a new consciousness of unity all over India.

GROWTH OF COMMUNALISM

The fifth important development was the growth of communalism. Once again the elections for the legislative assemblies, organised on the basis of restricted franchise and separate electorates, had produced separatist sentiments. Moreover, the Congress failed to win many seats reserved for the minorities—it won 26 out of 482 seats reserved for Muslims and even out of these 26 seats, 15 were won in the

North-West Frontier Provinces—though the Muslim League too did not capture many of these seats. The Hindu Mahasabha also failed miserably. Moreover, the landlord and moneylender parties fared badly in the elections. Seeing that the Congress had adopted a radical agrarian programme and the peasant movements were growing, landlords and moneylenders began to shift their support to the communal parties. They found that an open defence of their interests was no longer possible in the era of mass politics. It was now that the communal parties began to gather strength. The Muslim League, led by Jinnah, turned to bitter opposition to the Congress. It began to spread the cry that the Muslim minority was in danger of being engulfed by the Hindu majority. It propagated the unscientific and unhistorical theory that Hindus and Muslims were two separate nations which could, therefore, never live together. In 1940, the Muslim League passed a resolution demanding partition of the country and the creation of a state, to be called Pakistan, after independence.

The Muslim League propaganda gained from the existence of such bodies as the Hindu Mahasabha. The Hindu communalists echoed the Muslim communalists by declaring that the Hindus were a distinct nation. Thus they too accepted the two-nation theory. They actively opposed the policy of providing adequate safeguards to the minorities so as to remove their fears of domination by the majority. In every country, the religious or linguistic or national minorities have, because of their numerical position, felt at one time or the other that their social and cultural interests might suffer. But when the majority has by word and deed given proof that these fears are groundless, the fears of the minorities have disappeared. On the other hand, if a section of the people belonging to the majority becomes communal or sectional and starts talking and working against the minorities, the minorities tend to feel unsafe. Communal or sectional leadership of the minorities is then strengthened. For example, during the 1930s the Muslim League was strong only in areas where the Muslims were in a minority. On the other hand, in such areas as the North-West Frontier Province, Punjab, the Sindh and Bengal, where the Muslims were in a majority and, therefore, felt relatively secure, the Muslim League remained weak. Interestingly enough, the communal groups—Hindu as well as Muslim—did not hesitate to join hands against the Congress. In the North-West Frontier Province, Punjab, Sindh and Bengal, the Hindu communalists helped the Muslim League and other communal groups to form ministries which opposed the Congress. Another characteristic that the various communal groups shared was their tendency to adopt pro-government political attitudes. It is to be noted that none of the communal groups and parties, which talked of Hindu and Muslim nationalism, took active part in the struggle against foreign rule. They saw people belonging to other religions and the nationalist leaders as their real enemies.

The communal groups and parties also shied away from the social and economic demands of the common people which, as we have seen above, were being increasingly taken up by the nationalist movement. In this respect, they increasingly came to represent the upper-class vested interests. Jawaharlal Nehru noted this as early as 1933:

> The bulwark of communalism today is political reaction and so we find that communal leaders inevitably tend to become reactionaries in political and economic matters. Groups of upper-class people try to cover up their own class interests by making it appear that they stand for the communal demands of religious minorities or majorities. A critical examination of the various communal demands put forward on behalf of Hindus, Muslims or others reveals that they have nothing to do with the masses.

The national movement firmly opposed the communal forces, for its commitment to secularism was always deep and total. Yet it was not able to fully counter the communal challenge. In the end, communalism succeeded in partitioning the country. How is this failure to be explained? One answer that is often given is that the nationalist leaders did not make enough efforts to negotiate with and conciliate the communal leaders.

Our view is the very opposite. From the beginning, the nationalist leaders relied too much on negotiations with the communal leaders. But it was not possible to conciliate or appease communalism. Furthermore, efforts to appease one communalism invariably led to the growth of other communalisms in the form of a backlash. Between

1937 and 1939, the Congress leaders repeatedly met Jinnah to conciliate him. But Jinnah would not make any concrete demands. Instead, he put forward the impossible demand that he would negotiate with the Congress only if the Congress first accepted that it was a Hindu party and represented only the Hindus. The Congress could not possibly have accepted this demand, for it meant giving up its basic secular nationalist character. The fact is that the more communalism was conciliated, the more extreme it became.

What was required was not further appeasement but an all-out ideological political struggle against communalism. What was required was a massive campaign against communalism, a massive campaign of the kind that was carried on against colonial ideology since the 1880s. But the nationalists did not do so, except sporadically. However, the successes of secular nationalism should not be underrated. Despite the partition riots and the resurgence of communal forces during 1946–47, India did succeed after independence in framing a secular constitution and in building a basically secular polity and society. Hindu communalism did make deep inroads in society and even in the ranks of the nationalists. It remained a minority force among the Hindus. While many Muslims were swept away by the tide of religious fanaticism and communalism during 1946–47, others stood like a rock against communalism. The names of Abul Kalam Azad, Khan Abdul Ghaffar Khan, the firebrand socialist Yusuf Meherali, S.A. Brelvi the fearless journalist, the historians Mohammed Habib and K.M. Ashraf, Josh Malihabadi, Faiz Ahmed Faiz, Sardar Jaafri, Sahir Ludhianwi and Kaifi Azmi, the stormy petrels of Urdu poetry, and Maulana Madani readily come to mind.

National Movement during the Second World War

The Second World War broke out in September 1939 when Nazi Germany invaded Poland in pursuance of Hitler's scheme for German expansion. Earlier, he had occupied Austria in March 1938 and Czechoslovakia in March 1939. Britain and France, which had tried their best to placate Hitler, were forced to go to Poland's aid. The Government of India immediately joined the war without consulting the National Congress or the elected members of the

Central Legislature. The National Congress was in full sympathy with the victims of fascist aggression. It was willing to help the forces of democracy in their struggle against fascism. But, the Congress leaders asked, how was it possible for an enslaved nation to aid others in their fight for freedom? They therefore demanded that India must be declared free—or at least effective power put in Indian hands—before it could actively participate in the War. The British government refused to accept this demand and tried to pit the religious minorities and princes against the Congress. The Congress, therefore, asked its ministries to resign. In October 1940, Gandhi gave the call for a limited satyagraha by a few selected individuals. The satyagraha was kept limited so as not to embarass Britain's war effort by a mass upheaval in India. The aims of this movement were explained as follows by Gandhi in a letter to the Viceroy:

> The Congress is as much opposed to victory for Nazism as any Britisher can be. But their objection cannot be carried to the extent of their participation in the war. And since you and the Secretary of State for India have declared that the whole of India is voluntarily helping the war effort, it becomes necessary to make clear that the vast majority of the people of India are not interested in it. They make no distinction between Nazism and the double autocracy that rules India.

Vinoba Bhave was the first to offer satyagraha. By 15 May 1941, more than 25,000 satyagrahis had been jailed. Two major changes in world politics occurred during 1941. Having occupied Poland, Belgium, Holland, Norway and France in the West as well as most of Eastern Europe, Nazi Germany attacked the Soviet Union on 22 June 1941. On 7 December, Japan launched a surprise attack on the American fleet at Pearl Harbour and joined the war on the side of Germany and Italy. It quickly overran the Philippines, Indo-China, Indonesia, Malaya and Burma. It occupied Rangoon in March 1942. This brought the War to India's door-step. The recently released Congress leaders denounced Japanese aggression and once again offered to fully cooperate in the defence of India and the Allied cause if Britain transferred the substance of power to India immediately and promised complete independence after the War.

The British government now desperately wanted the active co-operation of Indians in the war effort. To secure this cooperation, it sent to India in March 1942 a mission headed by a Cabinet Minister, Sir Stafford Cripps, who had earlier been a radical member of the Labour Party and a strong supporter of the Indian national movement. Even though Cripps declared that the aim of British policy in India was "the earliest possible realisation of self-government in India," detailed negotiations between him and the Congress leaders broke down. The British government refused to accept the Congress demand for the immediate transfer of effective power to Indians. On the other hand, the Indian leaders could not be satisfied by mere promises for the future while the Viceroy retained his autocratic powers in the present. They were anxious to cooperate in the war effort, especially as the Japanese army endangered Indian territory. But they could do so, they felt, only when a national government was formed in the country.

The failure of the Cripps Mission embittered the people of India. While they still fully sympathised with the anti-fascist forces, they felt that the existing political situation in the country had become intolerable. Their discontent was further fuelled by war-time shortages and rising prices. The period from April to August 1942 was one of daily heightening tension, with Gandhiji becoming more and more forceful as Japanese forces moved towards India and the spectre of Japanese conquest began to haunt the people and their leaders. The Congress now decided to take active steps to compel the British to accept the Indian demand for independence. The All India Congress Committee met at Bombay on 8 August 1942. It passed the famous 'Quit India' Resolution and proposed the starting of a non-violent mass struggle under Gandhi's leadership to achieve this aim. The resolution declared:

> ... the immediate ending of British rule in India is an urgent necessity, both for the sake of India and for the success of the cause of the United Nations. ... India, the classic land of modern imperialism, has become the crux of the question, for by the freedom of India will Britain and the United Nations be judged, and the peoples of Asia and Africa be filled with hope and enthusiasm. The ending of British rule in this country is thus a vital and immediate issue on which depends the future of the war and the success of freedom and democracy. A free India will assure this success by throwing all her great resources in the struggle for freedom and against the aggression of Nazism, Fascism and Imperialism.

The Struggle for Swaraj: 1927–47 323

Addressing the Congress delegates on the night of 8 August, Gandhi said:

> I, therefore, want freedom immediately, this very night, before dawn, if it can be had.... Fraud and untruth today are stalking the world. ... You may take it from me that I am not going to strike a bargain with the Viceroy for ministries and the like. I am not going to be satisfied with anything short of complete freedom. ... Here is a *mantra,* a short one, that I give you. You may imprint it on your hearts and let every breath of yours give expression to it. The *mantra* is: "Do or Die". We shall either free India or die in the attempt; we shall not live to see the perpetuation of our slavery. ...

But before the Congress could start a movement, the government struck hard. Early in the morning of 9 August, Gandhi and other Congress leaders were arrested and taken to unknown destinations, and the Congress was once again declared illegal.

The news of these arrests left the country aghast, and a spontaneous movement of protest arose everywhere, giving expression to the pent up anger of the people. Left leaderless and without any organisation, the people reacted in any manner they could. All over the country there were *hartals,* strikes in factories, schools and colleges, and demonstrations which were lathi-charged and fired upon. Angered by repeated firings and repression, in many places the people took to violent action. They attacked the symbols of British authority—the police stations, post offices, railway stations, etc. They cut telegraph and telephone wires and railway lines, and burnt government buildings. Madras and Bengal were the most affected in this respect. In many places, the rebels seized temporary control over towns, cities and villages. British authority disappeared in parts of Uttar Pradesh, Bihar, West Bengal, Orissa, Andhra, Tamil Nadu and Maharashtra. In some areas, such as Ballia in eastern Uttar Pradesh, Tamluk in Midnapore district of Bengal and in Satara district of Bombay, the revolutionaries set up 'parallel governments'. In general, the students, workers and peasants provided the backbone of the 'revolt', while the upper classes and the bureaucracy remained loyal to the government.

The government on its part went all out to crush the 1942 movement. Its repression knew no bounds. The press was completely muzzled. The demonstrating crowds were machine-gunned and even bombed from the air. Prisoners were tortured. The police and secret police reigned supreme. The military took over many towns and cities. Over 10,000 people died in police and military firings. Rebellious villages had to pay huge sums as punitive fines and the villagers had to undergo mass floggings. India had not witnessed such intense repression since the Revolt of 1857.

In the end, the government succeeded in crushing the movement. The Revolt of 1942, as it has been termed, was in fact short-lived. Its importance lay in the fact that it demonstrated the depth to which nationalist feeling had reached in the country and the great capacity for struggle and sacrifice that the people had developed. It was evident that the British would no longer find it possible to rule India against the wishes of the people.

After the suppression of the Revolt of 1942, there was hardly any political activity inside the country till the War ended in 1945. The established leaders of the national movement were in jail, and no new leaders arose to take their place or to give a new lead to the country. In 1943, Bengal was plunged into the worst famine in recent history. Within a few months, over three million people died of starvation. There was deep anger among the people for the government could have prevented the famine from taking such a heavy toll of life. This anger, however, found little political expression.

The national movement, however, found a new expression outside the country's frontiers. Subhas Chandra Bose had escaped from India in March 1941 to go to the Soviet Union for help. But when the Soviet Union joined the allies in June 1941, he went to Germany. In February 1943, he left for Japan to organise an armed struggle against British rule with Japanese help. In Singapore he formed the Azad Hind Fauj (Indian National Army, or INA for short) to conduct a military campaign for the liberation of India. He was assisted by Rash Behari Bose, an old revolutionary.

Before the arrival of Subhas Bose, steps towards the organisation of the INA had been taken by General Mohan Singh (who had been a Captain in the British-Indian army). The INA was joined in large numbers by Indian residents in Southeast Asia and by Indian soldiers and officers captured by the Japanese forces in Malaya, Singapore and Burma. Subhas Bose, who was now called 'Netaji' by the soldiers of the INA, gave his followers the battle cry of 'Jai Hind'. The INA joined the Japanese army in its march on India from Burma. Inspired by the aim of freeing their homeland, the soldiers and officers of the INA hoped to enter India as its liberators with Subhas Bose at the head of the Provisional Government of Free India.

With the collapse of Japan in the War during 1944–45, the INA too met defeat and Subhas Bose was killed in an aeroplane accident on his way to Tokyo. Even though his strategy of winning freedom in cooperation with the fascist powers was criticised at the time by most Indian nationalists, by organising the INA he set an inspiring example of patriotism before the Indian people and the Indian army. He was hailed as Netaji by the entire country.

Post-War Struggle

With the end of the War in Europe in April 1945, India's struggle for freedom entered a new phase. The Revolt of 1942 and the INA had revealed the heroism and determination of the Indian people. With the release of the national leaders from jail, the people began to look forward to another, perhaps the final, struggle for freedom.

The new struggle took the form of a massive movement against the trial of the soldiers and officers of the INA. The government decided to put on trial in the Red Fort at Delhi Shah Nawaz Khan, Gurdial Singh Dhillon and Prem Sehgal, officers of the INA, who had earlier been officers in the British-Indian army. They were accused of having broken the oath of loyalty to the British Crown and thus of having become 'traitors'. On the other hand, the people welcomed them as national heroes. Huge popular demonstrations demanding their release were held all over the country. The entire country now seethed with excitement and confidence that this time the struggle would be won. They would not let these heroes be punished. And the British government was this time in no position to ignore Indian opinion. Even though the Court Martial held the INA prisoners guilty, the government felt it expedient to set them free.

The changed attitude of the British government can be explained by several factors.

First, the War had changed the balance of power in the world. Not Britain, but the United States of America and the Soviet Union emerged from the war as the big powers. Both supported India's demand for freedom.

Second, even though Britain was on the winning side in the War, its economic and military power was shattered. It would take Britain years to rehabilitate itself. Moreover, there was a change of government in Britain. The Conservatives were replaced by the Labour Party, many of whose members supported the Congress demands. The British soldiers were weary of war. Having fought and shed their blood for nearly six years, they had no desire to spend many more years away from home in India suppressing the Indian people's struggle for freedom.

Third, the British-Indian government could not any longer rely on the Indian personnel of its civil administration and armed forces to suppress the national movement. The INA had shown that patriotic ideas had entered the ranks of the professional Indian army, the chief instrument of British rule in India. Another straw in the wind was the famous revolt of the Indian naval ratings at Bombay in February 1946. The ratings had fought a seven-hour battle with the army and navy and had surrendered only when asked to do so by the national leaders. Naval ratings in many other parts had gone on sympathetic strike. Moreover, there were also widespread strikes in the Royal Indian Air Force. The Indian Signal Corps at Jabalpur also went on strike. The other two major instruments of British rule, the police and the bureaucracy, were also showing signs of nationalist leanings. They could no longer be safely used to suppress the national movement. For example, the police force in Bihar and Delhi went on strike.

Fourth, and above all, the confident and determined mood of the Indian people was by now obvious. They would no longer tolerate the humiliation of foreign rule. They would no longer rest till freedom was won. There was the Naval Mutiny and the struggle for the release of INA prisoners. In addition, there were during 1945–46 numerous agitations, strikes, *hartals* and demonstrations all over the country, even in many princely states such as Hyderabad, Travancore and Kashmir. For example, in November 1945, lakhs of people demonstrated in the streets in Calcutta to demand the release of the INA prisoners. For three days, there was virtually no government authority left in the city. Again, on 12 February 1946, there was another mass demonstration in the city to demand the release of Abdur Rashid, one of the INA prisoners. On 22 February, Bombay observed a complete *hartal* and general strike in factories and offices in sympathy with the naval ratings in revolt. The army was called in to suppress the popular upsurge. Over 250 people were shot dead on the streets in 48 hours.

There was also large-scale labour unrest all over the country. There was hardly an industry in which strikes did not occur. In July 1946, there was an all-strike by the postal and telegraph workers. Railway workers in south India went on strike in August 1946. Peasant movements acquired a fresh thrust after 1945 as freedom approached. The most aggressive of the post-war struggles was the Tebhaga struggle by the share-croppers of Bengal, who declared that they would pay not one-half but one-third of the crop to the landlords. Struggles for land and against high rents also took place in Hyderabad, Malabar, Bengal, Uttar Pradesh, Bihar and Maharashtra. Students in schools and colleges took a leading part in organising strikes, *hartals* and demonstrations. Many of the princely states—Hyderabad, Travancore, Kashmir and Patiala, among others—were enveloped by popular upsurges and revolts. Elections to provincial assemblies, held in early 1946, provided another major political development. The Congress won an overwhelming majority of general seats, while the Muslim League did the same for seats reserved for Muslims.

The British government, therefore, sent in March 1946 a Cabinet Mission to India to negotiate with the Indian leaders the terms for the transfer of power to Indians. The Cabinet Mission proposed a two-tiered federal plan which was expected to maintain national unity while conceding the largest measure of regional autonomy. There was to be a federation of the provinces and the states, with the federal centre controlling only defence, foreign affairs and communications. At the same time, individual provinces could form regional unions to which they could surrender by mutual agreement some of their powers. Both the National Congress and the Muslim League accepted this plan. But the two could not agree on the plan for an interim government which would convene a constituent assembly to frame a constitution for the free, federal India. The two also put differing interpretations on the Cabinet Mission scheme, to which they had agreed earlier. In the end, in September 1946, an Interim Cabinet, headed by Jawaharlal Nehru, was formed by the Congress. The Muslim League joined the Cabinet in October after some hesitation; but it decided to boycott the constituent assembly. On 20 February 1947, Clement Attlee, British Premier, declared that the British would quit India by June 1948.

But the elation of coming independence was marred by the large-scale communal riots during and after August 1946. The Hindu and Muslim communalists blamed each other for starting the heinous killings and competed with each other in cruelty. Mahatma Gandhi, engulfed in gloom at this total disregard of elementary humanity and seeing truth and non-violence cast to the winds, toured East Bengal and Bihar on foot to check the riots. Many other Hindus and Muslims laid down their lives in the effort to extinguish the fire of communalism. But the seeds had been sown too deep by the communal elements, aided and abetted by the alien government. Gandhi and other nationalists fought vainly against communal prejudices and passions.

Finally, Lord Mountbatten, who had come to India as Viceroy in March 1947, worked out a compromise after long discussions with the leaders of the Congress and the Muslim League: the country was to be free, but not united. India was to be partitioned and a new state of Pakistan was to be created along with a free India. The nationalist leaders agreed to the partition of India in order to avoid the large-scale blood-bath and communal riots threatened by the separatists. But they did not accept the two-nation theory. They did not agree to hand over one-third of the country to the Muslim League as the latter wanted and as the proportion of Muslims in the Indian population would have indicated. They agreed to the separation of only those areas where the influence of the Muslim League was predominant. Thus, Punjab, Bengal and Assam were to be partitioned. The Muslim League was to get 'a moth-eaten' Pakistan. In the North-West Frontier Province, and the Sylhet district of Assam where the influence of the League was doubtful, a plebiscite was to be held. In other words, the country was to be partitioned, but not on the basis of Hinduism and Islam.

The Indian nationalists accepted partition not because there were two nations in India—a Hindu nation and a Muslim nation—but because the historical development of communalism, both Hindu and Muslim, over the past 70 years or so had created a situation where the alternative to partition was the mass killing of lakhs of innocent people in senseless and barbaric communal riots. If these riots had been confined to one section of the country, the Congress leaders could have tried to curb them and taken a strong stand against partition. But unfortunately, the fratricidal riots were taking place everywhere and actively involved both Hindus and Muslims. On top of it all, the country was still ruled by foreigners who did little to check the riots. On the other hand, the foreign government rather encouraged these riots by their divisive policies, perhaps hoping to play the two newly independent states against each other. Referring to communalism, Jawaharlal Nehru had written in 1948 in his *The Discovery of India*: "It is our fault, of course, and we must suffer for our failings. But I cannot excuse or forgive the British authorities for the deliberate part they have played in creating disruption in India. All other injuries will pass, but this will continue to plague us for a much longer period." Even Jinnah was in the end forced to revise his two-nation theory lying at the heart of communalism. When asked by Muslims who were staying on in India what they should do, he asked them to become loyal citizens of India. And he told the Constituent Assembly of Pakistan on 11 August 1947: "You may belong to any religion or caste or creed—that has nothing to do with the business of the state." He was, in vain, trying to put back in the bottle the genie he had released to practise communal politics.

The announcement that India and Pakistan would be free was made on 3 June 1947. The princely states were given the choice of joining either of the new states. Under the pressure of the popular States People's movements and guided by the masterful diplomacy of Sardar Patel, the Home Minister, most of them acceded to India. The Nawab of Junagadh, the Nizam of Hyderabad and the Maharaja of Jammu and Kashmir held back for some time. The Nawab of Junagadh, a small state on the coast of Kathiawar, announced accession to Pakistan, even though the people of the state desired to join India. In the end, Indian troops occupied the state and a plebiscite was held, which went in favour of joining India. The Nizam of Hyderabad made an attempt to claim an independent status, but was forced to accede in 1948 after an internal revolt had broken out in its Telengana area and after Indian troops had marched into Hyderabad. The Maharaja of Kashmir also delayed accession to India or Pakistan, even though the popular forces led by the National Conference wanted accession to India. However, he acceded to India in October 1947 after Pathans and irregular armed forces of Pakistan invaded Kashmir.

On 15 August 1947, India celebrated with joy its first day of freedom. The sacrifices of generations of patriots and the blood of countless martyrs had borne fruit. Their dream was now a reality. In a memorable address to the Constituent Assembly on the night of 14 August, Jawaharlal Nehru, giving expression to the feeling of the people, said:

> Long years ago we made a tryst with destiny, and now the time comes when we shall redeem our pledge, not wholly or in full measure, but very substantially. At the stroke of the midnight hour, when the world sleeps, India will awake to life and freedom. A moment comes, which comes but rarely in history, when we step out from the old to the new, when an age ends, and when the soul of a nation, long suppressed, finds utterance. It is fitting that at this solemn moment we take the pledge of dedication to the service of India and her people and to the still larger cause of humanity ... We end today a period of ill fortune and India discovers herself again. The achievement we celebrate today is but a step, an opening of opportunity, to the greater triumphs and achievements that await us.

But the sense of joy, which should have been overwhelming and unlimited, was mixed with pain and sadness. The dream of Indian unity had been shattered and brother had been torn from brother; what was worse, even at the very moment of freedom a communal orgy, accompanied by indescribable brutalities, was consuming thousands of lives in both India and Pakistan. Lakhs of refugees, forced to leave the lands of their forefathers, were pouring into the two new states.

Writing of those months, Nehru wrote later:

> Fear and hatred blinded our minds and all the restraints which civilisation imposes were swept away. Horror piled on horror, and sudden emptiness seized us at the brute savagery of human beings. The lights seemed all to

go out; not all, for a few still flickered in the raging tempest. We sorrowed for the dead and the dying, and for those whose suffering was greater than that of death. We sorrowed even more for India, our common mother, for whose freedom we had laboured these long years.

The symbol of this tragedy at the moment of national triumph was the forlorn figure of Gandhiji—the man who had given the message of non-violence, truth, and love and courage to the Indian people, the man who symbolised all that was best in Indian culture.

He had been touring the hate-torn parts of the country, trying to bring comfort to people who were even then paying through senseless communal slaughter the price of freedom. He had come to Calcutta from the Punjab and proposed going to Noakhali. He stayed in Calcutta in a locality which had been one of the worst affected by the communal riots. He spent the Independence Day by fasting and spinning. The celebrations had hardly died down when, on 30 January 1948, an assassin extinguished the light that had shone so bright in our land for over 70 years. Thus Gandhi "died a martyr to the cause of unity to which he had always been devoted."

Earlier, in reply to a journalist on the occasion of his birthday in 1947, Gandhi had said that he no longer wished to live long and that he would "invoke the aid of the Almighty to take me away from this 'vale of tears' rather than make me a helpless witness of the butchery by man become savage, whether he dares to call himself a Muslim or Hindu or what not".

In a way, with the achievement of freedom, the country had taken only the first step: the overthrow of foreign rule had only removed the chief obstacle in the path of national regeneration. Centuries of backwardness, prejudice, inequality and ignorance still weighed on the land and the long haul had just begun. For as Rabindranath Tagore had remarked three months before his death in 1941:

> The wheels of fate will some day compel the English to give up their Indian empire. But what kind of India will they leave behind, what stark misery? When the stream of their centuries' administration runs dry at last, what a waste of mud and filth will they leave behind them.

The freedom struggle had, however, not only overthrown colonial rule, it had also evolved a vision of what free India would be like. This vision was that of a democratic, civil libertarian and secular India built on the foundations of an independent self-reliant economy, social and economic equality, and a politically awakened and politically active people—an India which would live in peace with its neighbours and the rest of the world, basing itself on an independent foreign policy.

The first effort to give expression to this vision was the framing of the Constitution of Free India by the Constituent Assembly under the guidance of Jawaharlal Nehru and B.R. Ambedkar. The Constitution, introduced on 26 January 1950, laid down certain basic principles and values. India was to be a secular and democratic republic with a parliamentary system based on adult franchise, that is, on the right of all adult men and women to vote. It was also to be a federation with demarcation of spheres of action between the Union government and the governments of the states forming the union. It guaranteed all Indian citizens certain fundamental rights: freedom of speech and expression, freedom to assemble peaceably and to form associations, freedom to acquire and hold property. The Constitution guaranteed all citizens equality before the law and equality of opportunity in government employment. The state was not to discriminate against any citizen on grounds of religion, caste, sex or place of birth. 'Untouchability' was abolished and its practice in any form forbidden. All Indians were given the right to freely profess, practise and propagate any religion. At the same time, it forbade imparting of any religious instruction in any educational institution wholly maintained out of state funds. The Constitution also laid down certain 'Directive Principles of State Policy', which were not enforceable in a court of law but which were to guide the state in the making of laws. These included the promotion of a social order based on social, economic and political justice in all areas of national life, prevention of concentration of wealth and means of production, equal pay for equal work for both men and women, organisation of village panchayats, right to work and education, public assistance in case of unemployment, old age and sickness, a uniform civil code throughout the country, and promotion of the educational and economic interests of the weaker sections of the people, in particular of the Scheduled Castes and Scheduled Tribes.

With confidence in their capacity and their will to succeed, the people of India now set out to change the face of their country and to build a just and good society and a secular, democratic and egalitarian India.

Books for Further Reading

I. General

1. Desai, A. R. *Social Background of Indian Nationalism,* Popular Book Depot, Bombay.
2. Chand, Tara. *History of the Freedom Movement in India,* Vols. I to IV, Ministry of Information and Broadcasting, New Delhi.
3. Chandra, Bipan et al. *India's Struggle for Independence,* Penguin, New Delhi.
4. Chandra, Bipan. *Nationalism arid Colonialism in Modern India,* Orient Longman, New Delhi.
5. Sarkar, Sumit. *Modern India, 1885-1947,* Macmillan; New Delhi.

II. Decline Of Mughal Empire and 18th Century India

1. Habib, Irfan. *Agrarian System of Mughal India, 1556-1707,* Oxford University Press, Bombay.
2. Chandra, Satish. *Parties and Politics at the Mughal Court, 1707-1740,* People's Publishing House, Delhi.
3. Chand, Tara. *History of the Freedom Movement in India,* Vol. I, Ministry of Information and Broadcasting, New Delhi.
4. Alavi, Seema. *The Eighteenth Century in Indian History,* Oxford University Press, New Delhi.
5. Alam, Muzaffar. *The Crisis of Empire in Mughal North India,* Oxford University Press, New Delhi.
6. Ali, Athar. 'The Eighteenth Century: An Interpretation', *Indian Historical Review,* Vol. 5, No. 1-2, 1978-79, ICHR, New Delhi.
7. Raghuvanshi, VPS. *Indian Society in the Eighteenth Century,* Associated Publishing House, New Delhi.
8. Sardesai, G.S. *New History of Marathas,* Vols II and III, Munshiram Manoharlal Publishers, New Delhi.
9. Hasan, Mohibul. *History of Tipu Sultan,* World Press, Delhi.

III. European Penetration and The British Conquest Of India

1. Bandopadhyaya, Sekhar. *From Plassey to Partition*, Orient Longman, Hyderabad.
2. Gupta, Brijen K. *Siraj-ud-daullah and the English East India Company*, Leiden.
3. Chaudhary, Sushil. *From Prosperity to Decline: Eighteenth Century Bengal*, Manohar Publications, New Delhi.
4. Majumdar, R.C. (ed.) *The British Paramountcy and the Indian Renaissance*, Bhartiya Vidya Bhawan, Bombay.
5. Dodwell, H.H. (ed.) *The Cambridge History of India*, S. Chand, Delhi.

IV. Administrative Organisation and Social and Cultural Policies

1. Dodwell, H.H. (ed.) *The Cambridge History of India*, Vol. V S. Chand, Delhi.
2. Chand, Tara. *History of the Freedom Movement*, Vol. I, Ministry of Information and Broadcasting, New Delhi.
3. Misra, B.B. *Central Administration of the East India Company*, Manchester University Press, Manchester.
4. Misra, B.B. *The Administrative History of India*, Oxford University Press, London.

V. Social and Religious Reform Movements

1. Joshi, VC. (ed.) *Rammohun Roy and the Process of Modernisation in India*, Vikas Publishing House, Delhi.
2. Panikkar, K.N. *Studies in History: Special Issue on Intellectual History of Colonial India*, Vol. 3, No. 1, January-June 1987, JNU, New Delhi.
3. Panikkar, K.N. *Culture, Ideology and Hegemony*, Tulika, New Delhi.
4. Majumdar, R.C. (ed.) *British Paramountcy and Indian Renaissance*, Vol. X, Bhartiya Vidya Bhavan, Bombay.
5. Sen, Amit. *Notes on the Bengal Renaissance*, People's Publishing House, Bombay.

6. Datta, K.K. *Social History of Modern India*, Macmillan, New Delhi.

VI. REVOLT OF 1857, AND PEASANT AND TRIBAL REVOLTS

1. Sen, S.N. *Eighteen Fifty-Seven*, Publications Division, Delhi.
2. Chattopadhyaya, Haraprasad. *The Sepoy Mutiny: A Social Study and Analysis*, Bookland Private, Calcutta.
3. Chaudhuri, S.B. *Civil Rebellion in the Indian Mutinies 1857–59*, World Press, Calcutta.
4. Joshi, PC. (ed.) *Rebellion 1857: A Symposium*, People's Publishing House, Delhi.
5. Desai, A.R. *Peasant Struggles in India*, Oxford University Press, Bombay.
6. Mukherjee, Mridula. *Peasants in India's Non-Violent Revolution: Practice and Theory*, Sage Publications, New Delhi.

VII. REVOLUTIONARY MOVEMENTS

1. Gupta, D.N. *Bhagat Singh: Selected Speeches and Writings*, National Book Trust, New Delhi.

VIII. INDIAN ECONOMY IN THE 18TH, 19TH AND 20TH CENTURIES

1. Dutt, R.C. *The Economic History of India under Early British Rule*, Trubner & Co., London.
2. Dutt, R.C. *Economic History of India in the Victorian Age*, Trubner & Co., London.
3. Sinha, N.K. *The Economic History of Bengal: From Plassey to the Permanent Settlement*, Firma K.L. Mukhopadhyay, Calcutta.
4. Chandra, Bipan. *The Rise and Growth of Economic Nationalism in Modern India*, People's Publishing House, Delhi.
5. Chandra, Bipan. *Essays in Colonialism*, Orient Longman, New Delhi.
6. Kumar, Dharma and Raychaudhuri, Tapan. (eds) *Cambridge Economic History of India*, Vol. II. Cambridge University Press, Cambridge.

7. Islam, Siraj-ul. *The Permanent Settlement in Bengal, 1793-1819*, Bangla Academy, Dacca.
8. Gopal, S. *Permanent Settlement in Bengal and its Results*, G. Allen & Unwin, London.
9. Bagchi, A.K. *Private Investment in India 1900-1939*, Cambridge University Press, Cambridge.
10. Thorner, Daniel and Thorner, Alice. *Land and Labour in India*, Asia Publishing House, Bombay.
11. Gadgil, D. R. *The Industrial Evolution of India in Recent Times*, Oxford University Press, Oxford.
12. Dutt, R. Palme. *India Today*, People's Publishing House, Bombay.

IX. NATIONAL MOVEMENT

1. Chandra, Bipan et al. *Freedom Struggle*, National Book Trust, New Delhi.
2. Chandra, Bipan. *The Epic Struggle*, Orient Longman, New Delhi.
3. Chandra, Bipan. *Communalism in Modern India*, Vikas Publishing House, New Delhi.
4. Pande, B.N. (ed.) *A Centenary History of the Indian National Congress*, 3 Vols, AICC, New Delhi.
5. Nehru, Jawaharlal. *An Autobiography*, Allied Publishers, Bangalore.
6. Gopal, S. *Jawharlal Nehru: A Biography*, Vol. I, Jonathan Cape, London.
7. Nanda, B.R. *Mahatma Gandhi: A Biography*, George Allen and Unwin, London.
8. Mehrotra, S.R. *Emergence of Indian National Congress*, Vikas Publishing House, New Delhi.
9. Pradhan, G.P and Bhagwat, A.K. *Lokamanya Tilak: A Biography*, Jaico Publishing House, Bombay.
10. Sarkar, Sumit. *The Swadeshi Movement in Bengal 1903-1908*, People's Publishing House, Delhi.
11. Bose, Subhas. *The Indian Struggle*, Asia Publishing House, Calcutta.
12. *The Communal Problem: Report of the Kanpur Riots Enquiry Committee*, 1931, National Book Trust, New Delhi.

Index

A

Abdali, Ahmed Shah, 9, 17, 26, 33, 38, 43
Abdul Rasul, 252, 266
Abdullah Khan, 4, 6
Abhinava Bharat, 255
Abu Mohammed, Syed, 251
Act of Parliament (1858), 158–59
administrative, changes after 1858, 158*ff*; and economic unification of the country, 202; organisation and social and cultural policy of British, 108*ff*; and other reforms, 213–14; and revenue system of Mughals, 19–20, 27
Afghanistan, and British relations after 1858, 178–80; Russian influence, 178
Aga Khan, 267
Agarkar, Gopal Ganesh, 222
Agra, 30, 31–32; occupied by British, 79; invasion by Jats, 43
agricultural, agriculture, 214; labourers, 183; loans (*taccavi*), 22; stagnation and deterioration during British rule, 189–91, 210, 212, 261, 294, 304–05
Ahmedabad mill strike, 282–83
Ahom kings, 49
Ahrar movement, 268

Ajit Singh, 253, 255
Ajit Singh, ruler of Marwar, 1–2, 3, 5, 31
Ajmal Khan, Hakim, 266, 268, 287
Akali Movement, 29–30, 290
Akbar, 10–11, 15, 121, 204, 265
Al Hilal, 268, 274
Ali Brothers, 274, 287
Aligarh, 32; occupied by British, 79
Aligarh Muslim University, 227
Aligarh School, 226–28, 268, 274
Alivardi Khan, Nawab of Bengal, 22, 26, 60, 61, 65
All India Depressed Classes Association, 241
All India Federation, 309
All India Harijan Sangh, 240–41
All India Hindu Mahasabha, 270, 297, 302–03, 318
All-India Khilafat Conference, 287
All-India Kisan Sabha, 314
All-India People's Conference, 317
All India Progressive Writers Association, 314
All India Scheduled Castes Federation, 241
All India Students Federation, 314
All India Trade Union Congress (AITUC), 299

All India Women's Conference, 238
All Party Convention, 303
Ambedkar, B.R., 235, 241–42, 332
Ambur battle, 62
Amichand, 66
Anglo-Afghan War, First (1838–42), 142, 146, 179; Second, 180
Anglo-French struggle, 67; in south India, 60–64
Anglo-Maratha War, first (1782), 39, 73; second (1803–05), 40, 80; third (1816–19), 40
Anglo-Mysore War, second, 27, 74; third, 74
Ansari, M.A., 266, 268, 295, 302
Arakan, 175, 176
army, 108, 111–12; reorganisation after 1858, 163–65
Arrah, revolt of 1857, 151, 153
artisans and craftsmen, ruined under British rule, 181–84, 193, 200
Arya Samaj, 224–25, 240, 286
Asaf Jah, Nizam-ul-Mulk, 5–6, 21, 26, 32, 37, 61–63
Ashraf, K.M., 320
Attlee, Clement, 328
Aurangzeb, 1, 3, 5, 10–12, 15, 21, 31, 33, 35–36, 59, 61, 121, 265
Awadh, 19, 24–26, 32, 38, 85, 96; annexation by Lord Dalhousie, 142–43; Nawab of, 26, 77, 85, 143; revolt of 1857, 149, 152
Azad, Chandra Shekhar, 299–300, 301
Azad, Maulana Abul Kalam, 252, 266, 268, 274, 279, 287, 320
Azmi, Kaifi, 320
Azizuddin, Fakir, 34

B

Bahadur Shah Zafar, 1–3, 13, 143–44, 149, 151–52, 156
Baji Rao I, 36–37
Baji Rao II, 40, 79, 143, 152
Balaji Baji Rao, 37, 39
Balaji Vishwanath, 35–36
Banda Singh Bahadur, 2, 33
Banerjea, Surendranath, 135, 172, 206, 209, 249, 250, 279
Banerjee, Sasipada, 235
Bangash Pathans and Rohelas, 26, 32
Bardoli Satyagraha, 299
Bareilly, revolt of 1857, 151
Bengal, 7, 19, 22–24; dual system of administration, 71–72, 86; British occupation, 64–71; East India Company acquired control over revenue, 65, 67, 70, 102; customs administration, 23; famine (1770), 72, 196; modern education, 124; Nawabs, 22–23, 24, 37, 64–71, 98; partition, 243, 243, 248–49, 257, 267;— movement against, 249–50, 253–54, 265; sepoy mutiny, 146
Bentinck, William, 113, 114, 121, 131, 183
Besant, Annie, 225–26, 271, 289
Bethune School, 137
Bezbarua, Lakshminath, 204
Bhagat Singh, 300–01, 307
Bhakti movement, 51
Bhandarkar, R.G., 138, 222
Bharati, Subramanya, 204
Bharatpur, 31; Raja of, 79
Bhave, Vinoba, 321
Bhonsle, 37, 39, 78–80

Bihar, 153; East India Company acquired control over revenue, 67, 70, 102
Bolshevik (Communist) Party, 277
Bombay, Bombay Presidency, 80; was given as dowry to Prince Charles II, 57
Bombay Presidency Association, 207
Bose, Ananda Mohan, 206, 209, 250
Bose, Khudiram, 255
Bose, Rajnarain, 247
Bose, Rash Bihari, 273, 324
Bose, Subhas Chandra, 266, 291, 298–99, 309, 312–13, 324–25
Brahmo Samaj, 130, 133, 135, 220–21, 222, 225, 240
British, British rule, 20, 39–40, 84, 143–46, 155–57, 200, 206, 243–45, 257, 326; administration in India, 119;—changes after 1858, 158*ff*; annexed Jullundhar Doab, 83; commercial policy (1757–1857), 91–98; economic exploitation, 140, 181, 210–11, 244;—policies in India (1757–1857), 91–107; expansion under Lord Wellesley, 74–80; Labour Party, 326; occupation of Bengal, 64–71; power consolidation, 1818–57, 81–85; wars under Warren Hastings and Cornwallis, 72–74
British India Association, 206–07
Bundelkhand, 7; revolt of 1857, 149; won by Marathas, 37
Burke, Edmund, 118
Burma, British-India war (1824), 175–76; (1852), 176; (1885), 176, 178; annexation by British, 213
Buxar battle (1764), 70, 85

C

Cabinet Mission, 327–28
Canning, Lord, 144, 153, 164
Cape of Good Hope, 54, 55, 60
capitalism, 158, 301, 316
Carnatic, 21, 61, 62, 74, 77, 78
caste system, 121, 132, 138, 210, 221, 235; rules in eighteenth century, 45–46; struggle against, 238–42
Champaran satyagraha (1917), 282
Chand Bibi, 237
Chanda Sahib, 62–63
Chandernagore, 23, 65–66
Chandragupta Vikramaditya, 204
chapattis, 148. See also Revolt of 1857
Chariar, C. Vijayaraghava, 209
Charter Act (1813), 90; (1833), 90, 110, 114
Chatterjee, Bankim Chandra, 125, 204
chaukidari tax, 305
Chauri Chaura, 291
chauth, 2, 3, 5, 26, 35–37, 61
Chelmsford, Lord, 275, 278–79
Chhatarsal, Bundela chief, 2, 3
Chikka Krishna Raj, King of Mysore, 27
child labour, 171
child marriage, 47, 221, 236
Chiplunkar, Vishnu Shastri, 204, 247
Christian missionaries, 122, 144, 235
Christianity, Christians, 120, 122, 130, 144, 145, 148, 222, 228, 239, 259, 287, 290
Churaman, 2, 3, 31

Civil Disobedience Movement, 292–94, 304–09, 314, 317
Civil Service, 108, 109–11, 165–66
Clive, Robert, 63, 66, 67–68, 70, 87–88
colonialism, 23, 93, 155, 158, 268
communal riots, 328–29
communalism, 121, 235, 225, 228, 258, 258–70, 275, 303, 317, 329; (1927–47), 317–20
Communist International, 298
communist movements, 272
Communist Party, 313
Comrade, 274
Congress, 169, 178, 199, 206, 207–09, 215, 217, 237, 240, 249, 261, 263–64, 266–67, 270–71, 279, 287–88, 298–99, 302, 305, 307–09, 310, 311, 313, 314–16, 320–21, 323, 327; (1905–14), 256–58; All India Congress Committee, 322; Faizpur, 313; Karachi session, 312; Lucknow session (1916), 273–75;— (1936), 312, 315; Ministries, 310–11; and Muslim League pact, 274–75, 286; predecessors, 205–07; Working Committee (CWC), 289, 291, 313; and world affairs, 314–16
Congress-Khilafat Swarajya Party, 295
Congress Socialist Party, 313
Constitution of India, 236, 238, 242, 293, 332
Cornwallis, Lord, 72–74, 91, 103, 108–10, 112–13
corruption and bribery, 13–14, 17, 21, 23–24
Crimean War (1854–56), 142, 179

Cripps, Stafford, 322
Curzon, Lord, 158, 167, 217, 244, 248, 252, 256

D

da Gama, Vasco, 53
Dalhousie, Lord, 100–01, 142–44; and the policy of annexation (1848–56), 84–85
Dandi March, 304
Darpan, 138
Das, C.R., 266, 288, 295–97
Dayanand Sarswati, Swami, 224–25, 231
Deccan, 2, 6, 10, 21; and the Marathas, 35–36, 37, 43
Defence of India Act, 275
Delhi, 31–32; occupied by British, 79; invasion by Nadir Shah, 43
Derozio, Henry Vivian and Young Bengal Movement, 133–35
Desai, Mahadev, 282
Deshmukh, Gopal Hari, 139, 221, 224, 235
divide and rule policy of the British, 168–69, 260, 269
Doab, revolt of 1857, 149
Doctrine of Lapse, 84–85
Dogra, Raja Gulab Singh, 83
Dominion Status, 308
Dost Muhammad, 178–79
Duff, Alexander, 133, 217, 237
Dupleix, Lord, 62–63
Dutch East India Company, 55, 57, 62
Dutch gained control over Indonesia, 55, 57
Dutt, Akshaye Kumar, 135
Dutt, Ashwini Kumar, 247, 253
Dutt, B.K., 300

Index

Dutt, Romesh Chandra, 209
dyarchy system, 278
Dyer, General, 285

E

East India Association, London, 206
economic: backwardness/underdevelopment, 198–200, 210–12, 258, 266; crisis, 14, 20; critique of imperialism, 210–12, 218, 294; drain, 98–99; emancipation, 312
education, 122–27; eighteenth century, 44–45; (1858–1905), 202–03; and unemployment (1905–1918), 245–46; Western, 125–26, 138, 144
Elizabeth, Queen, 57
English and Mughals, hostility, 59
English East India Company (EIC), 1, 9, 23, 34, 39, 62, 64–68, 70–74, 76, 78–80, 86–93, 95, 97–98, 102–06, 108–12, 120, 122, 123, 126, 135, 140–41, 143, 145, 158–59, 182; trade and influence (1600–1714), 57–60
Europe, European (s), 18 eastern trade, new phase, 53–57; economy, 162; penetration and British conquest of India, 53*ff*

F

Faiz Ahmed Faiz, 320
family system in eighteenth century, 46–47
famines, under British rule, 195–98
Farrukh Siyar, 4–5, 30, 32, 36, 60

fascism, 316, 321–22
foreign policy, foreign relations, 77, 81, 315; after 1858, 174–80
foreign service allowance (*batta*), 146
Forward Bloc, 314
France and England war (1742), 62
French: East India Company, 61–63; lost their possessions in India, 64; power in South India, 61–63; Revolution, 28, 117, 133

G

Gaekwad, 37, 39, 78
Gandhi, M.K., 203, 214, 240, 254, 264, 266–67, 279–86, 287, 288, 290–95, 303–04, 307–09, 312, 321, 323, 328, 331; South Africa, campaigns, 282
Gandhi-Irwin Pact, 307, 308
Ganguli, Kadambini, 208
Gardi, Ibrahim Khan, 38
Ghadar (Rebellion) Party, 271, 272
Ghose, Aurobindo, 245, 247, 251, 253. 254, 265
Gobind Singh, Guru, 2, 32–33
Gokhale, Gopal Krishna, 209, 212–13, 215, 216, 244, 256
Gopalakrishnayya, Duggirala, 290
Government of India Act (1919), 278, 296; (1935), 309–10, 317
Grand Trunk Road, 99–100
Gujarat, 7, 30; invasion by Maraths, 37, 43
Gurudwara Act (1922), 230

H

Haidar Ali, 27, 28, 30, 39, 73–74, 78. See also Tipu Sultan

Hali, Altaf Hussain, 204, 228
Har Dayal, Lala, 255, 271, 273
Hardinge, Lord, 83, 121, 255
Hare, David, 131, 133
Harishchandra, Bhartendu, 204
Hasan Imam, 268, 279
Hasrat Mohani, 274, 287
Hastings, Warren, 45, 72–74, 80, 88, 102, 108–09, 113, 118, 122, 184, 188
Havelock, General, 157
Hawkins, Captain, 58
Heer Ranjha, 49
Hindu(s), 23, 24, 26–27, 34, 51–52, 83, 137, 168, 205, 217, 225, 227–29, 234, 236, 250, 253, 258–64, 267, 286, 288, 290, 328; caste rules, 45–46; chiefs and rajas, 1, 11; communalism, 266; education, 44–45; and Muslims, relations, 11–12, 51; and Muslims unity, 265, 274–75, 283, 285,287, 291, 297; Marriage Act (1955), 238; Succession Act (1956), 238
Hindu College, 131, 133, 134
Hinduism, 130, 138, 144, 223, 225, 237, 329
Hindustan Socialist Republican Association (HSRA), 299–300
Hitler, Adolf, 320
Holkar, 37, 39, 40, 78, 80
Holkar, Ahilya Bai, 47, 237
Holkar, Madhav Rao, 80
Holkar, Yeshwant Rao, 79
Home Rule League, 271, 274
Home Rule movement, 178, 237
humanism, 117–18, 121–22, 144, 232
Hume, A.O., 207–08, 217
Hyderabad 7, 19, 21, 62, 73, 326, 327, 330; French intervention, 62–63; invasion by Maratha chiefs, 61; Nizam, 73, 329, 317;—defeated at Udgir, 38

I

ijarah, 15
Imad-ul-Mulk, 38
Imperial Legislative Council, 212, 257
imperialism, 156–57, 201, 218, 261, 277, 315–16, 322; economic and political consequences, 269
import duties, 96–97
Indian Association of Calcutta, 206
Indian Civil Service (ICS), 206
Indian Councils Act (1861), 159; (1892), 212, 244; (1909), 257
Indian Factory Act (1881), 171; (1891), 171
Indian Liberal Federation, 279
Indian National Army (INA), 324–27
Indian National Congress (INC). *See* Congress
Indian Official Secrets Act (1904), 244
Indian Penal Code, 114
Indian states and society in the eighteenth century, 19*ff*
Indian Statutory Commission, *See* Simon Commission
Indian Universities Act (1904), 244
industry, industrial, 15, 200; capitalism, 116–17, 172; and commercial backwardness, 168;

Index

development under British rule, 91–95; social consequences, 195; and trade in eighteenth century, 43–44
Industrial Revolution, 54, 92–94, 116–17, 158, 162, 197
Iqbal, Muhammad, 229
Irwin, Lord, 301, 307
Islam, 130, 144, 223, 237, 329
Iyer, G. Subramaniya, 172, 207, 209

J

jagir system, jagirs, 14–15, 20, 24, 40, 42
Jai Prakash Narayan, 313
Jai Singh, Sawai Raja of Amber, 1–2, 3, 5, 11, 12, 31, 121
Jallianwala Bagh massacre, 284–86
Jamia Millia Islamia, 289
Jaswant Singh of Marwar, 11
Jats, 5, 11, 12, 14–16, 19, 31–32, 39
Jhansi, 84; revolt of 1857, 151, 152–53
Jinnah, Muhammad Ali, 263, 266, 274, 289, 318, 320,329
jizyah (pilgrim tax), 3, 5, 11
judicial organisation under British, 113–16, 132, 213
Junagadh, Nawab of, 329

K

Kakori Conspiracy Case (1925), 299
Kanpur, 32; Conspiracy, 298; revolt of 1857, 152
Kashmir, 327, 330; conquered by Ranjit Singh, 33; invasion by Pakistan, 1947, 330
Kerala, 29–30
Kesari, 247
Khalisah (crown) lands, 14–15, 17, 22
Khan Abdul Gaffar Khan, 266, 305, 308, 320
Khan Bahadur Khan, 157
Khan, Sayyid Ahmad, 142, 146, 203, 217, 226–28, 231–32, 261–62
Kheda satyagraha, 282–83
Khilafat, 269; and Non-Cooperation Movement (1919–1920), 286–95
Khilafat Committee, 287
Khudai Khidmatgars, 305, 308
Kitchlew, Saifuddin, 285–86
Krishak Praja Party, 310

L

labour legislation after 1858, 171–72
Lahore Treaty, 83
Lajpat Rai, Lala, 172, 231, 247, 253, 297, 289, 300
Lakshmibai, Rani of Jhansi, 143, 152–53, 157
land holdings, fragmentation, 189–90
land revenue system: landed aristocracy in Bengal, 23; of British, 102–07, 140, 185–86, 211; Mughal, 15, 33; in Punjab, 33
Lansdowne, Lord, 158, 166
Latif, Nawab Abdul; 262
Latif, Shah Abdul, 49
law and order, 5, 108, 211–12
Legislative Councils, 159–60, 212
Lenin, Vladimir I., 277

local bodies, administration after 1858, 161–62
Lucknow, revolt of 1857, 149–51, 152
Lytton, Lord, 158, 161, 170

M

Macaulay, Lord, 114, 123, 125–26
Madhav Rao, 39
Madhav Rao II, 73
Madhav Rao, Sawai, 39
Mahalwari System, 106–07, 184, 186
Mahmud, Ghalzai chief of Qandahar, 7
Mahratta, 247
Malaviya, Madan Mohan, 172, 209, 226, 297
Malcolm, John, 50, 118, 166
Malihabadi, Josh, 320
Malwa, 7, 30; won by Marathas, 37
Manick Chand, 66
mansabdars (nobles), *mansabs*, 2, 3
Maratha(s), 2, 5, 9, 12, 16, 19, 23, 61, 74, 76; chiefs, 14, 73, 79; power, rise and fall, 34–41; *sardars*, 2, 3, 8, 10, 12, 24–26, 27, 35–39
Marathi Dhyan Prasarak Mandalis, 138
Martanda Varma, ruler of Kerala, 29–30, 49
Marxism, 298, 311
Masulipatnam, 57–59, 62
Mathura, 31–32
Mazhar-ul-Haq, 268, 282
Meerut Conspiracy Case, 302
Meerut, revolt of 1857, 148–49
Metcalfe, Charles, 118, 172

militant nationalist school of thought, 247–48, 253–54
military training, in eighteenth century, 50; in the time of Tipu Sultan, 29
Mill, John Stuart, 202
Mir Jafar, 66–68, 70, 72
Mir Qasim of Bengal, 9, 68, 70
Miran, 67
misls (confederacies), 33
moneylenders (*mahajans*), 23, 154, 185–86, 187, 200, 269
Montagu, Edwin, 278–79
Montague-Chelmsford Reforms 275, 278–79
Moplahs rebellion, 291
Morley-Minto Reforms, 257–58
Mountbatten, Lord, 328
Mughal(s), Mughal Empire, 42; administrative and revenue system, 19–20, 27, 32; army, 17; decline/disintegration, 19, 34, 43, 19;—causes, 10–18; system of *jagirs*, 40; politics, 3; wars with Marathas, 35–37
Muhammad Shah, 4, 6–9, 21, 30
Muhammedan Anglo-Oriental College, 227
Muhammedan Literary Society 226
Muinuddin Chisti, Sheikh, 51
Murshid Quli Khan, Nawab of Bengal, 22, 26, 60, 65
Muslim(s), 22, 24, 26, 34, 51–52, 83, 168, 217, 227–29, 234, 236, 250, 254, 258–61, 263–64, 269, 286–87, 288, 290, 293–94, 317; backwardness of the Muslims, 262; caste divisions, 46; criminal law, 113; education, 45; nationalism, 266

Muslim League, 267–68, 269, 274–75, 297, 302–03, 310, 318–19, 327–29
Mustafa Kamal Pasha, 293
Muzaffar Jang, 62–63
Mysore, 19, 27–29, 73, 76–78. *See also* Haidar Ali. Tipu Sultan

N

nabobs, 87–88
Nadir Shah, 7–9, 17, 32, 33, 43, 61
Naicker, E.V Ramaswamy, 235
Naidu, Sarojini, 237
Najib-ud-Daulah of Rohilkhand, 38
Nambiar, Kunchan, 49
Nana Phadnis, 39–40, 73, 78, 84, 143, 152, 157
Nanabhoy, Cowasjee, 191
Nanak, Guru, 32
Naoroji, Dadabhai, 139, 172, 203, 206, 219–12, 215, 229, 256, 264
Narayana Guru, 235, 241
Narendra Dev, Acharya, 289, 313
Nasir Jang, 62–63
National Planning Committee, 313
nationalism, nationalist movement, 194; (1858–1905), 167–69, 199*ff*, 234; (1905–18), 243*ff*; (1919–27), 276, 278; (1927–47), 317; all-India aspect, 252; and the First World War, 270–75, in nineteenth century, 135; during the revolt of 1857, 156; revolutionary character, 255–56; during the Second World War, 320–25; role of students, women, Muslims and masses, 251–52
Naval Mutiny, 326

Nazir Ahmad, 228
Nazism, 321–22
Nehru, Jawaharlal, 170, 173, 232, 263, 266, 294, 298, 304–05, 308, 313, 315, 317, 319, 328–30, 332
Nehru, Motilal, 266, 288, 292, 295, 297, 303–04
Nepal war (1814), 174–75
Nizam-ud-Daulah, 70–71
Noakhali, communal riots, 331
Nomani, Maulana Shibli, 228
Non-Cooperation Movement (1919–20), 286–95, 299
North West Frontier Province (NWFP), 308, 318–19

O

Olcott, H.S., 225
Oriental learning, 123
Orissa, 79; East India Company acquired control over revenue, 67, 70, 102; famine, 196
Ottoman Empire, 53, 268, 286–87

P

Paine, Thomas, 202
Pakistan, 328–30
Pal, Bipin Chandra, 172, 235, 245, 247, 253, 254, 289
Pande, Mangal, 149
Panipat, Third Battle, 1761, 9, 38–39
Paramahansa Mandali, 138, 221
parliamentary system, 257, 332
Parsi Law Association, 139
Parsis, 228, 234, 263, 290; religious reforms, 229
Patel, Vallabhbhai, 266, 283, 295, 299, 329

Patel, Vithalbhai J., 296, 309
Pathans, 26, 305
peasant discontent and movements, 15, 140–41, 308, 314, 318, 327
peasantry, impoverishment under British rule, 20, 184–87, 189
Pegu, British annexation, 176
Permanent Settlement, 102–05, 132, 188
Peshawar, conquered by Ranjit Singh, 33
Peshwas, 26, 35, 37–40, 73, 78–80, 121
Phule, Jotiba Govind, 139, 235, 241
Pillai, Champakaraman, 273
Pillai, Chidambaram, 253
Pitt's India Act, 1784, 89–90
Planning Commission, 194
plantations, 97, 171–72, 193, 211
Plassey battle (1757), 67, 92–93
police, 108, 112–13, 213
poligars (warrior chieftains and zamindars), 27, 28
politics: (1858–1905), 215–18; (1905–18), 260; (1935–39), 309–14; in eighteenth century, 19–20, 21, 43
polygamy, 131, 135, 137, 236
Poona Sarvajanik Sabha, 207, 215
poorna swaraj, 303–04
Portugal, Portuguese, 37, 53–55
postal system, 202
poverty and famines, under British rule, 195–98; (1858–1905), 210–11, 214
Prarthana Samaj, 222, 225, 240
press and literature, role (1858–1905), 203–4; restrictions after 1858, 172–73

princely states, 326–30; and British relations after 1858, 166–67; people's struggle, 316–17
provincial administration after 1858, 160–61
Provincial Legislative Council, 278
Pundit, Vishnu Shastri, 138
Punjab, 19; conquest by British, 83–84; under Ranjit Singh, 33–34; Wars (1845–49), 142
purdah, 47, 236

Q

qazis and *muftis*, 24
Quit India Resolution, 322

R

racial dominance and discrimination, 173, 201, 205, 271
railways, 100–01, 192, 202
Rajagopalachari, C., 266
Rajendra Prasad, 266, 282, 295
Rajput: princes and chiefs, 5, 10–12, 14, 16, 26; States, 30–31, 39
Rajputana states, 38, 80
Rama Varma, ruler of Kerala, 30 48
Ramakrishna Mission, 224, 240. *See also* Vivekananda
Ramakrishna Parmahamsa, 222–24
Ranade, Mahadev Govind, 172, 203, 207, 209, 215, 222, 224, 231, 235
Ranjit Singh, Maharaja of Punjab 33–34, 83
reason (rationalism) and humanism, 128, 230

religion, 7, 210; in eighteenth century, 51–52; religious and social reforms after 1858, 219*ff*; policy of Aurangzeb, 11, 12
revenue system: in Awadh, 24; of Mughals, 21; of Marathas, 41
Revolt of 1857, 140*ff*, 173, 187, 260, 262
Revolt of 1942, 323–25
Roberclaw, Henry, 80–81
Rohelas, 26, 32, 39
Rohilkhand, 32, 38, 77; revolt of 1857, 149
Round Table Conference, 307; Third, 309
Rowlatt Act, 279, 286
Roy, M.N., 298
Roy, Raja Rammohun, 52, 121, 123, 128–33, 135, 172, 205, 220–21, 232
Royal Indian Air Force, 326
rule of law, 114–15, 279
Russia and Turkey treaty, 7
Russian Revolution, 180, 277, 298, 312
Ryotwari Settlement, 103, 105–06, 184, 186, 188

S

Saadat Khan Burhan-ul-Mulk, 24, 26
Saadutullah Khan, Nawab of Carnatic, 21, 78
Sabarmati Ashram, Ahmedabad, 281, 304
Safavi dynasty, 7
Safdar Jang, 24, 26
Sahajanand Saraswati, Swami, 314
Sahir Ludhianwi, 320
Saiyid brothers, 4–6, 21, 36

Saiyid Hussain Ali Khan, 36
Salbai Treaty (1782), 73
Sanskrit studies, 44, 135–36
Santhal rebellion, 142
sardeshmukhi, 2, 3, 5, 35–37
Sarfaraz Khan, 22
Satara, 84
sati, 47, 121, 130–1, 144, 170, 231, 236
Satnamis, 11,15
Satyagraha Sabha, 284
satyagraha struggles, 240–41; against the Rowlatt Act, 283–84
Savarkar, V.D., 255
science and technology, 15, 49–50, 117
secularism, 218, 266, 319
Sehgal, Prem, 325
self-respect and self-confidence, 225, 245
Self-Respect Movement, 241
Sen, Keshub Chandra, 219, 220–21, 224, 232
Sen, Rajani Kant, 251
Servants of India Society, 235
Shah Alam, 39–40
Shah Alam II, 9, 70, 71
Shahu, king, 2, 3, 12, 35–36, 37
Shahul Hamid, Shaikh, 51
shaikhzadas, 26
ship-building and navigation in eighteenth century, 43–44, 53
Shiva Prasad, Raja of Varanasi, 217, 261
Shivaji, 5, 35–36, 80, 247, 265
Shivaji II, 35
Shore, John, 28, 104, 110
Shradhanand, Swami, 286
Shringeri temple, 29, 52
Shuja-ud-Daulah, Nawab of

350 Index

Awadh, 9, 38, 70–71
Sikh League, 303
Sikhs, 2, 11–12, 14, 15, 32–33, 38, 42, 83, 234, 239, 259, 287, 290; religious reforms, 229–30
Simon Commission, 297, 299, 302–03, 307
Sindh, British conquest, 81
Sindhia, 37, 39, 78–80
Siraj-ud-Daulah, Nawab of Bengal, 23, 64–71
Sirhind, invasion by Sikhs, 43
social and cultural: awakening in the first half of nineteenth century, 120*ff*; backwardness, 170–71, 197–98; life in eighteenth century, 45–52; policy of British, 116–21
social and economic conditions: in eighteenth century, 41–44; under Mughals, 12, 18
Social Conference, 235, 240
social evils: in eighteenth century, 47–48, 120–1, 130–31. *See also sati*
social reforms, 121–22, 135, 170; after 1858, 219*ff*; socialism, 117, 298, 301, 311–14, 316
South African colonies, 280
South India, Anglo-French struggle, 60–64
Spanish America, Revolution, 133
Spice Island, 53, 55
St George Fort, 58
Student's Literary and Scientific Society, 138
'Subsidiary Alliances' system, 76–78
Subsidiary Treaty, 76, 79, 81
Sufism, 51
Surat, 57, 59, 77; invasion by Marathas, 43

Swadeshi and Boycott movements, 173, 211, 250–1, 254, 266; in Bengal, 256
swaraj, 248; struggle for (1919–27), 276*ff*; (1927–47), 298*ff*
Swarajist Party, 295–97

T

Tagore, Debendranath, 135–38, 220–21
Tagore, Dwarkanath, 133
Tagore, Prasanna Kumar, 133
Tagore, Rabindranath, 135, 139, 165, 204, 250–51, 286, 331
Tagore, Satyendranath, 165
taluqdars, 15, 143, 145
Tata Iron and Steel Works, 299
Tattvabodhini Sabha, 135
taxation policy of British, 102, 195, 201, 211, 212
Tayaumanavar, 49
Tebhaga struggle, 327
technological development, 93–94
Telang, K.T., 207, 235
Temporary Zamindari Settlement, 184, 188
textile industry, 43, 191, 193–94
Theosophical Society, 225–26, 240
Thibaw, King of Burma, 176–77
Tilak, Bal Gangadhar, 172, 203, 209, 214, 244, 245, 247, 252, 253, 254, 265, 270–71, 273, 287–88, 293
Tipu Sultan, 27–28, 50, 51, 74, 77–78; infantry and warfare, 28–29
trade in eighteenth century, 43–44, 53–54
transport and communication, development, 99–101

Travancore, 29, 326, 327;
Maharaja of, 317
Trichinopoly, siege by French, 63
Tyabji, Badruddin, 207, 209, 261, 263

U

Udai Narayan, 22
unemployment, 200, 245–46, 276
uniform civil code, 332
Unionist Party, 310
United Nations (UN), 322
untouchability, 239–42, 290–91, 332
Upanishads, 130, 221

V

Vedanta, 129, 223
Vedanta College, 131
Vedas, 129, 130, 221, 224
Vellore, sepoy mutiny, 146
Vernacular Press Act (1878), 173
Victoria, Queen, 167
Vidyasagar, Ishwar Chandra, 122, 135–38, 139, 172, 220, 224
Vijaynagar Empire, 27, 57
Viresalingam, 222, 235
Vivekananda, Swami, 219, 222–24, 229, 230, 234, 245

W

Wajid Ali Shah, 85
Wandiwash battle (1760), 64
Warris Shah, 49
wars of succession, 3, 61
watans and *saranjams (jagirs)* system of Marathas, 36, 40
Wellesley, Arthur, 74–80, 108–09
Western knowledge, 120, 124, 202–03
Western trading companies, 23
widow, in eighteenth century, 47–48; remarriage, 122, 135–38, 144, 170, 221
Widow Remarriage Association, 138
Wilberforce, William, 119
Willingdon, Lord, 308–09
women, in eighteenth century, 47–48; emancipation, 236–38; status, 131, 139
Wood, Charles, 125, 160, 164
Wood's Dispatch, 124–25
World War I, 178, 180, 270–77
World War II, 178, 320–25; postwar struggle, 325–33

Y

Yandabo treaty, 175–76
Young Bengal Movement, 133–35
Yugantar, 255

Z

Zafar Ali Khan, Maulana, 268
zamindars, zamindari, 5, 15–17, 19, 20, 22–24, 26, 31, 41, 43, 44, 46, 48, 102–07, 109, 116, 132, 135, 140,142, 147, 150, 152, 153–56, 184, 186, 196, 200–01, 262, 268–69, 290; and British relations after 1858, 169–70; ruin of old zamindari and rise of new landlordism, 187–89
Zamorin of Calicut, 29–30
Zoroastrianism, 139, 225, 237
Zulfiqar Khan, 3–4, 35